THE FRENCHMEN

Or, My Life in Theory

Emily Eakin

PENGUIN PRESS
New York
2026

PENGUIN PRESS
An imprint of Penguin Random House LLC
1745 Broadway, New York, NY 10019
penguinrandomhouse.com

Image credits appear on pages 453–54.

Designed by Amanda Dewey

LIBRARY OF CONGRESS CONTROL NUMBER PERMALINK:
https://lccn.loc.gov/2025053042
ISBN 9781594206320 (hardcover)
ISBN 9780698183261 (ebook)

Printed in the United States of America
1st Printing

The authorized representative in the EU for product safety and compliance is Penguin Random House Ireland, Morrison Chambers, 32 Nassau Street, Dublin D02 YH68, Ireland, https://eu-contact.penguin.ie.

For Mark, Isabel, and Sadie

What civilization, in appearance, has shown more respect towards discourse than our own?

—*Michel Foucault*

CONTENTS

Part Four • EVASIONS

Lives of
The French Philosophers

One dreamed of becoming a novelist. One was championed by the Surrealists, who considered him one of their own. One was expelled from his school because he was Jewish. One published anti-Semitic articles in a pro-Nazi newspaper. One repeatedly failed the university entrance exams. Two had children with women who were not their wives. A third was a bigamist. One worked at an experimental psychiatric clinic where patients and staff lived together as equals. One was obsessed with knots. One swindled his friends and was sentenced to prison. One dabbled in S/M. Two attempted suicide. One died after being hit by a dry cleaner's van while crossing a street. One killed himself by jumping out a window. One murdered his wife.

If you had read only their philosophical writings, you'd never have known any of these things. You might not have guessed that these philosophers experienced love, lust, madness, hope, envy, hatred, and deep despair. You might not have guessed they had bodies as well as minds.

Reading them, I nearly forgot I did.

INTRODUCTION

The classicist Allan Bloom called deconstruction "a circus performance." The conservative columnist Roger Kimball called it "linguistic subterfuge." Others called it much worse. One commentator, an admirer, couldn't decide whether deconstruction was a "tyrannicide" or a "game." Another said it was "the most bankable product ever to emerge on the market of academic discourses."

Everyone had a notion of what deconstruction was and all the wonderful or terrible things it could do. Everyone, that is, except Jacques Derrida, the French philosopher who coined the term. Derrida defined deconstruction rarely, usually when pressed, and then typically in a negative sense. It denoted a set of "non-concepts." Or, more ambiguously: "Deconstruction, if there is such a thing, takes place as the experience of the impossible." There was no formula for deconstruction, no blueprint, no rules. You could call it a style of reading, an approach in the loosest possible sense since it existed only in relation to something else—typically a classic work of Western philosophy—that it took apart and left in pieces.

This elusive phenomenon, responsible for so much confusion and agitation, was a hallmark of the intellectual movement known as French theory, or more frequently, theory. Strangely, the movement took shape not in France but in America, beginning in the late 1960s, just as existentialism, the last big French intellectual import, was fading from view. Theory entered the United States through college literature departments and spread across the culture—"like kudzu," *The New York Times Magazine* marveled.

For more than two decades, through the pitched battles of the 1980s "canon wars" over which books were essential to a college education, theory, an eclectic body of philosophical writings by a handful of middle-aged Frenchmen (for better or worse, most of the theorists were both French and male) held sway on campuses and, more remarkably, in the American imagination where it loomed almost comically large. "Students in our best universities do not believe in anything, and those universities are doing nothing about it," declared Bloom in 1982, sounding the alarm in an essay that laid the groundwork for his subsequent bestseller, *The Closing of the American Mind*. "The heads of the young are stuffed with a jargon derived from the despair of European thinkers, gaily repackaged for American consumption."

Thanks to his book, Bloom, a bald, chain-smoking, nattily dressed, hitherto obscure translator of Plato and Rousseau, became nearly as famous as Derrida himself. (Also much wealthier: Bloom's book, which spent forty-five weeks on *The New York Times* bestseller list and sold more than one million copies, made him a millionaire.) Other critics soon joined the fray. "Behind the transformations contemplated by the proponents of feminism, deconstruction, and the rest is a blueprint for a radical social transformation that would revolutionize every aspect of social and political life," warned one in an influential 1990 book. Deconstruction is "blighting the most promising minds of the next generation," yet another concluded two years later. "This is a major crisis if there ever was one, and every sensible person must help bring it to an end."

Leading political figures weighed in, including Lynne Cheney, wife of the future Republican Vice President Dick Cheney who, under President Ronald Reagan, had served as chair of the National Endowment for the Humanities. In a 1995 takedown of the intellectual currents then gripping academia, Cheney decried "French thinkers" guilty of importing "to this country the effort begun by their German predecessors of undercutting the defining principles of the modern world."

What was everyone so worked up about? The Frenchmen themselves—Derrida, Louis Althusser, Roland Barthes, Gilles Deleuze, Michel Foucault, Félix Guattari, Jacques Lacan, and Paul de Man (this last technically not a Frenchman but a French-speaking Belgian who taught in the French department at Yale)—were serious, often brilliantly original thinkers, if barely accessible to the lay reader. (For the purposes of this book, I'll focus on these eight men, arguably among the most influential in the United States and certainly the ones who figured most prominently in my education, but this list is not meant to be exhaustive.) It wasn't just that their preoccupations were abstract; their writings often seemed intentionally rebarbative, as if the labor required to grasp their ideas was somehow in part the point.

In retrospect, the passion they aroused among a generation of Americans—including me, a college student at the time—seems as improbable as it was extraordinary. Take Derrida, whose brand of deconstruction came to stand for both the grandest insights and worst excesses of theory on American soil. A shy, Algerian-born Jew, he was often regarded in France as an outsider and iconoclast, a philosopher whose esoteric considerations and neologism-pocked wordplay relegated him to the margins of the academic establishment. Moreover, deconstruction as he conceived it was notoriously slippery, its targets, at least in the beginning, narrowly scholastic and forbidding: Husserl, Heidegger, Nietzsche, and other continental thinkers who were known for their extreme difficulty and had little currency in the United States.

In short, the barriers to entry could hardly have been higher. Yet American students and scholars flocked in droves to theory, perceiving in its recondite abstractions a thrilling new way of understanding the world—even, some believed, of changing it. And in many respects they were right: The Frenchmen challenged some of our most fundamental assumptions, from our beliefs about power, truth, and the individual to reality itself.

At the center of their concerns was language. Intellectually and temperamentally, they were a diverse group, forever being lumped together and divided up under various, shifting labels—Marxism, psychoanalysis, structuralism, poststructuralism, postmodernism. But language, they could all agree, was paramount. In this, they were united in opposition to existentialism, the philosophy championed by Jean-Paul Sartre that dominated France during the first two decades after World War II. Where the existentialists promoted a humanist creed with, at its heart, a heroic individual imposing meaning on a senseless world, the structuralists ditched the idea of the human altogether, replacing it with a vision of language as an all-powerful, impersonal system whose formative effects on our lives had been poorly understood and routinely underestimated.

The French philosophers who followed in Sartre's wake dedicated much of their careers to showing how they believed language actually worked: molding our thoughts and behavior, constraining and compelling us, tripping us up and deluding us—in a word, *creating* us. And not just us, but the world too, everything we liked to imagine was out there, beyond us. In the new dispensation, there was little room for physical existence. *Non*, the Frenchmen said, language is all there is. Or, more precisely, it's what matters: What we know about the world is inseparable from our discourse about it. As Derrida famously put it, "*Il n'y a pas de hors-texte." There is nothing outside the text.*

As the Frenchmen's work was embraced by American scholars, the distinction between the philosophy and political action gradually collapsed. Literature professors who'd come of age during the Civil Rights Movement and the Vietnam War thought they saw in the French thinkers' writings a tool for protest and, the ultimate goal, social transformation. Applied with care to a literary text, like a jeweler's loupe to a precious gem, theory uncovered hidden angles and surfaces, all shimmering with movement, along with fractures and flaws invisible to the casual eye. Wielded like a cudgel aimed at social norms and institutions, theory became something else, the weapon of choice for a politically exercised generation of scholars intent on remaking society along more equitable lines: Change the discourse, change the world!

Enlisted in this way, theory was used to expose contradictions and omissions regarding gender, race, or class in nearly every form of cultural expression—philosophical treatises, novels, poems, speeches, movies, TV shows, art, architecture, clothes, music, advertisements, cartoons. For professors who studied literary themes and metaphors for a living, theory endowed their scholarship with an armature of larger purpose, transforming textual analysis into jargony skirmishes in a crusade for social justice. So pronounced was theory's metamorphosis in the United States, so distinctive the uses to which it was put, that the French sociologist François Cusset refers to "the *American* invention of *French* theory."

◆ ◆ ◆

It was a heady time. Years later, after the fixation on theory had subsided, and its critics had moved on to other targets, a wise professor summed up what had transpired: "A bunch of people threatening all kinds of subversion by means that couldn't possibly produce it, and a bunch on the other side taking them at their word and waging cultural war. Not comedy, not tragedy, more like farce, but farce with consequences. Careers made and ruined, departments torn apart, writing programs turned into sensitivity seminars, political witch hunts, public opprobrium, ignorant media attacks, the whole ball of wax."

The story of theory, from its birth in France to its unlikely domination of America, where I became one of legions of devotees, is the subject of this book. It is a tale rich not just in ideas but, ironically, given the Frenchmen's generally antihumanist stance, human drama. By personal choice and historical circumstance, these philosophers' lives were as far from ordinary as their beliefs. Exposed only to their writings in college, I had no notion of the theorists as actual people, or how their experiences might have influenced their work. If it's true that, as one scholar puts it, "French intellectual life is among the most ideological and politicized in the world," the French theorists were no exception. They were profoundly shaped by the genocide of World War II; the disappointments of the postwar period as the world was divided up between two flawed superpowers, the capitalist United States and the communist Soviet empire; the social upheaval of the 1960s, culminating in France in the mass protests of May '68; and—for those among them who lived long enough to see it—the fall of the Berlin Wall and the end of the Cold War.

More intimately, the French theorists nursed grand ambitions and old wounds. At least one observer has ascribed their distinctive takes on the world in part to the fact that they "were typically outsiders who did not readily fit within traditional disciplinary and institutional boundaries, and they were often scarred by personal traumas." They struggled with illness, depression, moral failure, emotional betrayal, and singular proclivities—for "the overwhelming, the unspeakable," and "the limits of the possible," as Foucault said about the literature he admired.

Some of these thinkers were good friends; a few were hardly acquainted. But each was acutely aware of the others' work. They followed one another's professional ascents and stumbles, and came to one another's rescue in times of need. Their careers were marked by the jockeying for power and position that the hothouse world of the Parisian intelligentsia encouraged, as well as by shifting allegiances and fallings out.

My goal in this book is to re-embody these men—to recover the hidden human element beneath their often stringent antihumanism. To do so has required an approach that is less linear than thematic. To capture the defining incidents and contours of each thinker's life, and explore suggestive areas of overlap, I sometimes circle back to major events or key encounters, considering them anew, in a different light, and guided throughout by these underlying questions: What was it about the Frenchmen that led them to see language and the world in the peculiar way that they did? What was it about France in the 1960s and America in the 1980s that made first one and then the other so receptive to their work? Finally, I want to know what it was that led me to come under theory's sway—and nearly lose myself there.

But there is another, more urgent, reason to tell this story now. The

Frenchmen, it turns out, are crucial for understanding the world we inhabit today, one that in decisive ways they bequeathed to us. Their influence ran deep, permanently altering how we think not only about bedrock philosophical ideas but about the role of language in shaping those beliefs and everything else.

Caught up in the culture wars of our day—disputes over the "death of truth"; over the nature of scientific knowledge; over the collapse of a binary conception of gender; over the rights to the "authorless" content generated by AI chatbots; over whether appeals to universal notions of reason, justice, or freedom any longer make sense—we rarely acknowledge these conflicts as, in part, the legacy of the postwar French philosophers. These thinkers weren't nihilists (as their critics often accused them of being). They didn't claim that reality is an illusion, or that truth doesn't exist. (They would have been horrified by the misinformation and conspiracy theories saturating our political discourse today.) Their aim was to enlighten us about language's very real and powerful, if mostly invisible, effects. By showing, through rigorous close readings of literary and philosophical texts, how language operates as an inescapable force, shot through with ideology, and in which intention and meaning often fail to coincide, they taught us to be deeply wary consumers of signs.

We have learned the Frenchmen's lessons for both good and ill. In the wake of their teachings, we no longer regard language as innocent or natural, a mirror reflecting the world as it is or even necessarily our thoughts as we think them. The theorists instructed that no single person, institution, or state power can fully control the narrative about our world; language is far too unstable, too self-aware, too contradictory for that. And where no one can claim jurisdiction over meaning, interpretations inevitably proliferate—multiplying, diverging, competing.

The French philosophers are not alone responsible for the crisis of authority in which we find ourselves, or the demise of what is often called, with understandable despair, "a shared reality." The rise of cable news, podcasts, and social media—of a world in which anyone can say almost anything on a public platform at any time—along with the ability to customize the content we consume to filter out inconvenient facts and reinforce preexisting beliefs: All have played a part in turning theory's revelatory insights to destructive ends. Yet it's fair to say that, for better and for worse, we are in some ways all like the Frenchmen now, expert decoders of our tirelessly signifying universe.

Part 1

Murder

Chapter 1

DERRIDA'S PIPE

I came under the Frenchmen's spell in the late 1980s, as an eighteen-year-old Harvard sophomore at the height of America's theory craze. In the spiral notebook my roommates and I kept under a corner of our living room rug—our "Under the Rug Book"—we recorded jokes, fragments of conversation, passages from our reading. My roommates, English majors both, jotted lines from Milton and *Wuthering Heights*. I, a literature concentrator—the college's name for theory-centered studies—copied out paragraphs from Derrida. References to theory crept into my papers, so that an essay on Wordsworth for a course on nineteenth-century

English poetry included an allusion, indecipherable to me now, to a "sunny Derridean plateau."

By then, I had concluded that the English department was tweedy and old-fashioned, a bastion of conventionality and received wisdom. By contrast, the literature department, just a few years old when I got to campus, struck me as cutting edge, attracting some of the most brilliant students around. They were also a little intimidating. These were the students who lingered in the dining hall after dinner, discussing Nietzsche's *Übermensch* and logical aporias in Plato's *Symposium*. The way they talked about language, they seemed to know things the rest of us didn't—how slippery meaning was, how words didn't express or reflect reality so much as fashion it. Maybe reality was just that, they implied: *words*. And theory was what they talked *with*—a constant touchstone. It was their common currency, their secret code, their drug.

In the beginning, I was like Madeleine, the heroine of *The Marriage Plot*, Jeffrey Eugenides' comic novel about a senior at Brown in the 1980s, an earnest suburbanite who comes to college intent on studying English literature because of her love of Dickens, Wharton, and James. She soon finds herself surrounded by students dressed in "Doc Martens and anarchist symbols" who casually name-drop thinkers she's never heard of. "Derrida is my absolute god!" Madeleine's roommate declares in a typical—and, to Madeleine, baffling—aside.

Determined to understand this strange cult, Madeleine signs up for Semiotics 211, an upper-level seminar. Derrida was in the air, godlike, at Harvard and, like Madeleine, I wanted access to the sanctum. I was from Bloomington, Indiana, a midsize Midwestern college town—so not the suburbs, and hardly the boondocks, but still sorely lacking, it seemed to me, in intellectual hipness. Who was this one-name Frenchman, anyway?

I was interested in French, and I was interested in intellectuals, or at least in being mistaken for one. Toward this end, I had taken a first step the year before college, spending it on a program for high school students in Rennes, in northwestern France, from which I'd returned nearly fluent. I'd found the flier advertising the program in the wastebasket of my father's study (an unexpected perk of having to collect the family trash—a chore I shared on a rotating basis with my three siblings). My teenage fantasies about France were vague and romantic, inspired as much by real estate ads at the back of *The New York Times Magazine* ("17th-century château in Limoges; 15 bdrms, 4 baths, 29 forested hectares, family-owned for more than 300 years!") as any book I happened to have read.

But there was also Suzy, a girl in my high school who had gone with her family to Geneva for a year and come back not only fluent in French but transformed, with a black leather jacket, a nose ring, a handmade zine operation, and a low tolerance for us, her former friends, who, it was clear, she now found hopelessly provincial. Suzy had turned punk and urbane while the rest of us were giggling in sleeping bags on someone's rec room rug and trawling the mall for fuzzy cardigans on markdown. As it had been for so many Americans before me—including characters in the novels by Henry James that my father, an English professor, taught at the local university—Europe beckoned as an essential stop on the road to worldly sophistication and glamour.

My parents implicitly encouraged this view. For my father's first sabbatical, when I was four, we had lived in Paris, where my little sister and I attended the *maternelle* and my older sister completed first grade at a local public school. Seven years later, another sabbatical, this one in Athens, where we went to a British school, now with the addition of my baby brother. In both cities, weekends and holidays were for touring museums and archaeological sites—in a word, for Culture, the thing that lurked in Doric capitals and within six-foot gilt frames, the ones we peered at over stanchions and red-velvet rope. Our French had grown rusty since that first trip, but the muscle memory was there, resurfacing at random in phrases that had blended unremarked into the family idiom—"*On y va, alors?*" "*À table!*" "*Dégueulasse!*"

Yet there was something particular about France, something I could not have expressed at the time but that as I grew older factored into its allure: the idea that it was the country—and French the language—of intellectuals. I had seen photos of my father in Paris from January 1960, during a postcollege year abroad. Seated in his student hotel room in the Latin Quarter, in a dark turtleneck sweater and black frame glasses—the signature existentialist look, though I didn't know it then—he is holding up a copy of the leftist newspaper *Combat,* with the shocked headline: ALBERT CAMUS EST MORT. I had never heard of Camus. But that the death of such a person was front-page news made an impression.

My father in Paris, 1960

I could not have put the thought into words, but the message wafting subliminally from those photos was that what was meant by "life of the mind" was France. And by this logic there was little more French than theory.

As it turned out, I did not meet any intellectuals, French or otherwise, during my senior year of high school in Rennes. Instead, I got to know a couple dozen students from East Coast prep schools—the majority of the kids in the program. These encounters supplied more confirmation that Suzy had been right: I was provincial. I had cut my hair in a Louise Brooks bob before the trip, but no one was fooled by my Jazz Age veneer. The other students had clearly read more, drunk more, smoked more—done more—than I had. As far as I could tell, the main reason some had come to France was to be able to indulge more freely: no drinking age, no dorm proctors, no parents, no prohibitions. Many had credit cards. John, pale, blond, and bony, from New York City via Exeter, slunk around the nineteenth-century villa where we took our classes, wearing a secondhand red-satin smoking jacket and strumming a guitar. The nickname for Prescott, the long-lashed, dark-haired boy, from New York City via Andover, who became my first serious boyfriend, was "Marlboro Man." We spent hours after school in the café down the street, which had both a foosball table and beer on tap—a seductive combination for teenagers playing at being adults.

"You are a babe in the woods among tigers," the wife of the program's director told me, with what I took to be motherly concern. For the most part, though, my new friends were protective, not scornful, of my innocence. When John acquired a few tabs of LSD, and a group of us went to the sprawling green Parc du Thabor in the city center to take them, it was decided that I, alone, would not be getting high. "I don't think it would be a good idea," John said, not unkindly. "You're already tripping."

John wasn't wrong. My journal from that year overflows with exclamation points—"I'm running out of new superlatives," I exulted early on. The French franc was at ten to the dollar; American high school students with unfettered access to their parents' Visas could live extremely well, and my friends were nothing if not generous. When the midterm

Me, on the right, with two friends, in Rennes

break arrived that fall, we took the train to Paris, where we drank Scotch, dined at Michelin-rated restaurants and overpriced tourist joints ("P. had snails, I had artichoke hearts, and beef with olives," I dutifully recorded about a meal at La Coupole), toured Notre Dame, climbed the Eiffel Tower ("cliché but true: breathtaking, awesome, beautiful at night!"), went to the ballet and a disco, and slept four to a room at the Grand Hotel Oriental off the rue des Écoles. Except for the night when we arrived at the front door in the wee hours to find it locked and were forced to retreat down the hill to the banks of the Seine, where, tipsy and shivering, we watched the sunrise in the company of some local drunks. I was sixteen years old and living in a chapter from Hemingway's *A Moveable Feast*, the one where he declares: "All Paris belongs to me."

"I tried to express how lucky I felt to know them, because of my middle-class Hoosier normality," I wrote in my journal about my new friends. "I realize how different, how much less deep and wide, I would be had I remained at home. Last night I took a big step away from Mini, Erika, Janet, and Jean"—high school friends back in Indiana—"a step I had taken long ago, but only now am I able to look back and see the imprint of my feet yards behind me."

◆ ◆ ◆

Theory would be another giant step along my path to worldliness, a bildungsroman I was only dimly aware I was writing. In the spring of my freshman year in college, I was cast in an experimental adaptation of Chekhov's *The Seagull*, which is how I met Mark, a sophomore literature concentrator, and his roommate, Jason, a history major and pianist who spoke accentless French and was obsessed with Huysmans, Baudelaire, and other exemplars of the nineteenth-century French Decadent Movement. The plot of *The Seagull*, which revolves around the romantic triangles of a group of struggling writers and actors, in our version became a series of striking tableaux. Dressed in black formal wear, we rushed onstage to the jubilant opening chords of Mendelssohn's Italian Symphony. At one point, the stage directions called for Jason to deposit me atop a baby grand piano; there may have been a rose in his hand or my mouth.

"It was unmistakable that you were an innocent," Mark told me recently, "high culture laminated on Midwestern innocence." Tall, dark, artistic, and brainy, Mark was from suburban Massachusetts via Exeter (do you see a pattern here?) and already into theory. "It would be hard to overstate how simply cool theory was," he says. "The aura surrounding that stuff was pretty intense." He doesn't recall the circumstances of his "first contact," nor do I mine, but I'm pretty sure that his enthusiasm for theory was a draw. We soon embarked on an on-again, off-again romance, and by the following fall, I'd declared myself a literature concentrator too.

Like many theory heads, Mark and Jason lived in Adams House, a red brick Victorian pile off Harvard Yard, originally intended as luxury accommodations for the college's wealthiest students. In the 1980s, housing for upperclassmen was still assigned according to student-ranked choices in a lottery system (rather than randomly, as it is now), and Adams, known for its literary and artistic bent, was the place I wanted to be. In 1978, a young Peter Sellars staged *Antony and Cleopatra* in the ornate marble-lined swimming pool in the basement. ("At one end floats Cleopatra's sturdy raft; at the other, the diving board extends over the water like an erect phallus," the reviewer for *The Harvard Crimson* wrote.) A decade later, in the humid half-darkness, I attended a hypnotic performance of "Inlets," a composition by John Cage featuring the otherworldly sound of water flowing through conch shells. By the end of the concert, I was floating on my back in the pool, along with the rest of the audience. That must have been one of the last such aquatic extravaganzas in Adams House. Notorious for late-night skinny-dipping parties, and a source of paranoia about AIDS in the days before the disease was well understood, the pool was closed for good the year after I graduated.

In Adams House, whose rooms were occupied by actors, musicians, and performers of every stripe, everyday life could take on a theatrical air. My roommates and I met the boys across the hall when they slipped a folded piece of paper under our door. Featuring a hand-drawn image of a flower, its petaled head snapped and tumbling from its stem, the card was an invitation to a "deflowering" party for a woman in the house named Elizabeth. She had recently lost her virginity, and, with her blessing, her friends had organized a public celebration. (She would go on to fame as the author of *Prozac Nation*, an early memoir of life on the antidepressant.)

Theory, too, could have a self-conscious, performative aspect, along with a whiff of rebellion. After all, we were a generation embarking on adulthood at a moment of unusual quiescence. Ronald Reagan, president when we began high school, would still be president until a few months before we graduated from college, when he would be succeeded by his former vice president in an election suggesting widespread public approval of his conservative revolution. The anti-war demonstrations that had roiled campuses the decade before we arrived had disappeared, as well as, apparently, any organized opposition. The culture wars had yet to ignite; the AIDS crisis had not yet penetrated the national consciousness. Politics seemed to have gone dormant, its focus elsewhere, expressions of dissent reduced to a "shantytown" in Harvard Yard protesting the university's investments in apartheid South Africa. In an era of complacency and self-satisfaction, theory was a symbol, however small, of intellectual nonconformism, a badge, like a pink mohawk, that marked you as a member of the counterculture, different from—and critical of—the docile horde.

Directly across Bow Street from Adams House's rear façade was Café Pamplona, or, as Mark recalled it, "a useful simulacrum of Parisian space": a tiny, subterranean coffee shop with an even tinier kitchen and a black-clad, male-only waitstaff that serviced an equally black-clad student clientele, a species conversant in theory. The only thing anyone seems to remember eating there is gazpacho. Mostly we went for the espresso frappé—served cold, in a tall skinny glass topped with whipped cream—and to check out who else was there. Mark and Jason both waited tables there, though no one worked at Pamplona for the money—a piddly $2.01 an hour before tips. Like theory, the job was something you did because it was cool; working there was another way of advertising to the world your superior status.

That we were hardly as original or as special or as independent-minded as we thought didn't occur to us. That an entire generation—now our professors—had gotten there first seemed not to register. As the late British historian Tony Judt wrote, "During the middle third of the twentieth century, every aspiring thinker from Buenos Aires to Bucharest lived in a Paris of the mind. Because French thinkers wore black, smoked Gitanes, talked theory, and spoke French, the rest of us followed suit."

Theory was cool. Theory was French. Theory was also, strange though it might sound, sexy. It wasn't just that those who practiced it tended to skew—like the waiters at Pamplona—youthful and attractive, though surely this was part of it. See, for example, Lorrie Moore's novel about a young woman from the rural Midwest who, arriving in a big city for college, finds her brain "on fire" in literature class: "Twice a week, a young professor named Thad, dressed in jeans *and* a tie, stood before a lecture hall of stunned farm kids like me and spoke thrillingly of Henry James's masturbation of the comma. I was riveted. I had never before seen a man wear jeans with a tie." Commenting on this passage, the critic Nicholas Dames suggests that it captures "the moment of initiation into Theory," when theory is experienced purely as "style"—jeans with a tie!—and not yet as thought. I would add only that central to that style was an erotic charge, the masturbation reference here (an allusion to a famous, much debated paper about Jane Austen by the gender theorist Eve Kosofsky Sedgwick) serving as shorthand for the way theory transposed sex to the realm of discourse, sometimes to ridiculous effect—the ridiculous part being how seriously many of us took it.

In theory, there were no bodies per se, let alone sex. But there was plenty of high-minded discussion *about* bodies and sex, Sedgwick's paper on the motif of "the masturbating girl" being a prime example. (Of course, there was no literal masturbation in Jane Austen; Sedgwick's argument, based on a reading of Austen's novel *Sense and Sensibility*, was that contemporary readers, for whom Austen is an exemplar of the heterosexual marriage plot, miss considerable evidence of her female protagonist's homoerotic and autoerotic passion.) The point was that bodies *were* discourse, starting with the body of the author, which the French philosophers had famously killed off. As Roland Barthes put it in "The Death of the Author," a legendary 1967 essay, literature is "the trap where all identity is lost, beginning with the very identity of the body that writes."

The novelty of this approach—the cold, impersonal braininess of it—was unmistakable. For a young woman like me, raised in a Protestant ethic of hard work, self-improvement, and sexual sublimation, it was irresistible. Smart talk was sexy, and none sexier than theory. There was a libidinal rush at seeing reality, language, the human psyche, pried open and ripped apart. "I took one critical theory class in college," a journalist I know confided recently. "I understood pretty much nothing. But everyone in the class was there to get laid, in intellectual fashion." When Mark told me I had "intellectual breasts," I took it as a compliment.

That theory could also compensate for shameful gaps in my education—the fact that I had arrived at college without having read *Paradise Lost* or *Hamlet*, James Joyce or James Baldwin—was another attraction. There were no prerequisites for studying theory. What mattered, my professors suggested, was not *what* I'd read but *how* I read. Like the little black dress that confers on its wearers a chicness belying its modest price tag, theory offered users automatic membership in an intellectual elite.

"You wanted to be in the group that had some kind of esoteric knowledge separating them from the squares," my friend Tony, another literature major, a few years ahead of me, said. "There was a certain type, which I was," he explained, "someone who has read some theory and then goes into another class and debunks everything—bringing all this half-digested stuff to bear. Because everyone else was still talking in traditional, literal-minded, naïve, or undertheorized ways." Need I add that Tony, too, was a waiter at Café Pamplona, the one who trained Mark for the job?

In truth, theory was very hard. For a lot of my peers, it probably seemed like too much work for too little payoff. The sense of superiority theory conferred—a smug feeling of being in the know—could go a long way toward camouflaging insecurity. But not every student needed such a prop. My roommates, one a serious actress, the other a gifted poet and fiction writer, were not tempted by theory. Neither, for all his love of French history, was Jason. Even for Mark and Tony, theory was just one component of a much broader intellectual diet. Both went on to graduate school at Johns Hopkins, a university that had been a center of high theory but by the time they got there, in the early 1990s, was becoming ground zero for the dawning backlash against it. "I realized the shortcomings of a theoretical education," Tony told me recently. "There was all this literature I hadn't read." And yet today I know few people who are *better* read than Tony. No one was surprised when he became a well-known cultural critic, admired for his witty, deeply literate movie and book reviews, or when Mark became a prominent professor, admired for his incisive scholarship on the contemporary novel.

My relationship with theory was more fraught. Maybe I expected too much from it. I didn't have a plan for after graduation. I didn't know what I wanted to be; I was hung up on something more basic: what it meant *to* be. I lacked confidence and, more to the point, skepticism. I didn't know how to take theory in small doses—and John wasn't around to warn me about getting high. Instead, I doubled down. "I had this euphoric moment at Widener Library tonight, sitting in a remote carrel reading a Marxist critique of Lacanian psychoanalysis," I wrote in my journal halfway through college. "It was thrilling. To read, to think, to walk through the cavernous halls of Widener after 10pm, alone!"

The experience of reading theory could be like that—vertiginous, as when the bottom of the Gravitron at the amusement park falls away and you are pinned by centrifugal force to the spinning wall. Deconstruction, especially, had this effect. "It's kind of exciting," explains a "deconstructionist" professor in *Small World*, David Lodge's 1984 satire of academic life. "The last intellectual thrill left. Like sawing through the branch you're sitting on." Deconstruction, then, meant violence. Derrida's mission was to show that philosophy's preoccupation with first principles, its determination to capture reality, truth, being, Kant's *Ding an sich*—or, more pretentiously, "the transcendental signified"—was doomed. How could we possibly make claims about such weighty things when the only way to do so was with *words*, flimsy surrogates for what we were really after? As Derrida's fellow theorist the psychoanalyst Jacques Lacan put it in his tongue-twisting way: "No language can say the truth about truth, since truth is grounded in the fact that truth speaks and that it has no other means by which to become grounded."

The Frenchmen, I began to see, were right. Language was a trap that even the most agile philosophers couldn't escape. They might treat words as vehicles for expressing their intuitions about the world and human existence, but this approach rested on illusion. The name for this illusion was *metaphysics*—a term the French theorists uttered like an insult. Whenever philosophers invoked such fundamental notions as truth, being, reality, or consciousness, they were engaging in metaphysics: assuming meanings that were impossible to prove.

To be fair, numerous thinkers before the Frenchmen had wrestled with the problem of language; Nietzsche, Heidegger, and a handful of others had tried their best to solve it—but to little avail. According to the Frenchmen, language was practically thinking our thoughts for us. It wasn't a window onto reality; it was a scrim over the surface of the world, sealing it from us. Exactly what lay beneath or beyond language hardly mattered since we could only gesture helplessly toward it via language itself, this intricate symbolic system of our own invention. Or maybe it had invented us?

You might think that the theorists' questions about foundational ideas were also being hotly debated in American philosophy departments, but this was not the case. In the United States in the late 1980s, the field was dominated by the so-called analytic school, which favored highly technical arguments rendered in formal logic—philosophy that resembled mathematics. A classic analytic hypothesis at the time went like this: "Possibly there are blue swans if and only if, for some world W, at W there are blue swans." As Mark put it to me, "If you wanted philosophy to be a discourse about how to live in wisdom, the field itself, especially at a place like Harvard, would have seemed repellent." By contrast, the Frenchmen, philosophers of the so-called continental school, continued to probe the big existential problems, even if only to show the impossibility of resolving them. Theory's suspicion of anything resembling human beings or human feelings was hardly a deterrent. "That didn't seem to matter because we could convert theory into a kind of melodrama nonetheless," Mark said. "We were young people! We wanted it to matter! We wanted ourselves to matter within that discourse!"

Theory made *thinking* feel like *doing*. There was a rigor and beauty to it, an athletic strenuousness. What seemed merely an intellectual exercise was actually a way of being. Doing theory, I felt I was perched at the frontiers of thought. I felt I'd become someone, or rather, something, else—that I'd escaped my body and become pure mind, that I'd left small-town Indiana far behind and entered a rarefied stratum.

The thing about French theory, though, was that its general thrust was negative. Some people talked about the productive tension implicit in the combination of "construction" and "destruction" in the word "deconstruction." But really, deconstruction was about undoing. Moreover, it was parasitical. It existed only in an encounter with a piece of writing, one it typically left in ruins, or, at best, in an equivocal state. Derrida's fellow deconstructionist Paul de Man argued that it was the fate of every critic to misread—that "blindness" was built into the act of interpretation, and so all readings were doomed to err.

Of course, deconstruction was just the most famous version of French theory. But Lacanian psychoanalysis, with its emphasis on the loss and lack that Lacan believed characterized a child's transition to what he called the "symbolic order" of language, was hardly more affirming. Then there was the Marxist Louis Althusser, who described the process by which social institutions and even human consciousness were infiltrated by the ideology of the state. Michel Foucault showed how power coerces and constrains, reaching its tentacles into schools, prisons, hospitals, and people's bodies to shape us into docile, law-abiding citizens. Roland Barthes exposed capitalist society's manipulation of words and images to promote consumerist values. Only the exuberant writings of Gilles Deleuze and Félix Guattari, unfolding a fantastical vision of unimpeded desires and "flows" as means of resistance—hands down the weirdest stuff in the French theory canon—seemed to express a modicum of hope for human progress and freedom.

In sum, I had spent my college years imbibing the work of thinkers whose main message appeared to be that our notions of reality and the self were naïve illusions, and that language, meaning, even my thoughts were not necessarily under my control. So who, or what, was I? And who were they?

◆ ◆ ◆

Nietzsche once remarked that every great philosopher left behind "a kind of involuntary and unconscious memoir." Sartre wrote that "my life and my philosophy are one and the same." And yet in the teaching of philosophy, biography is still widely considered irrelevant, if not taboo. Students are not even taught philosophers' first names. Quick: What's Hegel's? Not long ago, a scholar writing in *The New York Review of Books* marveled that the biography of Hegel he was reviewing was the first of substance to appear since 1844. He speculated about the obstacles the book's author had had to overcome, not least having to do with the philosopher's name, "which strikes one not as that of a person but of a thing: an asteroid, perhaps." This is in keeping with how philosophy as a discipline has tended to regard its most famous contributors: not as people, but as objects—receptacles for abstract ideas. The notion of a philosopher's life is still somehow vaguely embarrassing or preposterous.

"As you know, traditional philosophy excludes biography," Derrida once observed. "You'll remember Heidegger's reference to Aristotle: 'What was Aristotle's life?' Well, the answer lay in a single sentence: 'He was born, he thought, he died.'" About his own life, Derrida was cagey. "No one will ever know the secret from which I write and the fact that I say it changes nothing," he declared. Yet, a couple years before his death, when he was asked by a pair of filmmakers what he would want to learn from a documentary about a famous philosopher, he replied: "Their sex lives. . . . What is the sexual life of Hegel or Heidegger? . . . Why did these philosophers present themselves as asexual in their work? Why have they effaced their private lives from their work? And why do they never talk about personal things? . . . I'm not saying someone should make a porn film about Hegel or Heidegger. I want to hear them talking about the part love played in their lives."

To us as students, the idea that any of the Frenchmen had a body, let alone a love life, was unfathomable. Which is why we were tantalized by the story a college friend told about encountering Derrida in a men's bathroom. This friend, now a professor of French literature himself, attended a lecture by the philosopher while studying in Paris. The lecture was on the theme of mourning (in Derrida's view, a predictably paradoxical activity that could only fail to successfully commemorate the dead person while serving to underscore the mourner's state of being very much alive). Throughout the talk, about which my friend said he understood next to nothing, he had been fighting a desperate need to pee. As soon as the lecture ended, he made a beeline for the men's room, only to discover that it was already occupied, by Derrida himself. As they stood side by side at the urinals, my friend willed himself not to look down.

"The funny thing is that in my memory Derrida was smoking a pipe," he said. "That seems so unlikely. Is it possible that I displaced the 'transcendental signified' onto the pipe?" Confronted with the prospect of glimpsing Derrida's naked appendage, my friend could not permit himself to puncture the illusion of the philosopher as a disembodied mind.

Only much later did I discover how rich and varied were the lives of the French theorists on whose ideas I had labored so hard. This was long after I'd overdosed on theory and fled graduate school for journalism, a profession, it occurred to me then, that was theory's antithesis and antidote—one in which the concrete realness of the world, and of the ability of language to represent it, went largely unquestioned. Journalism offered me something else too: a sense of physical solidity, the chance to be a body again, not just a mind.

Eventually my youthful foray into theory came to seem embarrassing, if not kind of nuts, a multiyear breakdown I hadn't realized I was having. And yet the breakdown wasn't just mine; the entire culture had been touched by it. The wise professor who called America's theory craze a "farce with consequences" was right. It was a farce rooted in misunderstanding. What seemed abstract in the work of the French philosophers—the quality that made it so adaptable to American agendas—had its origins in lived experience.

Hélène Cixous, one of the few women to accede to their rank, called the philosophers of Derrida's generation *les incorruptibles*, the incorruptibles. But what she perceived as purity—men uncompromised by politics, ideology, or self-interest, aloof from the world of appetites and cravings—belied just how much they were products of their time, and of their own particular stories. Even Foucault, rigorously discreet and evasive about himself in public, nevertheless conceded a few years before his death: "Each time I have attempted to do theoretical work it has been on the basis of elements from my experience." In this, he might have been speaking for all of them.

Chapter 2

"CONDEMNED TO BE FREE"

Nineteen-eighty was a bad year for French philosophers. In February, Roland Barthes was struck by a dry cleaner's van while crossing rue des Écoles in the Latin Quarter. He died from his injuries that March, at sixty-four. In April, Jean-Paul Sartre, a chain-smoker and heavy drinker, his body wracked by strokes and diabetes, died at seventy-four. Then, in November, Louis Althusser, who had a history of bipolar disorder, strangled his wife and, judged unfit to stand trial for murder, was committed to a mental hospital. These incidents were unrelated, but it was hard not to see in them a dark symbolism. As a headline in the Parisian weekly *Les Nouvelles Littéraires* put it that fall: LA THÉORIE C'EST FOUTU!—theory is finished.

In America, theory was going strong. But the magazine had a point. Both existentialism, which Sartre had made famous, and Marxist theory, for which Althusser had been a leading mouthpiece, were in steep decline. These doctrines had enjoyed extended (and sometimes intersecting) postwar vogues, offering damaged and demoralized people hopeful new ways of conceiving of their lives and societies. And both had gradually fallen from favor, as their respective promises of social transformation on a grand scale failed to materialize—at least not in the manner their adherents had hoped. Of the three French philosophers who made headlines in 1980, only Barthes, whose groundbreaking essays on the subliminal power of words and images—he called them "signs"—seemed to speak directly to the emerging forces of globalization and consumerism, would continue to experience an uptick in readership, achieving a level of posthumous adulation in the United States that eluded him in France during his lifetime.

For each country, 1980 marked not just the beginning of a new decade but a shift in political mood. In the United States, the defeat of a weak Democratic president by the Republican populist Ronald Reagan signaled the ascendency of neoliberalism—financial deregulation and sweeping tax cuts, along with reductions in social welfare programs, increased defense spending, and escalating Cold War rhetoric. While America veered right, France veered left, electing François Mitterrand in May 1981 to head the first socialist government of the country's postwar Fifth Republic. Mitterrand remained in power for the next fourteen years, even as his socialist policies nearly ran the French economy aground and he was forced to abandon them.

On a more global scale, too, the 1980s were characterized by seismic geopolitical shifts: the fall of the Berlin Wall, the beginning of the end of the Soviet empire, the bloody crackdown on the Chinese democracy movement at Tiananmen Square, and a flurry of treaties cementing the agreement by the countries of Europe to trade independent nation status for membership in the EU. By 1993, when the Maastricht Treaty went into effect, France was no longer a sovereign nation in the traditional sense but one of eleven member states with which it shared borders, foreign policy, military defense, a central court, and, eventually, a currency and central bank as well.

Following an initial explosion of optimism in the aftermath of the war—the three decades of wondrous economic growth that the French call "*les Trente Glorieuses*"—the setbacks began to outpace the victories. The communist revolutions in Russia and China had led not to more human freedom but to less; the conflicts in Algeria and Vietnam had entailed hundreds of thousands of deaths and exposed Western powers' complicity in torture and other war crimes; and the collapse of the Soviet

Union seemed to portend the global triumph of a neoliberal order in which the intrepid individual of Sartrean existentialism was, like France itself, no longer an actor on the world stage, but a paltry thing buffeted by inhuman forces. As the American critic Fredric Jameson put it, "What appeared when the dust settled, when the fog of war cleared away, was not a transformed world, not even the world of decolonization, of independent nations, but the world of transnational corporations, nascent globalization."

In such a world, what could a person be?

◆ ◆ ◆

This, of course, was the question that the French philosophers had assigned themselves to answer. Sartre had crafted his philosophy in the 1930s, after careful study of German phenomenology, in particular the dense work of Edmund Husserl and Martin Heidegger. In retrospect, though, existentialism seemed to have burst forth overnight from the ruins of World War II. In October 1945, five months after the war's end in Europe, Sartre delivered a lecture to a crowd of rapt Parisians at the Salle des Centraux, distilling the theory he'd elaborated two years earlier in his seven-hundred-page magnum opus, *Being and Nothingness*, as well as in one novel (*Nausea*) and two plays (*The Flies*, *No Exit*). Together, these works had given the French under Nazi occupation their first taste of existentialist ideas. In his lecture, Sartre boiled down his philosophy to its essential tenets, stressing what he argued was the defining attribute of human existence: freedom. Humans, alone among animal species, he maintained, were free to determine the direction and meaning of their lives. In his view, freedom was thus both a blessing and a curse, for with it came responsibility—the responsibility to *act*. Existentialism "defines man by his actions," Sartre explained. "It tells him that the only hope resides in his actions and that the only thing that allows him to live is action." Moreover, he went on, there were no excuses for not acting. "That is what I mean when I say that man is condemned to be free."

The idea of freedom as an inviolable human trait resonated powerfully with the French, who'd endured a humiliating surrender and four years of German rule. Even the Nazis could not take that kind of freedom away. In September the previous year, weeks after Paris was liberated, Sartre had published a rousing paean to his fellow citizens, declaring, "Never were we freer than under the German occupation. . . . Because the Nazi venom seeped into our very thoughts, every accurate thought was a triumph. Because an all-powerful police force tried to gag us, every word became precious as a declaration of principle. Because we were wanted men and women, every one of our acts was a solemn commitment." This was a message the French—including those who'd done little to support the Resistance—thrilled to hear: They were not victims but heroes.

Arriving at the Salle des Centraux on the night of his lecture, Sartre saw that an unruly crowd had formed at the door. He feared it was a protest by the French Communist Party. Given existentialism's emphasis on individuals and their struggle for meaning, the philosophy could sound suspiciously bourgeois—as if it had nothing to do with actual workers or basic human needs. (It would be seven years before Sartre publicly backed the French communists.) As it turned out, the crowd consisted of a couple thousand people fighting to get inside. The event was so oversubscribed that riots broke out in the hall and, as a caption in *Time* magazine cheekily put it, beneath a mugshot of the famously homely philosopher: "Women swooned."

Sartre and his philosophy garnered a two-page spread in *Time*'s foreign news section—twice as much space as the latest developments at the Nuremburg trials. The magazine pronounced the philosopher "France's most discussed writer," adding that "in Paris since liberation, Existentialism had called forth more words and more ink than any intellectual movement since Dadaism ushered in Europe's 'lost generation' after World War I."

By the time the story appeared, in January 1946, Sartre was on a speaking tour of the East Coast, preaching the gospel of existentialism at Harvard, Yale, and Princeton. Throughout the 1940s and '50s, his name and ideas circulated like an electric current among intellectuals on both sides of the Atlantic. Here was a school of thought that, against the backdrop of bombed out cities and still-fresh memories of genocide and totalitarianism, insisted that we are never powerless casualties of circumstance. More pointedly, it spoke to survivors' guilt and nagging consciences, to personal and collective failures: collaboration, betrayal, indifference. Even in the most challenging situations, Sartre maintained, we have *choices*, and those choices have moral consequences. We are compelled to become *engaged*—a favorite existentialist term—with the world around us, and to act to change it.

William Leftwich
PHILOSOPHER SARTRE
Women swooned.

By the early 1950s, Sartre had moved decisively to the left, joining the wave of French intellectuals smitten by Marxism. Unabashed in his commitment to revolutionary politics, he lent his support to the French communists, then in thrall to Stalin, and to African independence movements. Horrified by the brutal tactics—torture, rape, executions—employed by the French Army against local militias in Algeria, he decried "the crimes being committed in our name," insisting, in existentialist fashion, that French citizens were "of necessity personally implicated because it is in our power to stop them."

His hectic travel schedule notwithstanding, Sartre was an intellectual whose activism was largely confined to words: an unceasing flow of petitions, books, op-eds, and interviews, as well as articles in *Les Temps Modernes*, the journal he founded after the war with his partner, the feminist thinker and novelist Simone de Beauvoir, and his former classmate the philosopher Maurice Merleau-Ponty. In one of his first pieces for the journal, Sartre explained that for the *engagé* writer, words *were* action—they were "loaded pistols." His radical rhetoric, and support for Soviet Russia, won him hundreds of admirers and lost him a few friends. Albert Camus, the Algerian-born philosopher who had once been a close confidant, accused him of recklessly endorsing violence from the safety of his study, complaining, in a letter to *Les Temps Modernes*, of "having to put up with endless lessons in effectiveness from censorious folk who have only ever placed their armchairs to face the way history is going."

In 1964, when Sartre turned down the Nobel Prize in Literature—on the principle that an *engagé* writer must "refuse to let himself be transformed into an institution"—he was world-famous. Yet, despite his scruples, Sartre *had* become something of an institution. He was no longer a philosopher but an icon: France's most celebrated intellectual, its national conscience; the tireless, pipe-smoking, wall-eyed little man whose signature gave an automatic stamp of moral authority to revolutionary struggle the world over. When, in 1960, Sartre signed a petition defending the right of French soldiers to refuse to fight in the Algerian war for independence, others who had signed were punished. But not Sartre. "You do not imprison Voltaire," the French president, Charles de Gaulle, explained.

Yet in the French capital, few people talked of existentialism anymore; philosophy had moved on. As Sartre's biographer Annie Cohen-Solal wrote of his fading stature: "He was the man of scandal, man of wisdom, man of freedom, man of truth. He was the one who had refused the Nobel, a hero, the one nothing could touch. But never, during his entire literary career, had he had as few contacts with other intellectuals, his contemporaries. In Paris, in the Latin Quarter, he seemed rather a has-been."

◆ ◆ ◆

Among those contemporaries, one of the first to dare make this point to his face was Sartre's fellow leftist Louis Althusser. Within a decade, Althusser's idiosyncratic readings of Marx—the work that made his reputation—would also begin to seem *depassé*. But in 1961, when he challenged Sartre after a lecture at Sartre's alma mater, the elite École Normale Supérieure, the famous existentialist still appeared untouchable and Althusser had yet to make his public mark. He was then serving as the École Normale's supervisor in philosophy—the *caïman* in the school's nomenclature, after a man who had previously held the post and was said to resemble an alligator. The *caïman*'s job was to prepare students for the rigorous *agrégation* exam, the first step toward becoming philosophy professors themselves. Althusser had brought his students to hear Sartre's lecture, and there were several prominent philosophers in the audience as well, including Sartre's former classmate Merleau-Ponty, with whom he had fallen out over politics, just as he had with Camus.

Sartre's subject was "The Possible in History," and by all accounts he acquitted himself in masterly fashion, declaiming on the necessity of human beings to shape world events through their actions, to mold history into a narrative of ever-expanding freedom. When he had finished, Althusser got up to speak. No recording of their exchange was made, and Sartre's lecture was apparently never published. But for those in attendance the event was decisive: the moment when existentialism was publicly dethroned and a new dispensation, soon to be known as structuralism, took its place. In its various guises, structuralism would rule French philosophy for the next decade, becoming the paradigm with which aspiring young scholars were obliged to grapple, even as several made their reputations by arguing against its claims.

Chapter 3

PRISONERS OF WAR

Compared with Sartre, Althusser was a virtual unknown, at least outside the academic world of the École Normale. Already in his mid-forties, he'd published little—a monograph on Montesquieu, a couple of articles on Feuerbach and Marx. Physically, he was Sartre's opposite: six feet tall with blue eyes, a thicket of sandy brown hair, and a high, handsome forehead. He was also from another continent and class. Sartre was a doted-on son of Parisian intellectuals; Althusser hailed from a family of lower-middle-class *pieds-noirs*—French citizens living in Algeria. (The *pied-noir* population was a fertile source of French philosophers, yielding Camus and Derrida as well as the political theorist Jacques Rancière and the feminist Hélène Cixous.) Moreover, unlike Sartre, who claimed he'd lost his belief in God at eleven while waiting at a bus stop, Althusser never fully relinquished the militant Catholicism of his youth. Even after he'd joined the Communist Party, at the age of thirty, he continued to make regular, if secret, visits to a group of nuns in his Parisian neighborhood, and in 1979 he sought an audience with Pope John Paul II. Catholicism and communism, he insisted, with their mutual focus on solving social problems and establishing "universal fraternity," were naturally compatible.

Yet Althusser and Sartre had more in common than they had differences, starting with their commitment to radical politics. For one thing, they'd both been taken prisoner during the war and spent most of it on the sidelines. Called up to serve in September 1939, Sartre was posted to a meteorological station in Alsace, Althusser to a unit of reserve officers in the Auvergne. They were captured the following spring and sent to POW camps—Sartre for nearly a year, Althusser for five. For both, the experience was transformative.

Louis Althusser as a POW

Althusser, held at a gigantic Luftwaffe base in northern Germany, learned about Marxism from a lawyer who was passing through and met his first communist, a self-appointed inmate leader who dazzled Althusser with his skill at eliciting concessions from their German captors and establishing a tranquil ambiance in the camp. Observing this man, Althusser later wrote, was what converted him to communism. "I began to feel quite at home as a prisoner," he admitted. "I found life easy because I enjoyed the comradeship of real men"—by which he seemed to mean men who were not intellectuals—"and I was happy because I was well protected."

He was also living apart from his parents for the first time, a fact he came to believe was essential to his happiness. For Althusser, who never had children, belatedly married his longtime partner when he was in his late fifties, and devoted many ambivalent pages of his memoir to his relationship with his mother and father, the family was a treacherous institution. Though he said he believed his parents loved him, he also harbored strong negative feelings for them, especially his mother, whose attentiveness he found oppressive. In one incident that he recalled as a "form of rape and castration," his mother brought him, then barely thirteen, into his bedroom to congratulate him on his sheets stained with the evidence of a wet dream.

Where Marx suggested that the ruling class ensures its dominance over the working class in part via ideology, understood as a set of abstract values and beliefs that are spread through a culture, Althusser viewed ideology as a material force, shaping people's behavior in concrete ways. A state typically relied on visible means of coercion—the army, the police, the courts—what Althusser called "repressive state apparatuses." But no state, he argued, could endure by force alone; it was obliged to rely on surreptitious forms of manipulation and control, what he called "ideological state apparatuses." These included schools, churches, social clubs, the media, and, most insidiously, the family.

The disconcerting thing about ideology, Althusser wrote, was that it acted invisibly, insinuating itself into every cranny of our lives, including inside our minds. (Roland Barthes's definition, expressed with his signature panache, was similar: Ideology is "what-goes-without-saying.") And the worst ideological state apparatus of all—the one that most effectively transmitted the values and beliefs of the ruling class—was the family. In a memoir Althusser wrote in 1985, he made his disgust for the family emphatically clear: "What I also discovered during my captivity was how much I enjoyed living with people other than my father and mother and away from the world (without any outside) of books, the classroom, and the family flat. In short, I was free from that most *frightful, appalling, and horrifying of all the ideological State apparatuses*, in a nation where the State exists, namely the *family*." Because his parents were "trapped" in the same "ideological structure," they had unwittingly instilled in him the "supreme values prevailing in the society in which I was growing up: absolute respect for absolute authority and above all for the State." Like all citizens in the clutches of ideology, his parents failed to recognize that the state protected the powerful and exploited everyone else.

◆ ◆ ◆

Sartre's imprisonment was much briefer but equally momentous. In his POW camp at Trier, in western Germany, he reread Heidegger's *Being and Time.* A major intervention in the field of ontology—the study of what it means to be—by the most prominent German philosopher of the day, the book had been the talk of intellectual circles since its publication in 1927. Sartre took detailed notes, and on the floor of his barracks began to draft his prodigious response: *Being and Nothingness.* After he was freed and had returned to Paris, he discovered that he missed the regimented order of camp life: the shared spaces, the rows of tightly packed sleeping bodies, everyone reduced to the same simple patterns of existence. Walking into a Parisian bar again for the first time as a free man, he took in the roomful of boisterous strangers, all drinking, talking, and thinking about different things, and felt a surge of fear.

Such episodes, along with a close reading of the Danish philosopher Søren Kierkegaard's writings on anxiety, fueled Sartre's conviction that fear was inextricable from freedom. Being free at every moment to choose—where to have a drink, whom to have it with, what profession to pursue, whom to marry, or even simply what thoughts to occupy your mind with for the next few minutes—was an uncertain prospect, one whose outcome could hardly be guaranteed in advance. This was scary enough. But, Sartre insisted, we are also responsible for our uncertain choices, no matter how they turn out—no excuses. Overwhelmed by his freedom on being released from prison, Sartre was also, then, overwhelmed by anxiety. No wonder at least one biographer suggests that he "would rarely be as relaxed and happy again as he had been as a prisoner of war." The same might be said of Althusser.

The two philosophers had shared yet another important experience: the École Normale Supérieure. Initially conceived during the French Revolution—its founding date on the revolutionary calendar, *9 brumaire, an III* (October 30, 1794), is inscribed on the transom over the front door—the school had been intended as a national training facility for secondary school teachers. A century later, having moved to its present location on the rue d'Ulm, it had become one of France's most eminent institutions of higher education, whose mission was to produce the country's elite.

By most indications, it has succeeded, having supplied a disproportionate share of French statesmen, politicians, Nobel laureates, and philosophers—including, in this last category, in addition to Sartre and Althusser, Henri Bergson, Georges Canguilhem, Raymond Aron, Derrida, Foucault, and, a rare woman graduate, Simone Weil. (By tradition, the school did not admit women and officially barred them from 1940 until 1985.) Foucault's biographer James Miller called the school "a kind of monastery for boy geniuses," while the French American philosopher George Steiner (who did not attend) called its students "the freemasonry of cultural politics." "Who will ever write . . . the history of this 'house' and its filiations?" Derrida mused in 2001. "This would be an almost impossible but indispensable task for beginning to understand the various 'logics' of French intellectual life in this century."

The mystique of the École Normale, like that of Ivy League colleges in the United States, stems in large part from how hard it is to get in. Though the school now confers a diploma equivalent to a master's degree, most students obtain their degrees from affiliated universities across Paris, with the École functioning instead as a kind of exclusive residential society. Once admitted, students become national civil servants in training; they are paid a monthly stipend and expected, after passing the *agrégation* exam in their chosen field, to teach high school or college or otherwise work for the state for six years, though a company may buy them out if they choose to join the private sector instead. For decades, one effect of the system was to ensure that even high school students in the provinces were taught by some of France's most brilliant minds, who rotated through their towns on state-sanctioned tours of duty.

To apply to the École Normale, students complete two years of grueling *classes prépas* (preparatory classes) after high school, culminating in an inordinately difficult *concours* (contest) featuring, for students in the literary or philosophy track, written and oral portions in Latin or ancient

Greek as well as French. Only the top-scoring two hundred applicants are admitted, half of them in the sciences, half in the humanities. Many promising students don't get in on the first try. Derrida failed the entrance exam twice before obtaining a passing score. After his first attempt he may have contemplated suicide. He was so panicked during his second that he choked and turned in a blank sheet of paper. Between the nightmare of getting in and the nightmare that awaited him once there—the *agrégation*—the École left Derrida with grim memories. Like many gifted thinkers before and after him, he failed the *agrégation* the first time around. "The threat of the guillotine—at least that's what it seemed like—turned those years into years of hell as far as I was concerned," he said later. "This past was really painful, I never liked the École."

Each spring for decades, the names of the admitted students were posted by rank on a window looking out onto the school's courtyard—an obsession with rank being a Cartesian ordering impulse that recurs again and again in French intellectual life. (In the 1960s, Foucault would analyze this French rage for classification in one of his most beautiful books, *The Order of Things*.) Sartre was admitted to the school in 1924, placing seventh, not quite as high as Simone Weil, who, four years later, became one of the first women to attend the school. (Known for her rigorous ethics and her religious mysticism, Weil died in an English sanatorium in 1943, of tuberculosis allegedly abetted by principled self-starvation: French citizens under German occupation were going hungry, she reasoned; why should she eat when they could not?) Weil's equally brilliant contemporary Simone de Beauvoir did not attend the École, but in 1929 she placed second after Sartre on the philosophy *agrégation*. Sartre had failed *that* exam the year before, but this time he and Beauvoir, who first met in cram sessions as they prepared for the test, dazzled their examiners. One witness later said that the jury had been exceedingly hard-pressed to decide which of the two deserved top honors.

By the time Althusser arrived at the École, in October 1945, Sartre was long gone—off living the life of a local literary sensation. That life was made possible in part by his mother, with whom he shared a flat in Saint-Germain-des-Près from which he ventured out to cafés and night-clubs as a celebrated novelist, playwright, and, increasingly, existentialist sage. (Unlike Althusser, Sartre was more than happy to be coddled by his twice-widowed mother, who, according to Beauvoir, also delighted in the arrangement, calling it "my third marriage.") In fact, Althusser had been admitted to the École with the class of 1939, but the war had intervened, and when he finally showed up six years later, he felt "irremediably old and overtaken by events," no longer a student yet hardly a scholar. He was given a room in the infirmary by the school doctor, who must have sensed his fragility.

Chapter 4

A MARRIAGE OF THEORY AND PRACTICE

Nearly a half century later, I spent a year after college at the École on a fellowship. My friend Nick had received the fellowship the previous year and encouraged me to apply. I'd known Nick since Rennes, and we had gone on to college together; he graduated in three years instead of the usual four, thanks to a raft of high school AP class credits. Nick and I shared a love of French and France, but Nick hadn't caught the theory bug. His intellectual passions were solidly grounded in the empirical: He'd spent his postcollege year in Paris earning a *maîtrise* (master's) in history with a thesis on the centralization of political power and punishment in medieval France. He had then moved across the Channel to study law at Oxford.

I figured I, too, would eventually go to graduate school. But as an immediate prospect, the thought of returning to France was irresistible. Besides, Nick said, the fellowship came with few strings attached. Knowledge of French was a prerequisite, but if I wanted to spend the year sitting at the Café de Flore or strolling around Paris, no one would complain. As it turned out, I spent the year diligently earning a *maîtrise* as well, typing in French, with the aid of a generous font and margins, on a hulking desktop PC in the *salle des ordinateurs*—computer room—at the École Normale, the hundred-page thesis required for the degree in comparative literature. Mine was on the novels of the dissident Czech writer Milan Kundera, whom I had discovered in college. When I learned that Kundera himself would be teaching a seminar in Paris that fall, I immediately applied. Every week for several months, I sat with a couple dozen other students in a classroom at the École des Hautes Études en Sciences Sociales listening to the great man expound his theory of the novel. Aside from passing references to Hegel or Heidegger, Kundera did not dwell on the philosophers whose names I'd become accustomed to hearing. Tall and imposing, with large expressive hands and a broad, handsome face—his entire demeanor rough around the edges, even a little thuggish, in a way that defied my hothouse conception of the writer—he had his own ideas.

In Kundera's view, something tragic had happened to the novel in the nineteenth century, when naturalism became its dominant aesthetic. Until that moment, he argued, the genre had been rife with experimentation, encompassing the picaresque, the epistolary, and the novel of ideas, characterized by philosophical and essayistic digressions, the whole leavened with irony and humor. In Kundera's telling, it was as though the novel, once a bountifully leafing tree, had lost some of its most lustrous foliage as it grew. The modern novels he admired most—books by Kafka, Robert Musil, and Hermann Broch—were the ones he believed paid homage to this earlier, luxuriant period in the genre's history. Kundera, who had trained as a musician and worked as a jazz pianist in Prague in the 1970s after being expelled from the Communist Party, claimed that classical music had followed a similar trajectory. He said that the composers he loved best—Stravinsky and Schoenberg—were likewise those who acknowledged and somehow incorporated into their work the fruits of an earlier era of free experimentation.

Kundera did not discuss his own writing, but the eighteenth-century inspirations for his own playful, ironic, philosophical novels were clear. In my thesis, I made much of his formal adventurousness—his efforts to, as he put it, marry "utmost seriousness of question" to "utmost lightness of form"—as a promising model for a genre increasingly paralyzed by theory's generally nullifying insights into language and meaning. Kundera's novels, I wrote, "speak directly to the impasse in which literary theory and philosophical thought currently find themselves" while "offering a plausible way out of the cul-de-sac." (It sounded better in French.)

Clearly, I was working through some of my college theory trauma in the only way I knew how: via an academic paper. My *maîtrise* would not be my last word on the subject, though it proved therapeutic. The cafés proved therapeutic too. That fall, my friend Jennifer, a college classmate and free spirit—someone able to converse with anyone, anywhere, regardless of whether she had any language in common—moved into my room for several weeks, after her job as an *au pair* for a wealthy family in the 16th arrondissement came to a crashing end. Jennifer was appalled when the parents returned early from a weeklong getaway to Morocco complaining that there hadn't been enough sand on the beach. And she resented what she said were repeated abuses of the childcare schedule they had agreed to. The simmering tension erupted one night in November in a showdown during which slaps and obscenities were exchanged, and Jennifer was kicked out of the house. The next day, under the boisterous escort of nearly a dozen *normaliens* distributed across several cars—"cavaliers in cravats" I called them in my journal—Jennifer and I returned to the 16th to retrieve her belongings.

After that, everyone at the École Normale seemed to know *les Américaines* in Room 304. That winter, I had a fling with a floppy-haired physics PhD student from Lyon whom I met in the cafeteria. His area of academic specialty was the first three seconds after the Big Bang—to my relief, an utterly different, and to me incomprehensible, realm of theory from the one I knew. We sat in the Luxemburg Gardens sipping whipped cream–topped *cafés viennois* from slender glass mugs and talked about jazz and poetry instead. "This is the place I needed to come to," I wrote solemnly. "Where I am purged and begin anew."

◆ ◆ ◆

In some ways the École Normale hadn't changed much since Althusser first saw it. The menu at the *pot*—the cafeteria—had no doubt improved; when Derrida was a student, he filed a formal complaint about the food, objecting to the mushy peas and the Camembert that approached "the consistency of brick." The drab, dirty rooms lamented by students in Sartre's day had obviously been renovated. Arriving in the fall of 1989, in the wake of such storied history, I was disappointed to be assigned a *thurne*—literally "hovel" in the school's lexicon—across the street from the main building, in a banal modern addition devoid of character. I heard rumors about a room that had belonged to Samuel Beckett, who spent two years at the École as a lecturer in English in the late 1920s; he was said to have left lewd drawings, still visible, on a wall. Alas, I never saw them.

In appearance and ambiance, the main building remained as it had for decades. At its center, through a generous entrance hall (known as the "*aquarium*") was the *Cour aux Ernests*: a lushly planted courtyard with black locust trees, manicured hedges, and a twinkling fountain filled with goldfish—the *Ernests*. (The courtyard and the fish were named after Ernest Bersot, a late-nineteenth-century director of the school.) Running the length of the perimeter and connecting the *cour* to the classrooms, dormitories, cafeteria, and in the basement, a game room, was an enclosed arcade with large, arched windows. Evidently, I was confounded by the setting, writing (a little pretentiously) in my journal that the courtyard "gives off an air of tranquility more suited to a monastery or a Mediterranean villa for the wealthy in their dotage. One can hardly imagine the clamor of five hundred young intellectuals emanating from its sedately decaying façade. The peeling white lawn chairs scattered amiably around the fountain in little social clusters are unoccupied now but seem to speak of the aged fannies they once held—an inner sanctuary worthy of Freud, a natural healing ground for the hysterical Dora and the traumatized little Hans."

Looking back now, I am struck, not only by the florid drift of my prose—I was clearly much affected by my atmospheric surroundings—

***La Cour aux Ernests* at the École Normale Supérieure in 1929**

but by my impression of lurking infirmity. Sitting alone in the empty courtyard that day, shortly after my arrival, I noted a bell chiming somewhere, a crumpled cigarette carton abandoned on a nearby table, and, most remarkably, scribbled in chalk along one wall, some graffiti in ancient Greek. (Graffiti in ancient Greek was not something I had seen at Harvard, for all its scholarly ostentation.) But I seemed fixated on the aura of hidden malaise, writing, "My imagination reads illness into the invisible and the silent, as if I myself were a patient taking the cure"—which, in a sense, I was.

No one mentioned Althusser to me that year, and by the following October he was dead. But he had lived at the École Normale for three and a half decades, punctuated by frequent stints in psychiatric hospitals, until he was finally taken away by ambulance, never to return, on the morning in 1980 when he killed his wife. In retrospect, his life was so consumed by illness and its treatments—electroshock therapy, antidepressants, psychoanalysis, at one point on a daily basis—that it seems astonishing he had a career at all. Amid the dramatic mood swings and emotional instability, the École had been a soothing constant, in this respect not so different from the German *stalag*, where he'd found solace interned with other men.

In his memoir, he describes the school as a "'womblike' place, where I felt warm and at home and was protected from the outside world. . . . In essence it had a maternal ambiance, was like an *amniotic* fluid." Althusser's biographer declared that Althusser "was mad (*fou*) for the school, with a true love" even as he was also "symbolically 'the madman' (*le fou*) of the school. No other university setting would have suited him." Promoted to the post of *caïman* in 1948, after completing the *agrégation*, Althusser mentored Foucault and Derrida and later brought both back to teach there, along with Jacques Lacan, whom he befriended after discerning powerful similarities in their work. In 1961, when Althusser confronted Sartre at the school after Sartre's lecture on history, he was nearing the peak of his intellectual powers.

Though he was obscure to the broader public, among the school's philosophy students, he was revered as a teacher and leftist. Like thousands of other French citizens after the war, he had joined the Communist Party, which, for the next two decades routinely received between 20 and 25 percent of the vote in national elections. Initially inspired by the communist prisoner he'd met in the POW camp, Althusser was further converted by Hélène Rytmann, his girlfriend (eventually his wife) whom he met through a mutual friend during his second year at the school.

He was twenty-eight and sexually inexperienced, having never even kissed a woman. She was eight years older, a Parisian Jew whose parents had died when she was barely into her teens, leaving her virtually destitute. She had joined the Communist Party in the 1930s and then, during the war, the Resistance. At one point, she had been in charge of a group of Resistance fighters who captured, tortured, and summarily executed a senior Gestapo official. Though Rytmann insisted she had ordered her group to keep the man alive for questioning, she was blamed for his death. In his memoir, Althusser recounts how Rytmann was subjected to a weeklong trial by a Party committee in Paris, the upshot of which was a motion to expel her. "When it came to the vote, everyone raised their

Louis Althusser and Hélène Rytmann in the 1950s

hand," Althusser wrote, "and to my shame and astonishment, my own hand went up. I had known it for a long time: I was indeed a coward."

This remarkable admission is in keeping with the extreme ambivalence Althusser displays toward Rytmann throughout his book. Their first sexual encounter sets the tone: Althusser was immediately overwhelmed by a "deep-seated feeling of repulsion" and sank into a clinical depression. He ended up on a locked ward at Sainte-Anne Hospital, where he received twenty-four electroshock treatments. Rytmann visited faithfully, if illicitly, standing beneath a restroom window to talk to him and meeting him at the hospital's gate when he was released. Just as Sartre had found an intellectual life partner in Beauvoir, Althusser found one in Rytmann. Though they did not seem to have formally negotiated an open relationship, as Sartre and Beauvoir had, Althusser sought, and apparently was granted, Rytmann's approval for most of the numerous affairs he conducted on the side.

What the couple had in common—"a perfect understanding," Althusser claimed—was a political worldview. Theirs was quite literally a marriage of theory and practice: Rytmann was not a philosopher; she had never read Marx. "The only thing that mattered to her in politics was the working class," Althusser wrote. Her belief in communism as that class's best hope for salvation was absolute. It was a conviction they shared with a vocal majority of students at the École Normale, where being a communist was practically de rigueur.

Chapter 5

THE CULT OF MARX

It's hard to overstate the enthusiasm of French intellectuals for Marxist theory in the 1950s and '60s. If Sartre was the most important living philosopher, Marx was the most important dead one. And the École Normale, an institution filled with young men "overeducated in the art of interpretation," as Derrida put it, was a central incubator of Marxist zeal. Newspapers, literary journals, and bookstore shelves teemed with work by *normaliens* staking out their positions on Marx, Stalin, the working class, and the revolution—and attacking anyone who opposed them.

A lot of this work is almost unreadable now, the pained efforts of young eggheads twisting themselves into rhetorical knots over the moral conundrums posed by real-world applications of Marxist principles. It was impossible to deny that the Soviets' attempt to turn their country into a workers' paradise had fallen short. The French knew about some of Stalin's excesses—the show trials, the labor camps, the bloody purges of those who strayed from the party line. But for hardcore believers, this didn't mean that the philosophy undergirding the Soviet experiment was wrong. Certainly Soviet communism was preferable to the imperialistic capitalism of the United States. (The term *antiaméricanisme* first appeared in France in 1948 and quickly caught on, reaching a crescendo during the Vietnam War.) "Whatever the nature of today's Soviet society, the Soviet Union is, by and large, and given the balance of power, on the side of those who are struggling against the forms of exploitation we are so familiar with," declared *Les Temps Modernes* in an editorial in 1950. "The fact that Russian communism is decadent does not mean that the class struggle is a myth, that 'free enterprise' is either possible or desirable, or, more generally, that the Marxist critique is dated."

Yet by the time Derrida arrived at the École Normale in the fall of 1952, several of Sartre's closest friends had either renounced their commitment to communism or spoken out forcefully against it, and Sartre was publicly feuding with both Camus and Merleau-Ponty over the issue. These rifts were mirrored at the École, where students argued about politics and split into groups according to their leftist persuasions. Even so, a generally militant atmosphere prevailed, and few dared admit to harboring more conservative views. "Every morning, straight after breakfast, the members of the École's 'cell' would gather in the '*aquarium*' to read *L'Humanité*"—the Party newspaper—"and wave the best pages around," Derrida's biographer Benoît Peeters writes, adding that on the day in March 1953 that Stalin died, "the Communists—many of whom could not dry their tears—forced the École to observe a minute's silence, while trying to find out to whom in the USSR they could address a telegram of condolence." Put off by the militants, Derrida opted to join a non-communist leftist group.

The historian Tony Judt refers to the "holistic strain in French styles of thought," noting the attraction of French intellectuals to theories that emphasized "'totality' or the absolute" over partial or small-bore explanations, a tendency he traced to Descartes and his legacy of "distaste for intellectual doubt." Marxism was a prime example. "Because Marxism offered a way of recovering 'the illusion of total knowledge,'" Judt wrote, "modern French intellectuals were always likely to be susceptible to its appeal, appropriately packaged."

The same could be said about the appeal of French theory decades later to intellectually insecure American students (like me). With its grand explanatory ambitions, theory swept away doubt, offering in its place the certitudes of an all-encompassing system. In the case of Judt's

Parisian thinkers, the Marxism they embraced was one largely of their own making and, as pure theory uncontaminated by practice, it endured longer in France than elsewhere in the West. "In France, the owl of Minerva does not spread its wings at dusk but at mid-morning the next day," observed one historian, paraphrasing Hegel. "For all of France's stylishness, intellectual and political news arrives late."

The philosopher Raymond Aron, who had been Sartre's classmate at the École Normale (placing first in the *agrégation* the year Sartre failed it) was so alarmed by the French left's cultlike embrace of Marx and the Soviet Union—the latter as proof of the former's prophetic vision—that he devoted a book to the subject. As a young professor at the University of Cologne in the 1930s, he had witnessed Germany's transition to totalitarianism, and he was as appalled by the French intellectuals' reverence for Stalin as he was by the Germans for Hitler. For the title of his 1955 bestseller, *The Opium of the Intellectuals*, he took inspiration from a damning critique by Simone Weil: "Marxism is undoubtedly a religion, in the lowest sense of the word. Like every inferior form of the religious life it has been continually used, to borrow the apt phrase of Marx himself, as the opiate for the people."

Refusing to be cowed, Sartre responded to Aron with his own book on Marx, the nine-hundred-page *Critique of Dialectical Reason*, in 1960. By then, even Sartre had lost his enthusiasm for the USSR and had broken with the doctrinaire French communists. (In his view, the Soviets, in their violent suppression of the 1956 Hungarian Uprising, had finally crossed the line to indefensible.) His aim was to salvage Marxist theory from its corrupt application behind the Iron Curtain, and he opened the book with crusading words: "I consider Marxism to be the unsurpassable philosophy of our time." Even so, he was unwilling to abandon existentialism, and so the book became an uneasy attempt at reconciliation: a hugely ambitious but often contorted endeavor to join the anxiously free human actor of existentialist thought with Marx's determinist view of class-based conflict and of history itself. As Sartre poses the problem:

"How are we to understand that Man makes history if at the same time it is history which makes Him?"

For Sartre, the great limitation of orthodox Marxism was that it had nothing to say about individuals. He cited Engels's description of people as wholly formed by their class and its relations to production at a particular moment—people as products, not agents, of history. "Lacking Napoleon," Engels insisted, "another man would have filled his place." Not true! Sartre protested. By way of proof, he offered the case of Flaubert. (The book is peppered with allusions to Flaubert, a writer with whom Sartre was so obsessed that he went on to devote a four-thousand-page psychobiography to the novelist—at his death in 1980, he still had one volume to write.) The traditional Marxist framework may explain why Flaubert, the conflicted son of a successful provincial surgeon, wrote naturalistic novels mocking the grandiose aspirations of the rural bourgeoisie, Sartre conceded. But it failed to explain "why Flaubert preferred literature to everything else, nor why he lived like an anchorite, nor why he wrote *these* books rather than those of Duranty or the Goncourt brothers." To answer such questions, Sartre argued, we needed to consider Flaubert's childhood and the psychodynamics of his family life. Only then were we likely to learn why Flaubert negotiated the tensions of his social class in the precise way that he did and chose literature as his vocation—his "project," to use Sartre's term.

In this way, *Critique of Dialectical Reason* attempts an impossible balancing act, straining to acknowledge Marx's mechanistic model—dialectical materialism—on making us who we are while insisting on the fine-grained particulars of lived experience, all commingling to motivate and constrain us in our pursuit of freedom, our chosen "projects." The book meant a great deal to Sartre—he said it was the philosophical work for which he wanted to be remembered. He wrote it in haste, at the height of the Algerian War, propelled by irritation with Aron, animus toward the French Communist Party, and up to twenty pills of Corydrane, an amphetamine, per day. Unfortunately, the effects of this high-pressure, drugged performance show. At one point, Sartre left his voluminous manuscript—hundreds of handwritten pages—on a windowsill, where it was caught by the wind and scattered about the room. As Fredric Jameson, who wrote his dissertation on Sartre and became a leading Marxist cultural critic at Duke, tells the story, it took Sartre's friends nearly a week to reassemble the pages in the proper order. The book is that challenging—turgid, repetitious, and laced with technical jargon.

This is a shame, and not only because the book's style obscures its significance as the most high-profile effort by that date to marry what were then the two most important currents of French philosophy. It's a shame because Sartre's lasting contribution to the field, beyond existentialism itself, *was* stylistic. Moving fluidly among genres—from novels and plays to essays, and even a handful of screenplays—he showed that philosophy could be literary and literature philosophical. What his works shared was an attention to the everyday life of ordinary people, which he insisted should be at the center of philosophical endeavor. Even as Sartre's intellectual star began to dim, and existentialism fell into disrepute, this focus on lived experience endured, though recast in ways Sartre might not have recognized or approved.

Chapter 6

SARTRE GETS A DRUBBING

In his 1961 lecture at the École Normale, "The Possible in History," Sartre likely invoked some of the ideas he'd developed in *Critique of Dialectical Reason*. Yet as the philosopher Régis Debray, then Althusser's student, recalled years later, in one of the few detailed accounts of the event, Sartre's title for the lecture already signaled a problem. Among French intellectuals at the beginning of the 1960s, the existentialist individual freely reasoning his way through life had come to seem naïve, a relic of Descartes and the Enlightenment, of an obsolete, romantic past.

Sartre had failed to grasp just how much the landscape had shifted. The fight against fascism in Europe—arguably existentialism's original *raison d'être*—had been won. Like elsewhere on the Continent, France was rapidly advancing along a path toward modernization and prosperity; during the first half of the 1960s, at the peak of *les Trente Glorieuses*, its economy grew at an average rate of more than 6 percent a year—faster than any other in Europe. Moreover, the struggle for liberation had migrated to countries far away: The Korean War had ended in a standoff; the Algerian War was winding down in a victory for Algerians; France had granted independence to its former colonies in Indochina; and President de Gaulle had declared his opposition to the American war in Vietnam. The two great powers, the United States and the Soviet Union, appeared locked in a stalemate of words and images, having more or less carved up the world between them. The Berlin Wall, a potent symbol of that division, would go up five months after Sartre's lecture.

In such a world, humanist philosophy had little place. "Personalism," as some liked to call Sartre's theory, no longer made sense. The individual was a puny thing compared with the vast, impersonal forces rearranging the planet. From now on, the Western citizen would be relegated to the sidelines, a passive viewer of the history beamed into her TV set from somewhere else. "Our role, as smalltime profiteers of the peace at home in exchange for war elsewhere, was already fixed," Debray wrote, "always spectators, never actors."

Within a few years, this new culture shaped by proliferating images would be christened "the society of the spectacle" in an influential book by the French philosopher Guy Debord. But already by 1961, some French thinkers were turning to a novel way of conceptualizing reality, one seemingly more attuned to the workings of this media-saturated modernity. Drawing on ideas from anthropology and linguistics, some new, others decades old, these thinkers saw in place of Sartre's freely acting man vast interconnected networks of symbols and signs within which human beings were constrained. This was structuralism. In the 1950s, in a series of groundbreaking books, the anthropologist Claude Lévi-Strauss had given the French their first tutorial in structuralist concepts and vocabulary.

Lévi-Strauss had also been the first prominent intellectual to debunk existentialism, calling out its "over-indulgent attitude towards the illusions of subjectivity" and dismissing it as a "sort of shop-girl's metaphysics" in his 1955 memoir, *Tristes Tropiques*. In 1962, he would publish *The Savage Mind*, which ends with a chapter-long attack on Sartre, picking apart his *Critique of Dialectical Materialism* and its "mystical conception" of history. By then Barthes, Foucault, and Lacan had all gained acclaim with books announcing their allegiance to the new approach. Barthes's *Mythologies* (1957) elaborated a powerful analysis of mass media, showing how it served as a manipulative conduit of ruling-class culture, subliminally reinforcing bourgeois values. Foucault's *Madness and Civilization* (1961) introduced the idea that fundamental cultural distinctions—between sanity and madness, or reason and irrationality—were not natural or inevitable but products of shifting political and social realities. Finally, steadily larger crowds were flocking to Lacan's seminar at Sainte-Anne Hospital, where he painstakingly explained Freudian concepts as functions of language—a closed symbolic system in which we were all trapped.

Althusser, who remained in analysis virtually his entire adult life, was following Lacan's career with more than casual interest. In 1963, in a footnote to an article on Marx, Althusser suggested that in reworking Freud, Lacan was attacking the idea of a simple "homo psychologicus," just as Marx was attacking the notion of a simple "homo economicus." In other words, human beings were no more in charge of their own psychology than they were of the material conditions of their lives. Althusser was so taken with Lacan that he invited him to move his seminar from Sainte-Anne Hospital to the École Normale. "As a result, and for a good many years from that day on," Althusser recalled later, "there were expensive English cars all over the pavements of the rue d'Ulm on Wednesdays at midday, much to the annoyance of the local inhabitants."

How the individual—now renamed the "subject"—fit into the new structuralist paradigm, or whether he or she did at all, was a vexed question. It was in this charged context that Sartre delivered his lecture at École Normale. As Debray recounted the event: "At the very moment when French history was turning us into its puppets—and at the same time making Structure the foundation of all the dominant theories—the last philosopher of the Subject, with his booming voice and metallic timbre, which made you think for an instant that the great little man was hiding a megaphone in his mouth, held forth brilliantly on History and on our work, we little demiurges pushing events along before us at the head of our 'independent projects.'"

Few in Sartre's audience were buying it. "When he had finished, Althusser tried very politely to show him that Descartes was dead and we could not revive him by disguising the 'cogito' as 'praxis,'" Debray wrote. Sartre was baffled by the objection. He and Althusser spoke past each other, enacting a "dialogue of the deaf," while Merleau-Ponty, seated on a student bench, watched in stony silence. He died of a stroke weeks later, at fifty-three, making this encounter the last between him and his *Temps Modernes* cofounder and onetime friend—the "final bitter adventure of the Dialectic," as Debray ruefully put it. (Merleau-Ponty had seen what was coming: In a prescient book published the previous year, he had noted that the cultural tide had turned against the exponents of "revolutionary heroism and humanism.") The philosopher Georges Canguilhem, who was also in the audience that night, later recalled "the treachery" of Althusser's and his students' questions. The winner of the debate was clear. "Only one opponent managed, it seems, to corner Sartre—but only once—in a true intellectual confrontation, and that was Louis Althusser," Sartre's biographer Cohen-Solal wrote. "The Sartre-Althusser debate remains an extraordinary moment, one that none of those present ever forgot."

◆ ◆ ◆

Routing Sartre in front of an august crowd of *normaliens* must have been a thrill. Afterward, Althusser lost few opportunities to denigrate his opponent. "I have always thought that Sartre, though a brilliant mind and the author of wonderful 'philosophical novels' such as *Being and Nothingness* and *Critique of Dialectical Reason*, never really understood anything of Hegel, Marx, or needless to say, of Freud," he wrote haughtily in his memoir.

Of course, Althusser believed that he did understand these thinkers. He was determined to loosen the Soviets' grip on the French Communist Party by returning its members to Marx's own writings, as he, Althusser, interpreted them. His moment of triumph came in October 1965 when he published his two most influential books virtually simultaneously: *For Marx*, a collection of essays based on his close study of Marx's early work;

and *Reading Capital*, a synthesis by him and several of his students of a monthslong seminar on *Das Kapital* that he had led at the École Normale earlier that year.

Released by a left-wing press, as part of a series called "Theory," Althusser's books were a spectacular success. *For Marx* sold thirty-two thousand copies, an extraordinary number for an abstruse academic work, and both books were quickly translated into other languages. In *For Marx*, Althusser aimed to show that there were two Marxes: a young Marx inclined to humanist idealism, and a mature Marx, capable of rigorous, scientific thought. Althusser went so far as to posit a "*coupure épistemologique*," or epistemological break, between these two Marxes, pinpointing the event to the year 1845.

He proposed that we overlook the young, humanist Marx much as we should overlook the hopelessly humanist Sartre. This young Marx was still beholden to the Hegelian mindset of his day, which saw history as a conflict-ridden but purposeful process leading inexorably toward ever greater reason and freedom. Such a view was too mystical for Althusser. He did not believe, as the young Marx apparently did, that communism was mankind's inevitable destiny. Of course, he suggested, it would be grand if communism were to take root everywhere, but nothing about human history to date guaranteed such a future. Nor did Althusser believe the existentialist line about humans directing the course of their history. "It is impossible to *know* anything about men except on the absolute precondition that the philosophical (theoretical) myth of man is reduced to ashes," he wrote. (Take that, Sartrean man of action!) Althusser insisted that we concentrate on the mature Marx instead.

After 1845, and certainly in *Das Kapital*, he argued, what Marx was writing wasn't theory but *science*: the first science of history. Marx had identified the material variables—from natural resources, property, and human labor to the production and consumption of goods—around which society was organized. And in *Reading Capital*, Althusser and his students endeavored to tease out Marx's insights into how those variables governed relations among the social classes and shaped history. Using a method borrowed from Lacanian psychoanalysis that they called "symptomatic reading," the group suggested how the variables might combine in different ways at different times, yielding a range of effects. But the point was that the variables were always the same. Marx, they maintained, had grasped the grand interconnected system that underlay every aspect of existence, but he had left pieces of it half buried. It was the task of Althusser and his students to unearth the entire system and bring it into the light. This shift in emphasis from Marx himself to the act of interpretation was a hallmark of structuralism: The important thing was not the author or his intentions, but the *text*.

Althusser's Marxism was as doctrinaire as his Catholicism, as though he'd merely swapped one absolutist worldview—or "totality," to use Judt's term—for another. Stressing the objective nature of Marx's work, Althusser called it "theoretical anti-humanism." Much of Althusser's writing consists of mouthfuls like this suspended in paragraphs formatted with the logic of mathematical proofs and embellished with generous helpings of italics. He worried about Marx's use of descriptive language, including spatial metaphors, such as the suggestion of an edifice to evoke society's most basic arrangements—an economic "infrastructure" topped by a cultural "superstructure." He sought to sweep away the metaphors and expose with stringent clarity the bedrock of truth beneath them. (Not beholden to the same criteria, I am permitting myself a spatial metaphor here, because it seems—perhaps as it did to Marx—apt.)

Althusser worked doggedly to rid his prose of any taint of humanism. But when he reflected on his career a few years before he died, he insisted that the individual had been his primary concern. He wrote that he had been "a pure-minded student of the École Normale, an academic, and above all the author of a body of philosophical work which was abstract and impersonal, but passionately concerned with the self." Certainly the self that emerges from his pages looks nothing like the thinking, desiring, flesh-and-blood creature we typically associate with this word. And it looks nothing like Sartre's trembling existentialist.

Instead, the individual in Althusser's theory—as in the work of Barthes,

Lacan, Foucault, and the other structuralists—is faceless and nameless; it's hard to conceive of a sentient entity more abstract than the structuralist subject. In Althusser's conception, this subject is not born into a particular family or cultural milieu. Instead, he or she is "interpellated" by ideology into the larger social system. Althusser's usage of the word was apparently novel. His name appears in my dictionary in the entry for "interpellate," which includes this definition attributed to his work: "*Philosophy* [of an ideology or discourse] brings into being or give identity to [an individual or category]."

The process of interpellation is constant and never ending, flowing through every subject's experience of family, friends, school, church, books, television, jobs, marriage, children, and on and on. Ideology is acting on us and through us all the time, Althusser says. We are never outside it. It is even inside our heads, within our unconscious. This reality, Althusser believed, is what Freud and then, with greater rigor, Lacan aimed to demonstrate in their accounts of the human psyche.

To show how ideology exerts its effects in even the most banal circumstances, Althusser offered the example of a friend knocking on our door. "Who's there?" we say. "It's me," the friend replies. "And we recognize that 'it is him,' or 'her,'" Althusser writes. "We open the door, and 'it's true, it really was she who was there.'" His point is that it is *ideology* that makes such trivial rituals seem so natural and obvious—virtually beneath comment—while in fact they perform the important, unceasing work of situating us within the social system and thus making it easy for ideology to continue to act on us.

More sinisterly, by continually reminding us that you are you and I am I, ideology reinforces the fantasy that we are distinct and freely acting individuals. "You and I are *always already* subjects," Althusser writes, "and as such constantly practice the rituals of ideological recognition, which guarantee for us that we are indeed concrete, individual, distinguishable and (naturally) irreplaceable subjects." In this way, he says, ideology masks the fact that we are really just expendable cogs in a vast, exploitive, economic system.

This is why Althusser found Sartrean humanism so suspect: It perpetuates the illusion of freedom—in Althusser's view, little more than a bourgeois conspiracy ("bourgeois" being for French intellectuals steeped in Marxism the ultimate epithet, ubiquitous shorthand for the ruling class and its oppressive, conformist, consumerist values). Even the ease with which we formulate an opinion about Althusser's theory is conditioned by ideology, he insisted: "The writing I am currently executing and the reading you are currently performing, are also in this respect rituals of ideological recognition, including the 'obviousness' with which the 'truth' or 'error' of my reflections may impose itself on you." How Althusser himself was able to see through the comforting illusions of ideology with which the rest of us are brainwashed was a question he conveniently ignored.

To a citizen of the twenty-first century, with its freewheeling digital culture, multibillion-dollar social media companies, and relatively weak federal governments, the idea of a state ideology conditioning the thoughts and behavior of its citizens sounds faintly ridiculous, a quaint relic of the Cold War, of movies like *The Manchurian Candidate* rather than, say, *The Matrix*, in which human freedom is an illusion promoted not by an evil government but by artificial intelligence—technology run amuck. These days, it seems more likely that social media platforms, with their precision-targeted algorithms, are the entities doing the manipulating—turning us into "lab animals" in a "continuous behavior modification" experiment "on a titanic scale," as the internet pioneer Jaron Lanier once put it. But when I first encountered Althusser's theory of the interpellated subject in college, I reacted much as he says we do when ideology makes some notion seem obvious and natural: Of course, I thought, what he says is true!

By then, I had read a good deal of structuralist philosophy, and I was convinced the structuralists were right—there was little about our existence that wasn't shaped by impersonal networks of power and symbols in which we were all enmeshed. And Althusser's theory provided a clear account of how the enmeshing occurred. Having a brand-new word to describe this process made it seem only more powerful, as if I'd been let in on crucial secret knowledge. I pictured interpellation as something akin to what's endured by the anonymous workers in Fritz Lang's 1927 dystopian movie *Metropolis*. Enslaved to Moloch, a mammoth beast-like machine, the workers change shifts en masse and perform identical mechanical movements as they go about their jobs. In one scene, the movie's hero hallucinates a vision of the workers being fed into Moloch's gaping mouth—a nightmarish stand-in for capitalism's insatiable maw. I was pretty sure that these alienated workers were what Althusser had in mind. He might have added that whether the "subject" is a factory worker or a college literature student, the process by which ideology acts on us is the same.

The impersonal nature of Althusser's theory gave it a practical advantage: Scrubbed of human agency, his Marxism was impervious to human failing. If Stalin or Mao had committed terrible mistakes, or if the French Communist Party had looked the other way while they did so, well, that was on them. Marx, the rigorous antihumanist, was not to blame. Althusser's work galvanized a cohort of young French intellectuals, who, born in the shadow of World War II and coming of age during

Workers being fed to Moloch, the industrial machine in Fritz Lang's *Metropolis* (1927)

the dissolution of their country's far-flung empire, were eager to rearm the fight on behalf of the exploited classes with a true Marxist science, one unmarred by Soviet or Chinese perversions of doctrine. Régis Debray recalled the scene at the École Normale, with Althusser presiding inside a filthy office late into the night, "crushing under the tyranny of his rigor a cohort of students who would put up with anything just to be a part of it."

The historian Tony Judt, who was raised in England by Marxist parents, arrived in Paris as a graduate student in the late 1960s, after the Althusserian frenzy had taken hold. "Althusser was touted by everyone I met as a man of extraordinary gifts, who was transforming our understanding of Marx and reshaping revolutionary theory," Judt recalled years later. "His name, his ideas, his books were everywhere." Another Englishman, the philosopher Roger Scruton, was a PhD student at Cambridge at the time, with a girlfriend in Paris. When Scruton went to visit her, he discovered that Althusser had been "adopted as a foundational authority of the new curriculum, someone whose work it became instantly imperative to discuss." *Le tout-Paris*, it appeared, had been swept off its feet. In the breathless words of a French historian, Althusser had become "a new Marx," having "assigned himself the task, through a teaching both rigorous and collective, of awakening the soul of the world." As it turned out, however, neither Judt, a man of the left, nor Scruton, a man of the right, proved susceptible to Althusser's charms, both taking a dim view of his thought once they'd had a chance to study it.

Althusser himself was alternately elated and despondent over the reception of his work—a typical pattern. By his own tally, he suffered at least fifteen serious depressions during his years at the École Normale, many of which involved hospital stays and were preceded or followed by periods of near mania. In his memoir, he confessed that he had read only the first of *Das Kapital*'s three volumes closely and lived in terror of being exposed as a fraud. At the same time, he recalled with embarrassment how he had gloated about his public success, declaring at one point: "We are in the process of becoming hegemonic."

He chalked up the boast to hypomania—the prelude to a manic episode. Yet some of his acolytes took him literally. After passing the *agrégation* in 1965, Régis Debray left for Cuba, where, as a philosophy professor at the University of Havana, he published a Marxist analysis of Latin American revolutionary movements that became a handbook for guerilla groups fighting authoritarian regimes in the region. Arrested in Bolivia in 1967, Debray was convicted of being an associate of Che Guevara, who was helping to foment an insurgency there. He was sentenced to thirty years in prison but released after two following an international outcry led by President de Gaulle, Pope Paul VI, and Sartre.

Chapter 7

ALTHUSSER SLEEPS THROUGH THE REVOLUTION

Debray was in prison in 1968 and missed the events that convulsed France that spring. The violent student and worker protests that May brought the French economy to a halt, pushed de Gaulle's administration into a near-fatal tailspin, and left a permanent scar on the national psyche. In retrospect, May '68 marked a rupture in French history of the kind Althusser believed he had found in Marx: a *coupure épistemologique*. The demonstrations signaled the end of traditional French society—the conservative Catholic patriarchy embodied by the old general in charge. Politically, France did not change right away; de Gaulle's party and its allies gained 112 seats in the National Assembly that June, giving it an overwhelming majority, though de Gaulle himself resigned the following year. But socially, France was torn apart and remade. May '68 should have been Althusser's crowning moment. Instead, improbably, the day belonged to Sartre.

In November 1967, when students at the suburban Nanterre campus of the University of Paris held a weeklong strike to protest conditions at the school—overcrowded classes, strict sexual segregation in the dormitories, and an unpopular new curriculum—the issue appeared, to the de Gaulle administration at any rate, to be a local one. Over the following winter and spring, there was sporadic unrest on campuses elsewhere—in Paris, Bordeaux, and Nantes. At Nanterre, campus radicals—"*groupuscules*" of Trotskyists, Maoists, and Castroists—were said to be whipping up opposition to "the bourgeois university" and organizing students for action. There were reports of vans with "suspicious license plates" delivering pamphlets to the dorms, and rumors that student activists were receiving funds smuggled in from East Berlin and China and advice from Maoist cells at the École Normale.

Yet the French Communist Party denounced the students as "false revolutionaries," which de Gaulle's government interpreted as a sign that they could safely be ignored. In March, in the pages of *Le Monde*, a prominent journalist mocked the "boredom" of the French youth. While students the world over, from the United States to Egypt, were staging protests calling for revolutionary change, he scoffed, "French students were preoccupied with knowing whether the girls at Nanterre and Antony could freely access the rooms of boys, a frankly limited conception of the rights of man."

Less than two months later, Nanterre was shut down and the Sorbonne in Paris was occupied by protestors. On May 6th, more than twenty thousand students marched to the Sorbonne, which had been surrounded by police. The students' leaders saw themselves not simply as *engagés* in the Sartrean sense but, borrowing the name of French Revolution–era extremists, *enragés*. For nearly three weeks, Paris was mayhem. The *enragés* erected barricades in the streets, ripping paving stones from beneath their feet to hurl at riot police. The police responded with tear gas, water cannons, and truncheons. Hundreds of students were injured and arrested during street battles that went on all night.

By mid-May, trade union workers across France had joined the action, striking for better pay and working conditions. The Communist Party, which controlled one of the largest trade unions, decided it had no choice but to go along and belatedly declared its support for "the struggle of the students and teachers." With as many as ten million workers on strike, the French economy came to a standstill. There were no trains or buses, no mail service or gas for cars. Food was scarce. The rich fled to Switzerland. The CIA warned President Lyndon B. Johnson that France might be on the brink of civil war. On May 29th, de Gaulle, having failed to resolve the crisis, disappeared. For three days he kept out of sight. Even his staff didn't know where he was. It turned out that he'd flown in secret to a French Army base in Germany on the theory that he could terrify his country into submission through the shock of his sudden absence. "I will win them back through fear," he told his son-in-law.

To judge by France's swing to the right in the elections that June, the tactic worked. By the time the votes were counted, the revolutionary fervor had receded. The trade unions had called off the strikes, having secured pay increases and other small concessions. The police had retaken the Sorbonne.

Yet amid the chaos and violence, something extraordinary had happened. It was as though an entire generation of young people, along with some of their teachers, had gathered for an earnest, open-ended debate. What kind of society should France be? What kind of government should it have? Who had too much power, and who not enough? What was the proper place of women? Of immigrants? Of gay people? University classrooms turned into all-night seminars. Walls, courtyards, street signs, and lampposts were festooned with posters and graffiti promoting the movement's anarchic spirit: "Be realistic, ask for the impossible!" "It is forbidden to forbid!" "Underneath the pavement, the beach!"—this last inspired by the delightful discovery that beneath the cobblestones pried out of the streets to fling at the cops, there was sand.

"The feeling we had in those days, which has shaped my entire life really, was: We're making history," Daniel Cohn-Bendit, a student leader, recalled in 2018. "An exalted feeling—suddenly *we* had become agents in world history." If that sounds like textbook existentialism, it more or less was. Sartre wasn't the movement's inspiration or its guiding voice, but in some respects he was its spiritual father. At one point, two student leaders showed up at Beauvoir's apartment at two in the morning, just to talk. Sartre and Beauvoir graciously listened for hours to what they had to say. While Sartre's *normalien* classmate Raymond Aron decried the student movement as indulgent play-acting—a "verbal delirium with no casualties"—Sartre welcomed it as an authentic antiestablishment gesture. He and Beauvoir signed statements of support that were published in *Le Monde*, and Sartre interviewed Cohn-Bendit for *Le Nouvel Observateur*, telling him, "You have been able to create something that has astonished, upset, and denied all that has turned our society into what it is today."

On the night of May 20, Sartre went to an amphitheater at the Sorbonne and spoke to thousands of students who, as word spread of his arrival, pushed their way inside. Nearly twenty-five years after he had introduced existentialism to a postwar crowd, Sartre, now sixty-two and visibly haggard, sat onstage in front of a microphone and conversed with the offspring of that crowd—a new generation of Parisians also seeking change. This time, he was a beloved elder statesman—a "venerable relic," as the writer Sarah Bakewell put it—not the commander of the revolution. "He did not say much," Cohen-Solal recounts, "except that he was there in total intellectual communion with them inside this symbolic Bastille, the Sorbonne, they had seized from established power." After a while, he admitted he was tired and asked to leave before he uttered "a bunch of idiocies."

◆ ◆ ◆

Completely missing from the action was Althusser. His name may have been everywhere in the late 1960s, but when revolutionary fervor took over French universities that May, Althusser was under sedation at a mental hospital. "À QUOI SERT ALTHUSSER? ALTHUSSER—À RIEN" went a damning pun spray-painted on walls in the Latin Quarter. ("What is Althusser good for? Althusser is good for nothing.") While Sartre was holding forth at the Sorbonne, Althusser was writing from his sickbed to his partner, Hélène Rytmann. Noting that he was 50 kilometers from the turmoil in Paris, he told her that he could hardly fathom what was happening. "How can I get a handle on all that?" he grumbled. He said that he

Sartre at the Sorbonne on May 20, 1968

preferred to sleep, though it wasn't a true sleep cure they were putting him through, but rather, a kind of "Valium-induced, general stultification."

Althusser's absence from the events didn't stop him from weighing in on them when he had a chance. In his memoir, he excoriated the Communist Party for failing to respond to a historic opportunity. The Party could have mobilized its "organizational might" to catalyze a "strong mass movement," he wrote. Instead, out of fear of an uprising that it had not initiated and could not control, the Party did "everything it could" to prevent the striking students and workers from truly coming together. The result was a protest that accomplished nothing. Without the workers by their sides and united in their goals, he complained, the students were more or less what Aron had said they were: play-actors performing a harmless rebellion that was neatly contained by bourgeois ideology. True revolution, Althusser insisted grimly, exacts a price in blood: "When revolt ends in defeat without workers being massacred, it is not necessarily a good thing for the working class which has no martyrs to mourn or commemorate."

Of course, Althusser never managed to put himself in harm's way on behalf of any revolution, and it's tempting to see in his theoretical work a strenuous attempt at self-justification. To be fair, at least some of his students were inspired to political activism by his teaching—as in the case of Debray. France may be one of the few Western countries in which academically trained philosophers routinely go on to political careers. (It must also be one of the few countries in which philosophers routinely achieve public renown.) After being released from jail in Bolivia, Debray sought refuge in Chile, where he interviewed Salvatore Allende, the country's Marxist president, for an admiring book. After Allende died during a military coup in 1973, Debray returned to France, eventually serving as a foreign-policy adviser in the Mitterrand administration. The current French president, Emmanuel Macron, has a degree in philosophy from Nanterre (which he attended after twice failing the entrance exam for the École Normale), and likes to credit the philosopher Paul Ricoeur with encouraging him to enter politics.

Yet Althusser himself was strictly an academic. In his view, his scholarship *was* activism. Philosophy traditionally served the interests of the ruling class, he argued, but Marxist theory was different. He gave his philosophy a political patina, insisting that it "represents class struggle in the realm of *theory*." It, too, was subject to the laws of dialectical materialism and, properly analyzed and deployed, could be put to work for the greater good. "*All great philosophers* have sought to change the course of history," he wrote with typical hubristic flourish. "Either to transform the world, or to make it regress, or to preserve and reinforce the status quo so as to avert the threat of changes perceived as dangerous." As Tony Judt neatly summed up the implicit message of Althusser's teaching: "Scholars in their seminars were on the front line, and need feel guilty no more."

Chapter 8

"JE SUIS LE GRAND ALTHUSSER"

Throughout the 1970s, the structuralist movement that Althusser helped to launch inspired acolytes, revisionists, and detractors, and continued to spread overseas. But Althusser's own star seemed to fade nearly as quickly as it had risen. He was consumed with rearguard actions against critics who found his symptomatic reading of Marx selective and fanciful to the point of perversity. A British philosopher published a long, two-part critique in the journal *Marxism Today*, describing Althusser's work as a combination of insistent dogmatism and airy metaphysics. Althusser, he concluded, lacked a "healthy immersion in everyday affairs and current issues." He was prone to woefully, or willfully, naïve statements about Maoist China and the Soviet Union. He cheered China's Cultural Revolution, overlooking its violence and bloodshed, and after a 1974 trip to Moscow for a conference on Hegel, he gushed, "The USSR is different from the usual descriptions we read in this country. Any public involvement in politics is, of course, forbidden and dangerous, but as far as everything else is concerned, what a splendid life they lead!" Even former acolytes turned against him. "Althusserianism had died on the barricades of May '68," one wrote bitterly.

At the same time, the French left was gradually disentangling itself from the Marxist paradigm. The Communist Party steadily lost voters to the newly rebranded Socialist Party, launched in 1971 and increasingly home to a liberal, non-Marxist constituency. Two other developments helped hasten Althusser's philosophical work to obsolescence: the 1974 publication in French of Aleksandr Solzhenitsyn's harrowing account of the Soviet gulag, and the rise to prominence of a trio of telegenic and stridently anti-Marxist young French philosophers—Pascal Bruckner, André Glucksmann, and Bernard-Henri Lévy. (Lévy, who entered the École Normale in 1968, had been Althusser's student.)

But Althusser's public career was not yet finished. Early on the morning of Sunday, November 16, 1980, he committed the lethal act that ensured his name would once again inflame intellectual circles and come to overshadow all he had accomplished before that date. The story recounted by Althusser, the sole witness to the crime, begins *in medias res*: "Suddenly I was up and in my dressing-gown at the foot of the bed in my flat at the École Normale," he writes. "Hélène, also in a dressing-gown, lay before me on her back." Althusser found himself leaning over her body, massaging her neck, something he said he did frequently, using a technique he had learned from an inmate at his POW camp. "But on this occasion," he goes on, "I was massaging the front of her neck. I pressed my thumbs into the hollow at the top of her breastbone and then, still pressing, slowly moved them both, one to the left, the other to the right, up towards her ears where the flesh was hard." He was aware of his forearms beginning to tire, and of Hélène's face, "calm and motionless," her eyes "open and staring at the ceiling." And then the dawning realization: "I knew she had been strangled. But how? I stood up and screamed: 'I've strangled Hélène!'"

A scene of panic and confusion ensues. Althusser tears down the stairs, across a section of courtyard, and up another flight, to the apartment of the school physician, above the infirmary. Frantic, he bangs on the door. Finally the doctor appears. Althusser shouts that he has strangled Hélène. He begs the doctor to come see, threatening to burn down the school if he does not. The pair, both in bathrobes, hurry to Althusser's apartment. The doctor verifies that Hélène is dead. Althusser places a strip of tattered red curtain from the bedroom window across her chest. The doctor makes a phone call. He gives Althusser an injection. Then everything goes black until Althusser wakes up to find himself confined to a ward at Sainte-Anne Hospital.

All of this drama Althusser relates in the astonishing opening pages of his memoir, surely one of few published accounts by a man of murdering his wife. The memoir, *L'Avenir dure longtemps*, came out in 1992, two years after Althusser's own death, from a heart attack, and was an instant bestseller in France, making it without a doubt his most widely read work. On a handwritten title page found with the manuscript, he had scrawled and then crossed out a subtitle: "Brief History of a Murderer." The book, which was translated into English as *The Future Lasts Forever*, is mesmerizing: a surprisingly literary chronicle of narcissistic self-pity and recrimination mixed with candid self-appraisal, political score-settling, and snatches of poetic beauty.

Althusser's impetus to write his story was apparently an article that appeared in *Le Monde* in March 1985, by which time he had been released from the hospital and was living alone in an apartment in the north of Paris. The article was by Claude Sarraute, a journalist at the paper who happened to be the daughter of the experimental French novelist Nathalie Sarraute as well as the ex-wife of the philosopher Jean-François Revel, who had studied with Althusser at the École Normale. Titled "Petite Faim" (Little Hunger), the piece was a rebuke aimed at the French justice system—specifically, its deferential treatment of the "rich, famous, or powerful"—and at the media for abetting it.

Sarraute's primary exhibit was the shocking case of a wealthy Japanese student, Issei Sagawa, who in 1981, while studying for a PhD in literature at the Sorbonne, had lured a female classmate to his Paris apartment, and then proceeded to shoot her in the neck, have sex with her corpse, and, over the next two days, consume pieces of her flesh, which he sliced off her body with a butcher knife. More bits of flesh were found under aluminum foil on plates in his fridge, after he was arrested a few days later while trying to dump her remains in a lake at the Bois de Boulogne. Deemed mentally unfit to stand trial, Sagawa was remanded to a psychiatric hospital, and his case was declared, as Althusser's had been, a *non-lieu* (literally "no grounds"), a French legal term denoting ineligibility for prosecution.

While institutionalized, Sagawa wrote a memoir about his crime that became a bestseller in Japan, propelling him to celebrity status there. Eventually deported to his native country, he went on to a career as an author and actor, writing manga comics, giving interviews, and collaborating on numerous films about his life.

"I love stories that end well," Sarraute wrote sarcastically. "I'm also proud. Because at the end of the day, it's thanks to whom? Me. Once we in the media come across a prominent name—Althusser, Thibault d'Orléans—involved in some juicy trial, we make a huge deal out of it. The victim barely gets three lines. The star is the perpetrator. We zero in on his family, on his past as a poor little boy too rich or too intelligent. We explain away his behavior. We find all sorts of rationales."

Althusser was horrified to see his name linked to Sagawa's. (Thibault d'Orléans, the third man in Sarraute's piece, was a French aristocrat who, convicted of attempted robbery in 1981, was given a suspended sentence.) Friends urged him to write *Le Monde* in protest. He decided to write a memoir instead. The article had clarified for him a crucial matter: His failure to receive a trial—his *non-lieu*—had been condemning. Denied a chance to tell his story in court, he would tell it in a book. Only then, he wrote to a friend, could he "reappear in public." He was also sensitive to complaints in the right-wing press that he had benefitted from special treatment by the political establishment; Mitterrand's socialist administration had come to power just a few months after Rytmann's death.

Althusser worked on the book in solitude, largely cut off from his former life at the École Normale. He received occasional visits from a handful of former students and colleagues, but much of the time he was alone. According to one friend, he would sometimes walk the streets of his neighborhood, shouting despondently at strangers: *"Je suis le grand Althusser!"*

The anecdote seems to encapsulate the whole tragic, Icarus-like arc of his career. It also suggests a parodic inversion of his theory of ideological interpellation: Here is a subject outside the social system and desperate to get in—desperate to be recognized by it, to be granted the illusion of individual identity through which ideology enacts its effects. By Althusser's own account, he is a human shade, a ghost, a nonentity: "Even though I have been out of psychiatric hospital for two years, I am still a *missing person* for the public who have heard of me. I am neither alive nor dead and, though I have not been buried, I am 'bodiless.' I am simply *missing*." The "victim" in his book is not Rytmann but Althusser himself. The sole person "under a tombstone"—a recurring image—is him. If only he'd been an existentialist! Then maybe he could have taken comfort and inspiration from Sartre's insistence that we are free, even in horrific circumstances, to choose our destinies, to give our lives meaning and purpose.

◆ ◆ ◆

Rytmann is granted more than three lines—Sarraute's damning quota—in *The Future Lasts Forever*, but she remains as much an enigma in the book as she apparently was in real life. "For a long time, he hid his wife from us," Régis Debray recalled about Althusser. "At the École in the 1960s, when he would invite us over for a drink in the evening in his apartment: the sounds of a door, an embarrassed cough, a fleeting shadow at the end of a hallway. It took me a year or two to put a name to this mysterious person, with her penetrating stare, always discreet, who soon became my friend—this childless woman who was tender beneath her tough exterior, suffering in silence the malicious rumors that made her out to be our philosopher in chief's dragon lady and shrew, when in fact she was his nursemaid, punching bag, and big sister."

In his memoir, Althusser insists that he loved Rytmann; that he came to appreciate her "womanly smell," which he had "at first found disgusting"; that he worked hard to get his students and friends to like her, despite her "prickly nature"; that, recognizing her profound unhappiness, he persuaded his own psychoanalyst to take her on as a patient (a highly unorthodox arrangement). Finally, he declares that he murdered her not by choice or by accident but out of loving obligation.

By all accounts, the last few months they spent together were agony. Althusser had passed the summer of 1980 in a psychiatric clinic, following a severe depression. Prescribed nialamide, an antidepressant, he experienced terrifying side effects: persecution fantasies, suicidal impulses, even, at one point, the conviction that he should destroy all his papers, kill himself and his wife, and burn down the École Normale. Eventually stabilized on another drug, he was sent home, but remained extremely fragile. Rytmann, burdened as always with his care, was miserable. The couple, "shut up together in our own private Hell," were barely on speaking terms, Althusser writes. Rytmann threatened to move out. She threatened to throw herself under a bus or a train. She told him "there was no way out, given the 'monster' I was and the inhuman suffering I inflicted upon her, other than to kill herself." At one point, he claims, she asked him to kill her. "The very idea, which was both unthinkable and unbearably awful, made me tremble convulsively for a long time," he writes. "It still makes me shudder."

After endlessly rehearsing the circumstances of his wife's death with his analyst, Althusser says he came to believe that what he had done to her was more accurately something that had been done *for* her: It was, he says, "suicide via a third party." The phrase is shocking, the anonymity of "a third party" magically removing Althusser from the scene of death entirely. The murder becomes an act without human agency—the act of a man who is no longer himself, or is no one in particular, just another anonymous interpellated subject caught in the workings of an insidious regime, presumably one in which a suicidal woman has little obvious value.

Elsewhere, Althusser suggests that in killing his wife he was fulfilling her wish to die by his hand and that her death was, in the words of Régis Debray, who apparently accepted his strained logic, "a beautiful proof of love."

Chapter 9

THE MAD PHILOSOPHER

Was Althusser out of his mind? Should he be pitied as a madman or as a selfless husband? He appears to want it both ways. As he put it in 1982, in what may be the most succinct expression of his views on the matter: "The fact is I strangled my wife, who meant everything to me. . . . She loved me so much, and since she could not go on living, she wanted to die. Unaware of what I was doing and in a state of confusion, I must have 'done what she wanted,' which she did not resist and which caused her death."

The commingling of madness and reason in *The Future Lasts Forever* makes for unnerving reading. Eventually, it becomes impossible to disentangle the two strands. "The Facts," a memoir he began and abandoned in 1976, four years before Rytmann's death, is appended to the end of the book, and contains passages of flagrant delusion. At one point, Charles de Gaulle bums a light off Althusser in the street. At another, Pope John XXIII converses with Althusser in a garden at the Vatican. Still other passages describe Althusser's attempts to steal an atomic submarine on the Atlantic coast and stage a bank heist in Paris. He was clearly in the throes of mania when he wrote it. The later, longer memoir is more sober, but it includes multiple descriptions of psychological breakdown, institutionalization, and tenuous recovery. When the book's editors ask in the foreword, "How is it that such a story can move into the realm of madness, yet its author remain so aware?" you understand their unease. As the most extensive published record of Althusser's psychiatric history, *The Future Lasts Forever* introduced the variable of mental illness into the public assessment of his career and compelled a reckoning.

For some, including longtime Althusser skeptics, his illness was proof that his Marxist theory—with its "manic fancies"—was itself crackpot. Calling the École Normale's onetime philosophy *caïman* "one of the most powerful figures in the French intellectual establishment," the intellectual historian Mark Lilla wrote with apparent horror, "this means that from 1948 until 1980, two generations of French philosophers and intellectuals passed under Althusser's manic-depressive tutelage."

Althusser's own students tended to a more nuanced view of the relationship between his life and his work. "I loved Althusser because he wasn't Althusserian," Debray wrote, "containing within himself contradictions that seemed to me more worthy of attention than the right angles of his theoretical texts." According to Bernard-Henri Lévy, who passed the philosophy *agrégation* under Althusser in 1971, few at the École had any idea he was seriously ill. Many noticed his "not completely explicable" absences and the fact that he rarely taught classes, but, Lévy insisted, "we thought our weird professor was well."

For Lévy, Althusser's illness presents an insoluble quandary: "To imagine that when, with pounding heart, I pushed open the door to his office and found him at his desk, pensive, in his varnished wood armchair, his head in his hand, that he was thinking not of Hegel or Marx, nor even of the break between the two Marxes, but of the encroaching pain and madness, and of how long he could hang on before rushing off, for the umpteenth time since the beginning of the year, to the clinic. . . . What link, which no one suspected, is there between the work and the madness? What about this work, this very great work, has its source—or impediment—in the immense suffering that harassed him until the end?"

Althusser is hardly the first philosopher whose work forces us to confront the question of madness—of madness *in* philosophy. Madness occupies a distinctive place in the discipline's history. Nietzsche lost his mind in 1889, at the age of forty-four—according to legend after witnessing the flogging of a horse in the streets of Turin. David Hume and John Stuart Mill famously suffered breakdowns, as did, by his own account, Sartre. Wittgenstein struggled with suicidal urges (three of his brothers took their lives). "As though madness were the inevitable price of philosophy," Michel Foucault's biographer Didier Eribon suggests, adding Foucault, who was also afflicted by suicidal impulses, to the list of "mad" philosophers.

For the French philosophers, though, madness wasn't just a professional liability; it was a subject for investigation, one so important that it merits a section of its own. While Althusser was in and out of hospitals in the 1960s and '70s, his fellow structuralists were exploring madness as a philosophical problem. Lacan, who trained as a psychiatrist before becoming a psychoanalyst and published an influential thesis on psychosis and persecution, often lectured in a baroque style that some compared to the florid chains of associations typical of psychotic speech. He also brought psychiatric patients into the public seminar on Freud that he conducted at Sainte-Anne Hospital, just as Foucault brought his students to the same hospital to observe how such patients were treated. In *Madness and Civilization*, Foucault connected shifting conceptions of madness over the course of Western history to large social changes, arguing, to controversy and acclaim, that madness is a product of culture, not biology. And Lacan, Foucault, and Derrida all puzzled over the relationship between madness and reason.

When Althusser wandered the streets of Paris declaring, *"Je suis le grand Althusser"* to passersby, he was speaking from that place of silence to which as a "madman" he had been consigned by the French authorities. What gives the anecdote special poignancy is his longing to be recognized by a society in which, according to his own theory, such recognition is a strategic illusion. Althusser devoted pages in his theoretical work to showing how human subjects are not in charge of their actions or even their thoughts but are the products of ideology. In his memoir, he shows how a human being in the grip of madness isn't in charge of his actions either. Was it here, in his philosophical conception of the self, that Althusser's experience with mental illness—of debilitating mood swings, electroshock therapy, and mind-altering drugs, in short, of being "unaware of what I was doing"—reveals its influence on his work?

Had I known that Althusser killed his wife when I first encountered his theory of the interpellated subject in college, would I have thought about it differently? Had I been able to read his memoir then, would it have colored the way I understood his emphasis on the impersonal forces shaping our behavior? My guess is probably not. After all, Althusser was hardly alone in renouncing the individual as a romantic fiction; his stance was widely shared by other structuralists to whom I was unquestioningly in thrall—seduced by a worldview confident in its totalizing vision. Now, though, I think I have an inkling of what Althusser may have meant when he insisted that his work, however "abstract and impersonal," was nevertheless "passionately concerned with the self."

From the early, invasive attentions of his mother to the manias and depressions that chronically gripped him, the dozens of electroshock treatments and Valium-induced stupors that typically followed, and even the soothing cocoon of the stalag prison, the episodes from his life Althusser details most vividly in his book involve strikingly little agency and much submission to authority. In light of his memoir, it's possible to see his structuralist insistence on the abstract and the antihuman—on individual self-erasure—as borne out by profound personal experience. "Both in her presence and away from her," Althusser wrote of his mother, "I always had the overwhelming feeling that I did not exist in or for myself." He might as well have been talking about one of his ideological state apparatuses, of which he wrote near the beginning of his memoir: "I am surprised I have been unable to do without them in understanding what happened to me."

◆ ◆ ◆

In the wake of May '68 and its failure to catalyze dramatic social change, five young artists in Paris collaborated on a now-legendary painting that captured something of the public ambivalence toward the structuralist intellectuals. Titled *La Datcha*, and rendered in a pared-down, socialist realist style, the painting was exhibited in 1969 at the Salon de la Jeune Peinture, where it created a bit of a stir. It depicts Claude Lévi-Strauss, Lacan, Foucault, and Barthes in the living room of a Russian country house, or dacha, a term associated at the time with the pooh-bahs of Soviet leadership. The gathering has a stiff and formal air. This is clearly not a group of *enragés*, recovering from an all-nighter at the barricades: The men are dressed in suits, Lacan is wearing his signature bow tie, and Barthes is entering from the right bearing a tray of petits fours. The room is simple but elegant, its only decorations an indigenous mask mounted on one wall and a vase with a single pansy flower: allusions to Lévi-Strauss's anthropological work, including his book *La Pensée sauvage*—in French a double entendre meaning both "wild thought" and "wild pansy."

The men appear expectant, as though waiting for something—or someone. Behind them, in the red-orange twilight, through a sliding glass

***La Datcha*, 1969**

door, is the silhouette of a fifth man, his hand on the door handle, a couple books tucked under one arm. The inscription on the painting's frame resolves the mystery: "Louis Althusser, hesitating to enter Claude Lévi-Strauss's dacha, Tristes Miels, where Jacques Lacan, Michel Foucault, and Roland Barthes are gathered at the moment the radio announces that the workers and the students have joyfully decided to abandon their past." (The dacha's name, Tristes Miels, literally "Sad Honeys," suggests a mash-up of Lévi-Strauss's memoir *Tristes Tropiques* and his 1966 book *Du miel aux cendres,* or "From Honey to Ashes," the second volume in his series on mythology after the more famous *The Raw and the Cooked.*)

Althusser stands outside and alone, a blurry figure fading into the dusk. Evidently his moment of glory has passed. But what to make of the men lounging inside? Don't they look a little smug? Are they congratulating themselves on a revolution they watched unfold mostly from the comfort of their armchairs? What's so important about them, anyway?

Part 2

Madness

Chapter 10

SARTRE SEES A SHRINK

Sartre was having a breakdown. It was the spring of 1935, and he was sure he was going mad. Deeply depressed, he was beset by hallucinations. As Beauvoir later recalled the episode, "his visual faculties became distorted: houses had leering faces, all eyes and jaws, and he couldn't help looking at every clockface he passed, expecting it to display the features of an owl—which it always did." Worse was the near-constant sensation that he was being pursued by crabs. "I started seeing crabs around me all the time," Sartre said. "They followed me in the streets, into class."

He blamed the visions on a bad drug trip. In truth, he had been in a funk for nearly a year, having returned to France and to a job he loathed teaching high school in Le Havre, following a glorious nine months in Berlin—the transformative visit during which he immersed himself in the German phenomenology that would prove so critical to existentialism and to his philosophical first novel, *Nausea*. Now he was back in France and on the verge of turning thirty, painfully aware, as he watched a couple of his closest friends publish their first books, that he had yet to make his mark. "By the fall of 1934," Cohen-Solal writes, "Sartre is only a small, fat, aging provincial teacher."

So when a former professor of his at the École Normale commissioned him to contribute a volume to an academic series on philosophy, Sartre threw himself into the project. He proposed to write about the imagination, viewing the opportunity as a chance to test out some of the German phenomenologists' ideas about consciousness in the context of a subject that interested him: mental imagery. While he grappled with the philosophical differences between images conjured by the imagination (while reading a novel, say) and those resulting directly from perception (the omelet on your breakfast plate), he became fascinated by visual hallucinations—images that appeared to have no basis in reality. A *normalien* classmate who was a psychiatrist at Sainte-Anne Hospital offered to inject Sartre with mescaline, a known hallucinogen, with the thought that such auto-experimentation might give him some useful insights. The experience was likely to be "mildly disagreeable," the friend warned, but it would last just a few hours.

In fact, it was miserable. "He had not exactly had hallucinations," Beauvoir reported, "but the objects he looked at changed their appearance in the most horrifying manner: umbrellas had become vultures, shoes turned into skeletons, and faces acquired monstrous characteristics, while behind him, just past the corner of his eye, swarmed crabs and polyps and grimacing Things."

Sartre managed to finish his book, celebrating the imagination—what he called the "great 'irrealizing' function of consciousness"—in suitably existentialist style as an expression of freedom, enabling us to contemplate scenarios and possibilities beyond what currently exist. By contrast, he suggested, hallucinations were a confounding, pathological form of imagination, in which consciousness itself seemed to disintegrate. Yet as the weeks went by, the crabs were still following him, and he feared for his sanity. "I'm on the edge of a chronic hallucinatory psychosis," he complained to Beauvoir. Finally, he sought professional help. "I began to think I was going crazy," he told an interviewer in 1971. "So I went to see a shrink, a young guy then with whom I have been friends ever since, Jacques Lacan."

Pressed to recall Lacan's diagnosis, Sartre was vague: "We sort of concluded that it was fear of becoming alone, or to put it more in context, fear of losing the camaraderie of the group." The idea is striking given Sartre's insistence, in *Being and Nothingness*, on the crucial role of other people: In making us the object of their gaze, they inform our sense of self, and in their interactions with us, encourage, or just as often, limit our freedom. As the famous line from his play *No Exit* puts it, "Hell is other people." Then again, in 1935, Sartre had yet to formulate this theory and could never have guessed that the "young guy" he turned to for help would end up, like Sartre himself, a household name. (As for the crabs, Lacan's insights notwithstanding, Sartre said that they went away "the day I simply decided that they bored me and that I just wouldn't pay attention to them.")

In 1935, Lacan, then thirty-four, was a novice psychoanalyst. He had been in private practice for barely a year, having opted out of a more conventional medical career after completing his psychiatric training at Sainte-Anne, where he irritated his oral examiners by showing off his knowledge of philosophy. ("A tiresome young man," the examiners wrote.) It would be years before he achieved superstardom in the 1960s as part of the structuralist wave, but by then he had spawned a movement—some called it a cult—inspiring legions of followers.

Physically, Lacan was unmistakable, his dramatic features—beady eyes behind rimless glasses, bushy black brows beneath a shock of dark hair—conspiring with his bow ties and bespoke suits to give him a Dracula-like aspect. He was reputed to be both a genius and a tyrant, alternately lauded and reviled for his unorthodox analytic practices, his oversize ego, and his revolutionary reworking of Freud. Fixating on language as a grand impersonal system in which we are all entrapped, his theory, developed over decades, chimed neatly with the new structuralist framework—both its antihumanism and its linguistic turn. Lacanian psychoanalysis was, like Marxism, another holistic "total knowledge" philosophy. Lacan's vision of the individual in society was just as disillusioned as Althusser's, but he shifted the emphasis from the public sphere—a Marxist revolution that never seemed to materialize—to the private one, proposing that the quest to understand one's relationship with the world was a personal matter best illuminated by his teachings.

Jacques Lacan (*seated*) and two colleagues in the 1930s

After Lacan opened the École freudienne de Paris in 1964, the number of analysts in France climbed from fewer than one hundred and fifty in the late 1950s to more than five thousand (and by one estimate, as many as fifteen thousand) by the end of the 1980s. The American sociologist Sherry Turkle was so struck by the "infatuation with psychoanalysis" that took over France in the late 1960s and 1970s that she devoted a book to it, concluding that Lacan's "Cartesian, poeticized, linguistic, and politicized psychoanalysis" responded to a thirst in French culture for a new way of thinking about social life in the wake of May '68 and its failure to bring about sweeping change. The events of that famous French month were often summed up afterward as a revolution in *desire*, one whose unrealized goal was the liberation of human beings from repressive forces all around them, including in their own minds. (Recall the slogan "It is forbidden to forbid!") Lacanian psychoanalysis provided concepts for understanding this yearning and perhaps—though Lacan himself didn't seem to put much stock in the idea—for addressing it, beginning with one's own life.

Just as existentialism gave the French a way to comprehend the humiliations of Nazi occupation as a matter of individual choices, psychoanalysis offered a way to redeem the disappointments of May '68 through self-examination. In both cases, the emphasis was on a "politics of the person"—even if the visions of personhood were very different. You didn't do an analysis simply because you were distressed—though, as would-be revolutionaries pointed out, after May '68 there were plenty of depressed people around. You did a psychoanalysis because you had intellectual ambitions. You wanted a philosophical framework for making sense of your place in society—or at least the status associated with such a goal.

In 1969, the French government established the country's first academic department of psychoanalysis, at the University of Vincennes, a brand-new experimental campus conceived as a sop to the student protestors, Overseen by Lacan's son-in-law, staffed by analysts Lacan had trained, and with a curriculum cribbed from his ideas, the department was essentially made in Lacan's image. There was even a course devoted to a single page of his work. "They're the only visible intellectuals around," a philosophy student from the École Normale told Turkle. "The existentialists' cafés have given way to the psychoanalysts' couches."

Certainly, there was a crowd at Lacan's office on the rue de Lille, where the waiting room was often standing room only, and his roster of patients—whom he charged top dollar—included the singer Marianne Oswald, the photographer Dora Maar, and, briefly, Picasso. His reputation as a dandy and seducer grew in tandem with his fame. Among those who paid him regular house calls were a gym teacher, hairdresser, manicurist, pedicurist, and tailor—this last the chief executive of a high-end Parisian firm who arrived twice a year with fabric samples for Lacan to choose from for his custom shirts and suits. He wore a shirt the color of cotton candy, a velvet-and-silk striped jacket, a black mink coat.

Patients and paramours—these were sometimes one and the same—published detailed accounts of their analyses and affairs with him. One mistress, who became an analyst herself, lovingly recorded his unapologetic tendency "as a free man" to burp and fart in public. Beauvoir reported being so awestruck by the flow and vigor of his ideas when she met him, at a public reading during World War II of a play by Picasso, that she was reduced to little more in response than the "occasional liquor-induced platitude."

Lacan inspired at least one novel, *Le Pitre* (The Clown), by a former patient, and he appeared as a character in several others. Yet he rarely gave interviews and, with one or two exceptions, never went on TV. There was virtually nothing in the public record about his early life. Even his published writings weren't standard scholarly fare, consisting for the most part of write-ups of lecture notes and transcriptions by students of his seminars. As one scholar put it, "Lacan's prose aspires perpetually to the condition of speech." Like Socrates, he was a mythic teacher surrounded by acolytes who disseminated his word.

His most important venue was his public seminar, where every week, beginning in 1953 at Sainte-Anne Hospital, he presented his ideas. The forum eventually attracted most of the leading lights in Paris, including Althusser, Barthes, Derrida, Foucault, Lévi-Strauss, and Beauvoir, as well the novelist Philippe Sollers and his wife, the psychoanalyst and critic Julia Kristeva. During the 1960s, competition for a seat was so fierce that you had to arrive an hour early if you hoped to sit down. "You were so tightly packed in like sardines that people would drop ash from their cigarettes on your knees," recalled Fredric Jameson, who tried to attend once, in 1969, only for Lacan to appear briefly, announce that he was sick, and cancel class. As many as a thousand people regularly crammed into the seminar's final location, an auditorium at the University of Paris law school near the Pantheon.

Not that everyone understood what Lacan was saying. His lectures—riddled with neologisms, mathematical allusions, and slippery chains of associations—were inordinately hard to follow. Reading them has been described as an exercise "on a par with reading *Finnegans Wake*." If Sartre wrote philosophy like a modern novelist, Lacan wrote it like a member of modernism's avant-garde. "Lacan's whole teaching is metaphorical," two scholars of his work conceded. "The highly condensed language of his writing leads to the realm of the ineffable, reaching the enigma of poetry, or often just enigma."

Here's a Lacanism I like: *parlêtres*—a play on *parle êtres* ("speak beings") and *par lettre* ("by the letter"): It nicely captures the primacy of language in Lacan's conception of the human being. But wading through pages peppered with such novel coinage can quickly become overwhelming. As a character says in yet another story by Lorrie Moore, explaining why she dropped out of graduate school: "I did try. I read Derrida. I read Lacan. I read *Reading Lacan*. I read *Reading 'Reading Lacan.'*" Althusser, who grasped better than most the rudiments of Lacanian theory, called his style the "dumbshow equivalent of the language of the unconscious." What's remarkable, though, is how many who applied themselves to the task of untangling his words tended to agree that the picture of human existence they found there was a revelation.

Chapter 11

SCANDALOUS FREUD

That Lacan's teachings proved so influential is extraordinary given not only the difficulty of his work but also of his personality. "In Lacan's Paris, there was a general consensus that the problem was Lacan himself, and if the analysts could have the theory without the man, then all would be well," one of his students, an American who moved to France to do a training analysis with him, wrote. "Everyone would have loved to have the theory without the theorist." Élisabeth Roudinesco, a psychoanalyst who was a member of Lacan's inner circle and later his biographer, suggests that in his eccentricity and extremism, his indifference to accepted codes of behavior, and his obsession with obscure wordplay, he had more in common with some of the "mad" patients he treated early in his career, and with the Surrealists who initially embraced him, than with the rest of the medical establishment or his fellow intellectuals. He was a rebel and an upstart, driven in equal parts by disdain for convention and desire for acclaim. In Freud, Lacan found a perfect vehicle for his ambitions: a brilliantly original thinker who shocked bourgeois society by showing it to be founded on a tenuous illusion of civility and reason.

Born in 1901, into a strict, upper-middle-class Catholic family that had made a fortune in the vinegar trade, Lacan was sent to the top private

Parisian lycée for boys, the Collège Stanislas. A driven if not especially popular student—"arrogance was the keynote of his character," Roudinesco says—he horrified his parents by renouncing religion and reading Nietzsche in the original German. They may have been equally put out by the poster he hung on his bedroom wall: a chart diagramming the conceptual logic of Spinoza's *Ethics*—this philosophical treatise by a seventeenth-century Jewish heretic was the teenage Lacan's idea of a pinup. He, in turn, was appalled when his younger brother decided to join the priesthood.

In his spare time, he socialized with writers and artists at La Maison des Amis des Livres, the bookshop on the Left Bank that served as a de facto salon for the Parisian avant-garde. There, in December 1921, he heard the first public reading of passages from James Joyce's *Ulysses*. Lacan would go on to devote a year of his seminar in the mid-1970s to Joyce, whose ingenious wordplay he, like Derrida, admired and tried to imitate.

It was probably at La Maison des Amis des Livres that Lacan met André Breton, the founder of Surrealism, another young man in rebellion against French society. Older than Lacan by five years, Breton had trained to be a doctor while aspiring to become a writer. Assigned during World War I to the mental ward at the Val-de-Grâce military hospital, Breton and his friend (and future Surrealist) Louis Aragon had performed nightly recitations from *Les Chants de Maldoror*, an outré, nineteenth-century prose poem by the Comte de Lautréamont. The men's patients found the readings, and the readers, disturbing, calling out during their performances, "Help! They're crazy." For Breton, though, crazy was the point. He was dazzled by the traumatized soldiers' imagery and associations. As a friend noted in his diary, Breton "in his nut-case hospital is moved and horrified to see patients who are better poets than he is."

While working in the mental wards during the war, Breton learned about Freud's theories through the work of French psychiatrists. Freud's own work wouldn't appear in French until 1921, in part the result of entrenched anti-German and anti-Semitic prejudice. (When Lacan's future colleague Françoise Dolto told her family she was becoming a psychoanalyst, her brother accused her of "being kept by the Jews"—a common sentiment.) Gradually, however, Freudian concepts crept into French medical practice. Hysteria, for example, once considered a physical problem originating in the uterus, was redefined as a psychological disorder related to repressed childhood sexual trauma. At the same time, Freud's work was given a different spin by the French avant-garde, who greeted it with glee. As Althusser put it, "Freud's discovery represented a sort of scandal." He had punctured modernity's urbane façade and exposed the lust, aggression, and turmoil beneath. He had shown that human behavior was at the mercy of violent urges in the unconscious, a realm we could hardly access or hope to subdue.

These ideas are so commonplace now—and, thanks to advances in neuroscience, in some respects discredited—that it's hard to comprehend how radical they seemed a hundred years ago. Not only was Freud regarded with suspicion in predominantly Catholic France, but, worse, his teaching made a mockery of the prized French value of rationality. Every schoolchild knew the story of the birth of reason in the form of Descartes' cogito ("I think, therefore I am"), the cornerstone of Enlightenment philosophy. Freud knocked Descartes from his pedestal by exposing the triumph of reason over madness as just so much wishful thinking.

"Freud set out to show that it was necessary to have done with the bourgeois idealist representation of man as an entirely conscious being," Althusser wrote. "The most stupefying feature of Freud's work was and remains the *absolutely autonomous* character of the whole of this theory and mechanism. Everything happens in the mechanisms of the unconscious as if they led a life completely independent of *both* their biological condition of existence, although it underpins them, *and* their social condition of existence, although it indirectly commands them."

Freud himself audaciously compared the impact of psychoanalysis to both the Copernican revolution, which had displaced the Earth from the center of the solar system, and Darwinian evolution, which had displaced humankind from its throne above the animal kingdom. Now Freudian science, he said, had delivered the "third and most wounding blow" by showing "the ego that it is not even master in his own house." The twentieth century was supposed to represent the pinnacle of human progress, the ascendency of reason in public life. World War I had shaken that assumption, and Freud had dealt the knockout punch: Warring impulses existed not only between countries but within each of us, and reason was never guaranteed the upper hand.

To the existentialists, with their Cartesian emphasis on conscious choice and free will, Freud appeared to pose a threat. "We criticized the psychoanalysts for pulling man to pieces rather than understanding him," Beauvoir wrote. Yet their hostility soon faded. Not only did Sartre see Lacan about his crab problem, but in 1958 he even wrote the initial script (ultimately abandoned) for a John Huston biopic about Freud. Beauvoir admitted that she and Sartre found the prospect of the psyche's untamed hidden forces exciting—a potential source of revolutionary energy. Freud had convinced her "that in every person there lurks what André Breton called *un infracassable noyau de nuit*, an indestructible kernel of darkness, something that cannot break up social conventions or the common currency of human speech, but does, now and then, burst out in a peculiarly scandalous fashion. Every time one of these explosions took place, we believed, some truth was always revealed, and those which brought about an access of freedom we found especially impressive. We set particular store by any upheaval which exposed the defects and hypocrisy of the bourgeoisie."

Exposing the defects and hypocrisy of the bourgeoisie was just what Breton believed Surrealism could do. Some of the group's antics were simply juvenile. They were not above making prank phone calls, throwing food, or swinging from chandeliers in posh restaurants. But Breton harbored more serious ambitions. When he published his first Surrealist manifesto in 1924, he clearly had Freud as well as his wartime hospital experience in mind. Surrealism, he wrote, is "psychic automatism in its pure state." The goal was to tap directly into the unconscious, to uncouple thought from logic and sense—conventions that conspired to stultify and constrain creativity.

To this end, Breton recognized that certified madmen had a head start; everyone else would have to work at it. Chance encounters, coincidences, dreams, delusions: Such phenomena revealed the roiling underbelly of life stripped of its deadening bourgeois overlay. In 1928, the Surrealists celebrated the fiftieth anniversary of hysteria, hailing it as "the greatest poetic discovery of the late nineteenth century," and "in every respect a supreme means of expression." More than anything else, Breton was interested in language, which he called "the worst convention of all." He was convinced, his biographer writes, that "words and language could change the world, that the *mind* was the seat of any worthwhile revolution."

In this cause, the Surrealists saw Freud as a natural ally. After World War I, Breton and a friend had experimented with automatic writing. They met every night for a week, scribbling as fast as they could into composition notebooks, sometimes for more than eight hours at a stretch. Breton found the experiment so destabilizing that he ended it after eight

Sigmund Freud and André Breton in the 1920s

days, fearing for his sanity. The results, published in 1920 as *The Magnetic Fields*, included images of stark beauty ("Love deep in the woods gleams like a great candle") amid a flood of tedious nonsense ("The blood of earwigs encircles the plants whose leaves are held up by means of safety pins"). Breton promptly sent Freud a copy. It was one thing to analyze signs from the unconscious in the work of Shakespeare or Sophocles, as Freud had done, but here was a book-length transcription of the unconscious itself!

Soon after, Breton went to Vienna to see the great doctor in person. The meeting was a disaster. Freud, a scientist bent on curing the distressed, couldn't see the merit of Breton's poetic experiments. Severely disappointed, Breton poured his bitterness into an article, "Interview with Doctor Freud," in which he dismissed the analyst as "a little old man with no style who receives clients in a shabby office worthy of the neighborhood GP."

Chapter 12

THE PARANOIAC-CRITICAL METHOD

Yet there was one doctor who courted and returned the Surrealists' favor: Lacan. He, too, had read Freud, and at Sainte-Anne Hospital, where he began his internship in psychiatry in 1931, he befriended a group of philosophically inclined peers who closely followed the Surrealists' goings-on. Like Lacan, Breton was a controlling and demanding man; despite preaching a doctrine of spontaneity and freedom, he brooked no dissent from his followers. The Surrealists were required to attend daily meetings at the time and café of Breton's choosing, and even to order drinks according to his specifications, from a personal hierarchy of beverages ranging from the anise liqueurs Pernod and Ricard (the closest one could get to absinthe, which was banned) on down to beer and vermouth. Unsurprisingly, the Surrealists—not unlike the Lacanians later on—were constantly fighting and breaking up, founding and folding magazines. In July 1930, they unveiled a new journal, *Le Surréalisme au service de la révolution* (Surrealism in the service of the revolution). The first issue contained an essay by the artist Salvador Dalí that was to prove critical to Lacan's thinking on madness and language.

Freud, in his 1911 reading of a memoir by the German judge and paranoid schizophrenic Daniel Schreber, had defined paranoia as the projection onto the external world of private thoughts too shameful to admit to consciousness. Freud made much of Schreber's terrified fantasy that his doctor's treatments had as their goal to turn him into a woman, arguing that paranoia typically had its source in repressed homosexual urges. According to Freud's account, projection was not a straightforward process but instead involved distortion and transformation, so that, in Schreber's case, "what should have been felt internally as love" (homosexual desire) "is perceived externally as hate" (the doctor's persecution). Once externalized, projections took on the allure of truth, forming an intricate system of meaning rooted in delusion. Dalí had read Freud and saw in his description of paranoia inklings of a powerful creative tool.

When Dalí joined the Surrealists, he was twenty-five and had recently arrived in Paris from Spain, where he'd been kicked out of his parents' home for exhibiting art his father deemed sacrilegious. Manically inventive and a born provocateur, he naturally gravitated to Breton's circle. "*L'Âne pourri*" (The Rotten Donkey), his essay for *Le Surréalisme au service de la révolution,* was in essence another Surrealist manifesto, trumpeting a novel technique for upending convention. "The moment is near, when, by means of a deliberately paranoid thought process (as through automatism and other passive states), it will be possible to systematize confusion and contribute to the total discrediting of the world of reality," Dalí wrote with typical hyperbolic flourish. By employing what he later called the "paranoiac-critical" method, an artist could break down the flimsy barrier between himself and the world, endowing private fantasies with the attributes of objective reality.

In practice, Dalí explained, the method would yield a "double" or even "multiple" image, so that the representation of a donkey would simultaneously signify something else, completely unrelated—a woman, say—emanating from the artist's unconscious. Much of Dalí's work during this period plays with this conceit, including his 1928 painting *L'âne Pourri* and his celebrated 1929 film with Luis Buñuel, *Un chien andalou*, which teems with disturbing double images: a moon that becomes an eyeball, a cloud that becomes a razor blade, breasts that turn into buttocks, etc.

L'Âne pourri by Salvador Dalí (1928), in which the image of a donkey is also that of a woman

Like Judge Schreber in Freud's reading, Dalí projected onto the external world a cryptic set of private signs. "The only difference between me and a madman," he liked to say, "is that I am not mad." His obsession with paranoia would get him in trouble with the Surrealists when he became fixated on Hitler—in his view an icon of paranoiac possibility. In 1934, Breton, who was increasingly envious of Dalí's artistic success, put Dalí on trial for "counterrevolutionary acts tending to glorify Nazi fascism" and he was eventually expelled from the Surrealist movement.

Lacan was fascinated by Dalí's account of the hidden symbolism embedded in art and called the artist to request a meeting. He found Dalí in a hotel room, a bandage affixed to his nose. Lacan, interested only in the artist's ideas, made no comment on his appearance. (Forty-five years later, in the fall of 1975, Dalí ran into Lacan in the lobby of the Saint Regis Hotel in New York City and confronted him about this oversight. Why, at their first meeting, hadn't Lacan mentioned the bandage on the artist's nose? "Because I knew there wasn't anything wrong with you," Lacan replied; the bandage was a projection empty of meaning. Dalí was stunned. "Fantastic!" he said. "You're the only one who didn't say anything.")

Dalí's influence was apparent in Lacan's 1932 medical thesis, *De la psychose paranoïaque dans ses rapports avec la personnalité* (Paranoid psychosis and its relation to personality). Centered on the case of a patient at Sainte-Anne Hospital, the thesis was a brief for a new conception of paranoia. On an April evening in 1931, Marguerite Pantaine, a thirty-eight-year-old worker at a Parisian railway company, arrived at the Théâtre Saint-Georges and accosted Huguette Duflos, a star of France's budding film industry who was playing the lead in a stage comedy that night. Pulling a kitchen knife from her purse, Pantaine tried to stab Duflos, who caught the blade in her right hand, severing several tendons. Pantaine was arrested and, after a few weeks in jail, sent to Sainte-Anne's, where she was diagnosed with "systematic persecution mania" and became Lacan's patient.

Most psychiatrists at the time attributed psychoses to vaguely defined organic causes and disturbances of "constitution." But Lacan, inspired by Freud, Dalí, and a handful of other maverick thinkers, emphasized psychological factors, arguing that a patient's experiences and personality were key to explaining her illness. In his thesis, he reviewed Pantaine's history in painstaking detail, from her relationships with her parents, sister, husband, child, coworkers, and friends to her "ceaseless reading," and the "five or six cups of very strong coffee" she consumed each day.

Bolder still, Lacan combed Pantaine's writings for clinical insights—perhaps also relishing the chance to show off his literary expertise. "The patient had caught my interest because of the impassioned signification of her written productions, whose literary value struck many writers," he later recalled. Determined to become a successful author, Pantaine had transferred from her company's office in the suburbs to its Paris branch, leaving her baby son in the care of her husband and elder sister. In Paris, she succumbed to delusions, convinced that various well-known women, including the actress Duflos as well as the author Colette, were threatening her through the books of a popular male writer.

In the throes of this paranoid psychosis, Pantaine wrote two novels, which she tried in vain to publish. One was a rural idyll featuring a dreamy, maternal girl named Aimée (Beloved) who falls ill and dies after a decadent couple arrive in town and Aimée's family comes under their malign influence. Lacan discerned in Pantaine's novel conflicts that he believed were at the root of her psychosis. As if to underscore the point, he used her character's name—Aimée—as a pseudonym for her in his thesis. Quoting at length from her manuscript, he praised the "authentic poetic value" of her imagery, and her "pleasing balance of precision and suggestion." He called the novel's sensibility "Bovaryque." Like Flaubert's Madame Bovary, the fictional Aimée was a country woman whose romantic aspirations ill accorded with the mundane reality of her life and doomed her to disappointment.

So, too, Lacan argued, the real-life Pantaine was unable to resolve the conflict between her idealized notions of motherly love (represented in her novel by Aimée) and her fantasies of worldly success (represented in her novel by the sinister couple). Pantaine hated her sister for taking over her maternal duties but couldn't admit her hostility. Instead, she projected it onto famous women she didn't know, imagining that they were persecuting her and her son. She said she despised these women, regarding them as decadent and false, but at the same time, Lacan insisted, she desperately desired their fame.

According to Lacan's analysis, when Pantaine tried to stab Duflos, she was acting out her unconscious desire to punish *herself* for her shameful feelings and fantasies. Once she committed her crime and was sent to jail, her delusions subsided: She had received the punishment she unconsciously sought. Here Lacan was indebted not only to Freud, who had discussed the compulsion to commit crimes out of a sense of guilt and desire for punishment, but also, in the emphasis on symbolism, to Dalí. Pantaine's internal conflicts—those at the heart of her identity as a mother and aspiring author—were projected outside herself, onto symbolic surrogates in the world around her. The idea that the unconscious expresses itself via a symbolic logic, a radical notion at the time, became increasingly central to Lacan's thought. But there was also, in Lacan's approach to Pantaine's case, the germ of another idea for which he would one day become famous: Our identities are formed not within our minds but, to a paradoxical degree, outside our bodies, in our entanglement with other people.

From a medical perspective, the achievement of Lacan's thesis was to have identified a new type of psychosis—he called it "self-punishment paranoia"—along with its causes. According to the Lacan scholars Bice Benvenuto and Roger Kennedy, the thesis was "the first French attempt to interpret a psychosis in terms of the total history of the patient . . . including her conscious and unconscious intentions." Lacan claimed, a little disingenuously, that he had relied on Freudian concepts in his thesis "without realizing it." (In fact, he had included footnotes to Freud, sent Freud a copy, and begun his own analysis, with the highly respected Rudolph Loewenstein, a few months before the thesis was published.)

Pantaine apparently never forgave Lacan for appropriating her life story and her writings. In the first of a series of strange—or, more aptly, surreal—coincidences, around 1950, long after she had been released from the hospital and was working as a housekeeper in the Paris suburbs, she was hired as a cook by Lacan's father. When Lacan visited his father's house, Paintaine asked him to return her manuscripts, but he never did. At the same time, in another remarkable coincidence, Lacan began an analysis of Pantaine's son.

The son, Didier Anzieu, a philosophy graduate of the École Normale, had no idea that his mother, from whom he had been estranged for years, had been Lacan's patient. He made the connection only after his wife located Pantaine and facilitated a reunion. Upon hearing his mother's story, Anzieu rushed to the library to read a copy of Lacan's thesis, and then confronted Lacan, who confessed that he had deduced Anzieu's identity over the course of their sessions. Anzieu went on to become a prominent Parisian analyst himself, and a fierce critic of Lacan, accusing him in print of promoting a cult—"an unending dependence on an idol, a logic, and a language." As for Pantaine, Lacan's rising public profile was, as we say now, triggering, arousing old conflicts and animosity. "When he became famous, she resented it," Roudinesco writes, "and feelings of persecution again rose up strongly in her."

◆ ◆ ◆

The Surrealists hailed Lacan's "Aimée" as one of their own. Just as they had celebrated hysteria as a "supreme means of expression" a few years earlier, they now extolled paranoid psychosis as a similar accomplishment. Writing in *Le Surréalisme au service de la révolution*, the novelist René Crevel applauded Aimée's "wonderful convulsive state that is both appalled and appalling." The poet Paul Éluard included some of Aimée's words in a collection of "involuntary" poetry. Dalí, too, weighed in, in the first issue of a new Surrealist journal called *Minotaure,* which featured a sumptuous cover collage by Picasso. He commended Lacan for challenging "constitutionalist theories" and recognizing that "paranoid delusion is a form of interpretation."

Lacan himself had an article in the first issue of *Minotaure*, proof of how cozy his relations with the Surrealists had become. Titled "The Problem of Style and the Psychiatric Conception of Paranoid Experience," the piece reflected his growing interest in madness as a language. His thinking on the subject was not so different from the Surrealists' own. He described paranoid expression as a "syntax" formed from the projection of unconscious conflicts and fantasies into the social arena. "Understanding this syntax can, I think, provide an invaluable introduction to the symbolic values of art," he wrote. In a sense, Lacan was parroting Dalí's essay on the paranoiac-critical method, giving Dalí's ideas the imprimatur of medical authority. ("The scientist comes off as a timid disciple of the painter," a historian of Surrealism later observed.)

But Lacan was also beginning to see, in the symbolic projections of the paranoid patient and paranoid artist, clues to how the ego is constructed. In responding to the world as if it were an extension of her own mind, the paranoiac suggested the degree to which externalized images and other people shaped our sense of self. Within a few years, Lacan would argue that identity formation—the process of building an "I"—is rooted in projection and estrangement, in a fundamental but necessary confusion of self and other.

In the meantime, he was planting his flag on the side of the mad. Like the Surrealists, Lacan saw in madness a creative freedom he aspired to in his own work. His style—his sentence structure, his puns, his literary allusions—grew increasingly elaborate. He was careful never to define concepts in a straightforward or consistent way, preferring to keep them in play like a juggler ceaselessly tossing and catching balls. If they knew what I was saying, he joked in his seminar, with a hint of paranoia himself, they would never let me say it. Decoding his thought became a formidable task, one for which his audience, Lacan admitted, "must pay the price with elbow grease."

Chapter 13

MADWOMEN

Six months after Lacan's first essay in *Minotaure* appeared, he published a second. This one was about an episode of madness involving a sensational crime. On a February evening in 1933, in the provincial town of Le Mans, a retired lawyer left his club and went home to pick up his wife and daughter for dinner at his brother-in-law's place. To his surprise, he found his front door locked and the lights out, except for a faint glow from the maids' room in the attic. No one answered his knock. Alarmed, the lawyer rounded up his brother-in-law and several police officers, and together they broke in through a window.

The electricity in the house was out, but near the second-floor landing, illuminated by an officer's flashlight, they found a human eyeball, and then, a few feet further on, the bodies of the lawyer's wife and his daughter, Geneviève. Their grotesquely mutilated corpses attested to an act of breathtaking violence and inspired flights of purple prose from the journalists who soon converged on the story. "Beneath their provincial petticoats their modest limbs had been knife-notched the way a fancy French baker notches his finer long loaves," Janet Flanner, *The New Yorker*'s Paris correspondent, wrote. "Their fingernails had been uprooted; one of Geneviève's teeth was pegged in her own scalp. A second single orb—the mother's, this time, for both generations seemed to have been treated with ferocious nonpartisanship—rested shortsightedly gazing at nothing in the corner of the hall. Blood had softened the carpet till it was like an elastic red moss." In the attic, the police found the family's maids, the sisters Christine and Léa Papin, in bed together, naked under their dressing gowns. They immediately confessed to the killings, whose only discernible motive was a scolding by their employer over a minor infraction—a blown fuse.

By the time the case came to trial, it had become a national obsession. In Paris, leftist intellectuals fixated on reports that the sisters' employers had never spoken to them directly and that the lady of the house would vet the quality of their work by donning white gloves and testing surfaces for dust. Clearly the murders were an act of vengeance on behalf of the exploited working class. "The main outline of the Papin sisters' tragedy was at once intelligible to us," Beauvoir wrote. "In Rouen"—where Beauvoir was teaching high school at the time—"as in Le Mans, and, indeed, perhaps even among the mothers of my pupils, there was to be found, beyond any doubt, the sort of woman who would deduct the price of a broken plate from her maid's wages, and wear white gloves to hunt down the least grain of forgotten dust on the furniture: in our eyes such creatures deserved the death penalty a hundred times over." As for the Papin sisters, they were "the instruments and the martyrs of justice," Beauvoir declared. "Respectable folk execrated them as mad-women, monsters, murderers: but it was their orphaned childhood and subsequent enslavement, the whole ghastly system that had made them what they were."

The Surrealists agreed. "For six years, they bore observations, demands, insults with a perfect submissiveness," a pair of poets wrote in *Le Surréalisme au service de la révolution.* "Fear, weariness, humiliations, were slowly begetting hatred inside them. . . . When the day came, Léa and Christine Papin repaid evil in its own coin."

In prison and the courtroom, however, Christine Papin complicated the narrative of working-class retribution with flagrant displays of psychosis. She suffered from hallucinations, claimed that in a former life she

Léa and Christine Papin

had been her sister's husband, tried to pluck her eyes out, and then refused to open them in court. A psychiatrist for the defense argued that the girls were insane and had formed an incestuous "psychological couple." The jury was unmoved. Léa was sentenced to ten years in prison, Christine to decapitation in Le Mans's public square—an announcement she received by getting down on her knees and bowing her head. (Her sentence was subsequently commuted to life in prison.)

Lacan, fresh from his study of Aimée/Pantaine, sided with the defense. In his *Minotaure* essay, "Motifs of Paranoid Crime," he outlined his theory of the sisters' "*délires à deux*," or double delirium, drawing on both his concept of self-punishment paranoia and his budding ideas about the role of projection in the construction of identity. Other commentators had noted the sisters' striking physical resemblance; the psychiatrist for the defense said their depositions were so similar that it was "like seeing double." Lacan pushed the doubleness further still: The sisters, true "Siamese souls," suffered from a "*mal d'être deux*" (literally, "sickness from being two"), each perceiving the other as an idealized reflection of herself rather than as a distinct someone else. Their desire for each other was narcissistic. It was also, of course, taboo, and thus deeply shameful. This disavowed shame found expression in their horrific crime, one featuring what Lacan called "the most worn metaphors of hate": the plucking out of eyeballs—a deeply symbolic act, blinding the sisters' victims to their illicit relationship. Just as the actress Huguette Duflos was for Marguerite Pantaine the embodiment of *her* unconscious shame, so the murdered mother-daughter pair were for Christine and Léa the embodiment of theirs. "On the fateful evening, in the anxious expectation of imminent punishment, the sisters conflated the image of their mistresses with the mirage of their own affliction," Lacan wrote.

Lacan would soon have much more to say about the confusion of self and other he believed was at the heart of the sisters' case. If his emphasis on doubles and symbols and metaphors sounds suspiciously literary, as though he were analyzing a novel rather than the actions of real human beings, it's for good reason. At this point, the major concepts of his psychoanalytic philosophy were still in the larval stage, but they were beginning to gel. And nearly all had to do with language, the "symbolic order" in which, he came to believe, we are profoundly and irrevocably enmeshed. In this respect, Lacan's view of the world *is* literary. Language, he will argue, is an all-encompassing system, mediating every stage of our development. It's this conviction that will make him a structuralist. It's also what will make him a key theorist for literature students decades later, when I am in college. Already here, in his essay on the Papin sisters, he speaks of "the structure" of paranoia. Later, he will say: "There is no structure except that of language."

◆ ◆ ◆

At the same time, it's hard not to notice another pattern in these investigations of madness: The theorists and champions of psychosis were invariably men, while the troubled souls that filled their case studies were overwhelmingly women. It's a pattern that in France dates to the 1870s, to Jean-Martin Charcot's theatrical demonstrations of hysteria starring female patients at the Hôpital de la Pitié-Salpêtrière in Paris. When the Surrealists celebrated hysteria's fiftieth anniversary in 1928, they singled out not Charcot but his most famous hysteric, Augustine. We don't know what most of these women thought of their doctors, let alone their Surrealist fanboys, though Pantaine later made it clear that she was an involuntary participant in Lacan's thesis, telling her son that she found the psychiatrist "too attractive and too much of a clown to be trusted." Roudinesco's judgment is severe: "Lacan was interested in the woman only in order to illustrate his ideas on paranoia and write a theoretical work that would make him the founder of a new school of Freudian discourse."

In short, women served as convenient forms onto which seductive theories of madness could be projected without risk of protest. They functioned more or less like literary conceits in the hands of an author, infinitely pliable to his needs. As a freshman in college, I fell hard for a madwoman conjured by a man in thrall to madness: Nadja, the titular heroine of Bréton's 1928 novel, widely considered Surrealism's greatest literary creation. I read the book my freshman spring, in a class on experimental French literature that doubled as my initiation into theory. *Nadja*, you could say, was my gateway drug to hardcore French thought.

The book is autobiographical, narrated by Breton himself. Nadja doesn't appear until page sixty-four, but her delayed entrance is in part the point: She is by inclination a Surrealist. Since she has never heard of the movement, she may be the most authentic one around—an indigenous species. She has no obligations, no job. She is oblivious to convention, narrative and otherwise. Sometimes she shows up for her rendezvous with Breton, sometimes she doesn't. She is, he says, "*un génie libre*"—a free genius. There are hints that she has worked as a prostitute and, at least once, as a drug courier, though Breton glosses over these unsavory details. I didn't dwell on them either. Like him, I was enchanted by the idea of Nadja, by her iconoclasm, her freedom.

When he first spies her, on a sidewalk near the Paris opera, she is poorly dressed, her hair disheveled, her makeup slapdash. But she reels him in, first with her eyes ("What was it they reflected—some obscure distress and at the same time some luminous pride?") and then with her words. When, at a café near the Gare du Nord, she tells him that she spends evenings riding the Métro, trying to guess what the other passengers are thinking, you can practically see the drool collecting on Breton's lower lip. Nadja makes cryptic drawings—a woman's face emerging from a glove, a devil's head joined to a pointed shoe. These, along with moody black-and-white photographs of *objets d'art*, Parisian boulevards, and Nadja's eyes, give the book the air of an ethnography, or as Breton put it in a later edition, a clinical case history. Moreover, Nadja speaks a kind of Surrealist high pidgin, word salads of portentous metaphors and non sequiturs that bowl Breton over:

> About to leave her, I want to ask one question which sums up all the rest, a question which only I would ever ask, probably, but which has at least once found a reply worthy of it: "Who are you?" And she, without a moment's hesitation: "I am the soul in limbo."

Surrealism Q.E.D. That's what Breton thinks, anyway. He can't get enough of Nadja, though in the end she proves too much, too mad, even for him. After fewer than a dozen enchanted days, he breaks off their affair. Soon, she is confined to an insane asylum. "I do not suppose there can be much difference for Nadja between the inside of a sanitarium and the outside," Breton writes in a defensive coda. She was born to serve the cause of "human emancipation," he declares, showing us how "each individual must foment a private conspiracy, which exists not only in his imagination . . . but also—and much more dangerously—by thrusting one's head, then an arm, out of the jail—thus shattered—of logic, that is, out of the most hateful of prisons."

I underlined these thrilling words, and Nadja became, without much conscious reflection, a role model. Breton was right: Why be a slave to logic? Why wear sweaty snow boots just because it's snowing? Why bother with socks at all? Why organize my life around someone else's idea of good sense? Or of time? Why follow the dreary herd like the other sheep? For one long, miserably cold winter, I left my watch in a drawer and wandered the freezing Cambridge streets barelegged in ballet flats. My wardrobe veered to black. I wore a shabby, oversized, secondhand wool coat and elbow-length opera gloves in stretch satin—enhancing, or so I

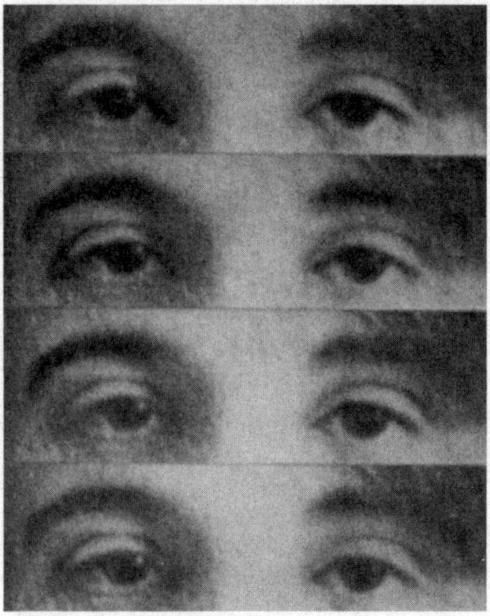

Nadja's eyes

thought, my otherworldly look. I was a seventeen-year-old waif teetering across the frozen snowbanks on Massachusetts Avenue. For the most part, I made it to class, but I was otherwise unreliable. I believed I was freeing myself from social expectation and conformism when in truth I was just flaky and lonely—and cold.

The real-life Nadja was a tragic figure: Léona Delcourt, a single mother from the French working class who died in a mental institution at the age of thirty-eight. Breton met her when she was on the brink of a psychotic break, and the enchantment he found in her incipient madness finally could not make up for the banal wretchedness of her existence. "She had no hesitation, as I have said, about telling me the most unfortunate vicissitudes of her life, not omitting a single detail," he complained. "How many times, unable to endure it any longer, desperate to restore her to a true conception of her worth, I virtually fled from her presence." Nadja's dejectedness is a turnoff, and Breton would rather end things than sully his Surrealist fantasy with her worldly woes. His heroine is a metaphor, not a human being. As one critic crisply put it, "The portrait left of Nadja is not so much of a living creature as of a philosophical concept."

At the time, I couldn't see this. With red pen, I circled Breton's description of Nadja as "*un génie libre*," scribbling in the margin "*pas une personne*" (not a person), an insight I chose to ignore. Months later, after I'd finally given up playing Nadja, I tried to make sense of the experience in a letter to a friend:

> I worshipped this mysterious woman. I wanted to emulate Nadja in my own life, I wanted to do wild and impulsive things. For a while it even sort of worked. I used to drive my roommates crazy because I could never be decisive about future plans. Tuesday night, Anne would say, "Do you want to see a movie on Friday?" and I would say, "Ask me on Friday at 9:30!" I was never punctual, and I hated watches and appointment books, but I was generally—at least superficially—carefree. I thought I was pretty cool.

The truth, I went on, was very different. "I had a sort of identity crisis, when I was forced to confront the fact that parading around as Nadja, the Surrealist heroine, was actually giving me a lot of stress. The real Emily was much less spontaneous and wild, and worried a lot about time, and the reputation for irresponsibility she was building. . . . I began to crack under the pressure of trying to be Nadja while really caring underneath about the way people conceived of me, about my grades, my future, etc."

It wasn't until I reread *Nadja* recently that I saw the book in a different light: as male philosophical fantasy, an instruction manual for how to become the object of that desire. It occurs to me now that in trying to "do" theory perfectly—in trying to get Lacan or Derrida just right, playing back their ideas to my professors in my college papers—I was no different from Nadja, telling the gurus what I thought they wanted to hear. When I mentioned my undergraduate obsession with Breton's novel to my friend Liesl, a critic and translator who'd also attended college in the heyday of theory, she told me the following story. Soon after graduating, she'd gone to a fancy party in Paris for an American journalist who covered France. Naturally, there were many French people among the crowd, including a tall, trim man with a striking mop of gray hair. Extending a hand in her direction, he leaned in close, and, in a seductive stage whisper, introduced himself: "André Glucksmann, *philosophe*."

"The French were philosophers because it got them laid," Liesl said. "We Americans never understood the erotic *frisson* associated with being a philosopher in France." It's true that in America philosophers were generally not sex symbols. It's hard to think of one whose love life (at least the part on public record) was comparable in its flamboyance to Lacan's—or to that of virtually every other Frenchman in this book, for that matter. According to one story, a Parisian taxi driver was so impressed by what was transpiring between Lacan and a woman in the back seat of his cab that he telephoned Lacan's office for an appointment the next day and remained in analysis with him for several years. Then there is Michel Foucault, who told the novelist Edmund White that he had spent his life "trying to do intellectual things that would attract beautiful boys."

As students, we intuitively grasped theory's sex appeal—we went to class to "get laid, in intellectual fashion," as my journalist friend had put it to me—but surely there was a role for women in French theory other than being an Aimée or a Nadja trapped in male fantasy. In its obsession with the female form, Surrealism seemed, perversely, to exclude the possibility of real women. Structuralism, on the other hand, appeared more promising. Like the Surrealists, the structuralists were overwhelmingly male, but the emphasis wasn't on men and women anymore, or even on human beings, but rather on that impersonal abstraction: the *subject*.

Ditching humanism had philosophical appeal in postwar Europe, where technology, commerce, and state power increasingly reigned supreme, and the notion of free will seemed more and more fanciful. But for me, the allure of structuralism was precisely its abstraction, which, rightly or wrongly, I associated with rigor and purity of thought—with truth. As a psychoanalyst, Lacan could hardly avoid talking about relations between men and women, but he managed to do so in a way that retained, for a while anyway, the impersonal trappings and Cartesian logic of the structuralist framework. Where Freud grounded his insights in narratives about particular people, Lacan relied on arcane wordplay and mathematical diagrams. Though he frequently invoked myths, novels, and plays, after his analyses of Aimée and the Papin sisters, he rarely mentioned case histories of actual people again.

Chapter 14

STRANGER IN THE MIRROR

Three years after the Papin sisters' trial, Lacan made his first major intervention as a psychoanalytic philosopher. On August 3, 1936, he presented "The Mirror Stage" at the annual congress of the International Psychoanalytic Association (IPA). It was his début appearance at the congress, held that year in Marienbad. Freud stayed home in Vienna, too sick to attend, but many of his leading disciples were there, including Ernest Jones, his future biographer, who was president of the association. Lacan was thirty-five, a newly minted analyst, completely unknown outside his own country. He was, Roudinesco says, "a mere nobody." The other attendees, consumed by a feud between the Viennese and British branches over methodology, hardly acknowledged him, even as he broke new ground.

Psychoanalysts had long been struggling with the problem of the Freudian ego. How did it form? Where did our sense of self come from? As Freud put it in a 1914 paper, "A unity comparable to the ego cannot exist in the individual from the start; the ego has to be developed." The problem was that Freud wasn't quite sure how the ego happened, whether it emerged gradually in childhood through an organic process of separation from the id, or, rather, in response to external cues. Lacan was convinced that the latter scenario was correct. We don't know exactly what he said at the congress that day, as his paper was subsequently lost. But he continued to work on its ideas for many years. He incorporated them into a landmark entry on the family for the *Encyclopédie française* in 1938, and he presented them in expanded form in a paper, also titled "The Mirror Stage," at an IPA congress in Zurich in 1949, the group's first meeting after an eleven-year hiatus because of World War II.

Lacan started with the observation that infants between the ages of six and eighteen months acquire the ability to recognize themselves in a mirror—proof, psychologists had suggested, of our species' superior intelligence. (There is now evidence that many great apes, as well as some elephants, dolphins, and even birds have this ability.) But what fascinated Lacan about this "mirror stage"—a concept he borrowed without crediting from a French psychologist—was not the demonstration of superior intellect it implied but, rather, the disjunction between how an infant experienced its body and what it saw in the glass.

At six months, he pointed out, a baby has yet to learn to walk, stand up on its own, or master motor control: It senses its body as fragmented and incoherent. Yet the body that meets its gaze in the mirror is a seamless whole. In short, the infant's perception of itself as a *unified self* occurs not through direct experience but through an act of looking, what Lacan called the infant's "jubilant assumption of his specular image." (According to Roudinesco, mirrors held special interest for Lacan throughout his life: He was a narcissist terrified of aging, she says, and could hardly pass one without glancing at himself.)

Lacan was staking out the terms of a grand ontological paradox. As the infant begins to grasp the world around it, it can see everything except itself. The self in the mirror is merely an image—a reflection. Thus the act of self-recognition is also a misrecognition, an error: My reflection is both me and, in a literal sense, not me. Lacan would eventually call this realm of idealized identifications and misidentifications "the imaginary." And as he worked on the mirror stage, he made clear that a mirror was not required for the process to take place. More generally, it marked the moment when we recognize ourselves in the form of another human being—a parent, sibling, or playmate would do. "A child who beats another child says that he himself was beaten," Lacan noted, "a child who sees another child fall, cries." This was Lacan's counterintuitive insight: Our awareness of ourselves as a *self* requires another person, or to use the Lacanian term, an *Other.*

Sartre, too, around the same time, was contending with what in *Being and Nothingness* he will call "the problem of the Other"—the fact that every individual is not only a subject but also an object for another individual, an "Other," whose gaze and behavior impinges on our freedom. But Lacan went further. Like the paranoid psychotic who finds messages to herself in the pages of a novel (Pantaine) or mistakes her sister for herself (Christine Papin), the infant in Lacan's analysis must contend with images and people outside his body merely in order to conceive of his own. In this sense, Lacan argued, the ego is wholly a creation of society—a patchwork of data supplied by the world around us, providing an illusion of coherence and unity where none exists. Successfully traversed, the mirror stage configures us as beings uneasily sublimating an experience of profound fragmentation and estrangement.

◆ ◆ ◆

Lacan eventually saw the mirror stage not just as a key feature of the imaginary but as the initial step toward language—or what he called "the symbolic order." Like the reflection in the mirror, the "I" that stands in for the Freudian ego is merely an image, or, more precisely, a linguistic signifier. More radically, language is what *makes* the ego and what it is *made of.* Where Sartre saw an autonomous individual freely acting in the world, and Althusser saw a human subject as so much raw material to be molded (or "interpellated") by ideology, Lacan envisioned no experience of being prior to language. The moment we recognize ourselves in the mirror and are designated by other people ("That's you, baby!") marks our entry into both selfhood and language. For Lacan, there was no difference. Language was both the scalpel and clay of the self. "It is the world of words that creates the world of things," he declared. "Man thus speaks, but it is because the symbol has made him man." Of course, such a claim invites the question: If there is no human subject before language, where does language come from? Lacan essentially sidestepped the issue, suggesting that there is little practical use in pondering it. Language is simply there.

As a junior in college, I found Lacan thrilling. His work was proof that what I studied—literature, words—was the most important stuff around. When we read *Great Expectations* in literature tutorial, I was bowled over to discover on the novel's famous opening page an account of the orphan Pip's most formative early memory that was practically a transcription of Lacanian theory—recast with Dickens' inimitable wit. The book begins at dusk in the village churchyard, with a scene that Pip recalls as his "first most vivid and broad impression of the identity of things," the instant when, confronted with the graves of his parents, he grasps, as if for the first time, that they are dead. Having no memories of their ever having been alive, he derives his impressions of his parents solely from the inscriptions on their tombstones: "The shape of the letters on my father's, gave me an odd idea that he was a square, stout, dark man, with curly black hair. From the character and turn of the inscription, '*Also Georgiana Wife of the Above*,' I drew a childish conclusion that my mother was freckled and sickly."

Could there be a more comically literal description of language's decisive molding force? Or of the human subject's entry into the symbolic order? For Pip, the act of reading the tombstones is like the light dawning in Genesis—it's his initiation into consciousness, the moment he acquires a self:

> At such a time, I found out for certain, that this bleak place overgrown with nettles was the churchyard; and that Philip Pirrip, late of this parish, and also Georgiana, wife of the above, were dead and buried; and that Alexander, Bartholomew, Abraham, Tobias, and Roger, infant children of the aforesaid, were also dead and buried; and that the dark flat wilderness beyond the churchyard,

> intersected with dykes and mounds and gates, with scattered cattle feeding on it, was the marshes; and that the low leaden line beyond, was the river; and that the distant savage lair from which the wind was rushing, was the sea; and that the small bundle of shivers growing afraid of it all and beginning to cry, was Pip.

Overwhelmed by the discovery of who he is, Pip dissolves in tears, his outburst alerting the escaped convict Magwitch to his presence and setting the whole magnificent plot in motion.

Of course, language was Freud's principal tool, the medium from which—via his patients' dreams, jokes, and stories, as well as his readings of Greek myths and Shakespeare plays—he extracted evidence for his theory. Where Lacan departed from Freud was in suggesting that the most important attributes of language were its structure and social context. Drawing on linguistic theory, Lacan conceived of language as a vast decentralized matrix operating according to fixed rules to produce meaning and thus human beings. The unconscious itself could not escape language's organizing effects. "The unconscious is structured like a language" is among Lacan's most famous statements.

From the account he fleshed out over many years, a picture of human development gradually emerges. It is distinguished by rupture and loss, beginning with the trauma of birth itself. The infant's separation from its mother, while utterly dependent on her for survival, is the primordial experience of fractured unity, one repeated during weaning, inaugurating the infant's quest to restore its lost wholeness. (This, in essence, is Lacan's conception of desire: an unending quest for objects to compensate for the lost unity of our origins.) At the center of this picture is what Lacan called the "drama" of the mirror stage. It marks the birth of the subject but also, more broadly, of culture, the human social world. Given Lacan's dark view of this process, "drama" seems like an understatement.

The mirror stage tells a story of deception and alienation, in which we are doomed to chase symbolic representations of ourselves, fictions of coherence and unity papering over an unknowable and unnamable abyss of being. Lacan later called this chasmic register of existence beyond language "the real"—the final term, along with the imaginary and the symbolic, in his tripartite psychic schema, but he had little to say about it; like dark matter in the universe, the real defied knowledge. Our fate as humans is perpetually to mistake the symbols of self for the actual thing—just as Pip mistakes the letters on his parents' tombstones for evidence of their personalities. Under the influence of Lacan, intellectuals began to refer to the subject as "decentered" or "divided." As Lacan expressed this predicament, in a witty inversion of Descartes' famous maxim: "I am thinking where I am not, therefore I am where I am not thinking."

In its disenchanted grimness, the mirror stage hints at the horrors of two world wars. It also suggests why Lacan was a frustrating analyst, often at odds with his profession. To him, the idea that an analysis could exert a curative effect on psychological distress seems to have been philosophically untenable. He hated American ego psychology, with its optimistic emphasis on helping patients adapt to their environments by shoring up various "ego functions." Even Freud thought the ego served an important protective role, moderating the wildest impulses of the unconscious. But in Lacan's view, the ego was a fraud: To address an analysis to a patient's ego was to collude with its fantasy of coherence and reason.

He believed an analyst should refrain from offering patients interpretations or insights; his job was to listen closely for peculiar or illogical speech—a double entendre, a non sequitur or nonsensical phrase (Lacan encouraged analysts to do crossword puzzles)—and then get out of the way. "Tell me," was his typical, terse refrain. The moment he determined that something significant had been said, he would end the session. "Go and decipher the enigma of your own story," one patient quoted him as saying. "And come back and tell me what you have discovered." He continued to refine his practice of terminating sessions at will—known in Lacanian circles as "the cut"—over the course of his career, and it would eventually become a source of great conflict in his field. But he swore by the cut, in his view the most efficient means of bypassing resistance to the analyst while simultaneously empowering patients to generate the analysis on their own. In Lacan's conceit, the analyst was, like the ego, a fraud: "*le sujet supposé savoir*"—the subject presumed to know—endowed by the patient with magical powers of knowledge about the patient's unconscious that the analyst did not actually possess. Still, this fiction was necessary for facilitating the transference.

He offered the example of Antigone in Sophocles' play. After Antigone's brother Polynices is killed in battle, he is denied burial by Creon, the king of Thebes, against whom Polynices had rebelled. Knowing that the penalty for defying Creon's order is death, Antigone insists on burying Polynices anyway. Creon tries to talk her out of it, explaining why her action is unlawful and unreasonable, but she proceeds—in fact, she buries Polynices twice. She then hangs herself, calmly choosing the death she understood would be the consequence of her choice. Of these two figures, Antigone and Creon, Lacan suggested, Antigone, the embodiment of "pure" desire that, as it leads toward death, transgresses both self-interest and social norms, is the model the analyst should encourage in his sessions, while Creon, in his efforts to reason with Antigone and get her to adhere to social convention, serves only as an impediment to desire's expression.

Admittedly, this is a pretty remorseless description of the analytic encounter. More generally, Lacan seemed to believe that once a patient's unconscious desire—his symptom—found expression, the patient should reconcile himself to the fundamental alienation at the root of human experience. The sociologist Sherry Turkle calls his approach "therapeutically indifferent." The Lacan scholars Benvenuto and Kennedy maintain that "he was opposed to any notion that psychoanalysis is concerned with producing healthy, well-adjusted individuals." In sum, better to confront the primal lie on which the self is founded than to live an illusion.

In 1936, however, at the IPA congress in Marienbad where Lacan presented his first iteration of the mirror stage, no one was concerned with how he was or wasn't applying Freud's teaching to patients. No one paid him much attention at all. Precisely ten minutes into his talk, Ernest

Jones, who was chairing the proceedings, cut him off mid-sentence. Lacan never forgot the insult. He left in a huff the next day, heading for Berlin where Nazi Germany was hosting the Olympics. Preoccupied by the mirror stage, Roudinesco writes, Lacan couldn't help applying its concepts to the parade of athletic bodies he saw at the games. Revolted by fascism, he found the triumphant display of physical prowess against a backdrop of carefully choreographed propaganda deeply disturbing—a larger-than-life projection from the Nazi imaginary.

Chapter 15

"THE WOMAN DOES NOT EXIST"

In retrospect, Lacan's mirror stage theory was a blueprint for his entire career, encompassing nearly all the themes that would preoccupy him, with one notable exception: women. Simone de Beauvoir, who began working on her magnum opus, *The Second Sex*, a few years after she met him, at the alcohol-laced performance of Picasso's play during the Occupation, had read Lacan's entry on the family in the *Encyclopédie française*. Impressed, she telephoned him, hoping to discuss how it pertained to female development. Lacan told her they would need at least five months of meetings to cover the topic. Reluctant to make such a commitment—her book was already well underway—Beauvoir countered with a proposal for four interviews. Lacan rejected the offer as insufficient, and Beauvoir gave up.

Nevertheless, the mirror stage receives an elegant encapsulation in *The Second Sex*, just a page after her famous declaration "One is not born, but rather becomes, woman." Beauvoir grasped the existential stakes of Lacan's theory, in which the child "tries to compensate" for the "catastrophe" of separation from its mother's body "by alienating his existence in an image whose reality and value will be established by others." Then she went further, seeming to anticipate Lacan's later work on femininity, when she argued that by the end of childhood a woman "determines and differentiates herself in relation to man, and he does not in relation to her; she is the inessential in front of the essential. He is the Subject, he is the Absolute. She is the Other."

Jacques Lacan (*standing, far left*) and Simone de Beauvoir (*standing, second from right*) met at a staged reading of a play by Picasso (*standing with arms crossed, center*) in 1944. Sartre (*seated at left*) and Camus (*kneeling, center*) also attended.

Lacan, a libertine who loved women, was perplexed by the prospect of talking about them, especially their sexuality, within the context of psychoanalysis. In this, he was little different from Freud, who observed, "Throughout history people have knocked their heads against the riddle of the nature of femininity." For Freud, the sex drive was key to human behavior, and the crucial event of childhood was the discovery of sexual difference: the momentous realization of "the primacy of the phallus," and who does and doesn't have one. This discovery had very different implications for boys (who, in Freud's model, suffer from castration anxiety) and girls (who suffer from penis envy). Lacan transposed Freud's framework to the realm of language, arguing that it's only in the symbolic order that sexual difference acquires significance.

In the Lacanian schema, "male" and "female" name not anatomical differences but symbolic ones, with subjects primed to identify with one designation or the other. Yet being a subject in language always entails instability and loss. Men may identify with the phallus, but they have traded the actual organ for its linguistic signifier. Women have access to neither: The phallus is the *only* sexual symbol; there is no corresponding symbol derived from female anatomy. The upshot is a symbolic order organized around the phallus, in which we are all condemned to exist but in which no one, male or female, can ever feel completely secure. As a result, Lacan says, we are constantly seeking something, or someone, to compensate for our lack. Even so, language inherently favors men. "Woman" as a general concept can be defined only negatively, according to what she is missing. Woman is lack, loss—a "*pas-toute*" (not all), as Lacan put it, a phantasm like Nadja.

Precisely how desire for the phallus is baked into language and, in turn, into internalized conceptions of gender, is in Lacan's theory extremely complex, involving a lot of technical linguistic and psychoanalytic theory (not to mention inscrutable prose). It's telling that when Lacan's lectures on female sexuality were published in English in 1982, the book contained not one but two introductions, filling fifty-seven pages—nearly as many pages as the lectures themselves. Opening my copy recently, I found a faded yellow Post-it on which I had written: "Look especially at 'Introduction II' by Jacqueline Rose. It doesn't get more lucid than that." This is true, as far as it goes. Occasionally, though, even the trenchant Rose, a renowned British scholar who also translated the lectures, seems nearly defeated by the task of explication. As another astute critic lamented, even the smartest readers of Lacan have "the tendency, when the thought gets really difficult, to fall into the idiom of the master."

Lacan deferred talking about women in his seminar until the early 1970s, when he was over seventy—according to one report out of fear of triggering a feminist backlash. He was indeed attacked for, among other things, declaring, "The woman does not exist," by which he meant that within the symbolic order the category of "woman" is a negative, not that actual women did not exist. Nor did he know quite what to say about female sexuality. Lacan waxed wonderingly about "*jouissance*," his term for experience so intense that it exceeded representation—falling outside the symbolic order altogether—and which he associated with extremes of pleasure as well as suffering. (In French, *jouissance* can mean "enjoyment" but also "orgasm.") What he called "feminine *jouissance*" belonged to the inaccessible domain of the real, defying not just symbolization but knowledge. "We have implored our women psychoanalysts, on bended knee, to tell us about it, but mum's the word!" Lacan said.

Feminists couldn't agree on whether he was helping to expose the patriarchy as arbitrary and false or simply reinforcing its power, but as a group they were hardly mum. In the 1970s, feminist theorists began imagining what a non-phallic, woman-centered language might look like. For the philosopher Hélène Cixous, a true "*écriture féminine*" (women's writing) entailed a poetic, sidelong, nonlinear form of expression, one that undercut the Cartesian logic of "phallocentric tradition." By its very nature, *écriture féminine* resisted definition: "This practice can never be theorized, enclosed, coded," Cixous wrote; to do so would be to render it in phallocentric terms, defeating its purpose. But she stressed that having female anatomy was not a prerequisite. Just as most women "end up producing writing that's in effect masculine," men could produce *écriture féminine* too, though this rarely happened. Cixous counted the playwright and novelist Jean Genet as one of few such exceptions. Even so, and despite her caveats, women's writing for Cixous seemed implicitly connected to female biology: "She physically materializes what she's thinking; she signifies it with her body."

So, too, for the philosopher Luce Irigaray, who had trained at Lacan's psychoanalytic institute. A true women's writing would be based on the "at least double" nature of female genitalia and the "diffuse" quality of female sexual experience, Irigaray wrote. Whatever else *écriture féminine* was, or could be, it was intended to subvert Freudian chauvinism. As Cixous declared in "The Laugh of the Medusa," a landmark 1975 essay that became required reading in women's studies classes across the United States, "If they really need to believe that we're dying of desire, that we are this hole fringed with desire for their penis—that's their immemorial business."

The image of a bunch of cerebral philosophy PhDs crafting furious polemics about female genitalia as a source of authentically feminine expression doubtless seems goofy now. But no one giggled in my college class on French feminist theory when the professor distributed mimeographed copies of "The Laugh of the Medusa." We underlined key passages and earnestly debated whether a writing derived from the female body was desirable or even possible. No one I knew seemed to think the idea was absurd, or that it merited less than careful consideration.

Today we inhabit a world where personal identity is paramount—the prism through which speech and actions are routinely evaluated and granted significance. But identity is also no longer automatically assumed to be connected to biology in any meaningful way. Gender, sexuality, and race are widely understood to be products of culture, not nature, and as unstable, malleable, and context-dependent as everything else in our society (even as sexism and racism have proved dismayingly tenacious). Yet in the French intellectual world of the 1970s, under the influence of Lévi-Strauss's structuralist anthropology, culture was perceived as more of a monolith, the result of structures embedded in human social life—within the human mind!—since the dawn of time. And foremost among these structures was language. It was the stuff that philosophy PhDs were trained to analyze and manipulate, what Sherry Turkle would call their "object to think with."

It made sense that feminist intellectuals would see language as a central tool and target for reform, and that they would see Lacan, the man who brought structural linguistics and psychoanalysis together in one lecture hall—and who theorized "woman" as "lack"—as the person to argue with. Tellingly, one of the first feminist groups to form in France after May

'68 was called *Psychanalyse et Politique* (psychoanalysis and politics). The group, which also founded the publishing house *des femmes* (women), later changed its name to "*politique et psychanalyse*," apparently to reflect a reversal of priorities (as well as, perhaps, a dawning mistrust of capital letters). When Irigaray dared to attack Freudian and Lacanian theories of femininity in her 1974 philosophy doctoral thesis, *Speculum of the Other Woman,* she was kicked out of Lacan's École freudienne and lost her job in the psychoanalysis department at the University of Vincennes.

The Lacanian patriarchy could apparently tolerate only so much feminist pushback. But you can see the legacy of the '70s language debates in today's gender-fluidity movement and the accelerating collapse of the binary gender model. Recently, the *New York Times* columnist Ross Douthat, echoing other conservatives, suggested that the steep rise in the number of young people identifying as lesbian, gay, bisexual, or transgender now, compared with twenty years ago, was the result of "academic fashions laundered into psychiatry and education—one part Tumblr and TikTok mimesis, one part Judith Butler"—Butler being an important American disciple (and critic) of Lacan. Like an underground stream piercing the earth's surface miles from its source, the long-dead Frenchmen continue to haunt American life, seeping their way into some of our most contested cultural spaces, their influence no longer obvious because it is everywhere.

◆ ◆ ◆

Assigned to study Lacan in college, I encountered only his ideas: the mirror stage, the symbolic order, language as a system of meaning predicated on the male phallus and female lack. These concepts were presented to my classmates and me in the somber register of the lecture hall, as logical abstractions with great explanatory power. If we could only grasp Lacan's theory, it would help us understand how identities were formed and how language worked—and for whom. That his writings made their way into our hands sanitized of biographical details is testament to the hold of structuralism—or at least its main ideas—on the field of literary study at the time. Within the structuralist framework, an author was held to be of little account, a "fiction" perpetrated by the "linguistic system," so it was easy to ignore the philosopher (already more thing than person, having been reduced to a single name) and focus exclusively on his words. This approach had the effect of making the philosopher's theory seem self-evidently true. It came to us devoid of human context, as if imprinted on the sky just waiting for us to look.

And look I dutifully did. So when, in the spring of my junior year, I received a B on my Lacanian reading of *Lolita* for a seminar taught by an English professor of the pre-theory old guard, I was devastated. "I think you are a very good student," he wrote, "but perhaps you need a bit more irreverence toward theory." By then, I'd received similar feedback from Chris, the literature tutor in charge of my junior essay, a thirty-page paper viewed as a dry run for the senior thesis. My journal overflowed with self-pity. "My second folly-laden embrace of Lacan," I wrote. "Lacan as Master Code. Psychoanalysis as God. My methodology, my ideology, my instincts concerning the relationship between theory and fiction are fucked. A non-critical application of theory is a double no-no, a violation of the text, regardless of the theoretical issues at stake."

Chris, ruddy-cheeked and curly-haired, a pipe smoker of indeterminate young middle age, was fluent in theory. He was also everything I wasn't: skeptical, ironic, deeply read in French classical literature, and admirably allergic to the earnestness and dogmatism to which I was prone. Every literature student I knew had studied with him—Tony says he sometimes brought beer to Tony's class—and he was widely respected. I no longer have a copy of my junior paper, an attempt to analyze several novels by Marguerite Duras through a Lacanian lens, but my diary records the dismaying result: Chris took me to task over five, single-spaced pages and called me in for a meeting. "I was caught off guard and sat, lips quivering, for two hours while Chris explained and was moved to pity," I wrote afterward. "The worst moment was when he said, 'Poor Emily,' and instead of letting me go wordlessly off to sorrowful solitude, scribbled the address of two friends from college on a piece of paper and told me to look them up in Paris. I feigned gratitude and stumbled out to bawl on Jason's shoulder while stoic Mark typed away, Walkman turned up."

When I got back to my room, I called my dad but was so wracked by sobs I could hardly talk. The wound went deep, occupying pages in my journal. "This was a junior essay, not an article for *Signs* or *Critical Inquiry*," I fumed. "I looked at my ugly red face in the mirror and felt utterly purposeless. *Sans raison d'être.* Disgusted by both my delusions—about my ability to 'do' critical theory—and my incredible weakmindedness not to have defended myself, to have sat and absorbed the blows, a wet sponge afraid to speak back."

My dad convinced me to call Alice Jardine, the professor who'd taught my class on French feminism the previous semester and who had agreed to be my thesis adviser senior year. Alice was one of two female scholars on campus conspicuously associated with the latest currents in French thought—recent hires intended to underscore Harvard's entrance into the theory age.

Temperamentally, the two could not have been more different. Alice was petite and warm, with a warbling soprano, a cascade of blond curls, and a black leather jacket. She had studied in Paris with Julia Kristeva, Hélène Cixous, and other leading French feminists. The other professor, Barbara Johnson, was a protégé of Derrida's closest colleague in America, Paul de Man, at Yale. A translator of Derrida herself, Johnson was Harvard's first bona fide deconstructionist, a dry, lean woman with an angular blond bob as austere as her manner. Tony signed up for her class, "Deconstruction: Theory and Practice," as a seventeen-year-old freshman. It was a gutsy move. Johnson was brand-new on campus, and the centerpiece of her syllabus was *On Grammatology,* Derrida's intimidating magnum opus. At her first lecture, she invoked the story of Freud's arrival in America in 1909, when, standing on the deck of his ship in sight of shore, he allegedly commented to his traveling companion, Carl Jung: "They don't realize that we are bringing them the plague"—to which Johnson added ominously, "That's how I feel coming to Harvard, this very traditional scholarly environment."

Tony found her class exciting but also tough going. "I had been a good writer," he reflected. "I started writing these incomprehensible papers. I remember what Johnson wrote on my first one: 'You bring the reader to the very precipice of incomprehension and then push him off.'"

Not that Alice was a pushover. I had a bet with Mark, who was taking Alice's introduction to semiotics class, that she would award him an A for his forty-page paper on reading Harlequin romances from a straight male perspective, and that in the unlikely event she failed to do so, I would take him to dinner.

The unthinkable came to pass: Alice gave Mark's paper a B+, later changed to an A–. ("I'm sure the B+ was generous, also sure that I would have contested it," Mark says now.) We made a plan to eat Belgian waffles in Harvard Square—apparently one of the few "dinners" my budget would allow—but by the time we got to the restaurant, it had closed for the night. We ended up at Mark's parents' apartment in downtown Boston, stopping at a Store 24 on the way to load up on ice cream, M&Ms, and chocolate chips. Mark's parents were watching TV but received us graciously. His mom planted us at the kitchen table with mugs of milk and a stack of paper napkins to consume our sugary feast, while his dad turned his head from the screen to inquire genially in my direction, "So, Emily, do you do that English—I mean 'lit'—thing, too?"

I don't recall what Alice told me the night of my junior paper crisis, but in my journal I noted that she "obliged me with a fifty-minute phone call at 11 p.m." Whatever she said reassured me enough that I resolved to submit the same paper, buttressed by several new passages of justification for my apparently overdetermined Lacanian interpretations, to my comparative literature class on women and the avant-garde. (Apparently this was kosher.) The professor, an expert on French modernism, gave me an A, adding: "You have written a wonderfully rich and thoughtful paper, and synthesized a lot of theoretical reflection."

What was the right way to do theory? How could I tell?

Chapter 16

A PORTRAIT OF *JOUISSANCE*

Long before he tackled the mystery of feminine *jouissance*, Lacan bought a painting of it. In 1954, he paid 1.5 million francs (about $55,000 in today's dollars) for *L'Origine du monde* (The Origin of the World), a legendary canvas by Gustave Courbet depicting female genitalia in photo-realist detail. Commissioned in 1866 by Khalil-Bey, a wealthy, syphilitic Ottoman diplomat, the painting hung hidden behind a green curtain in his sumptuous bathroom on Paris's chic Boulevard des Italiens, within view of a pink-marble tub. It was here, in Khalil-Bey's bathroom, that the French writer Maxime Du Camp first saw the work. He left a detailed account of his shock: "When the veil was lifted, you were stupefied to see a woman of life size, glimpsed from the front, transported and convulsed, astonishingly painted *con amore*, as the Italians say, and constituting the last word in realism. But by an inconceivable oversight, the artist, who had copied his model from life, had neglected to depict the feet, the thighs, the legs, the stomach, the haunches, the chest, the hands, the arms, the shoulders, the neck, and the head."

The painting didn't linger long in Paris's scandalized consciousness. Two years after acquiring it, having exhausted his fortune on gambling and high living, Khalil-Bey was forced to sell it. After that, the painting disappeared, resurfacing just before World War I when it was bought in Paris by a Jewish Hungarian baron based in Budapest. During World

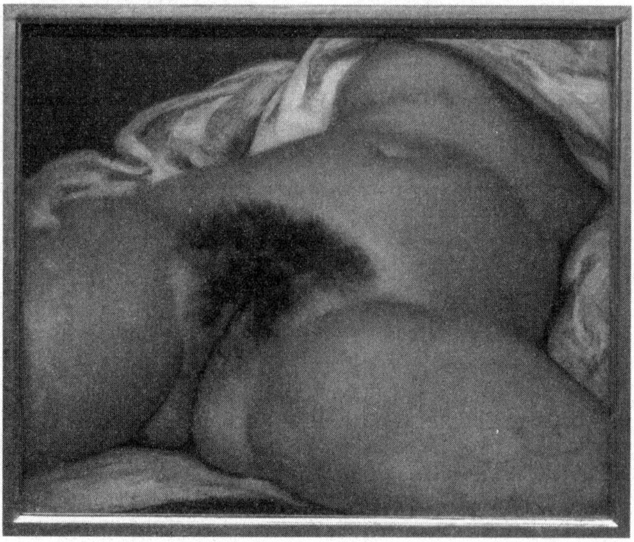

***L'Origine du monde* by Gustave Courbet (1866)**

War II, the baron's collection was pilfered, first by the Nazis, then by the Soviets. According to one report, in March 1944, after expelling the Nazis from the city, Soviet troops waved the painting from an open car as they rolled through Budapest's ruined streets. The baron, having survived the war, eventually succeeded in ransoming *L'Origine du monde*, along with nine other works, before fleeing to Paris as the communists took over his country.

How Lacan came to own the painting is not entirely clear. One theory is that he bought it on the advice of his friend the philosopher and novelist Georges Bataille. Bataille was another brilliant young man enamored of Nietzsche, madness, and Freud—or, as he summed it up, extremes of all kinds. Often overlooked by his contemporaries during his lifetime, he was rediscovered after his death in 1962 and hailed as a sort of proto-structuralist—though hardly a systematic one—by Barthes, Derrida, and Foucault. A once-devout Catholic who had considered becoming a monk, Bataille had a day job as a librarian at the Bibliothèque Nationale. But when he wasn't working or writing, he spent much of his free time in brothels or out drinking and gambling. "My true church is a whorehouse," he wrote, "the only one that gives me true satisfaction." A friend to whom Bataille showed drafts of his stories found the sexual fantasies in them so disturbing that he persuaded Bataille to go into analysis. Bataille did so for a year in the late 1920s, at the end of which he declared himself transformed from someone "unhealthy" into someone "relatively viable."

By the time Bataille befriended Lacan in the 1930s, he had edited a short-lived art magazine and published, under a pseudonym, his first book, *Histoire de l'oeil* (Story of the Eye), a novella of graphic sex and violence that Susan Sontag, in an admiring essay, called "the most accomplished artistically of all the pornographic prose fictions I've read"—she'd read quite a few. He had also fallen out with André Breton, who devoted several pages of his second Surrealist manifesto in 1930 to excoriating Bataille as a writer interested only in "that which is vilest, most discouraging, and most corrupted."

Breton wasn't wrong about Bataille's fascination with degradation, but he underestimated Bataille's intellectual seriousness—and his originality. Bataille shared with Dalí an interest in doubleness, in his case a fixation on overlapping extremes: the ways in which fantasies of sex and death, the sacred and the profane—all prominent motifs in his work—intersected. A few decades later, the deconstructionists Derrida and de Man would also become fixated on the way opposing terms bleed into one another, how insight goes hand in hand with blindness, for example. (De Man devoted a book of essays to this idea.) Bataille claimed his life was forever changed when his analyst gave him a photograph of a convicted Chinese murderer being tortured to death via a process of slow physical dismemberment called "the Hundred Pieces." The man had been given morphine and though he was experiencing an unimaginably brutal demise, the expression on his face appeared benign. "I have never stopped being obsessed by this image of pain, at once ecstatic and intolerable," Bataille wrote.

Years later, Lacan would also be haunted by a depiction of ecstasy and pain: Gian Lorenzo Bernini's statue of the sixteenth-century Spanish

***The Ecstasy of Saint Teresa*, by Gian Lorenzo Bernini (1598–1680)**

mystic Saint Teresa at the church of Santa Maria della Vittoria in Rome. A masterpiece of feeling engraved in marble, the sculpture shows the saint swooning in heavy-lidded rapture beneath a beaming seraph whose gold-tipped spear is aimed at her heart.

Teresa described this vision in her memoir:

> I saw in his hand a long spear of gold, and at the iron's point there seemed to be a little fire. He appeared to me to be thrusting it at times into my heart, and to pierce my very entrails; when he drew it out, he seemed to draw them out also, and to leave me all on fire with a great love of God. The pain was so great that it made me moan; and yet so surpassing was the sweetness of this excessive pain that I could not wish to be rid of it.

A photograph of the sculpture appears on the cover of Lacan's book of lectures from the 1972–73 academic year, during which he spoke about feminine *jouissance*. "All you have to do is go to see Bernini's statue in Rome to understand right away that she is coming [*jouit*], there is no doubt about it," he told his audience that term. "But what's she getting off on? It's clear from the essential testimony of the mystics that they experience it"—sexual pleasure—"but know nothing about it."

◆ ◆ ◆

Lacan probably met Bataille at a legendary seminar on Hegel taught by the Russian-born philosophy scholar Alexandre Kojève in the mid-1930s and attended by a sizable cohort of young Parisian intellectuals. (Bataille later wrote that he was "dumbfounded" by Kojève's lectures, though a friend claimed that Bataille often slept through them.) Lacan's relationship with Bataille is not well documented, but we know that he attended meetings of Bataille's anti-fascist journal *Contre-Attaque*, and may have been part of Acéphale, a secret society Bataille founded that was dedicated to a Nietzschean pursuit of "totality of being." The society's members gathered monthly under a full moon in a forest outside Paris where, led by Bataille, they engaged in philosophical discussions and mysterious rituals; thankfully, a plan to perform a human sacrifice never came to fruition.

Lacan's most lasting connection to Bataille, however, was via his wife, Sylvia Bataille, a talented film actress who became Lacan's second wife. By the time Lacan met Sylvia, in 1934, the Batailles' marriage was ending, a failure for which Bataille blamed himself. One disturbing scene from their life together made its way—twice—into his fiction: Staying at the home of his mother, who had just died, Bataille rose from his bed where Sylvia, pregnant with their only child, lay sleeping, and masturbated next to his mother's corpse.

Compared with the risqué Bataille, Lacan seemed dully conventional. This, at any rate, was Sylvia's impression when she and Bataille went to dinner at Lacan's home in February 1934. He had then been married for less than a month to Marie-Louise ("Malou") Blondin, the sister of a friend from medical school, a Catholic from an upper-middle-class family like his own. After that dinner, Lacan didn't see Sylvia again for a couple of years, and it wasn't until 1938, long after she had separated from Bataille, that they met by chance at the Café de Flore and, struck by a *coup de foudre*, began an affair. By then, Lacan and Malou had a young daughter and a son on the way.

Two years later, both Malou and Sylvia were pregnant, and France had effectively become two countries, one in the north, occupied by Nazi Germany, the other in the south, nominally under French rule. Malou and Sylvia remained on opposite sides of this divide, and Lacan spent the war shuttling back and forth over the demarcation line, between Paris (Malou) and Marseille (Sylvia) in his 5CV Citroën. Nearly everyone who knew him seems to have commented on his driving. The analyst Catherine Millot, a former patient who was romantically involved with Lacan for most of the 1970s, saw in his passion for speed and indifference to road rules an expression of his personal creed: Don't let arbitrary laws get in the way of one's desire. His son-in-law recalled making the mistake of stopping at a red light with Lacan in the passenger seat. Lacan got out of the car, crossed the intersection, and waited impatiently to be picked up on the other side.

It's not hard to picture him determinedly chugging across nearly five hundred miles of French countryside in the middle of the war. Fifteen years later, in 1955, Lacan's driving terrified Heidegger's wife, Elfride, when he took the couple to see the cathedral at Chartres on the occasion of Heidegger's first visit to France. The German philosopher had come to attend a conference on his work, to the dismay of many French intellectuals, including Sartre and Merleau-Ponty, who boycotted the event in protest of Heidegger's wartime Nazi Party affiliation. But Lacan, who had met Heidegger in Freiburg a few months earlier, offered to host him and Elfride at his country house and take them sightseeing. Heidegger was not known for his sense of humor—according to one account, he was observed to have laughed just once, at a picnic, when his friend the philosopher Ernst Jünger "leaned over to pick up a sauerkraut and sausage roll, and his lederhosen split with a tremendous crack." In the passenger seat of Lacan's car, Heidegger maintained a dogged silence, while Elfride, in the back next to Sylvia, complained the whole way, which only

Heidegger (*far left*), Lacan (*third from left*), with Elfride Heidegger (*second from right*), Sylvia Lacan (*far right*), and two colleagues at the Lacans' country house in 1955

spurred Lacan to drive faster. Miraculously, he did not have a serious accident until 1978 when he hit a crash barrier while exiting a highway and totaled his white Mercedes convertible. "The crash barrier was part of that real before which he bowed," wrote Catherine Millot. After that, he stopped driving.

◆ ◆ ◆

Lacan was still married to Malou when Sylvia gave birth to their daughter, Judith, in 1941. Since Lacan was legally prohibited from giving his name to a child born outside his marriage, Judith was given the last name Bataille. Seven months before Judith was born, Malou had also given birth to a daughter, Sybille, but by then the Lacans' marriage was over. After Lacan died, Sybille wrote an understandably sour, self-pitying memoir, *A Father: Puzzle*, about the man she never lived with and barely knew and whose entry in *Who's Who*, she learned as an adult, listed only one daughter: Judith.

The messy business of fathering two families simultaneously and assigning patronymics complicated Lacan's life in the 1940s. It may also, says Roudinesco, have influenced his conception of the "*nom-du-père*" (name of the father), which he introduced in his seminar in the early 1950s. The phrase, which in French plays on the homonyms "*nom*" (name) and "*non*" (no), was Lacan's clever shorthand for his structuralist reworking of Freud's Oedipus complex. Where Freud had figured a flesh-and-blood family drama, Lacan now featured words. The Oedipus complex marked the child's full transition to the symbolic order, the realm of laws and norms, with language assuming the role of the Freudian father who intercedes between the child and its desire for its mother, laying down the prohibition against incest while encouraging identification with the "paternal metaphor"—the phallus. The symbolic order not only shapes the self but serves as the ultimate enforcer, regulating desire in the name of phallic authority: "It is in the *name of the father* that we must recognize the basis of the symbolic function which, from the dawn of historical time, has identified his person with the figure of the law."

Like *écriture féminine*, Lacan's emphasis on patronymics seems dated in an era of much greater gender equality and fluidity, when a wife no longer automatically takes her husband's surname, and their children no longer automatically inherit it. Yet as the critic Rebecca Solnit points out in her recent memoir, *Recollections of My Nonexistence,* what we might call the patronymic mindset remains "built into the culture in so many ways." "Your mother's maiden name is often requested as the answer to a security question by banks and credit card companies," Solnit writes, "because it's assumed her original name is secret, erased, lost as she took on the name of a husband. It's no longer universal for women to give up their names but still rare to pass them on if they're married, one of the ways women vanish or never appear."

Feminist critics have suggested that *L'Origine du monde* depicts a similar erasure, since it portrays not a particular woman (debate is ongoing about the identity of Courbet's model) but only anonymous, eroticized body parts. According to this reading, the painting is a technically accomplished piece of pornography whose effect is to turn its viewers into

Peeping Toms. Moreover, the "origin" story the painting allegorizes is not the female act of giving birth but, rather, the male-centered version related in Genesis: "the creation of woman out of male materials"—in this case, Courbet's paints and brushes.

Lacan may have viewed *L'Origine du monde* in an allegorical light as well, as an expression of the Lacanian real, that place beyond, or before, the symbolic, which he associated with female *jouissance* and humanity's lost origins. He installed the painting in the office at his country house northwest of Paris, though Sylvia insisted that the work be covered up, ostensibly to protect the sensibilities of her cleaning staff and neighbors. She had her brother-in-law, the Surrealist artist André Masson, hide it behind a sliding wooden panel on which he painted a version of the original so abstract that it looked like a landscape, and no longer a female body.

Lacan loved to surprise guests by sliding back the panel and declaring that Courbet was Lacanian *avant la lettre*. Among those given a showing were Marcel Duchamp, the novelist Marguerite Duras, Lévi-Strauss, and Picasso, who exclaimed, somewhat cryptically, "Reality is the impossible!" It's fun to imagine Lacan treating Heidegger and his wife to a viewing during their 1955 stay, but if this happened, there is no record of it.

Chapter 17

KNOTS AND RINGS OF THE PSYCHE

In the early 1950s, around the time Lacan began shocking visitors with his Courbet, he began shocking colleagues with a new practice: the variable session. For decades, according to rules established by the IPA, an analysis was expected to involve four or five fifty-minute sessions each week for a period of at least four years. Lacan had been ignoring the fifty-minute rule, ending sessions when he judged they should stop. Eventually, the variable session gave way to the short session and sometimes, by the 1970s, to the very short session: a scandalous few minutes long.

"There was something of the horror of death in the short sessions," Stuart Schneiderman, the American who underwent a training analysis with Lacan in the mid-1970s, recalled. "The ending of the session, unexpected and unwanted, was like a rude awakening, like being torn out of a dream by a loud alarm. (One person likened it to coitus interruptus.)" Still, Schneiderman defended the practice, arguing that it eliminated inhibition: "When things come to mind they are spoken almost immediately, with spontaneity, for there is no time to mull them over, to find the nicest formulation."

Betty Milan, a Brazilian who also trained with Lacan in the mid-1970s and later published a memoir about her analysis, claimed that he "made abruptness a terribly effective analytic tool." In her account, her sessions—often just ten minutes long and turning on a single word or even just a syllable—lead with inexorable efficiency to revelation: about her longing for her native country, her shame regarding her family's immigrant past, her desire for motherhood. "Lacan did not interpret my speech by attributing this or that meaning to it," Milan wrote. "When he perceived that the unconscious had expressed itself, he sent me back to the solitude of the street so that I could interpret myself." Evidently, the ideal Lacanian analysand was an analyst.

Neither Schneiderman nor Milan was still a patient when, in the final years before Lacan died of colon cancer in 1981, the very short session morphed into its logical endpoint: the *nonsession*, during which he said not a word. By then, it was clear that he was suffering from cognitive difficulties; he was also frequently speechless at his seminar, and his behavior grew increasingly erratic. But his office stayed booked. After their sessions, Lacan's patients would often meet in bars or cafés to compare notes. Houda Aumont, an Algerian woman who continued to see Lacan during his decline despite increasing misgivings, reported that after one frightening encounter during which he pulled her hair, her café companions rationalized the incident with this gloss: "Lacan pulled your '*tifs*'"—French slang for "hair"—"and Sétif is the place where you were born!" As Aumont explained, "We were all really obsessed with signifiers. We ate and drank Lacan; he was with us all the time. If we went to the country"—*la campagne*—"we couldn't help calling it 'Lacan-pagne!'"

Roudinesco, to whom Aumont recounts this story, writes that between 1979 and 1980, Lacan "saw an average of ten patients an hour on an average of about twenty working days a month: i.e., the equivalent of eight hours of analysis a day for ten months of the year." She calculates that he was earning four million francs a year—about one million dollars—from his practice alone.

The heretical habits that helped make Lacan rich also got him in trouble. In 1953, he left the main French psychoanalytic society, joining a group of young analysts who felt the society had become rigid and authoritarian in its approach to training. In a paper Lacan gave in Rome that year he invoked a driving metaphor—an index of how strongly he felt about the matter—comparing French psychoanalysis's old guard to "a driving school, which not content to claim the unique privilege of issuing the drivers' licenses, also imagines that it is in a position to supervise car construction." Lacan and his liberal-minded young acolytes formed a new society: the Societé française de psychanalyse (SFP). Soon he was seeing a third of its students—about fifteen people—on his couch each week, in addition to private patients, an impossible schedule under the official rules.

Ultimately, his young colleagues concluded they could not support his use of the variable session, which, among other obstacles, prevented their society from being formally recognized by the IPA. In 1963, following a long investigation, the IPA ordered Lacan struck from the list of the society's training analysts, and the SFP fell apart. It was in December of that year that Althusser rang Lacan's bell and, finding him enraged and despondent over his "excommunication," took him to dinner.

By the following month, at Althusser's invitation, Lacan had moved his seminar from Sainte-Anne Hospital to the École Normale, trading the asylum for the university, the madwomen for the intellectuals. Buoyed by Althusser, Lacan went on to found his own school of psychoanalysis, the École freudienne de Paris, which soon attracted hundreds of members despite the controversy that inevitably followed in Lacan's wake. In the mornings, he often saw patients while still in his bathrobe and slippers. He thought nothing of treating multiple members of the same family. And not only did the school condone the variable session and allow anyone to become a member, but any member could become an analyst simply by declaring they were ready to be one, a procedure Lacan called "self-authorization." (One scholar says Lacan viewed the process of becoming an analyst as akin to that of becoming a poet, a sensitivity to language being the essential, and perhaps only, prerequisite.)

Althusser was in a position to play kingmaker. He talked up Lacan to his students, sent them to Lacan's seminar, and in December 1964 published a glowing article, "*Freud et Lacan*," in *La Nouvelle Critique*, the intellectual journal of the Communist Party. Expanding on his footnote the previous year comparing Lacan to Marx, Althusser explained how Lacan had revealed the revolutionary nature of psychoanalysis and its compatibility, hitherto in doubt, with Marxist thought. That compatibility seemed to hang mostly on Althusser's insistence that psychoanalysis was a science, just as Marxism was. And if Freud hadn't had access to all the scientific tools he would have needed to prove the point—here Althusser meant linguistic theory—well, Althusser reminded readers, don't forget that Marx had also been limited in his day by the reigning Hegelianism. We shouldn't hold these facts against either great man.

Althusser's essay helped legitimize psychoanalysis in the eyes of French Marxists, and foreshadowed the arguments he would make in his influential books, *For Marx* and *Reading Capital,* a few months later. More important, Althusser's public blessing marked Lacan's arrival in the inner sanctum of French intellectual life and his transformation from iconoclastic analyst to structuralist philosopher.

◆ ◆ ◆

One of Althusser's students helped midwife this metamorphosis: Jacques-Alain Miller, a nineteen-year-old aspiring philosophy *agregé* who went on to marry Lacan's daughter Judith and become Lacan's most trusted lieutenant and public mouthpiece—Plato to his Socrates. At Althusser's urging, Miller spent a weekend in the country poring over back issues of a Lacanian psychoanalytic journal. He returned to Paris electrified by what he'd read. In 1966, the year he married Judith, Miller published an article of his own, comparing some of Lacan's theoretical concepts to mathematical formulations of symbolic logic.

Miller also helped shepherd a collection of Lacan's essays and lectures into print in a nine-hundred-page book—his first since his thesis was published thirty-four years earlier. Astonishingly, the book, called simply

Écrits (Writings), sold out its first print run on advance sales alone and went on to sell nearly two hundred thousand copies. By the early 1970s, Lacan had transferred responsibility for publishing his seminars to Miller, who is credited on the books' title pages not merely with having "edited" the texts but with having "established" them—a more involved task. Miller's hands-on approach entailed tidying up Lacan's lectures, imposing a Cartesian clarity and consistency on ideas their author had purposely left contradictory, ambiguous, or open to various readings. Structuralist dictates demanded such rigor, but Miller "went furthest in the strictly 'structuralist' representation of the master."

Like many *normaliens* at the time, Miller was a militant leftist—a Maoist. With like-minded peers, he founded a structuralist journal, *Cahiers pour l'analyse*, that stressed the scientific nature of Lacanian thought. Though Lacan's theory hardly lent itself to practical politics, and he rarely addressed current events, his seminar acquired a reputation as a hotbed of leftism. Unlike Althusser, he emerged as a hero of May 1968. He signed a petition, declared his support for the striking teachers, and while the rebelling students debated the political utility of structuralism—one famously scrawled "A STRUCTURE CANNOT TAKE TO THE STREETS" on a chalkboard at the Sorbonne—Lacan arranged to meet Daniel Cohn-Bendit, the student leader. *The New Yorker* even reported a rumor that Lacan had helped Cohn-Bendit flee to Germany by smuggling him across the border in his Jaguar.

After the strike was over, the director of the École Normale asked Lacan to leave. Althusser claimed that the director believed cigarette smoke from Lacan's seminar was damaging the books in the school library. Others say he had tired of having fancy cars block the sidewalks on the rue d'Ulm every week and that, moreover, he found Lacan's work ridiculous. "Personally, all that business about the phallus, I find it obscene," the director reportedly told a colleague. Whatever the official reason, Lacan's ouster was met with outrage. A petition was circulated, and seminar attendees occupied the director's office until the police were called in. Inevitably, the affair made the press. Perhaps sensing that the political winds were blowing his way, Lacan slyly defended structuralism's role in the student strike, saying, "I don't consider it at all correct to have written that structures don't go out onto the streets, for if there's one thing the events of May prove, it's precisely that they do." He soon found a new, larger space for his seminar, the auditorium at the law school, which his acolytes immediately filled to capacity.

Jacques-Alain Miller brought logic and discipline to the public's encounter with Lacan's work, but Lacan was heading in an ever more structuralist direction on his own. By the early 1970s, he had developed a passion for topology, a branch of mathematics concerned with the properties of objects that are preserved even as the objects are bent, stretched, or deformed. He saw in the topologists' twisted shapes—the Möbius strip, as well as elaborate knots and rings—objective correlatives of his theory. At a dinner in 1972, a young mathematician told him about the Borromean rings, which figure in the coat of arms of the House of Borromeo, a Milanese noble family. Consisting of three interlinked circles in the form of a trefoil, the rings date to the Middle Ages and were often used to invoke the Holy Trinity. (In the case of the Borromeos, they apparently signified a local alliance with two other families.) Lacan was fascinated that the rings were linked in such a way that if just one is cut, the other two are also set free.

Catherine Millot, his lover at the time, went to the naval equipment aisle of a Parisian department store to buy him shipping rope in different colors, each corresponding to one of the Lacanian orders of experience—the imaginary, the symbolic, and the real—so that he could make rings as well as draw them. The rings were not mere symbols, but objects that could be arranged into knots emulating the structures of the psyche. Lacan rejected the dualist conception of consciousness based on notions of "inner" and "outer"—an interior mental life and an exterior world outside the self. The mind has no inside or outside, he argued, and we should stop thinking of it this way, as a sphere (like our heads), or as any sort of container. Instead, we should conceive of the mind as a Möbius strip or set of interlinked rings. If you placed a dot in the middle of a ring, the

Lacan drawing a Borromean knot at his seminar

inside/outside distinction broke down; the dot can be said to be inside *or* outside the ring. And if you linked rings together, they formed a chain or a knot; such structures, Lacan insisted, are truer models of our psyches.

The knots were also riddles, whose solutions, he believed, could yield insights for psychoanalytic theory. Lacan called his topological shapes *mathemes*, and to advance his study of them, he formed a *groupuscule* with a handful of eccentric young mathematicians whom he hounded for assistance. "Often, after spending hours drawing surfaces, twisting the inner tubes that they had delivered in large quantities, or filling baskets with bits of string and cutouts of colored paper," Roudinesco writes, the mathematicians "would get a message from Lacan asking them for the solution of a problem. Neither they nor he could find it, and the search went on. 'I'm going crazy,' he would say. 'Do please phone or come and see me.'"

A scholar who was helping Lacan learn to read Chinese at the time said, "I often wondered whether there was a single second in his daily life when he was not thinking of some serious theoretical problem." In a sense, you could say that through Lacan's work, structuralism achieved its apotheosis: The self had given way to the linguistic subject, and the subject to a series of geometric shapes.

In the fall of 1975, Lacan spoke about mathemes to scholars at MIT, Columbia, and Yale, explaining that he was trying to "invent another geometry," one corresponding to the chain of signifiers that structured human consciousness. The scholars were perplexed. At MIT, Lacan pressed Noam Chomsky on the significance of puns. Chomsky was dismissive, making clear the gap between his own linguistic science and Lacan's psychoanalytic theory. As a scientist, Chomsky explained, he was concerned with language's universal features, not with details peculiar to any one tongue. Humbled, Lacan conceded, "I am a poet."

That spring, Lacan, accompanied by Catherine Millot, had gone to visit Heidegger at his home in Freiburg. Heidegger had had a stroke and Lacan was eager to share his work on the mathemes with the German philosopher before he died. Lacan and Millot found Heidegger in his living room, lying on a chaise longue, his eyes closed. Undeterred, Lacan launched into a monologue about his knots and proceeded to draw some on a piece of paper he pulled from his pocket. Heidegger did not open his eyes.

Lacan never obtained the approbation he sought. A few years earlier, after *Écrits* came out, he had sent Heidegger an inscribed copy. Heidegger, in turn, wrote to a friend that he'd heard the book was "creating as much of a stir as Sartre's *L'Être et le néant* once did," but that he had been unable to make any sense of it. "It seems to me the psychiatrist needs a psychiatrist," he wrote.

Chapter 18

"I AM PSYCHOTIC"

Even in Lacan's most abstract structuralist phase, the problem of madness, first kindled in his Surrealist period, was never far from his thoughts. After all, it was in the paranoid projections and confusions of self and other of his early cases that he identified the building blocks of human identity. "Not only can man's being not be understood without madness, but it would not be man's being if it did not bear madness within itself as the limit of his freedom," he said in 1946. Nearly thirty years later, on his tour of the East Coast, he told an American colleague that he had been drawn to psychoanalysis out of a sense of vulnerability, the conviction "that it is possible for each of us to go mad." Presenting his mathemes to an overfull auditorium at Yale, he added that he considered himself psychotic: "Psychosis is an attempt at rigor. In this sense, I would say that I am psychotic. I am psychotic for the simple reason that I have always tried to be rigorous."

Did Lacan invoke madness the way the Surrealists did, on principle, as a provocation and counterweight to convention? Or did he genuinely suspect himself to be mad, as his outlandish language and behavior often led people to think? What was the difference between madness and reason anyway? Could the two ever be clearly distinguished? These last two questions entered French thought in the seventeenth century through the philosophical meditations of Descartes, and thread their way through the structuralists' and poststructuralists' work, preoccupying Lacan, Foucault, and Derrida in turn. Each brought his own private darkness to the subject. For all structuralism's pretense to objectivity—to rigor, systems, networks, and rules—there was no escaping the threat of instability, error, and delusion that haunted its claims. These threats would eventually be structuralism's undoing.

In 1946, Lacan delivered a keynote address at a conference organized by Henri Ey, a psychiatrist and friend from their days as interns at Sainte-Anne Hospital. After the war, French doctors had been horrified by the revelation that more than forty thousand people had died in the country's asylums during the Occupation, victims not of Nazi crimes but of starvation and neglect. Ey's conference was one of several responses to that horror, an attempt to bring together psychiatrists committed to developing more humane treatments for mental illness.

Lacan, however, devoted most of his talk to attacking Ey's approach to such illnesses. Ey, he said, had embraced an "organicist" doctrine, which held that mental disorders originated in the body and had nothing to do with the mind. In fact, Lacan suggested, Ey considered the mind and body to be a single integrated system. Moreover, Ey blamed French psychiatrists' failure to grasp this fact on the undue influence of Descartes, whose dualist view of mind and body, he believed, had been leading the French astray ever since.

Lacan vehemently disagreed: Ey's integrated theory made it impossible to distinguish between, say, a sane patient suffering from a brain lesion and, as a result, severe cognitive deficits (here he cited a famous case) and, say, a psychotic, who might exhibit similar symptoms but had no such neurological damage. Ey, Lacan protested, had misunderstood Descartes' theory of the mind. The philosopher had never said that "the mind is a mind without existence." Descartes' dualism was not about existence versus nonexistence but rather about two different kinds of *form*: The body was *extension* (meaning it took up space, occupying more than one dimension), whereas the mind was *thought* (it took up no space; it was incorporeal). Though the mind did not occupy space, existence was inconceivable without it: Descartes' famous proof, Lacan reminded his audience, was based entirely "on the consciousness that thinking has of itself."

Of course, his listeners knew all about Descartes. In France, Descartes was revered not just as the father of French philosophy but also of rationalism, the attribute that, perhaps more than any other, had come to define the French people's view of themselves. After a rocky start—the Catholic Church condemned Descartes' focus on human reason as a dangerous distraction from the primacy of God—his work entered the college curriculum in 1720, seventy years after his death, and never left. As Foucault once quipped, philosophy began in the French university with Descartes and so could only proceed in a Cartesian manner.

In some sense, you could say that Descartes was a proto-structuralist for whom the ultimate structure, the one to which all the others refer, wasn't language but God. Descartes was a mathematics prodigy who made seminal contributions to the field of algebra and who approached metaphysical questions with the same rigor he applied to math. Voltaire, born nearly fifty years after Descartes' death, pointed out some of the science Descartes had gotten wrong, mocking his "systematizing mind which blinds the greatest of men." He might have said the same about Descartes' structuralist descendants.

Descartes presented his celebrated proof of existence in Latin in 1639, as a series of "meditations" undertaken over the course of six days (though in fact he worked on them for several years), each narrated in a winningly earnest, confiding tone. In sum, the proof went something like this: *If I cast into doubt everything I believe to be true, what is left? Only my doubting thoughts. It follows that whatever is doing the doubting must exist. Therefore I must exist!* So indubitable was this logic, Descartes writes, that "I decided that I could accept it without scruple as the first principle of the philosophy I was seeking."

Lacan, in his talk at Ey's conference, recalled that Descartes had devoted the first step of his proof to madness. He quoted the relevant passage, which goes something like this: *How can I be sure I exist? How can I be certain that these hands and this body are real and that they belong to me? In believing these things to be true, I could be deceived. I could simply be mad. After all, mad people believe all kinds of things that aren't true—"that they are kings when they are utter paupers, or that they are arrayed in purple robes when they are naked, or that they have heads made of clay."* But, Descartes concludes, such people aren't thinking clearly: *They are mad, and "I would appear no less mad, were I to take their behavior as an example for myself."*

For Descartes, Lacan explained, madness is an error of thought that has taken on the guise of fact. The field of psychiatry could do worse than "to call for a return to Descartes," he declared. Psychiatry must not abandon mental processes for physiological ones. Already in 1946, we can see language—the substance of thought—acquiring for Lacan a formative materiality, a constitutive thingness. Madness, he insisted in true structuralist fashion, is a problem of language, a phenomenon "experienced entirely within the register of meaning."

Chapter 19

FOUCAULT'S ASYLUM

Fifteen years later, Foucault cast Descartes in a decisive role in his monumental book on the history of madness: *Folie et déraison: Histoire de la folie à l'âge classique* (initially published in English as *Madness and Civilization*). Foucault was just thirty-four when the book, his doctoral thesis in philosophy, appeared in 1961. The eldest son of a prominent surgeon in Poitiers, he was another precocious École Normale head case: fourth on the entrance exam in 1946 and preoccupied with Nietzsche, Sade, madness, and death. On the walls of his dorm room he hung etchings by Goya of men mangled by war and tormented by delusions. His nickname at school was "*Fuchs*"—German for fox. Solitary, smug, and argumentative, sometimes to the point of rudeness, he was respected for his formidable intellect and work ethic but also widely disliked. Some of his classmates thought he was nuts.

During his second year at the École Normale, he tried to commit suicide, prompting his father to take him to Sainte-Anne's for an evaluation. When he returned, the school doctor—the same one Althusser would turn to thirty years later, after strangling his wife—moved Foucault to the infirmary. Other suicide attempts followed. "He was obsessed by this idea," a friend said. (Later on, he often spoke about suicide in positive terms; in a 1979 article, he went so far as to imagine "suicide festivals" and "suicide orgies," calling death by suicide "a limitless pleasure.") He

Michel Foucault in the mid-1950s, when he was about thirty

was back in the infirmary in the spring of 1950, while studying for his philosophy *agrégation*. When he failed to pass, Althusser, by then the philosophy *caïman*, feared the worst and asked one of Foucault's classmates to keep a close eye on him.

The following year Foucault passed the exam and at Althusser's invitation became an instructor at the École in psychology, which had become for Foucault a consuming passion. He was a mesmerizing lecturer, fluently holding forth while pacing the stage, rarely obliged to consult his notes. "I was struck, like many others, by his speaking ability," remembered Derrida, who, just four years younger, took Foucault's class as a student at the École. "His eloquence, authority, and brilliance were impressive."

For the next several years, Foucault made frequent trips to Sainte-Anne's, both as a teacher who brought his students to observe the patients, and as an unpaid intern who learned to read patients' brain waves on an EEG. "I felt very close to and not very different from the inmates," he said years later. For a time, he also made weekly visits to a hospital attached to the French prison system, where he helped process patients, seeding a lifelong fascination with the experience of incarceration.

In addition, Foucault attended Lacan's seminar, then in its early days at Sainte-Anne's. But the place he spent by far the most time—by one estimate, more than he spent anywhere else over the course of his adult life—was the Bibliothèque Nationale, where he researched a short book on theories of mental illness. Madness and death by suicide, along with sadomasochistic sex and, later, mind-altering drugs, became enduring fixations. These were "limit experiences," dangerous and alluring, holding out the promise of some kind of transcendence or Lacanian *jouissance*—the possibility of glimpsing what in a preface to *Folie et déraison* Foucault called "that inaccessible primitive purity."

Foucault often used such language in his written work, hinting at hazy mysterious realms of existence that, owing to the repressive effects of state power, left little trace in the historical record. A voracious reader, he seemed to have an encyclopedic grasp of classical literature and art. At the same time, his primary interest was in the big picture, in the unconscious patterns he believed lurked beneath history's chaotic surface. Most of the patterns he identified were negative. History in his view was an insidious succession of restrictions undertaken in the name of reason and progress. What appeared to be advances in human liberty and tolerance almost always in Foucault's analyses turned out to be the opposite: new forms of coercion and control.

Equally significant, the patterns he uncovered were impersonal, embedded in the official discourses of institutions and governments, rather than the result of individual human actions. In this sense, his work in the 1960s was widely perceived as structuralist, a label he initially accepted but soon strenuously disavowed. In the original preface to *Folie et déraison*, he used the words "structure" or "structural" thirteen times. Five years later, he had begun avoiding the term, though arguments over whether he was or wasn't a structuralist continued, in one case prompting an entire book by a pair of American scholars who had taken different positions on the issue.

Foucault himself suggested that virtually the only thing the so-called structuralist philosophers had in common was an aversion to existentialism and its optimistic belief in human agency. "We have experienced Sartre's generation as a generation that was certainly brave and generous, one that had a passion for life, politics, and existence," he said in 1966. "But as for us, we have discovered something else, another passion: the passion for concepts and for what I will call 'system.'" Looking back on his student days in the late 1970s, he noted that his generation had come of age in the wake of France's capitulation to the Nazis and under the conservative regime of General de Gaulle. It was no wonder, he said, that so many of his peers joined the Communist Party (including, for a couple of years, Foucault himself). They wanted a social order completely different from the one they'd inherited.

◆ ◆ ◆

By temperament, however, Foucault was a philosopher, not a militant. Encouraged by his reading of Nietzsche, Sade, and, later, Bataille, he was in thrall to the idea that real freedom lay just out of reach, beyond the confines of so-called normal life. He was a young gay intellectual in a conservative Catholic society, the son of a man he described as a "bully" who had wanted him to also become a surgeon. Gangly and bespectacled, with intense blue eyes and fair hair that was already thinning, Foucault was also insecure about his looks, convinced that he was ugly. The doctor at the École Normale told Foucault's biographer Didier Eribon that Foucault suffered from "an extreme difficulty in experiencing and accepting his homosexuality."

Years later, when asked by an American colleague whether there had been a "specific event" in his life that had shaped his subsequent research, Foucault cited a meeting he'd had with the École Normale's director soon after he arrived: "The headmaster demanded to learn if there was anything unusual about me. When I informed him of my homosexuality, he replied with a horrified expression that such behavior was not normal and certainly unacceptable to the reputation of the school. . . . He told me that I must be reformed, that I would be confined, examined, and treated by an array of authorities—doctors, teachers, psychologists, psychiatrists, etc. At this instant I recognized in a flash how the system works. I perceived the fundamental impulse of our society: normalization."

Nearly all Foucault's books are variations on this insight, explorations of how power organizes and classifies human bodies in an effort to control or "normalize" them. Homosexuality was decriminalized in France during the French Revolution, but a 1960 law targeting gay people for "against nature" public indecency remained on the books until 1980. In the late 1960s, Foucault was nearly appointed to a high-ranking position in the French ministry of education only to be rejected at the last minute out of fear that his sexual identity would cause a public scandal. Like Bataille, whom he praised for elaborating a language of transgression—of "the experience of the limit" that "says what cannot be said"—Foucault turned a fascination with the socially impermissible into a scholarly vocation.

In 1955, he was hired to direct the Maison de France at the Uppsala University in Sweden. The university was Sweden's oldest and among its most prestigious, but the surrounding town was gloomy and cold, with few distractions. Foucault threw himself into his duties as director, teaching French language and literature to students, hosting visiting lecturers—Roland Barthes came twice—putting on French plays and showing French films. He discovered that the university housed an important archive on the history of medicine: thousands of documents dating from the sixteenth to the early twentieth centuries. His doctoral dissertation quickly took shape.

Foucault did make the occasional jaunt to Paris in his white Jaguar. Like Lacan, he loved to drive and drove very fast. Foucault's biographer David Macey called Foucault "one of the few French philosophers to have any competence at the wheel." Yet apart from a few road trips out of the country, he spent much of the next three years in Sweden, immersed in the library. He arrived each day by ten in the morning. Picture him there: the iconic egg-shaped head, still topped with a sparse layer of fine hair; the piercing blue eyes behind frameless glasses. He bends over a rare book, taking notes in longhand for five or six hours straight. In the evenings, at his apartment in the Maison de France, he continues to write, the pages

Foucault and his white Jaguar, at the Maison de France in Uppsala, Sweden, 1957

mounting while he listens to recordings of Bach or Mozart; his study of madness in the classical age was written to the accompaniment of music from the period.

The main thing to imagine is the incessant work. "He does not look well," an inspector reported to the French ministry of foreign affairs in 1956. "I have the impression that M. Foucault is overworking himself and not taking the necessary rest." The following year, another supervisor, another report: "There is some reason to fear that, a victim of his success and his constant availability, he might literally kill himself on the job."

After three years in Uppsala, Foucault spent one more in Warsaw, performing similar duties at a brand-new French cultural center until, caught in an affair with an informant for the Polish secret police, he was summarily fired and sent back to Paris. He returned home with a manuscript of more than nine hundred pages, the final chunk completed in Poland by candlelight.

The published book was pruned back but it was still a hulking tome, weighed down by its author's vast storehouse of research and stately prose. Laced with evocative imagery, it was also circular, repetitious, nuanced to the point of opacity, and sometimes contradictory. In a term that would come to define Foucault's career, he described it as an "archaeology" of madness "before it is captured by knowledge." For a scholarly work, the book was uncommonly vivid, freighted with the groans and murmurs (another Foucauldian word) of the madmen whose faint imprints on history he had disinterred from the shadows. But it was so dense with baroque flourishes that his excavations risked being buried under grandiloquence. Although he was awarded high honors by the jury of distinguished philosophers who granted him his degree, these scholars reproached him in their official report for a "tendency to go beyond the facts" in the interest of "creating an 'effect.'" Foucault later admitted to a friend who complimented him on the beauty of his prose, "If I had this book to write again today, I would be less rhetorical."

Gallimard, the publisher of Sartre's equally massive *Being and Nothingness* turned the book down. Then again, Gallimard had also rejected Lévi-Strauss's *Anthropologie Structurale* (Structural Anthropology), in 1958. That book, an influential manifesto for the new structuralist dispensation, had been published by Plon instead. But Plon very nearly passed on *Folie et déraison*. The manuscript landed in the hands of the eminent historian Philippe Ariès, who edited a series for the press. "I was dazzled when I read it," he said. "But I had to go through hell and high water to talk them into it." The slimmed-down American edition was no less forbidding; one reviewer, also invoking an aquatic image, likened reading it to "wading through several feet of water."

Yet even the grumblers conceded the book's originality. Tracing the status of the madman in European culture through royal edicts, institutional logbooks, court cases, medical treatises, philosophical tracts, paintings, and literature, Foucault advanced a startling argument: Madness had no objective reality. It had been invented by human beings under varied circumstances and its meaning had shifted radically over time. In the medieval period, the deranged of Europe occupied an ambiguous position, simultaneously shunned and feared as sources of dark revelation—the "nothingness that is life itself," the encroaching apocalypse. Some were permitted to roam the countryside or live on the fringes of town, Foucault wrote. Others were sent out to sea, plying the ports of Europe on a "ship of fools" of the sort made famous in a painting by Hieronymus Bosch.

Gradually, however, madness acquired a tamer silhouette—less otherworldly, more human. For Renaissance humanists like Erasmus, the author of the satirical treatise *In Praise of Folly* (1511), madness was not a conduit for eschatology or divine truths, but instead more earthly lessons. Erasmus saw madness in our capacity for self-delusion, hubris, pedantry, and other ordinary moral foibles. In short, madness was unreason—what reason defined itself against. As Foucault rephrased this idea, in the kind of binary formulation typical of structuralist thought: "Each is a measure of the other, and in this movement of reciprocal reference, each rejects the other but is logically dependent on it."

Human or alien, the madman hovered on the cultural threshold, in dialogue with reason but relegated to society's margins, to what Foucault, deploying another binary, called "the inside of the outside, or vice versa." For Foucault, a highly visual writer who found metaphor impossible to resist, the Renaissance madman is the archetypal liminal figure, embodying "the simple division into daylight and obscurity, shadow and light, dream and waking, the truth of the sun and the power of midnight." Such chiaroscuro is one of Foucault's signature traits; his work is filled with dawns and dusks, lightning bolts and penumbra—the visual correlatives of his love of paradox and contradiction, his Bataille-like attraction to intersecting extremes, his structuralist tendency to see the world through binary oppositions.

At this point in Foucault's book, there is a dramatic shift: As Europe entered the Enlightenment—Foucault's "classical age"—madness and reason go their separate ways. Madness, he says, moves from the ship to the hospital, which is really a prison. From now on, madmen will be locked up and forgotten. This event marks the book's climax, and Foucault is precise about when it occurred: between 1656, when the Hôpital Général was founded in Paris for the purpose of confining the poor and the deranged, and 1794, in the middle of the French Revolution, when the reformist physician Philippe Pinel unshackled the madmen at the Bîcetre asylum, thereby inaugurating a new era in which madness is reconceived as a medical problem—as mental illness. Foucault calls the period between these two dates "the Great Confinement," and he offers some data to back up his claim: In the seventeenth century, one of every one hundred residents of Paris was detained in a house of confinement, and one in ten arrests made for the Hôpital Général involved "'the insane,' 'demented men,' 'alienated men,' or people 'driven quite mad.'"

But Foucault's star witness, the expert with whom he opens his chapter on the Great Confinement, is Descartes. He quotes the philosopher's first *Meditation*—the same passage cited by Lacan a decade and a half earlier—in which Descartes considers, and quickly dismisses, the possibility that he is deceived because he is mad. "One cannot suppose that one is mad, even in thought," Foucault writes, paraphrasing Descartes' logic. "For madness is precisely a condition of impossibility for thought." For Foucault, Descartes' proof is decisive: Reason has triumphed, and "madness has been banished. While *man* can still go mad, *thought*, as the sovereign exercise carried out by a subject seeking the truth, can no longer be devoid of reason. A new dividing line has appeared, rendering that experience so familiar to the Renaissance—unreasonable Reason, or reasoned Unreason—impossible."

Ship of Fools, **by Hieronymus Bosch (c. 1490–1500)**

With this assertion, we have reached the crux of Foucault's argument. His aim, he declares in his original preface, is "to identify the moment of that expulsion," the event that "allows

Reason and Madness to fall away, like things henceforth foreign to each other, deaf to any exchange, almost dead to each other." Descartes' proof is that event. By the time the inmates are unshackled at Bicêtre, one hundred and fifty years later, madness will have long been severed from reason. From then on, Foucault says, madness no longer has a voice of its own; it will exist mainly as "the language of psychiatry, which is a monologue by reason *about* madness."

The only exceptions to this rule are a handful of avant-garde writers and artists, among them Nietzsche, Van Gogh, the German poet Friedrich Hölderlin, and the French playwright Antonin Artaud—all known to have struggled with mental illness. Their work, Foucault maintains, is shot through with a kind of lyrical unreason. As he explained at his dissertation defense, "To speak of madness one must have the talent of a poet." To which one awed scholar on the jury replied: "But you, sir, have it."

Like Lacan and the Surrealists before him, Foucault was clearly on the side of the madmen. What looked from the vantage point of the mid-twentieth century like successive steps toward a more humane conception of insanity became, in his account, the reverse. Madmen were perceived as foreign and threatening, in need of being sealed off from other people. Some said it was no accident that *Folie et déraison* was written at the height of the Algerian War—a conflict in which France was perceived to have betrayed the liberatory ideals that were its Enlightenment inheritance.

In the early 1980s, historians would begin challenging Foucault on his facts. The medieval ship of fools was declared to be more notional than real. The Great Confinement that Foucault identified was shown not to have ended with the French Revolution but to have continued well into the twentieth century. The swelling numbers of asylumed lunatics, critics argued, invited an alternate interpretation: Incarceration grew in tandem with democracy, not because madmen were regarded as radically *different* from other human beings but, on the contrary, because they were increasingly understood to be like everyone else, and therefore entitled to the protection of the state.

At the time of publication, however, Foucault's countercultural thrust accorded with the intellectual mood. Reviewing the book for *Le Mercure de France*, the philosopher Michel Serres remarked on Foucault's "almost religious" love for the mad. He also underscored Foucault's debt to Nietzsche, who in *The Birth of Tragedy* had praised the mingling of Dionysian (chaotic) and Apollonian (orderly) elements in Greek tragedy, just as Foucault celebrated the historic entanglement of madness with reason. When the English edition of *Folie et déraison* appeared in 1967, it included an introduction by David Cooper, a leader of Britain's burgeoning anti-psychiatry movement, who hailed Foucault's portrayal of madness as a fiction we "conjure up . . . in order to evade a certain moment of our existence—the moment of disturbance, of penetrating vision into the depths of ourselves."

Yet not everyone was persuaded by the dramatic tale of the expulsion of madness by reason. At Foucault's dissertation defense, Henri Gouhier, a Descartes specialist who was the jury's senior member, objected to his student's tendency to let historical figures like Descartes perform allegorical functions. Moreover, he failed to see how Descartes' words enacted the grand division between madness and reason. Hardly noticed at the time, Gouhier's reservations turned out to be prescient. Two years later, when Foucault's student Jacques Derrida took up the matter, they became the basis for a devastating takedown.

Chapter 20

DERRIDA THROWS A PUNCH

Like so many other momentous events in French intellectual life, the occasion for Derrida's takedown was a public lecture. In March 1963, Derrida was a thirty-two-year-old lecturer at the Sorbonne with a single book to his name: a forty-three-page translation of an obscure work by the German phenomenologist Edmund Husserl preceded by an introduction four times as long by Derrida himself. (Volubleness would become a Derridean trademark.) That book, *The Origin of Geometry*, hadn't sold many copies but it had impressed Derrida's colleagues and former teachers, including Foucault, who wrote to his "dear friend" that he was "filled with admiration" for it. Derrida in turn had read Foucault's *Folie et déraison*—twice. The first time, in 1962, he wrote Foucault a letter praising the book but also timidly expressing a feeling of "muted protest, unformulatable or as yet unformulated." A year later, the protest found its voice. Derrida wrote to Foucault again, to announce that he was drafting a paper that would focus on Foucault's reading of Descartes. Foucault could not have guessed what was coming.

Derrida presented "Cogito and the History of Madness" on the evening of March 4, at the Collège Philosophique in Saint-Germain-des-Prés. It was his first major appearance in Paris—his public début. With his square jaw, Byronic hair, and intense gaze, he was a striking presence: another French philosopher with sex appeal. (By the time he was forty, his hair had turned snow white, which seemed only to enhance his looks.) But his physical charisma belied a shy, gentle manner in turn at odds with the boldness of his work. "Cogito and the History of Madness" was a withering critique, and Foucault was in the audience to hear it. The awkwardness of the situation was immediately apparent. In an anguished preamble, Derrida identified himself as Foucault's "admiring and grateful disciple," now burdened with that disciple's "unhappy consciousness" as he embarked on a dialogue with his master, a dialogue "in danger of being taken—incorrectly—as a challenge."

Jacques Derrida in 1988

But Derrida's paper *was* meant as a challenge. After these strained opening remarks, his words contorted by embarrassment or guilt, he set about methodically demolishing Foucault's book. The paper merits pausing over, not only because of the ensuing psychodrama—the upheaval it caused in French intellectual circles—but because it's an exciting, virtuosic performance, revealing Derrida's singular methodology at an early stage in its development.

He began by admitting that just three pages of *Folie et déraison* were devoted to Descartes. Nevertheless, he declared, "the sense of Foucault's entire project can be pinpointed in these few allusive and somewhat enigmatic pages." This move, alighting on a single passage, a mere fragment of the whole, and using it to unravel the entire enterprise, will become a hallmark of Derridean deconstruction.

Even before he got to the key lines in Descartes, Derrida was already throwing punches. "Everything transpires as if Foucault *knew* what 'madness' means," he declared. Foucault claims to be attempting a history of "madness *itself*," but if madness is reason's opposite, it is "what by essence cannot be said"—at least not in the (reasoning) language of scholarship. Moreover, Foucault says he wants to let madness speak on its own behalf, but if madness has been silenced by thought, how can it possibly do so? "It is the most audacious and seductive aspect of his venture," Derrida went on. "But it is also, with all seriousness, the *maddest* aspect of his project." It simply wasn't possible to make sense of madness *and* hand it a microphone.

Foucault's structuralist methodology was equally problematic. He had linked Descartes' philosophical thought experiment to French government decrees ordering the confinement of mad people. But how were these things related? For Foucault, they were of a piece, neither causes nor effects but, rather, evidence of a single "event" in the history of thought. "Everything within the structural totality is interdependent and circular," Derrida pointed out. "But I wonder whether, when one is concerned with history (and Foucault wants to write a history), a strict structuralism is possible." As his talk progressed, he grew blunter, suggesting that Foucault's attempt to impose a binary framework on madness and reason verged on "structuralist totalitarianism." Pow!

By the time Derrida turned to Foucault's reading of Descartes, he had landed several such blows. He conceded that Descartes devotes only passing attention to madness in his *Meditations*, but, he insisted, this is not because Descartes summarily excludes madness from reason. On the contrary, Derrida said, Descartes concludes that madness simply isn't a very powerful threat to reason: Only some people are insane, and they are mad only about certain things, some of the time. In any case, Descartes tells us that he is not one of those people. ("I would appear no less mad, were I to take their behavior as an example for myself.")

Descartes needs a stronger threat to reason, something that will allow him to doubt the "*absolute totality* of ideas of sensory origin" (Derrida's words). And in the very next paragraph, one Foucault does not cite,

Descartes finds one: dreams. Dreaming strikes Descartes as a more promising avenue for doubt because it is a "more common, and more universal experience" (Derrida's words) than madness, and yet the dreamer "has all the same experiences while asleep as madmen do when awake—indeed sometimes even more improbable ones."

These last words are Descartes'. Over the course of one night in 1619, Descartes, then twenty-three, had a series of dreams so vivid and strange that when he opened his eyes he wasn't sure what was and wasn't real, or whether he was awake or asleep. He credited these dreams with inspiring his pursuit of philosophy, and the dreams became integral to his legend. Evidently Descartes was still thinking about those dreams when he tackled his proof of existence. And in Derrida's reading of the proof, madness for Descartes is just a subset of the more important category of *total sensory error* that is dreaming.

Yet, as it turns out, even dreaming can't cover the full spectrum of Descartes' doubt. He concedes it's possible that *particular* impressions—his sense of his body, his hands, the fire he is seated next to, etc.—might only be a dream, but he notes that his more *general* or abstract impressions appear consistent whether he is asleep or awake. Math, for example: Even in dreams, "two plus three" still "makes five" and "a square has only four sides." Unsatisfied, Descartes conjures a source of doubt more radical still, an evil genius:

> I will suppose not a supremely good God, the source of truth, but rather an evil genius, supremely powerful and clever, who has directed his entire effort at deceiving me. I will regard the heavens, the air, the earth, colors, shapes, sounds, and all external things as nothing but the bedeviling hoaxes of my dreams, with which he lays snares for my credulity. I will regard myself as not having hands, or eyes, or flesh, or blood, or any senses, but as nevertheless falsely believing that I possess all these things.

Here at last, Descartes arrives at what Derrida called "the possibility of a *total madness*": "This time madness, insanity, will spare nothing, neither bodily nor purely intellectual perceptions." With this last, theatrical stroke, Descartes' proof is transformed. It becomes the philosophical equivalent of a Matryoshka nesting doll, with the evil genius as the biggest doll, the one that contains the others—both the doll representing the world of dreams and, inside it, a smaller one representing mad people.

In this moment of total mad doubt, Descartes is left with just one certainty: that he is thinking. And it is now that he reaches his triumphant conclusion: *Cogito, sum* (I think, I am). Madness, then, is not banished from reason, but, on the contrary, exists *inside* reason. As Derrida put it, "Whether I am mad or not, *Cogito, sum*. Madness is therefore, in every sense of the word, only one *case* of thought (*within* thought)."

This was a lot to absorb. Imagine Foucault at this point, sweating in his seat, his distress mounting as he follows along intently, perhaps scribbling a few notes, trying to keep up. Had he flinched when Derrida invoked madness as lurking within thought, hearing in the phrase a damning echo of his student's opening statement, where he'd identified himself as the disciple challenged by "the master's voice within him," by "the master who speaks within him"?

Compared with Derrida's later work, "Cogito and the History of Madness" is relatively accessible, but to make sense of it at a public reading would have required serious concentration. The marginalia on the copy I've kept since college—first in red pen, then in pencil, finally in black pen—show how many readings it's taken me to grasp as much as I have. Derrida's argument was not intuitive to me the way it apparently was to Thurston Meems, the star student of Semiotics 211, the upper-level theory seminar in Eugenides' novel *The Marriage Plot*. "What Derrida's saying," Thurston explains to his baffled classmates, "is you have to use reason because, you know, reason is all there is. But at the same time you have to be aware that language is by its very nature *un*reasonable."

Derrida wasn't finished. In a bravura finale, he went on to declare that madness and reason do go their separate ways, just not in the manner Foucault claims. Madness and reason are divided only when thought begins to reflect on itself, at the moment, in short, when the act of thinking becomes philosophy. In this sense, he insisted, Foucault's book narrates a crisis not of history but of philosophy. What Descartes' *Meditations* attest to is not a historical event but an eternal predicament: the danger *always* posed to philosophy by madness, which it must constantly try to ward off or suppress. "I philosophize only in *terror*," Derrida said, "but in the *confessed* terror of going mad."

Chapter 21

"I'M REALLY AT THE END OF MY TETHER"

Terror" is an arresting word. The assertion seems histrionic even for Derrida, whose work is rife with emphatic italics and, to a surprising degree, emotion. He was speaking here not just for Descartes but for philosophers generally. Yet surely there was also a personal aspect to the confession. After all, Derrida's early life had been marked by exclusion and loss. Born in 1930 on the outskirts of Algiers, to French-speaking Sephardic Jewish parents whose families had been in Algeria for generations, he grew up feeling neither French nor Algerian nor particularly Jewish. In an interview the year before he died, he described himself as "a sort of child in the margins of Europe, a child of the Mediterranean, who was not simply French nor simply African, and who had passed his time traveling between one culture and the other feeding questions he asked himself out of that instability."

An older brother died in infancy less than a year before Derrida was born, and a younger one died of tubercular meningitis the year Derrida turned ten, leaving him with two siblings, a brother and a sister. While he was still in elementary school, a cousin he adored was run over by a car. Then, in October 1940, under the Vichy regime, Algerian Jews were stripped of French citizenship. Strict quotas on Jewish students followed, and in 1942 Derrida—"a little black and very Arab Jew," as he put it, who then went by his given name, "Jackie"—was expelled from his school. For six months, until Algiers, liberated by the Allies, became the capital of Free France and the anti-Semitic laws were revoked, he attended a school run by Jewish teachers and filled with Jewish students, all of whom had been pushed out of their former institutions. "The wound was of another order," he wrote later, "and it never healed."

At twelve, a sensitive, sentimental boy, already on familiar terms with death, racism, and war, he returned to his old lycée, where, in what would become a distressing pattern, he failed part of the baccalaureate exam on his first attempt. In the aftermath of that disappointment, he became a serious student, determined to leave Algiers for Paris and the École Normale. He changed schools and began reading philosophy in earnest, joining the extracurricular Cogito Club—Descartes' tentacles extended to the French lycées of 1940s Algiers—where he presented papers on Heidegger and Husserl, two of philosophy's "three H's" (the other being Hegel). All three would become important influences, but as a novice philosophy student Derrida found Heidegger's work a particular challenge. He accused the notoriously difficult German thinker of some of the same infractions that he himself would be charged with a couple decades later: "leadening and complicating his language, as if for fun," and "giving the most everyday, the simplest thoughts an appearance of profundity." Still, Derrida managed to rank second in his class of seventy. (The top place may have gone to the father of the American novelist Claire Messud, a contemporary of Derrida's and a fellow *pied-noir* at the lycée, who told Claire: "I always did better than him in philosophy.")

In 1949, Derrida moved to Paris. If he had a shot at the École Normale, he needed the best preparation he could get: He entered the *khâgne* (prepatory class) as a boarder at the Lycée Louis-le-Grand, Sartre's alma mater. There he earned high marks in philosophy, terrible ones in gym, and made a couple of close friends. He was good at friendship, and his letters from this period have a touching warmth and tenderness, capturing his tendency to nostalgia. But he found the regimented boarder's life—the barracks-style dormitory, the mandatory gray smock, the cold-water showers, and the meager, inedible food—more like prison than school. When exam week arrived, he showed up unslept and strung out on amphetamines. He failed the written portion and, like so many other students, had to spend another year gearing up to take the test again.

Jacques Derrida in his gray boarder's smock at the Lycée Louis-le-Grand, 1949–50

"As for madness, Jackie sometimes felt he was on the verge of succumbing to it as he started his second year in *khâgne,*" his biographer Benoît Peeters writes. "The cold, the lack of hygiene, the horrible food, and the absence of any privacy had become intolerable. Some evenings he fell into a crying jag and was unable to work or even talk to his friends. . . . He was constantly on the edge of a nervous collapse." Alone in Paris over the Christmas holiday in 1950, he was so depressed that, according to Peeters, he may have considered suicide. He retreated to his parents' home in Algeria in a dire state. "I'm really at the end of my tether here," he wrote to a friend. When, the following spring, he finally returned to Paris and sat for the exam a second time, he choked, submitting a blank sheet of paper.

That year, he earned middling results on exams for his philosophy *license* (the equivalent of a BA degree) at the Sorbonne. One of his examiners was Henri Gouhier, the Descartes scholar who, a decade later, as chair of Foucault's dissertation committee, would share some of Derrida's own objections to Foucault's reading of the *Meditations.* But evaluating Derrida in the spring of 1951, Gouhier was harsh, awarding him a humiliating 5/20 for an essay on the philosopher Malebranche. "These answers are brilliant in the very same way that they are obscure," he wrote, neatly encapsulating the impression Derrida's work would one day leave on many readers. "An exercise in virtuosity, with undeniable intelligence, but with no particular relation to the history of philosophy. . . . Can come back when he is prepared to accept the rules and not *invent* where he needs to be better *informed*."

But Derrida could not conform to the rules. Throughout his career, his rhetorical style, his intellectual method, even the subjects he chose to write about, often put him at odds with the French academic establishment. He had wished to become a novelist, and his elaborate, elliptical, decidedly un-Cartesian prose frustrated more traditional colleagues. After hearing him present a paper, one admonished him by observing that it might be better if "the way of saying things went unnoticed." How insulted Derrida must have felt; the way of saying things was entirely the point.

Other French intellectuals found his inability to produce a declarative sentence morally suspect, and he, in turn, found their tendency toward easy dogma alarming. When, after the events of May 1968, one newly radicalized philosopher asked him to explain "the enigma of his silence on Marx," Derrida was apologetic. "I will never emerge from this silence until I have done the work. And this work, I can sense, knowing as I do my style and my rhythms, will never give rise to a 'conversion,' but to oblique incisions, sideways shifts, following this or that unnoticed vein in the Marxist text"—hardly a response likely to satisfy his correspondent. In 1967, after enduring a particularly acrimonious defense of part of his dissertation, he wrote to another friend, "I don't feel at home either in the university system . . . or outside the university system." The four years he spent as an instructor at the Sorbonne in the early 1960s would be the only time he held a university job in France.

◆ ◆ ◆

In 1952, Derrida finally gained admission to the École Normale on his third attempt, but his spirits did not seem markedly improved.

Politically, he inclined to the left, but he identified neither with the *Talas* (the Catholics, so-called because they "*vont à la messe*"—"go to mass") or the *Stals* (the Communists, who, Derrida said, "dominated in a very tyrannical manner"). He cautiously supported Algerian independence but was horrified by the terrorist campaign of the Algerian insurgents. When other *normaliens* enthusiastically signed on to Althusser's Ahab-like pursuit of Marx's "scientific antihumanism," Derrida, despite his affection for the *caïman*, a fellow *pied-noir*, didn't join them, put off by what he saw as Althusser's ungrounded rhetoric.

At home in abstraction, drawn to philosophy's thorniest foundational conundrums, and, perhaps above all, to the paradoxes involved in trying to capture the world in language, he remained emotionally fragile, prone to depression, anxiety, and hypochondria. In the late 1960s, he developed a phobia of flying so intense that for several years he avoided planes altogether. He was fascinated by writers who pushed the limits of what language could do—James Joyce, the playwright Antonin Artaud, and the novelist and critic Maurice Blanchot—but their work frightened him too. In a letter to one experimental French author in the mid-1960s, Derrida hailed the man's latest book as "writing at its most radical." He went on: "And that's why it allures me, and that's why it is only painfully and impotently that I renounce that type of writing. . . . Standing near this limit is *threatening* . . . and that's why I am keeping away from it as much as *possible* so as not to be destroyed by the threat (feast or death) and as close as *possible* so as not to doze off. . . . I often have the feeling that through my '*fear*,' which one day I will be able to put behind me, I have fled from the route of the *heart* that you have managed to follow."

The extreme experiences that Foucault so aggressively pursued, Derrida recoiled from in fear—of madness, or worse. If experimental novels involved writing from the heart, then philosophy was writing from the head. But if this was a safer place from which to contemplate the limits of thought, it was not by much. "I am trying to do the same as you," Derrida concluded his letter, "with an extra mask—that is to say, between my 'life' and my 'thought' an extra detour."

In 1955, he failed the philosophy *agrégation*, having taken the exam in his usual state of nervous exhaustion, this time on a mix of amphetamines and sleeping pills. "There is no question at all of your talent," the head juror explained in what had become a familiar ritual. "We had to allow candidates to pass who were of a significantly lower intellectual 'quality' than some who fell victim to the written or oral exams, since the former students played by the rulebook and were successful by dint of their conscientiousness and patience."

Althusser, who had befriended Derrida on his first day at the school, had warned him not to cite Husserl during his exam, as the German phenomenologist was not "a 'familiar thinker' for the jury." (Within a few years this would no longer be the case.) But Derrida couldn't help himself. Husserl was the philosopher who excited him most. When, in preparation for the exam, he'd submitted to Althusser a paper influenced by Husserl's conception of time, the *caïman* said, "I can't grade this, it's too difficult, too obscure for the *agrégation*." Already, the word "obscure" was beginning to stick to Derrida like a burr. Althusser passed the paper to Foucault, who read it and told Derrida, "Well, it's either an F or an A+." Undeterred, Derrida devoted his master's thesis to "The Problem of Genesis in Husserl's Philosophy," a three-hundred-page study that seemed to have poured out of him over the course of a few months. The paper was dense and highly technical, clotted with Husserl's phenomenological jargon. But to a degree that in retrospect astonished even Derrida, it established the core elements of his signature approach.

◆ ◆ ◆

In an introduction Derrida wrote when the thesis was finally published, in 1990, he said he was shocked to recognize a conceit that had recurred throughout his work: "an originary complication of the origin" and "an initial contamination of the simple." The problem of the origin, or genesis, related to philosophy's tendency to posit as true something that hadn't been proved and then to erect an argument from that shaky foundation. Descartes was guilty of such maneuvering when he asserted that the existence of God can be deduced from God's nature, which is perfection: Since existence is perfection—it's clearly better to exist than not to exist—God, being perfect, must therefore exist. The circular logic here was obvious even to a contemporary of Descartes, who immediately pointed it out: "Existence is not a perfection in God or anything else; it is that without which no perfections can be present." Derrida was adept at detecting such missteps in other philosophers' work, but in his thesis on Husserl his concern with beginnings was also quite literal.

Like Derrida, Edmund Husserl was prone to bouts of depression, which he countered by immersing himself in his work. Long after his retirement from the University of Freiburg in 1928 he continued to make important contributions to phenomenology, the field he had pioneered. His most famous student was Martin Heidegger, who went on to repudiate Husserl's teaching, eclipse his renown, and, most appalling to many of his followers, embrace Nazism. When Husserl, a Jew who had converted to Lutheranism in his early twenties, was required to give up his affiliation with his university in 1933 in accordance with Nazi racial laws, Heidegger (by then Freiburg's rector) did not intervene. Moreover, that same year, he published a new edition of his 1927 masterwork, *Being and Time,* with Husserl's name excised from the dedication page.

Sartre was studying in Berlin at the time, and read both Husserl and Heidegger. Back in France, he remixed their theories with his own to produce existentialism. Two decades later, Derrida traced Sartre's course in reverse, proceeding from Sartre's novels and his treatise, *Being and Nothingness*—which Derrida judged "philosophically weak"—to his original German sources. Like Descartes, Husserl was transfixed by the question of how we know the things we believe to be true. He initially focused on math. A mental process was obviously involved in the concept of multiplicity, for example, according to which we perceive that a set of objects constitutes a particular number—five teacups, for example. But on what basis is five an objective fact, independent of our consciousness? Torn between what he called the "world of the purely logical" (objective

Edmund Husserl

reality) and the "world of actual consciousness" (private psychological experience), Husserl devoted his career to studying the relationship between the two. Clearly, he said, our minds don't simply think, as Descartes would have it; they think *about* things. Moreover, he concluded, it's absurd to dwell on "what is really there," since everything, real or imagined, is filtered through consciousness; instead, we should focus on how we perceive the various phenomena.

Husserl introduced a number of technical terms to explain how to undertake the work he proposed. The first step was to "bracket" off what he called "the natural attitude": the underbrush of emotional associations, cultural baggage, prejudices, and assumptions that color, without our being aware of it, our encounters with the world. After setting aside all that we take for granted about our interactions with reality, we can drill down to the essential, unvarying features of experience—" go back to the 'things themselves,'" as he memorably put it. It sounds simple, but to do phenomenology as Husserl envisioned it entailed extremely rigorous description and analysis. It was no easy feat to capture experience in its original neutrality, uncontaminated by the distortions of personal bias and collective history.

Derrida was enthralled by phenomenology, but he found Husserl's enterprise problematic, especially the way it dealt with time. He noticed that most of Husserl's examples involved objects existing in space (an ink pot, a piece of paper, a table). Husserl included far fewer descriptions of events existing in time (a three-note melody, an approaching stagecoach).

Moreover, he seemed unable to capture the precise moment of apprehension that inaugurates experience, despite repeatedly invoking its importance. According to Husserl's account, an experience in the present always includes the residue of an experience in the past and the anticipation of an experience in the future. This, Husserl argued, is how consciousness operates: as an uninterrupted stream. He called this process "flow" and referred to human life, wonderfully, as "the flowing thisness."

He acknowledged the challenge of isolating a moment and subjecting it to phenomenological analysis, since the illusion of unbroken flow is an inescapable aspect of consciousness: "But is not the flow a succession? Does it not have a now, an actually present phase, and a continuity of pasts which I am now conscious in retentions? We can say nothing more than the following: This flow is something we speak of *in conformity with what is constituted*, but it is not 'something in objective time.'" In other words, the experience of unbroken flow is an effect of consciousness, but it is not how time really works. "In the actuality-experience," Husserl insisted, "we have the primal source-point and a continuity of moments of reverberation. For all of this, we lack names."

Ultimately, Husserl's description of a conscious mind engaged in the act of perception depended on unprovable assumptions. What looked like a single instant of experience always contained within it other, prior instances of experience, and an already existing mind with a history of such experiences. There was no way to stop time in its tracks, to step outside it, or reach "the primal source-point"—the beginning of the flow. Husserl was unable to separate a concept of *being* from one of *time*, and vice versa. There was no way to explain one without presuming the other. "In spite of the immense philosophical revolution that Husserl undertook, he remains the prisoner of a great classical tradition," Derrida wrote. "Discovering the *a priori* synthesis of being and time as foundation of any genesis and every meaning, Husserl, to save the rigor and purity of 'phenomenological idealism' . . . did not adjust his method." Husserl himself conceded that time-consciousness was the "most difficult of all phenomenological problems."

In demonstrating that the problem of origin was never convincingly addressed by Husserl's philosophy, Derrida committed his first notable act of deconstruction. He wouldn't use the term for another decade, but the approach was clearly in formation. "It was Husserl who taught me a technique, a method, a discipline, and who has never left me," he reflected years later. He had followed Husserl's phenomenological logic to its limits and showed where it unraveled. In the future, he would do the same with the writings of other philosophers, elaborating his conviction that Western philosophy since Plato had conceived of foundational ideas by clinging to an illusory "metaphysics of presence."

In this respect, Derrida was building on the work of Nietzsche, Heidegger, and to a lesser extent Freud, all thinkers who had questioned deeply held assumptions about knowledge, truth, and the human self. All three—we might call them anti-idealists—had tried in different ways to solve the problem of foundational claims. Heidegger, who brought impressive technical rigor to the problem of how to understand "being," lamented that merely posing the question opens up an "abyss." We naturally endow our ideas about being with concrete attributes—with presence and essence—since we experience being alive and being ourselves (as opposed to being someone else or nothing at all), just as we experience events in the world as having a beginning and an end. Again and again over the course of his career, Derrida would show how philosophers had stumbled, assuming the very qualities they were trying to prove. When Husserl evoked the act of phenomenological perception, he ended up falling into a metaphysical trap.

◆ ◆ ◆

It was Husserl who sparked Derrida's interest in writing as a subject for philosophical investigation. An elliptical remark by the phenomenologist got him thinking about how writing worked. "How is it that writing can disturb the very question 'what is'?" he wondered, "and even 'what does it mean'?" Derrida shared the structuralist view of language as an all-powerful system standing between us and the world, but his belief that meaning was unstable—that words never meant simply what they appeared to mean—set him apart and would eventually be seen as a distinguishing feature of theory's next incarnation: poststructuralism. He stressed the extent to which Western philosophy tended to be organized around binary pairs—not unlike Bataille's opposed extremes—with one term in the pair privileged over the other: presence/absence, inside/outside, center/margin, origin/end, writing/speech, etc. Foucault's great error in *Folie et déraison* was to embrace such rigid logic in chronicling reason's triumph over madness. Derrida was at pains to show that these supposed opposites were constitutionally unstable, never behaving as philosophy assumed they did.

At the only lecture I saw Derrida give, in a genteelly dilapidated classroom at the École Normale in the fall of 1989, he wore a purple silk shirt and a richly patterned tie and discussed the relationship between *manger* (eating) and *aimer* (loving), which, under his idiosyncratic scrutiny, turned out to be vexingly paradoxical. The lecture was one of a series on "the politics of friendship" and drew on a disparate array of sources: from Holy Communion (the consumption of tokens symbolizing the body and blood of Christ) and the female praying mantis, which devours her male partner after mating ("the paradigmatic and emblematic case of animal cannibalism") to Freud (who described the "oral stage" in terms of the ego wanting to "incorporate the other" by "devouring it); and *Penthesilea*, a tragedy by German playwright Heinrich von Kleist, which, extravagant even by the Romantic standard of the day, recounts the mad passion of the mythical Amazon queen Penthesilea for Achilles, her warrior opponent, whom she attacks first with an arrow, then with her hands, and finally with her teeth, exclaiming that such a woman desires her lover so much "that she could eat him from love." (Derrida did not mention the Japanese murderer Issei Sagawa, whose bestselling memoir of his "cannibalistic love" had lately caused such a sensation.)

To love is to love the other as ourselves—"*aimer l'autre comme soi*"—Derrida said. By the end of the lecture the difference, and distance, between self and other, lover and beloved, not to mention between eating and loving, had pretty much disappeared. Yet it seemed to me that his listeners had spent a lot of the hour looking around to see who else was in attendance—perhaps because by this time Derrida was so famous, and his methodology so well known, that acolytes in the crowd already knew where his ruminations were likely to lead and everyone else was there mainly to gawk at the legendary thinker and his entourage. I had attended the lecture alone, and didn't recognize anyone. None of my *normalien* friends were interested in theory, and I was in the process of working it out of my system—through my class with Milan Kundera and in the research for my *maîtrise* on ways out of theory's paralyzing cul de sacs.

Listening to Derrida, though, I was struck anew in spite of myself by his argument that in philosophy's cherished hierarchal pairs, the less favored term never really disappears but continues to haunt the favored term—notwithstanding the philosopher's strenuous efforts to suppress it. Thus, love is always already contaminated by death, just as any description of genesis or "primal source" in Husserl is contaminated by history, by the past. And where Foucault claimed madness had been banished from reason, Derrida found madness still there, lurking inside. In a sense, as Fredric Jameson observed, "all of Derrida is the same. He's going to do the same thing with everything."

It wouldn't be farfetched to see in Derrida's thinking about excluded binary terms something of his experience as a French Algerian and a Jew, and perhaps also as an academic in France, even if Derrida himself didn't draw such stark parallels. In May 1956, writing to a friend from the École Normale infirmary, where he spent a week racked by anxiety as he prepared to take the *agrégation* a second time—thankfully he passed—he said: "I'm not good for anything except taking the world apart and putting it together again (and I manage the latter less and less frequently)." This sounds like the sentiments of a man struggling with depression, but at the same time, taking the world apart and failing to put it back together again is not a bad description of deconstruction.

And in this respect, Derrida was right: Aside from its ability to cast a sharp light on philosophy's missteps and mystifications, deconstruction really wasn't "good" for much, though that didn't stop American literary critics from trying to turn it into a political weapon during the culture wars of the 1980s and '90s. Among deconstruction's central implications was that certainty, at least in philosophy, was all but impossible. And uncertainty—about identity, about cultural origins and affiliations—was something Derrida knew well. By the end of the 1950s, he had begun taking Anafranil, one of the first commercially available antidepressants, which had just come on the market.

Chapter 22

FOUCAULT STRIKES BACK

Whatever Foucault felt listening to Derrida's takedown of his book, by all accounts he retained his composure. A week later, he sent his former student a gracious letter. "Off the cuff, I was taken aback and pretty clumsy in what I managed to say," he admitted, explaining his wish to thank Derrida for "the immense and marvelous attention you gave to my words." With what appeared to be sincere humility, he went on, "This relationship between the Cogito and madness is something that, without the least doubt, I treated too cavalierly in my thesis" adding, "You have magisterially showed the right road to take."

Several months later, Derrida announced that he planned to publish "Cogito and the History of Madness" in a philosophy journal, and Foucault approved the idea, writing, "only the blind will find your critique severe." Four years after that, in 1967, he sent another friendly note when Derrida included the paper in his book *L'écriture et la différence* (*Writing and Difference*) and gave Foucault a copy. But in the interim much had changed. Foucault had just published a surprise bestseller: *Les mots et les choses* (published in English as *The Order of Things*). In it, he proposed that the history of knowledge could be divided into discrete eras, each beholden to a hidden framework of understanding embedded deep within the culture. These hidden structures determined not only the likely objects of study at any given period but, just as important, the limits of what could be thought.

The book, undoubtedly Foucault's most structuralist work, appeared at the peak of the movement's influence and was hailed in *L'Express* as the "greatest revolution since existentialism." It made Foucault instantly famous. Some saw it as proof that he had taken Derrida's critique of *Folie et déraison* to heart. Derrida had attacked Foucault for claiming that he could make madness speak despite its having been silenced by reason and banished to the asylum. Now, Foucault had switched focus, from the voices of the marginalized and excluded to the large-scale structures responsible for the excluding.

He had also gotten hip. He'd shaved his head and traded his coat and tie for a mod wardrobe: black corduroy suits, white turtlenecks, a loden green cape—attire that by the mid-1970s expanded to include a black leather motorcycle jacket and chains. His love life had become public, too. Foucault had shocked colleagues by having his lover Daniel Defert, a young philosopher who became his life partner, appointed to the university in the Auvergne where he was then serving as chair of the philosophy de-

Michel Foucault in 1975

partment. According to *Le Monde*, the two most frequently cited names in the philosophy *agrégation* of 1966 were Althusser and Foucault.

But Derrida was nipping at his heels. By the fall of 1967, the once-obscure translator of Husserl was suddenly everywhere. At Althusser's invitation, he had become a lecturer at the École Normale, and then, after Althusser had a breakdown and wound up in the hospital, the new philosophy *caïman*. Astonishingly, he published three books that year, first *Writing and Difference* and then *Speech and Phenomena* and *Of Grammatology*, in which he elaborated his theory of deconstruction by means of a rigorous critique of structuralism. He won awed reviews in the major journals and newspapers, and, via literary scholars in the United States, dozens of new readers in America.

"Philosophy is in crisis," a reviewer for *Le Monde* declared. "This crisis is also a renewal. In France, a whole constellation of (relatively) young thinkers are transforming it: Foucault, Althusser, Deleuze, etc. We now need to add to these names that of Jacques Derrida. Known to a small group of enthusiastic *normaliens,* he has just revealed his talent to a wider public by publishing three books in six months. . . . Derrida's aim is not the destruction, but the 'deconstruction' of metaphysics." Imagine *The New York Times Book Review* devoting a page to anointing the newest young star in academic philosophy.

For Foucault, the last straw was a reverential essay on Derrida's three new books in *Critique*, a leading intellectual journal founded by Georges Bataille in 1946. "Already a whole oeuvre," the reviewer, a philosopher name Gérard Granel, marveled in his opening sentence. "Already an entire body of writing in a single year, unfurled above our heads like a banner. Beautiful to behold in the sky and new in its colors." Both Foucault and Derrida sat on *Critique*'s editorial board, and when the essay came in, Foucault took exception to a paragraph applauding Derrida's now famous takedown of his book. In Derrida's assessment of Foucault, Granel suggested, we can see how deconstruction works, how "a 'particular point,' initially lost in the middle of the work, allows us to penetrate, little by little, then suddenly and completely, the whole." And then "all we need to do is to transport (not even transpose) the now evident inadequacies of *Histoire de la folie* to *Les mots et les choses* for the basically undefined notion of archaeology underlying the whole enterprise to fall apart." Mortified by this derision, Foucault asked Derrida to intervene, but Derrida refused. The essay went to press essentially unchanged. One of the few concessions may have been a footnote to the offending passage in which Granel explained that Derrida was invariably "respectful and gentle" in his assessments of others' work, and if there was any "meanness" in Granel's essay, the fault was his alone.

In 1971, Foucault saw his chance for vindication. A Japanese journal was planning a special issue on his work and the editor hoped to include a piece on Derrida's takedown. Foucault suggested that the journal publish an essay by him instead: "Reply to Derrida" In it, he tried out several lines of attack, from declaring that his analysis of Descartes "was no doubt the most expendable part" of his book and should have been omitted—indeed, an abridged version published in 1964 left those pages out—to arguing that Derrida, blinded by his vantage point in philosophy, could not conceive of historical events, let alone those of a singular nature, such as occurred in seventeenth-century France involving the confinement of tens of thousands of people.

Foucault wasn't done. A few months later, to mark his book's tenth anniversary, Gallimard republished *Folie et déraison* at its original length. Foucault took the opportunity to add as an appendix an expanded version of his rebuttal (now called "My Body, This Paper, This Fire"), sharpening his tone and digging in his heels. Returning to the original Latin of Descartes' text, he pummeled Derrida over the course of thirty pages, showing how Derrida had constructed his argument on the basis of telling omissions, elisions, and inventions. By the end of the essay, Foucault was no longer bothering to conceal his rage. He dismissed Derrida as the leading exemplar of a style of reading that reduced history and culture to mere "textual traces." "I would not say that it is a metaphysics," Foucault wrote, hurling the term as an insult, philosophy's synonym for naïveté. "I would go much further: I would say that it is a historically well-determined little pedagogy, which manifests itself here in a very visible manner. A pedagogy which teaches the student that there is nothing outside the text . . . that it is never necessary to look beyond it. . . . A pedagogy that inversely gives to the voice of the masters that unlimited sovereignty that allows it indefinitely to re-say the text." In short, Derrida's deconstruction was nothing more than authoritarian quackery. Foucault sent him a copy of Gallimard's anniversary edition, along with a note that read "Sorry to have answered you so late." The two men didn't speak for nearly ten years.

A casual reader picking up a copy of that new edition of Foucault's book might have been baffled by the diatribe tacked on to the end. But to scholars, the hostile exchange between these two intellectual titans was like a match between Muhammad Ali and George Foreman, or Novak Djokovic and Rafael Nadal: riveting—and too closely fought to judge the rightful winner; they have been dissecting the play-by-play ever since. (The fifty-year anniversary of Derrida's attack in 2013 prompted the publication of at least two new collections of essays on the subject.) In many respects, the quarrel previewed the fork looming for theory in the road ahead: Along one path stretched rhetorical analysis, obsession with paradox, and the scrupulous close readings proposed by Derrida; along the other, investigations of political and social power in the form of "discourse," championed by Foucault. Both thinkers subscribed to what the French philosopher Paul Ricoeur called a "hermeneutics of suspicion," but they had different ideas about where to direct their mistrust, toward language itself or toward society's most powerful institutions, whose activities left a trail of evidence buried in their official pronouncements.

These divergent tendencies would soon become more clearly demarcated.

Chapter 23

"WE ARE ALL SCHIZOS!"

Just as the Foucault-Derrida feud was settling into a tense stalemate, a new philosophical quarrel over madness broke out, this one involving Lacan. It was more fodder in the growing backlash to structuralism. In March 1972, a book with the strange title *L'Anti-Oedipe* (Anti-Oedipus) was published in Paris. The title wasn't the only striking thing about it. The book had two authors who made an unlikely pair: Gilles Deleuze, an up-and-coming academic philosopher, and Félix Guattari, a militant leftist and onetime protégé of Lacan who helped run an experimental psychiatric clinic in the Loire. Then there was the prose. The opening lines went like this: "It is at work everywhere, functioning smoothly at times, at other times in fits and starts. It breathes, it heats, it eats. It shits and fucks. What a mistake to have ever said *the* id. Everywhere *it* is machines—real ones, not figurative ones: machines driving other machines, machines being driven by other machines, with all the necessary couplings and connections." The book sold out in three days.

In a Paris infatuated with psychoanalysis, and still coursing with the rebellious energy of May '68, Deleuze and Guattari struck a nerve. Their language was exuberant, anarchic, trippy—philosophy on psychedelics. "We are all schizos! We are all perverts!" they declared, seeming to channel the student protestors who had coated the city with absurdist slogans just a few years before. At the same time, their intellectual bona fides were solid and their message, however cheekily delivered, was serious: Psychoanalysis had devolved into structuralist dogma, for which the Oedipus complex was a prime example. First Freud and then Lacan had reduced the story of human development to a "daddy-mommy-me triangle" and imposed it willy-nilly on everyone, finding evidence for it everywhere they looked. The Oedipus complex—what did it mean to say that Freud had "discovered" it during his self-analysis in 1897, anyway?—was a structure, and its effect was repression. It constrained desire and boxed it in, turning psychoanalysis into a negative tale of frustration and lack, about objects of desire forever off-limits or beyond reach. In short, the Oedipus complex was a buzzkill.

Psychoanalysis was wrong, Deleuze and Guattari insisted. The unconscious was a happy place! There was nothing lacking about it. It wasn't structured like a language, as Lacan would have it. It didn't follow a logic or syntax. It wasn't even an "it," but, rather, a machine—or, really, lots of machines. The unconscious was a factory, and what it produced was desire, flowing every which way, all the time, from one machine (a mouth, say) to the next (a breast, say) and out into the world.

Desire in this conception was a potentially revolutionary force. It was the nature of desire to flow, and it was the nature of human society to try to stop the flow, to contain it in orderly structures like the family, the church, the state, the human subject—in Deleuze and Guattari's view the self was just an arbitrary collection of desiring machines—and the symbolic order. Psychoanalysis, too, was guilty of stanching desire. In this respect, *Anti-Oedipus* was a damning *J'accuse* aimed at the profession. "Instead of participating in an undertaking that will bring about genuine liberation," Deleuze and Guattari wrote, "psychoanalysis is taking part in the work of bourgeois repression at its most far-reaching level, that is to say, keeping European humanity harnessed to the yoke of daddy-mommy."

In its most extreme form, repression of desire was fascism, the authors suggested, borrowing the idea from the Austrian psychoanalyst Wilhelm Reich. But capitalism—the regime under which psychoanalysis was born—was hardly better. Capitalism unleashed desire, allowing it

Gilles Deleuze and Félix Guattari in 1980

(or rather, its surrogates: money and labor) to flow toward one place, only to dam it up again somewhere else in an endless, schizophrenic cycle of production and consumption, fleeting satisfaction and recurring frustration.

Like "machine," "schizophrenic" was a key word in *Anti-Oedipus.* Deleuze and Guattari saw schizophrenia not only as the "characteristic malady" of their day, but as a window onto desire in its unhindered, "deterritorialized" state. The schizophrenic Judge Schreber, whom Freud had diagnosed as suffering from repressed homosexual urges, was recast in *Anti-Oedipus* as a heroic truth teller, testifying—in his baroque descriptions of "sunbeams in his ass" and breasts on his torso—to the reality of desire as pure production, unimpeded by social and economic constraints.

"A schizophrenic out for a walk is a better model than a neurotic lying on the analyst's couch," the authors proclaimed. If schizophrenia was a scourge of capitalism, the schizophrenic was nevertheless exemplary, an embodiment of desire in its natural state. In Deleuze and Guattari's giddy description, the disease sounded like an ecstatic drug trip, a path to enlightenment. In place of psychoanalysis, they proposed "schizoanalysis," which promised to free desire from the social structures in which it had been caged.

After the book was published, Guattari was inundated with requests from people clamoring for treatment. According to one account, among his patients was briefly the beat poet Allen Ginsberg, whose epic poem "Kaddish," about his mother's mental illness and death, Deleuze and Guattari had praised—an example of schizophrenic "flux" as opposed to Oedipal "territoriality." Deleuze later told an interviewer that he and Guattari were worried about being misread as encouraging mental breakdown and dysfunction. "This book is extremely prudent," he insisted, a little disingenuously. "Don't become wrecks. We were terrified of producing hospital products."

Probably the closest Guattari got to practicing schizoanalysis was in his work at La Borde, the experimental clinic where he spent most of his career. Slight and high-strung, teeming with ideas but lacking discipline, he was a man in constant motion, getting by on little sleep. If he were alive today, he might be diagnosed with ADD and put on Ritalin. His second wife, Arlette Donati, a nurse at the clinic, said that when she met him there in 1967 he looked, in his cardigan and heavy black-frame glasses, like an old man, and that his table manners needed work. None of these apparent liabilities prevented him from a champion career as a womanizer; he considered monogamy another form of capitalist repression.

He was born in 1930, the same year as Derrida, and his family moved around France, from tiny towns in the provinces to Paris, as his father pursued a series of business endeavors with varying success: managing a chocolate factory, raising sheep and then angora rabbits (after the angora fur market collapsed, the family ate the rabbits), selling coffee pots and potatoes, and, finally, returning to chocolate, as the founder of a company. By the time his father was making steady money as a chocolatier, Guattari had joined the Communist Party, dropped out of school, and become a Lacanian.

Introduced to the master's work in the early 1950s by a psychiatrist mentor, Guattari was an early convert. He knew several of Lacan's essays practically by heart, including the one on the mirror stage—no small feat. Soon he was in analysis with Lacan himself, who, impressed by his intellect—or, equally likely, his devotion—invited him to attend his seminar, then in its early days at Sainte-Anne Hospital. For an additional fee, Lacan sometimes allowed Guattari to drive him home, explaining that the experience was "part of the analysis." In 1964, Guattari became a founding member of Lacan's École freudienne de Paris. By then he was working as an analyst himself at La Borde, which was housed in a nineteenth-century *château* surrounded by parkland not far from the grand Loire estates of Chambord and Blois.

Only a couple years old when he moved there in 1955, La Borde grew out of the postwar reform movement in psychiatry, and its practices were some of the most radical in France. Patients and staff lived together on site, mingling socially and sharing tasks. Medical personnel rotated from clinical work to manual labor, and patients were given administrative jobs. Guattari felt immediately at home, quickly gaining the trust of La Borde's equally radical Lacanian director, Jean Oury. "Félix really liked declassifying people, like having a doctor come work in the office," one former colleague said. "He had the psychologists doing the dishes."

Decisions were made by committee, and everyone had a say. There

La Borde, the experimental clinic in the Loire where Félix Guattari spent most of his career

was a newspaper and a social club. According to Deleuze and Guattari's biographer, François Dosse, during the mid-1960s La Borde was a hub of cultural activity, hosting as many as five thousand guests an evening for theatrical productions, as well as celebrities like the filmmaker Jean Renoir, who showed his movie *La Marseillaise* at the clinic. One staffer, an amateur magician, started a circus at La Borde and on a whim wrote to Charlie Chaplin's daughter Victoria—a known circus aficionado—in Switzerland, inviting her to visit. Victoria came to La Borde and ended up marrying the magician on the premises. Together, they ran the circus and got patients involved, including a catatonic man who, when Victoria wrapped him up like a mummy, was able, for the first time in years, to move his body.

On Wednesdays, the clinic emptied out as patients and staff took the train to Paris to hear Lacan's seminar. "They practically filled an entire car," Dosse writes, adding that everyone on the clinic's medical team spent time on Lacan's couch. Caught up in the era's "ambient structuralism," Oury, La Borde's director, claimed that the clinic was organized in "signifying units," by which he apparently meant the way different spaces were assigned different functions (the laundry room, the insulin unit, etc.) and how those spaces related to one another. But for Guattari, at least, loyalty to Lacan and his structuralist precepts was not to be rewarded in the way he had envisioned. By the mid-1960s, Jacques-Alain Miller had married Lacan's daughter and taken charge of prepping the master's lectures for publication, sidelining Guattari as the heir apparent.

In 1969, Guattari's disenchantment spilled into public view. That spring, at the École freudienne de Paris, he presented "Machine and Structure," a paper that previewed several of the ideas in *Anti-Oedipus,* in particular the attack on Lacanian structuralism. In his paper, Guattari cited Deleuze, who had just published a major book, *Difference and Repetition*, criticizing philosophy's tendency to value identity and sameness over difference and multiplicity. Guattari placed "structures" in Deleuze's category of identity and sameness, as elements defined by their relationship to one another within a fixed system, and he placed "machines" in the category of difference and multiplicity. Then, risking apostasy, Guattari went on to hint that "machine" was more apt than "structure" for conveying the way the unconscious worked. "The unconscious subject as such will be on the same side as the machine, or better perhaps, *alongside* the machine," he declared. Moreover, he suggested, true revolution could occur only if "the machine for institutional subversion" were able to resist "any attempt to 'structuralize'" it.

Perhaps the paper's opaque theoretical language afforded Guattari momentary reprieve from orthodox Lacanians, who may not have immediately grasped its import. But when Roland Barthes offered to publish the paper in a journal he edited, Lacan quickly extended a counteroffer—to publish it in *his* journal instead. This turned out to be a ruse. Lacan's goal was to suppress the offending document altogether, and it never appeared in his pages.

Guattari had written his heretical paper but not yet delivered it when he met Deleuze in person for the first time. Deleuze had just had a lung removed, following a recurrence of tuberculosis, and was recuperating at his country house in the Limousin. The two men immediately hit it off, an odd couple bound by common philosophical interests, complementary talents, and an intuitive understanding of the restive cultural mood—a nation of young people still smarting from the previous year's failed revolution. Guattari, unsurprisingly, had been delighted by the events of that May, swanning through the streets of Paris on a motorcycle at four in the morning, before zooming back to La Borde to goad staff and patients to action.

Soon, the pair began collaborating through the mail, with Guattari sending rough drafts to Deleuze, who revised, edited, and polished them. They worked well at a distance, cementing a professional relationship that yielded several more books as well as one of the few dual biographies in philosophy: Dosse's informative *Gilles Deleuze and Félix Guattari: Intersecting Lives*. Even so, their friendship retained an element of reserve; they never stopped addressing each other using the formal "*vous*."

Deleuze, five years older, had been raised upper-middle-class in Paris, a brilliant student who attended the Lycée Louis-le-Grand and, after failing the entrance exam to the École Normale, the Sorbonne. He came in second in the philosophy *agrégation* in 1948 and eventually wound up back at the Sorbonne teaching the subject. Married to a woman who worked for the fashion designer Balmain, he was a sharp dresser with a beaked nose and unusually long fingernails, which fascinated his students. Behind his back, they called him a dandy and whispered that he had homosexual tendencies, to which he responded, "So?" Despite chronic respiratory ailments—a friend compared him to Marcel Proust—he chain-smoked through his classes. He loved monster movies and French literature, but considered himself first and foremost a metaphysician, producing excellent studies of Nietzsche, Kant, and Henri Bergson. In 1967, he'd written an important essay, "How Do We Recognize Structuralism?" in which he defined the movement according to half a dozen criteria embodied by a similar number of figures, including Althusser, Barthes, Foucault, and Lacan. Two years later, he saw in Guattari's concept of the machine the promise of moving beyond structuralism to something even more radical.

Deleuze also shared Guattari's view that psychoanalysis had failed to come up with an adequate account of psychosis. He was phobic about actual madness—a friend said he "couldn't have spent even an hour at La Borde." But he was interested in schizophrenia as a philosophical problem, a name for expression that was unremitting and unimpeded, and thus something to be celebrated—a constant flow! The pair's ideas about schizoanalysis grew out of Guattari's experiments at La Borde with a form of psychotherapy he called "transversality." Convinced that mental illness was never simply a product of individual pathology or family dynamics but had important social and economic causes, Guattari favored treatment that stressed group interactions and forming new social relationships. At the same time, he sought to subvert the kind of vertical and horizontal power arrangements by which groups tended to be organized. Any approach that upset conventional structures (or, in the language of the day, "binary structural oppositions") might help to free up the desiring-machines of the unconscious.

Guattari wrote a theoretical paper on transversality, but, as with schizoanalysis itself, how the concept translated into practice was unclear. Ultimately, *Anti-Oedipus* was less interested in actual people than in ideas. It remained a work of theory, a dazzling provocation that had little effect on Guattari's profession other than to raise hackles. Though both Deleuze and Guattari believed that capitalism was making people sick, they insisted that *Anti-Oedipus* was not preaching Marxism as the solution. They saw the book's philosophy in more general terms, as a kind of liberation theology for the unconscious.

Foucault, probably as a favor to Deleuze, whom he deeply admired, wrote a preface for the English edition of *Anti-Oedipus* in 1977, praising it for exposing "the fascism in us all, in our heads and in our everyday behavior, the fascism that causes us to love power, to desire the very thing that dominates and exploits us." Being anti-Oedipal was to embrace a revolutionary new way of life: rejecting the "old categories of the Negative (law, limit, castration, lack, lacuna)" and opting instead for "what is positive and multiple, difference over uniformity, flows over unities, mobile arrangements over systems."

Inspired by *Anti-Oedipus*, Guy Hocquenghem, a philosopher friend of Foucault's, promoted the idea in a 1972 book, *Homosexual Desire*, that homosexual practices more closely approximated the ideal of free-flowing desire—of the "plugging in of organs subject to no rule or law"—than heterosexual ones. To others, however, *Anti-Oedipus* sounded like rhetoric, nothing more. One reviewer, complaining that the book made little sense, acknowledged that "criticizing in the name of logic a book that defends delusional discourse seems pointless."

When I first read *Anti-Oedipus*, in graduate school in New York, where I headed after my year at the École Normale, I was excited by the book's rebellious erotic energy. It figured prominently in the essay I wrote for my master's degree, a long paper on *Nightwood*, an intriguingly strange 1936 novel by the American writer Djuna Barnes. Set mainly in Paris, where Barnes lived during the 1920s and '30s as fascist ideology spread through Europe, and populated by a bohemian cast of lesbians, transvestites, Jews, and circus freaks—all potential targets of fascism's obsession with racial and gender purity—*Nightwood* struck me as a bold experiment in Deleuzian "deterritorialization" as political resistance.

One character, an Irishman named Doctor O'Connor, presents as a parody of a psychoanalyst, holding forth in a woman's nightgown and makeup under a wig of blond curls from his bed in a sordid Parisian garret. Another character, so existentially elusive that, Barnes writes, "thinking of her, visualizing her, was an extreme act of the will," migrates through a succession of identities—heterosexual wife, mother, lesbian lover, and, finally, dog—in a seductive approximation of deterritorialized desire. (In a rather defensive introduction, T. S. Eliot, who edited the novel, removing some of the explicit content before publication, confessed that "it took me, with this book, some time to come to an appreciation of its meaning as a whole.") But for all its inventiveness, I concluded, *Nightwood* underscores the limits of anti-Oedipal fantasy as a "dubious sort of non-existence." What the novel ends up showing is that even "to write or speak is to be immediately complicit with one's own repression by participating in a system of coded investments—words, images, representations, the logic of narrative itself." So much for the Deleuzian revolution.

To read *Anti-Oedipus* today is to encounter a glorious utopian curio bearing a late 1960s time stamp—a book best read, as Foucault suggested, as "art." And yet its conception of fascism as a psychosexual manifestation has proved suggestive. In the late 1970s, Klaus Theweleit, a young German literature scholar, found evidence for this idea in dozens of novels and memoirs by members of the Freikorps, the hard-right private militias that fought German communists in the wake of World War I and went on to form a core of Nazi support. Theweleit's mammoth dissertation, "Male Fantasies," was a surprise bestseller in Germany in 1977, and, after it was translated into English ten years later, a cult hit among theory-minded Americans.

Theweleit traced the Freikorps' celebration of aggression and violence to a fear of sex, which the men associated in their writings with loss of control and dissolution of the self—and, ultimately, with women. In the Freikorps' fantasies, women figure again and again as objects of dread and hatred that threaten to engulf them. "Desire, if it flows at all, flows in a certain sense *through women*," Theweleit wrote. "Flow," that key Deleuzian term is, in the Freikorps' literature, a feminized phenomenon, like all substances "produced by the body and flowed on, in, over, and out of the body." These Theweleit spells out in a passage of memorably baroque description: "the floods and stickiness of sucking kisses; the swamps of the vagina, with their slime and mire; the pap and slime of male semen; the film of sweat that settles on the stomach, thighs, and in the anal crevice, and that turns two pelvic regions into a subtropical landscape; the slimy stream of menstruation" as well as "the floods of orgasm."

It's not much of a stretch to see a version of the Freikorps' gender anxiety and sexual preoccupations in the inflamed rhetoric emerging from today's ascendant authoritarian right. On the campaign trail in 2024, Donald Trump spun nightmare scenarios about transgender identity, telling attendees at his rallies, "There are some places, your boy leaves for school, comes back a girl," and his campaign spent millions of dollars on anti-trans and anti-LGBTQ ads (despite polls in which voters ranked gender issues among their lowest priorities).

Trump's administration and the ranks of his supporters are stocked with men fixated on threats to masculinity and disparaging of women, from Senator Josh Hawley of Missouri, the author of *Manhood: The Masculine Virtues American Needs* (2023), to political appointees like Darren Beattie, an undersecretary for global diplomacy at the State Department with a PhD in political theory and a dissertation on Heidegger, who tweeted: "Competent white men must be in charge if you want things to work. Unfortunately, our entire national ideology is predicated on coddling the feelings of women and minorities, and demoralizing competent white men." On Fox News, panelists discussed whether Trump's tariff-driven global trade war would solve the "crisis in masculinity" by returning "manly" jobs—in construction and manufacturing—to the United States. And in a viral speech and essay, the conservative writer Helen Andrews argued that an overrepresentation of women in the workplace was to blame for the country's affliction with "wokeness," declaring, "Everything you think of as 'wokeness' is simply an epiphenomenon of demographic feminization."

The Trump administration's embrace of what has come to be called the "manosphere" and its naked (a word frequently invoked in this context that seems ever less metaphoric with passing time) assertion of power appear hardly unrelated. As the journalist Katherine Stewart writes, "Manliness on the New Right comes with a distinctive—and extremely dangerous—politics. It defines the imaginary enemy around which the movement is united—and it also marks out the political endpoint of its fantasies. What the New Right wants to destroy is in essence democratic government; what it wants to create is the rule of the strongman."

You can be sure that Deleuze and Guattari would have been all for the gender fluidity the manosphere fears and abhors. What Foucault might have thought is less clear. Deeply skeptical of state power, and resolutely opposed to its incursions into private life, he was temperamentally more cautious than Deleuze and Guattari. Privately, he told friends that he didn't care for *Anti-Oedipus*. Deleuze was the first person Foucault tried to hire in 1968 when he was named inaugural director of the philosophy department at the new University of Vincennes. (Deleuze was too ill to accept the offer, though he did move to Vincennes two years later.) Stylistically, however, *Anti-Oedipus* could not have been more different from Foucault's own books, with their magisterial prose and archival references, and though he was taken with the idea of schizophrenia as an anti-structuralist conceit, he found the book baffling.

The person most clearly irritated by *Anti-Oedipus* was Lacan. Eager to hear his reaction, Deleuze and Guattari sent Deleuze's wife to Lacan's seminar for three weeks running after the book came out. But Lacan never mentioned it. "Lacan was really furious and gave instructions forbidding any organized debates about the book in his school," his lover Catherine Millot said. According to François Dosse, Lacan considered *Anti-Oedipus* such a terrible betrayal that he never spoke to Guattari again and encouraged colleagues to spread rumors about Guattari's incompetence as an analyst. In truth, the rebellion by Lacan's former acolyte was a sign of the times. Lacan was aging along with structuralism, and neither the philosopher nor the movement would remain in vogue much longer.

Chapter 24

"I *NEVER* TALK ABOUT FREEDOM"

By 1970, Lacan had begun referring to himself in the third person. Over the course of the decade, he retreated into silence. Some weeks, he would arrive at his seminar, draw a complicated knot on the chalkboard, and then leave the room without a word. A scholar working with Lacan at the time described him as "pure thought." But by the end of the decade, diminished by cancer and neurological issues, he was no longer able to fend off a mounting backlash. In 1979, an editor at *Les Temps Modernes* subjected him to a book-length takedown, mocking his seminars as unintelligible and comparing his followers to brainwashed cult members. The reviewer for *Le Monde*, endorsing the book's message, accused Lacan of "intellectual terrorism," likening his ruinous influence on psychoanalysis to the Ayatollah Khomeini's on Iran. Even Althusser turned against him, denouncing him as a "magnificent and pitiful Harlequin." The following year, Lacan closed his school and went to live with his daughter Judith and son-in-law Jacques-Alain Miller.

After Lacan's death in 1981, Phillipe Sollers put him into a novel, his 1983 bestseller *Women*, in which Lacan appears as "Fals," a very famous, very rich, and very eccentric psychoanalyst—his name an echo of Shakespeare's Falstaff—who "inspired both absolute devotion and implacable hate." Fals's teachings are credited with provoking French women to form FAM—the Front for the Autonomy of the Matrix—the national chapter of a secret global conspiracy to overthrow the patriarchy and replace it with all-female rule. To my mind, however, the character Lacan most resembles at the end of his life is the King Lear of Act III: dethroned and half-mad, nursing his betrayals as he wanders the heath through the raging storm. A former patient of Lacan's who made the same association pointed out that, like Lear, Lacan was supported in his final years by his youngest daughter and her husband.

Lacan's charisma and vulnerability are both on display in a rare film recording of a lecture he gave at the Catholic University of Louvain, in Belgium, in the fall of 1972, about six months after *Anti-Oedipus* came out. He is in a large hall packed with students. Many are sitting on the floor; some are standing. Lacan enters to a burst of applause. He makes his way to a long table at the front of the room, removes the cigar from his mouth, and beams at the crowd. He is wearing a patterned silk shirt with a matching cravat and frameless glasses. His hair is snow white, his head enormous. He speaks slowly, quietly, his hands in his pockets, pausing between phrases to look around, his cigar resting, still lit, in an ashtray.

"The 'speaking subject' is a pleonasm"—or redundancy—"isn't it?" he intones calmly. "It's as if because one is speaking that one is *being*, since there is only being in language." He's riffing, reprising old hits, evidently he hasn't prepared a talk. But it doesn't matter; the crowd is riveted. "The least we can say is that everything that is built up between these animals called humans is constructed, fabricated, and founded on language."

Moments later, he is shouting: "Death! It belongs to the domain of faith. Of course, you are right to believe you are going to die!" He plants his forearms on the table and glares at the room. He arrives at his point: "Nevertheless, it's only an act of faith," he yells. "The paradox is that you cannot be sure!" Life, he continues, that's a solid thing; there's no doubting that we are alive. "Yet as soon as we begin to talk about 'life' as such . . . it becomes a matter of thought." And this, he suggests, is the crux of the human predicament: We are trapped in thoughts, in words, and can never truly see beyond them.

Suddenly, a young man—shaggy-haired and wrapped in a heavy coat—approaches the table. He plunges his hands into a pitcher of water perched at one end. He is clutching something—it looks like bits of bread—which he proceeds to scatter, now soaking wet, over the table. Then he picks up the pitcher and pours its contents onto the table, too. Lacan steps to one side, puffing on his cigar, observing the young man with interest. The audience is entranced. A woman grasps the young man's wrists to try to stop him, but he shrugs her away.

"I was just expressing myself, like this gentleman, do you understand?" he says to the crowd. He gives a short speech about modern life, its alienation, its relentless "spectacle."

Lacan sucks on his cigar and paces silently for a few moments. "Expressing yourself like this," he says finally. "What do you want?"

"One thing," the young man says. "To make revolution."

"Yes," Lacan agrees.

Lacan lecturing at the Catholic University of Louvain, Belgium, in 1972

The young man continues speaking, gesturing with his hands. "One of our main targets will be those moments when people like you bring to all the people like these the justifications for their miserable lives. Isn't that what you do?"

"Not at all," Lacan says in a small voice.

The young man manages to throw one last piece of bread at Lacan as he is escorted from the room.

Before returning to Paris the next day, Lacan sat for an interview on camera with the filmmaker, a woman whose voice we can hear but whom we cannot see. At the end of the interview, channeling Deleuze and Guattari, she asks, "Doesn't psychoanalysis entail a repression of freedom?" Lacan has been sighing heavily during her questions, responding slowly, sometimes looking pained. Now he becomes animated. He looks at the camera and breaks into a huge grin. "These words make me laugh," he says. "I *never* talk about freedom."

Part 3

Words

Chapter 25

LACAN READS POE

The French structuralists may not have talked much about freedom, but they talked about everything else. And to a degree perhaps not matched before or since, the outpouring of words by 1960s Parisian intellectuals was about language itself. The fixation on language was extreme, even if language as they described it hardly resembled what we mean when we casually invoke the term today. To the structuralists, language was practically a living thing, a seismic, shadowy, even sinister force not only more powerful than anyone had previously suspected, but by itself almost entirely constitutive of human existence.

In this way, the structuralist revolution was really two revolutions in one. First, the freely acting, deeply feeling, existentialist self was banished, replaced by the impersonal regime of the system and the subject. Then, of all possible systems, it was language that rose to the fore. Althusser, Barthes, Foucault, and Lacan grumbled about being labeled structuralists, but they generally agreed about language: It was the thing that determined all the rest. As Deleuze put it in his 1967 essay "How Do We Recognize Structuralism?": "Language is the only thing that can properly be said to have structure." Foucault gave this notion a characteristically baroque spin: "Language exists," he wrote, "in the innumerable words spoken by men—whether they are reasonable or senseless, demonstrative or poetic—a meaning has taken shape that hangs over us, leading us forward in our blindness. . . . We are doomed historically to history, to the patient construction of discourses about discourses, and to the task of hearing what has already been said."

As with the trends that preceded it, though, the ascendency of the word in French intellectual life happened gradually, over a period of years. In retrospect, the key players and events are possible to discern, forming, as the structuralists themselves might have put it, a single signifying chain. Tracing the links in the chain backward—patiently hearing what has already been said—we soon arrive at Lacan, at a lecture he presented in the spring of 1955 on "The Purloined Letter," a short story by Edgar Allan Poe. The lecture is intricate and demanding, a bravura demonstration of Lacanian theory in peak structuralist mode.

Despite Lacan's Surrealist roots and love of wordplay, he rarely devoted entire lectures to literary subjects (James Joyce and *Hamlet* being notable exceptions late in his career). But Poe was a natural choice. A Francophile who set several of his stories in Paris during the French Restoration despite never having set foot in France, Poe was well known to French readers, thanks in large part to the poet Charles Baudelaire, who spent sixteen years translating and promoting his work. Moreover, the macabre obsessions of Poe's fiction had inevitably drawn the attention of psychoanalysts. In 1933, Princess Marie Bonaparte, a prominent French Freudian, had published a seven-hundred-page psychobiography of Poe, uncovering the effects on his writing of childhood trauma. (Poe's father had abandoned the family and his mother had died of tuberculosis, all before he turned three.) Bonaparte's name, wealth, and social connections granted her an outsize influence on her chosen field. She was a great grandniece of Napoleon and, through her marriage, an aunt to Prince Philip, the husband of Queen Elizabeth II. Most important, she had been analyzed by Freud himself. She had also translated Freud's work into French, helped found the first French psychoanalytic society, and financed Freud's escape from Nazi Vienna to London in 1938.

With good reason, then, Bonaparte considered herself to be Freud's designated representative in France. Not that the two agreed on everything. To Freud's horror, in an effort to cure a sexual frigidity that resisted even his ministrations, she twice underwent operations to move her clitoris closer to her vaginal opening. It was to Bonaparte that Freud directed his famous question "that has never been answered and which I have not yet been able to answer, despite my thirty years of research into the feminine soul": "What does a woman want?" (Bonaparte recorded the remark in her diary but not her response, if she gave one.) Though she engaged in some unorthodox practices of her own—sending her chauffeur to pick up her patients, whom she listened to in her garden while crocheting in a chaise longue—Bonaparte found little to admire in the perpetually insubordinate Lacan. He in turn regarded her with disdain.

Yet in performing a close reading of Poe, Lacan was up to far more than simply goading his nemesis. (He settled for mocking her in a footnote.) In his view, "The Purloined Letter" wasn't about Poe at all; it was about language. The context for Lacan's lecture was a yearlong seminar on Freud's *Beyond the Pleasure Principle*, in which Freud considered the repetition compulsion, the notion that our unconscious is primed to return again and again to a negative experience—in the form of a recurring nightmare, say—despite our attempts to repress it. Lacan's twist was to stress how unsuccessfully repressed material inevitably plays out in language. Words didn't merely represent symptoms; words *were* symptoms, and they behaved in predictable ways, according to the logic of the symbolic order. In Poe's story Lacan believed he had found an exemplary illustration of this process.

Published in 1844, "The Purloined Letter" was, along with "The Murders in the Rue Morgue" and "The Mystery of Marie Rogêt," the third in a series Poe called his "tales of ratiocination," a group often regarded as the first modern detective stories. Like the others, "The Purloined Letter" featured Poe's recurring cast of gentlemen crime busters: the hapless but dogged prefect of the Parisian police; the brilliant, eccentric Dupin (a proto–Sherlock Holmes); and Dupin's awed sidekick (his Watson), who narrates the tale. The story concerns a theft—the one announced in its title—with the befuddling twist that both the thief and the location of the stolen item are known from the outset. And yet the crime remains unsolved. Humiliated by this fact, the police prefect is obliged to seek Dupin's counsel.

Lacan zeroed in on two set pieces. The first, which he labeled in Freudian fashion "the primal scene," takes place in the "royal boudoir" and involves a group of three—that magic Oedipal number: the queen, the king, and a royal minister. The queen is reading a private letter in the boudoir when she is interrupted by the arrival first of the king and then of the minister. In her haste to conceal her letter, which, if discovered, we are told, would severely compromise her honor, the queen is forced to leave it face down on a table. There, it goes unnoticed by the king, but not by the minister, who, recognizing the handwriting on the address, immediately "fathoms her secret." As he reviews affairs of state with the royal couple, the minister stealthily places a similar letter of his own on the table. When, his business completed, he departs from the boudoir, he pockets the queen's letter, leaving his own in its place. The queen sees all this but is unable to protest without giving herself away.

Once in the minister's possession, the queen's letter becomes an instrument of blackmail: For months, the prefect tells Dupin that the minister has been wielding it "for political purposes." In desperation, the queen has enlisted the prefect to retrieve it. But despite searching every inch of the minister's office, where the letter is assumed to be hidden, his officers have failed to find it.

And so we come to Lacan's second key scene, which takes place in the minister's office and also involves a group of three. This time, however, the figures are the minister, Dupin, and—implicitly, Lacan says—the prefect of police, who has confided his failure to Dupin and sought his help. Accordingly, Dupin dons a pair of dark glasses and pays a visit to the minister on the pretense of making a social call. He engages the minister in small talk while at the same time, under cover of his tinted glasses, he conducts a visual inspection of the minister's office—the same office the police have searched twice to no avail. Immediately, Dupin spots the queen's letter: hiding in plain sight in a card rack that dangles from a ribbon below the mantelpiece.

Dupin returns to the minister's office the next day, on the excuse of having forgotten his snuffbox. This time he has arranged for a pistol to go off in the street below, and with the minister's attention diverted to the commotion outside his window, Dupin quickly claims the queen's letter from the card rack and replaces it with a worthless "facsimile." Once again, Dupin solves a mystery that has stymied the police, and to reclaim the queen's letter, the chagrined prefect is obliged to write Dupin a check for fifty thousand francs.

For Lacan, the story was further proof that "it is the symbolic order that is constitutive for the subject." In his reading, the "letter" of Poe's title is not only the epistolary kind: It is also an alphabetical letter—a linguistic notation. (In French, the word "*lettre*" has the same double meaning as "letter" in English.) The letter is what Lacan called "a pure signifier," a symbol detached from any specific meaning. After all, he pointed out, we never learn anything about the letter's content. Love letter? Compromising intelligence about the king? We don't know. What matters is that the letter travels along a symbolic circuit, or signifying chain, in a particular way. It changes hands, migrating from an unidentified sender to the queen, on to the minister, and then to Dupin, the prefect of police, and, eventually, back to the queen. The letter's movement is what directs the plot, Lacan argued, slotting the people whose paths it crosses into predictable arrangements and causing them to interact in predictable ways—without their ever being conscious of this process.

Arriving at this moment in his lecture, Lacan might have turned to the blackboard to diagram the tale. If he did, he would have drawn two triangles. When, in the preface to *Écrits*, his mammoth collection of writings, he praised Poe's fiction for being "so powerful in the mathematical sense of the term," it was "The Purloined Letter" he had in mind. As he explained in his lecture, the story's pivotal scenes form the same triangular structures, with the characters performing one of three roles determined by their relationship to the stolen letter. In each scene, there is: (1) a "blind" person, who sees nothing of what transpires; (2) a person who sees that the first person sees nothing but, unaware of being seen by a third person, "deludes himself as to the secrecy" of the letter he is hiding; and, finally, (3) "the robber," a person who sees everything and exploits this fact by stealing the poorly hidden letter.

In the scene in the boudoir, the king occupies the role of the blind person, the queen the role of the deluded hider who believes her secret is safe, and the minister the role of the all-seeing robber. In the scene in the minister's office, the cast changes and the roles rotate. Now the prefect of police (a surrogate for the queen) occupies the role of the blind person, searching the minister's apartment but failing to see the letter hidden in plain sight; the minister occupies the role of the deluded hider, mistakenly believing the letter he has stolen is safely concealed; and Dupin occupies the role of the robber, stealing the queen's letter out from under the minister's nose and, just as the minister did in the first scene, replacing it with a fake.

In Lacan's account, the story's logic is as tidy as a geometry proof and the implications of its comical merry-go-round crystal clear. He allowed himself a few rhetorical flourishes beyond his usual number to underscore the point: "The displacement of the signifier determines the subjects in their acts, in their destiny, in their refusals, in their blindnesses, in their end and in their fate, their innate gifts and social acquisitions notwithstanding,

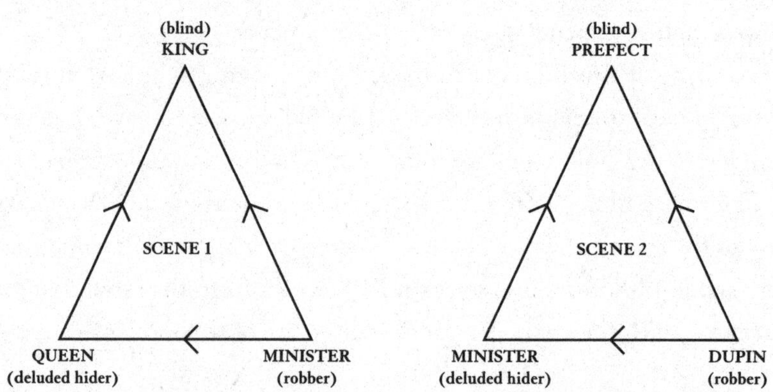

without regard for character or sex. . . . Falling in possession of the letter—admirable ambiguity of language—its meaning possesses them."

In Marie Bonaparte's analysis, the purloined letter is a physical object, a stand-in for the "missing maternal penis" and of Poe's longing for his dead mother. For Lacan, the letter is an abstraction—as the structuralists would put it, a signifier without a signified. It has no particular meaning, and yet as it migrates through the story it confers meaning, configuring the human beings who come into contact with it into particular roles in relation to it and one another. In this sense, Poe's tale was a ready-made allegory of the symbolic order, showing how language operated within a fixed structure and according to a fixed set of rules, and how it embedded human beings within its matrix, shaping our identities and behavior.

Lacan made his interpretation sound ridiculously obvious. Moreover, he implied that "The Purloined Letter" was also an account of a successful psychoanalysis, with Dupin in the role of the analyst, the queen as the (deluded) patient, and the missing letter as her symptom. In Lacanian theory, symptoms *were* words or, more precisely, words that had become trapped in the body. The analyst needn't try to ferret out his patient's unconscious secrets, Lacan said; he simply had to follow the chain of signifiers, or linguistic patterns, in their speech.

Following signifiers is an apt description of how he conducted his private practice. His Brazilian patient Betty Milan recounted a typical session during which she told Lacan about thinking she had seen an enormous rat that turned out to be a hallucination. "What?" he pressed. "A rat, *um rato*," she replied, inadvertently slipping into her native Portuguese. As she repeated the word, she writes, "the first syllable took on sudden importance" and she "made an unexpected association." "Ra," she told Lacan, was the first syllable of her father's name, Rachid, which she had trained herself never to say for fear of exposing her family's Lebanese immigrant roots; in Brazil, such an identity made them vulnerable to racism. Lacan immediately terminated the session.

"It was the name of the father, the object of a permanent denial, which had appeared in the hallucination," Milan wrote. "It had emerged in reality, and thanks to the cut, which obliged me to listen to myself, it was now impossible for me to deny my origins."

As Lacan triumphantly summed up this process in his lecture on Poe: "A letter always arrives at its destination." Never mind that he seemed to be wanting to have things both ways. On the one hand, Poe's tale was not *about* anything; it merely showed how language worked in the abstract. On the other, it was a tale *about* psychoanalysis, a concrete illustration of Lacan's professional practice. In this respect, the fifty thousand francs Dupin receives for his services in the tale might have seemed to Lacan only fitting—in keeping with his own handsome proceeds from patients.

Chapter 26

LÉVI-STRAUSS HEADS FOR THE JUNGLE

Lacan was so pleased with his lecture on "The Purloined Letter" that he chose to lead the otherwise chronological *Écrits* with it, "offering" it to the reader, he explained, "as an easy entryway into my style." Of course, "easy" is a relative concept. Let's be honest: Lacan's close reading of Poe was abstruse, relying on some specialized notions, the signifier and the signified primary among them. Borrowed from linguistics, these concepts play an outsize role in the structuralists' theories of language. Compared with the drama of the mirror stage, with its biblical overtones of cosmic creation, the signifier and the signified were a dry and technical business. Yet this was part of their appeal.

By the middle of the twentieth century, psychoanalysis was struggling to assert its legitimacy in a world where empirical science increasingly had the upper hand. (The migration of Lacan's seminar in 1964 from Sainte-Anne Hospital, the symbolic home of medical science, to the École Normale, the symbolic home of philosophy, seems indicative in this regard.) From radar, jet engines, and synthetic rubber to commercial antibiotics, color television, computers, satellites, and the atom bomb, scientific research and innovation in the wake of World War II were occurring at a breathtaking pace, with results that were transforming daily life.

How could psychoanalysis or philosophy compete with such concrete, verifiable achievement when what these fields had to offer were seemingly squishy theories and subjective claims? One solution was simply to declare that one's work *was* science, as Althusser did of his reading of Marx, and Lacan did of his reading of Freud.

At the same time, owing to a series of fortuitous encounters, the emerging structuralist dispensation got a boost from an unexpected source: linguistics. With its specialized vocabulary and technical account of how language made meaning, linguistics offered scholars in the humanities and social sciences a veneer of objectivity in which to dress their work. The structuralists' medium was language, but language, they argued, could be understood scientifically, with mathematical precision—in the case of Lacan, with math itself. Besides, they insisted, there was nothing *but* language. There was no realm of human experience language didn't touch—even physicists and engineers were beholden to it.

For their discovery of linguistics, the structuralists were indebted to a single man: the anthropologist Claude Lévi-Strauss—the next big link in our retrospective signifying chain. Lévi-Strauss had trained to be a philosopher, and in hindsight this may be the best description of what he was: a philosopher of human culture. Born in 1908, into a distinguished French-Jewish family with roots in Alsace, Lévi-Strauss grew up in Paris, where he completed one year of *khâgne* before opting not to apply to the École Normale. He enrolled at the Sorbonne instead, studying alongside Simone de Beauvoir and Maurice Merleau-Ponty. In 1931, he passed the philosophy *agrégation*. Like nearly everyone else in our story, Lévi-Strauss recalled the experience as one of inhuman ordeal and unexpected triumph. He spent the seven hours before the oral exam violently sick from a drug—morphine? cocaine? he never knew what, exactly—prescribed for his nerves by a doctor who was a family friend. "I appeared before the jury looking like death, without having been able to prepare a thing, and improvised a lecture that was considered brilliant, in which I believe I spoke of nothing but Spinoza," he said later. All these brainy nervous wrecks at the *agrégation*! It's tempting to see a correlation between degree of personal torment and future success: In the end, Lévi-Strauss, then only twenty-two, the youngest in his cohort, placed third. "Perhaps the drug had done its job, after all," he said with false modesty.

His conversion to anthropology began with an unexpected phone call in the fall of 1934. He was teaching philosophy at a lycée in Laon, in northeastern France—a coveted assignment since the town was within commuting distance of Paris. Even so, Lévi-Strauss was bored, a feeling that turned to dismay when he learned that he was expected to teach the same course year after year for the foreseeable future. (Sartre, who took the post in Laon a year and a half after Lévi-Strauss left it, also felt hamstrung by the rules, which he did his best to ignore. Reprimanded for missing a staff meeting he had assumed would be tedious, he got into a fistfight with a colleague in the faculty lounge.)

When the call came from a mentor encouraging Lévi-Strauss to apply for a job teaching anthropology at the brand-new University of São Paulo, in Brazil, he leapt at the chance. It was a "way of escape" from French academic routine—in particular from philosophy, a discipline he feared had lost touch with reality. "Philosophy was not *ancilla scientiarum*, the servant and auxiliary of scientific exploration, but a kind of aesthetic contemplation of consciousness by itself," he wrote years later in his elegant memoir *Tristes Tropiques*. "The signifier did not relate to any signified; there was no referent. Expertise replaced the truth."

Early in 1935, he sailed for Brazil, propelled by fantasies of "twisted palm trees concealing bizarrely designed kiosks and pavilions," and of air thick with "burning perfumes." He could not have predicted that his own work would supply French philosophy with the scientificity he reproached it for lacking—the reason he wanted to leave it behind.

Between 1935 and 1938, while teaching at the University of São Paulo, Lévi-Strauss made two expeditions into central Brazil. Armed with notebooks, typewriter, and a Leica camera, he spent several months with the Nambikwara, an Indigenous group that had had almost no

Claude Lévi-Strauss in Amazonia, Brazil, circa 1936

contact with Europeans. At first, he was shocked by the meagerness of the group's material culture. On a previous journey to visit other tribes, he had returned with a haul of more than six hundred artifacts, which he brought back to Paris, exhibited at an art gallery, and deposited at the Musée de l'Homme. By contrast, the Nambikwara seemed to make almost nothing: no pottery, no headdresses, no canoes, no intricate rituals. "Among the Indians of tropical America, to whom we owe the invention of the hammock," he wrote in *Tristes Tropiques*, "poverty is symbolized by the non-possession of this device, or of any other form of bed or bedding. The Nambikwara sleep naked on the ground."

But Lévi-Strauss gradually changed his mind. He came to see in the Nambikwara's pared-down existence a revelatory purity: Here was human society at its most elemental. The tribe's kinship and matrimony customs were starkly apparent, exposing a template that could perhaps be applied to other, more complex societies. In his notebook, he wrote almost wistfully of the Nambikwara's "immense kindness," their "profoundly carefree attitude," and a general outlook that struck him as "the most truthful and moving expression of human love."

Lévi-Strauss's time in the bush cemented his horror of racism. In France, his 1952 pamphlet "Race and History," arguing that differences among cultures are routinely mistaken for inequality among races, is considered a classic of anti-racist literature. But from a contemporary vantage point, his approach to fieldwork (not to mention indigenous artifacts) can seem to verge uncomfortably on the neocolonial. For one thing, he was not much for roughing it. As he confessed in the famous first sentence of *Tristes Tropiques*: "I hate travelling and explorers." For his trip to the Nambikwara, which lasted six months, including stops among two other Indigenous groups, he set out with thirty oxen, fifteen mules, three thousand kilos of food, hammocks, soap, toilet paper, medicine, and a doctor. The expedition ended up being his last.

Years later, a Brazilian anthropologist who had accompanied Lévi-Strauss on the trip was scornful of his timidity in the field, calling him "a philosopher among the Indians." (The Brazilian was more complimentary of Lévi-Strauss's wife, Dina Dreyfus, whom he called a "true" anthropologist. Unfortunately, Dina's trip was cut short by an eye infection that resulted in her evacuation, first to Paris, and soon after, from her marriage.) There's no question that by the time Lévi-Strauss's first major book, *The Elementary Structures of Kinship*, finally appeared in 1949, he had spent innumerably more hours in the library reading about Indigenous groups than he had in the field living among them.

A birdlike, bespectacled intellectual, he was drawn to big abstract ideas, not local observations. His gift was for the grand synthesis. As a perceptive teacher noted during Lévi-Strauss's single year of *khâgne*: "Knows a lot. A fine, penetrating mind. But these qualities are often spoiled by a rigor that is, as a rule, almost sectarian, assertion of absolute, black-and-white theses." Then, too, World War II played a determining role, upending his life just as it had those of Sartre, Althusser, and Derrida. The war propelled Lévi-Strauss to New York City and into the now-defunct Americana reading room at the New York Public Library. There he discovered a vast, undigested ethnographic literature on the Indians of

North America. And, in a second serendipity with historic repercussions, he met the Russian linguist who would help him make sense of all the research—while providing the future structuralist movement with its essential paradigm. French structuralism, it's not an exaggeration to say, was born in America.

Chapter 27

A TUTORIAL IN STRUCTURAL LINGUISTICS

No sooner had Lévi-Strauss returned to France from Brazil in 1939, hoping to launch a career as an anthropologist, than the country began mobilizing for war. He was called up to serve as a liaison agent near the Maginot Line but saw no combat before France surrendered to the Germans. Assigned to teach philosophy at a lycée in Paris during the Occupation, he approached an official in Vichy for permission to travel to the capital. "With a name like yours, to Paris?" the official replied. "You can't be serious!" Lévi-Strauss understood that his best bet for surviving the Nazis was to get the hell out of Europe.

In March 1941, he embarked from Marseilles on a ship bound for Martinique, with an invitation to teach anthropology at the New School in New York City. The boat had three hundred and fifty passengers but just two cabins—a total of seven bunks. Somehow, Lévi-Strauss managed to snag one. Striding up and down the deck one day, he recognized André Breton, who keeps popping up in our story as if in a game of Whac-A-Mole, or, perhaps more fitting, as an unconscious symptom, disrupting the orderly procession of the signifying chain with his insistence on unreason and nonsense. Wrapped in a heavy wool coat, he looked to

Lévi-Strauss like a blue bear, "very much out of place *dans cette galère*"—in the chaos. During a stop at Casablanca, the anthropologist introduced himself to the Surrealist, and the two passed the remainder of the voyage exchanging letters on art, beauty, and other lofty themes.

Both men eventually arrived in Manhattan. (Lévi-Strauss was briefly detained in Puerto Rico when American customs officials mistook his Native language vocabulary lists and German bibliographic notes for coded, possibly seditious, messages.) And both ended up living on the same street in Greenwich Village—West 11th. Breton tried, with limited success, to reassemble his Surrealist troops in exile, and Lévi-Strauss gamely hung out with the group, playing tarot cards and charades with the artists Yves Tanguy, Max Ernst, and Marcel Duchamp. Like Lacan before him, he even contributed an article—on face-painting by a Brazilian tribe—to a Surrealist journal, a new one that Breton was trying to launch in New York.

But Lévi-Strauss's heart wasn't in Surrealism. Like Foucault, he organized his days around long stints at the library. What he found there enthralled and flummoxed him: "a mass of documents," the whole "in such disarray that one didn't know where to begin or how to utilize it." Back at his studio on West 11th Street, he painstakingly plotted the kinship patterns of various Indigenous peoples onto sheets of paper, determined to find a way to synthesize the material. Consultations with mathematicians, including Simone Weil's brother, the number theorist André Weil, failed to solve his dilemma, even if the mathematicians were intrigued by the exercise. About one numbers specialist, Lévi-Strauss wrote, "This flirtation with the savages has got him all excited as if he was doing crossword puzzles or solving a murder mystery."

The breakthrough came in the spring of 1942, when Lévi-Strauss was introduced to the linguist Roman Jakobson. Both men had been recruited to teach at the brand-new École libre des hautes études, in Greenwich Village, a makeshift French university in exile financed in part by the Free French government in London. Jakobson, a peripatetic Russian-born Jew, had crisscrossed Europe before the war and spoke more than half a dozen languages. At their first meeting, he dazzled Lévi-Strauss with a crash course in structural linguistics.

The Swiss linguist Ferdinand de Saussure

Formulated at the turn of the twentieth century by the Swiss linguist Ferdinand de Saussure, the principles of structural linguistics were largely derived from a collection of Saussure's lectures published by his students in 1916, three years after his death. A major component of Saussure's teaching was his theory of the sign. Philosophers as far back as Plato's day had debated the relationship between words and things. Saussure declared that the relationship between the two was entirely arbitrary and made this claim the centerpiece of his theory.

Saussure was teaching linguistics at the University of Geneva at about the same time that Husserl was teaching phenomenology at the University of Freiburg. But where the German philosopher bracketed off reality as beyond the scope of human experience, Saussure understood reality as, practically speaking, a product of language, or at least thoroughly mediated by it. When we refer to objects in the world, the names we use—Saussure called them "signs"—are purely a matter of convention. A given sign had no intrinsic meaning; it had value only in so far as it could be distinguished from other signs within the same language system. On this point, he was insistent: Language wasn't a *referential* system; it was a *relational* one. "Everything is based on relations," is how he put it.

Different language systems carved up the world in different ways. The French word *mouton* can be translated into English as *sheep*, Saussure offered by way of example, but these two words aren't equivalent, because in French *mouton* can mean either the animal or its meat, while in English *sheep* refers only to the animal. (For the meat, we have *mutton.*) A sign only acquires value within the context of the system as a whole.

Moreover, signs concealed more arbitrariness within them. Each was made up of two parts: a signifier, or sound image (the written or spoken word *sheep*, say), and a signified, or mental concept (in this case, that of a small woolly ruminant). But these two parts "have nothing in common in essence," Saussure said. There is nothing inherently sheeplike about the letters s-h-e-e-p. Like signs themselves, signifiers have value only in so far as they differ from other signifiers: *Sheep* is different from *steep*, *sleep*, *sheer*, *sheen*, *shell*, and a slew of other words that vary by one or two letters. Once conjoined in the sign, however, the signifier and the signified are inseparable, like the front and back of a "sheet of paper." "Sheep," an arbitrary designation for a bleating four-legged creature, seems entirely natural and preordained.

Saussure is most famous for his theory of the sign, but his work encompassed all aspects of language. He distinguished between *diachronic* and *synchronic* approaches to linguistics, for example, emphasizing the latter (the study of language as an abstract system of rules) over the former (the study of language evolution over time, the traditional approach). And he postulated a horizontal *syntagmatic* axis, based on the principle of combination (words associated sequentially, such as within this sentence) and a vertical *paradigmatic* axis, based on the principle of selection (words associated by similarity, or their ability to substitute for one another). Lacan would later transpose Saussure's linguistic axes to psychoanalysis (finding equivalences in Freud's concepts of displacement and condensation), and literary critics would do the same in their field (finding equivalences in figures of speech such as metaphor and metonymy). But we don't need to get so technical. What's important is that Saussure provided a compelling account of language's key properties that was true for all cultures and tongues. His was a grand theory of meaning-making distilled to a system, a set of rules, and a series of neat binary oppositions: signifier/signified, diachronic/synchronic, syntagmatic/paradigmatic, etc. It was just the kind of template that Lévi-Strauss thought he needed to make sense of human social organization.

◆ ◆ ◆

Emerging from his tutorial with Jakobson, Lévi-Strauss felt he had grasped something extraordinary. Language operated according to laws that were both universal and largely unconscious, giving human social existence shape and meaning. And yet language was also infinitely rich, able to contain all of human experience thanks to the way its various elements could be associated or combined to generate sense. Saussure hadn't used the term "structure" to describe how language worked, but Jakobson frequently did. "At the time, I was a kind of naïve structuralist, a structuralist without knowing it," Lévi-Strauss said later. "Jakobson revealed to me the existence of a body of doctrine that had already been formed within a discipline, linguistics, with which I was unacquainted. For me it was a revelation."

For a few years, Lévi-Strauss nursed his revelation in private. Intent on isolating the underlying patterns in the hundreds of ethnographic studies he'd read at the library, he, too, undertook an act of transposition, reimagining relations among social groups according to Saussurean principles. At the time, anthropology was particularly focused on a few topics: gift-exchange rituals, the incest prohibition, and kinship and genealogy, with ethnographers dutifully recording who married whom and how group members were related. Lévi-Strauss painstakingly knitted these themes together, giving them a novel twist. At the center of his theory were women. Kinship customs were predicated on marriage rules, which in turn revolved around the exchange of women. In his schema, the incest prohibition existed not for negative biological reasons—to prevent a brother from marrying his sister—but for positive social ones: to compel the brother to exchange his sister for a woman from another group. By exchanging women, families fostered blood-tie connections that bound them together in larger groups and enhanced their chances of survival.

In this way, Lévi-Strauss turned the field of anthropology upside down. The incest prohibition was held to be a universal phenomenon—a product of nature. But here was Lévi-Strauss insisting that, to the contrary, the incest prohibition was just as much a product of culture, an effect of social norms guiding the exchange of women. In his view, the exchange of women marked humanity's transition from nature to culture. It seemed to him only logical that kinship systems should function much the way Saussure said language did. After all, kinship systems were by definition relational. Just as linguistic signs circulated according to the rules of syntax and grammar, acquiring value through their relations to other signs, so women acquired value as objects of exchange according to the mostly unspoken rules of social alliance.

Women served as "gifts" that men offered one another, ensuring that whenever a brother gave away a sister, he earned a wife in return. Kinship systems varied in their details, but they all obeyed the laws of a universal kinship grammar. "Although they belong to *another order of reality*," Lévi-Strauss wrote, "kinship phenomena are *of the same type* as linguistic phenomena." A few years later, he would apply the same framework to his analysis of myths across Indigenous cultures, coining the term "mytheme" to represent a myth's smallest unit of meaning. Human social organization, he believed, was based not on biological or sexual imperatives, but on the same arbitrary, if unconscious, conventions as language.

This was the bold theory at the heart of *The Elementary Structures of Kinship,* a book otherwise so technical that had it not been for a few fortuitously placed reviews by prominent intellectuals, its influence might never have extended much beyond the discipline of anthropology. Encompassing granular discussions of tribes on five continents, along with elaborate charts and diagrams of alliance patterns, as well as an appendix by André Weil showing how a particularly intricate set of Aboriginal marriage laws could be "interpreted algebraically," the book was clearly not intended for the general reader.

Lévi-Strauss returned to Paris from New York in the fall of 1947. He submitted his manuscript to the Sorbonne as the major thesis for his doctoral degree the following June, when he defended it before a skeptical jury. A scholar in the audience that day jotted down comments by the jury's president, a sociologist who was also dean of the Sorbonne. "A monumental work, the work of a philosopher—but why systematize so furiously?" the dean grumbled. "Like Descartes you begin with self-evident truth, but unlike Descartes, your self-evident truth is neither clear nor self-evident." Despite these doubts, after more than five hours of discussion, Lévi-Strauss was awarded high honors.

In June 1949, *The Elementary Structures of Kinship* was published in a small print run by an academic press. Alerted in advance by a mutual friend, Simone de Beauvoir, who was just completing her work on *The Second Sex*, asked Lévi-Strauss whether she could see a copy. She ended up reading the galley proofs at his apartment. (Lévi-Strauss was evidently more gracious than Lacan had been when Beauvoir asked to speak with him about the mirror stage.) *The Second Sex* appeared that May and, unlike Lévi-Strauss's book, was an immediate sensation, selling more than twenty-two thousand copies in a week. Still, Beauvoir gave Lévi-Strauss's career a big boost later that year when she published a rave review of *The Elementary Structures of Kinship* in *Les Temps Modernes*. Calling the book "a major event," she declared that Lévi-Strauss had unraveled "the mystery of society as a whole," comparing him to a young Karl Marx. "*Il faut la lire*," she wrote in conclusion. *It must be read.*

Beauvoir didn't mention structural linguistics. Neither did Georges Bataille, who reviewed the book in his journal, *Critique*. He also had mainly nice things to say. But he was disappointed that Lévi-Strauss, in reducing kinship systems to a dreary mathematical formalism, had "paid so little attention to the bearing of eroticism on the potlatch"—gift-giving—"of women." As it is, Bataille complained, the anthropologist's discussion of marriage rules "goes on and on and alas, it is desperately tedious."

◆ ◆ ◆

The year 1949 was also when Lévi-Strauss met Lacan. They bonded at a dinner party over their shared love of art and became close friends. Lacan even bought part of a collection of Indian artifacts that Lévi-Strauss, strapped for cash after separating from his second wife, Rose Marie Ullmo, was obliged to sell. It was at another dinner party at Lacan's house that Lévi-Strauss met the woman who would become his third wife, Monique Roman. (Like Lacan, Lévi-Strauss was an active participant in the Parisian social circuits that facilitated the exchange of women.) The friendship between the two men lasted a decade, until the pressures of their respective celebrity pulled them apart. Recalling their relationship years later, Lévi-Strauss, unsurprisingly, cited a road trip in Lacan's car—a brand-new one that the analyst had been itching to drive. Lévi-Strauss's other memory of the trip was equally characteristic: the travelers arriving at "a shabby provincial hotel" and Lacan "in his most regal manner ordering that his bath be run that very instant."

Intellectually, the pair had much in common: a fascination with symbols and mathematical formulas; a belief that human existence was profoundly shaped by universal if unconscious structures; a general skepticism toward traditional approaches to history (or at least a marked preference for the Saussurean synchronic over the diachronic); and finally, a desire for their work to be regarded as science. Some scholars have pushed the congruences further still, finding in Lévi-Strauss's writings on Indigenous tribes—the West's cultural "Other"—an analogy for Lacan's theory of identity formation: the "Other" in the mirror that both is and is not us. But Lévi-Strauss did not see things this way. A close reader of Freud from his days at the *lycée* in the 1920s, he had no patience for Lacan's convolutions. "I always had the impression that, to his fervent admirers, 'understand' meant something different from what it meant to me," he confessed. "I'd have had to read everything five or six times. Merleau-Ponty and I used to talk about it and concluded that we didn't have time."

For Lacan, however, the friendship was transformative. He began citing the anthropologist in his talks from virtually the moment they met. In 1950, Lévi-Strauss introduced Lacan to Roman Jakobson, who soon began making guest appearances at Lacan's seminar. By the early 1950s, Lacan had incorporated into his lectures an expansive structuralist lexicon of grids, rules, signifiers, and signs. "The primordial Law is therefore the Law which, in regulating marriage ties, superimposes the reign of culture over the reign of nature," he declared in 1953, in a baroque seventy-page manifesto outlining his structuralist approach to Freud. "Marriage ties are governed by an order of preference whose law concerning the kinship names is, like language, imperative for the group in its forms, but unconscious in its structure. Now, in this structure, whose harmony or conflicts govern the restricted or generalized exchange discerned in it by ethnologists, the startled theoretician refinds the whole logic of combinations."

The passage doesn't read much better in French, but Lacan was essentially parroting Lévi-Strauss: We are molded, individually and collectively, by rules that have nothing to do with nature and everything to do with culture. He later clarified that it wasn't women per se that men exchange in marriage, but rather women as signifiers of the phallus, just as the Oedipus complex wasn't about the desire of young boys literally to sleep with their mothers but, rather, about their desire to be what their mothers lacked and most desired: the phallus. "Lacan's encounter with the thought of Lévi-Strauss meant he had at last found a theoretical solution to the problem of how to make a complete overhaul of Freudian doctrine," Roudinesco writes. Where Freud had tried to ground his theory of the mind in biology, even Darwinian evolution, Lacan posited a human subject who, mirror stage aside, was largely a creation of timeless and impersonal symbolic forces.

As the vanguard of the new structuralist linguistics, Lévi-Strauss and

Lacan were impossible to ignore. Looking back on this period in an interview a decade later, Foucault summed up the thinkers' appeal to a generation disenchanted with existentialism and its emphasis on freedom and choice. Sartre believed "there was *meaning* everywhere," Foucault scoffed. He pinpointed the moment he had ceased to accept that message: "The break came the day that Lévi-Strauss demonstrated—about societies—and Lacan demonstrated—about the unconscious—that 'meaning' was probably only a sort of surface effect, a shimmer, a foam, and that what ran through us, underlay us, and was before us, what sustained us in time and space, was the system."

By the time Lacan delivered his lecture on "The Purloined Letter," he'd scrubbed his work of any residue of biology or Darwin. There were no more references to developmental stages or comparisons of humans to other species. And there were fewer and fewer allusions to the world of things. Lacan had abandoned Earth for the theoretical firmament. Henceforth, he would devote himself to untangling the laws of the unconscious and its signifying chains, those "links by which a necklace firmly hooks onto a link of another necklace made of links." By the mid-1960s, Lacan's former analyst Rudolph Loewenstein was writing to a colleague in exasperation about his onetime patient: "He shows penetrating imagination in pursuit of the signifier but has no interest in the signified. With this defect, no scientific discourse, aspiring to be a branch of knowledge, can claim to be complete. And so when I read his work I can't help thinking, 'Words, words, words.'"

Chapter 28

BARTHES DISMANTLES THE DOXA

Words, words, words, indeed. You'd be hard pressed to come up with a better slogan for the decade. When Tony Judt wrote of "the disproportionate amount of intellectual time in France devoted to the Word, the structuralist wave is what he meant: "The intoxication with the power of the spoken and written word (notably the abstract noun) took off into the stratosphere with the discovery by Saussure (discovered anew in the 1960s) that language itself can be an infinitely renewed subject of investigation for those who live by deploying it." In Paris, rumor had it that merely adding "structuralist" to a book title could turbocharge sales. In short, Saussurean linguistics was proving thrillingly elastic, claiming among its natural acolytes not only Marxists (Althusser), psychoanalysts (Lacan), and historians (Foucault), but also, with new prestige, literary critics and theorists. Of this last group, no one embodied the linguistic turn in French philosophy with greater facility and panache than Roland Barthes.

Barthes made Saussurean linguistics look not just easy but fun, a kind of game. Words weren't the only signs, he pointed out. Food, furniture, clothing, buildings, photos, gestures, music—the entire universe of objects, sights, and sounds all belonged to "the vast field of signifying media." Like his structuralist peers, Barthes regarded signs with suspicion. He devoted much ink to dismantling what he called the "doxa"—received opinion, stereotypes, ideas so commonplace they went unquestioned and unremarked. The doxa was for Barthes what ideology was for Althusser, a force both ubiquitous and insidious, but for Barthes it seemed almost a living, breathing presence. He compared the doxa to "Medusa"—"a gelatinous mass which sticks onto the retina." The doxa coated words and images in a sheen of naturalness, smoothing over their relationship to history and politics, bathing them in the false glow of eternal verity.

It was the job of the semiologist—a term Barthes helped popularize—to expose the doxa for the seductive fiction it was. To do so required scrutinizing signs, breaking them down into their component parts, showing how ideologically charged signifieds became attached to innocent (meaningless) signifiers to yield images of "petit bourgeois culture" that seemed timeless and universal.

Barthes's breakout book, *Mythologies* (1957), a collection of short essays originally published in mainstream monthlies, was a stylish demonstration of such analyses across a formidable range of cultural phenomena. He briskly tackled wrestling, cleaning products, steak frites, Billy Graham, Greta Garbo's face, and the brand-new, sleekly engineered Citroën DS (the letters "DS" in French being a play on the word "*déesse*," or "goddess"). "Cars today are almost the exact equivalent of the great Gothic cathedrals," Barthes wrote, "the supreme creation of an era, conceived with passion by unknown artists, and consumed in image if not in usage by a whole population which appropriates them as a purely magical object."

"I resented seeing Nature and History confused at every turn," he explained, "and I wanted to track down, in the decorative display of *what-goes-without-saying*, the ideological abuse which, in my view, is hidden there." These sound like fighting words. In truth, Barthes was no militant. His dismantling of mass culture was a labor of love; he adored signs in all their forms and enjoyed little more than thinking about the magical uses to which they were put. "One felt that he could generate ideas

The Citroën DS, 1955

about anything," his friend Susan Sontag wrote. "Put him in front of a cigar box and he would have one, two, many ideas—a little essay." Whatever the immediate inspiration before him, his thoughts would invariably circle back to language, his great subject. "I have a disease," he wrote. "I *see* language."

Barthes's evident joy in his work may be what made him in the end a fickle structuralist, at odds with the movement's rigorous antihumanism. In Philippe Sollers's novel *Women*, the narrator says of the Barthes character: "Jean Werth was a humanist, and it wasn't a time for humanism." If "doxa" was a recurring word in his lexicon, so, too, was "pleasure." One of his books was called, without irony, *The Pleasure of the Text*. In yet another, he declared: "Nothing is more depressing than to imagine the Text as an intellectual object (for reflection, analysis, comparison, mirroring, etc.). The text is an object of pleasure." In 1946, when he was thirty, he wrote in a letter to a friend, "*Happiness* is perhaps what I understand best in the world."

How many of our French philosophers could say such a thing? Unlike Foucault and Derrida, Barthes was never suicidal. Unlike Althusser and Lacan, he didn't worry about going mad. Yet when Barthes wrote to his friend about happiness, he was confined to a sanatorium in Switzerland, recovering from a pneumothorax. This gruesome procedure, which involved surgically collapsing a tubercular lung to allow it to rest and heal, was performed in cases of severe disease before the advent of targeted antibiotics. It makes an appearance early in Thomas Mann's *The Magic Mountain*, when Hans Castorp, newly arrived at his cousin's sanatorium in Davos, is alarmed to hear whistling sounds emerge from the chest of a young woman as she walks by. "Oh!" his cousin says, laughing at Castorp's horrified face. "That was Hermine Kleefeld, she whistles with her pneumothorax."

Barthes underwent the procedure twice, once in 1941 and again in 1945, and spent most of World War II in sanatoriums, where he was subjected to therapies that sound nearly as terrible as his illness. For three months in 1943, he was given a "reclining cure," which, his biographer Tiphaine Samoyault writes, required him to "lie at an angle to the horizontal for eighteen hours out of twenty-four, his lower limbs raised above the level of his thorax and his head, which made it difficult even to read."

Samoyault maintains that "tuberculosis was incontestably the major event of his life." Given his experience with the disease, is it any wonder he was drawn not just to literary pursuits but to a philosophy that conceived of history and human beings largely as discursive effects? If structuralism seemed intuitive for Barthes, it may have been in part because it provided a means of escape from life in a physical straitjacket. His career was given over to reading and writing, and his preferred form of the latter was the fragment. He kept notes on index cards—at his death he had amassed more than twelve thousand—and his books are typically organized in short, loosely connected chunks. His autobiography, *Roland Barthes by Roland Barthes*, published three years before he died, takes literally the structuralist idea of the self as a linguistic construction, treating "Roland Barthes" as a series of disjointed fragments—a text to be deciphered.

Both he and Sartre had in common fathers who were officers in the French Navy and who had died when their sons were infants. In Barthes's case, the result was an unshakable attachment to his mother—by far the most important relationship of his life. When, in 1948, he began his first real job, a yearlong stint as the librarian at the French Institute in Bucharest, his mother accompanied him to Romania. When, twenty-two years later, he took a position teaching literature at the University of Rabat, she went along to Morocco. During the intervening decades, they lived together in Paris and vacationed together in the South of France. "No father to kill, no family to hate, no milieu to reject," Barthes wrote gleefully. "Great Oedipal frustration!" His mother's death, three years before his own, left him completely bereft.

◆ ◆ ◆

Barthes's life was not an adventure story," Samoyault says, with what can only be wry understatement. Physically, too, Barthes was unprepossessing. He was tall, dark, and slim (though prone to a potbelly and, as a consequence, frequent dieting), with a large, expressive face whose blunt features—wide mouth; long, slanted nose; bushy brows—gave him a vaguely humorous appearance, like a cartoon drawing of a face.

Yet he inspired adulation—a response immortalized in at least half a dozen novels in which he figures as a character. In Laurent Binet's 2015 satirical thriller, *The Seventh Function of Language*, a bestseller in France, Barthes's fatal collision with the laundry van is no accident but, rather, an attempt at assassination. Barthes in this conceit is a literary critic of towering reputation, a grieving mama's boy with "sad spaniel eyes," who has come into possession of a secret manuscript by Roman Jakobson detailing a hitherto unknown linguistic "function." Here, too, Binet was playing off real life: Jakobson's famous theory that language could be divided into six functions ("referential," "emotive," "poetic," and so forth), several of which are combined in a typical speech act or communication. In an ingenious twist, Binet, taking literally the structuralist insistence on language's omnipotence, conjures a seventh ("performative") function, more formidable than all the rest: Whoever masters it is able "to convince anyone to do anything in any circumstances." Word of Jakobson's manuscript has leaked, and various parties—the Soviets and the Japanese, the

Roland Barthes in 1979

French president Giscard d'Estaing, his rival the Socialist candidate François Mitterrand, and the married critics Philippe Sollers and Julia Kristeva—are all trying to steal it for their own use.

On the notorious day in February 1980 when Barthes is hit by the van, he has just come from lunch at Mitterrand's home (this much is true), where (and now we're back in the realm of fiction) he solemnly informs the candidate and his advisers that "the real power is language." While Barthes, unsuspecting, slurps his fish stew, the manuscript is stealthily removed from his jacket pocket and—shades of Poe!—replaced with a fake hurriedly composed by Derrida, who is lurking in another room. But by the time, days later, the injured Barthes expires decorously in his hospital bed, the fake manuscript has disappeared, leaving a bewildered police investigator and his semiologist sidekick struggling to unravel the rapidly multiplying subplots.

The novel is peppered with allusions to French philosophy and inside jokes—secret agents driving a Citroën DS, a college band called "Anti-Oedipus," an academic lecture titled "Stayin' Alive, Structurally Speaking," a sickly little man with a frog-like face glimpsed "squinting through thick glasses" at the Café de Flore. Even Althusser's murderous act gets incorporated into the storyline. He is one of two characters (the other a gigolo) to whom Barthes has entrusted copies of Jakobson's secret manuscript. Althusser—more shades of Poe!—hides his copy inside an envelope of junk mail lying in plain sight on his desk, where his wife finds it and throws it out with the trash. In a fit of pique, the philosopher accidentally strangles her.

The book ends in 1981, with the French Socialists' historic victory: When Mitterrand trounces Giscard in the presidential debates and goes on to win the election, it's clear he owes his "*abnormally* good" rhetorical skills to the secret seventh function. This leaves Barthes's gigolo as the only other possessor of the manuscript. He, it turns out, has been in New York, taking classes at Columbia University, where he's met a talented American student—"a black guy from Hawaii." "I have a feeling he can go far, if I help him," the gigolo confides to the semiologist back in Paris. "I think I can make him a senator."

By the time Binet wrote his Barthes novel, Julia Kristeva had long since written hers. In *The Samurai* (1990), a steamy, cerebral roman à clef about Paris in the 1960s, Barthes is Armand Bréhal, a celebrated literary scholar with a nose "like a can opener." Kristeva's alter-ego protagonist, Olga, is barely off the plane from an unnamed Slavic country that sounds a lot like Kristeva's native Bulgaria, when she is whisked by Ivan, a friend from back home, to a Chinese restaurant and given the rundown on the Parisian intellectual scene. "Do you know the word?" Ivan says breathlessly. "I go to Armand Bréhal's seminars at the École d'Études Supérieures—he's the neatest prof there is, an artist in concepts."

Clued in by Ivan, Olga shows up at Bréhal's seminar and is immediately hooked. "You felt you were becoming *someone* just by listening to Bréhal," she reflects. She is captivated by his "slow, lascivious vibrato," by his ability to weave "individual vagaries into a tolerance so perfectly expressed it resembled rhapsody." The lecture hall is so crowded that Olga is forced to listen from the corridor. "I've never heard anyone so irresistible," the young woman next to her confides, straining on tiptoes to catch a glimpse of the master. "I think I'm in love with him."

In fact, Barthes was gay, a detail he kept from his mother, but despite the prejudices of his day he was remarkably equanimous. He was gentle and sociable, temperamentally conflict-averse: a man with many friends who, a rarity among our theorists, didn't engage in acid takedowns of his peers. For a decade beginning in the mid-1950s, he and Foucault were close—two intellectual iconoclasts pursuing subjects and methods that put them outside the academic mainstream. When both were in Paris, they would often hang out at night, meeting for drinks followed by cruising at gay bars and clubs. Some say they were occasional lovers. Together, they took trips to Marrakesh and Tangiers, where, according to some reports, they sought out minors for encounters that would certainly not be legal or tolerated today. (In 2021, a French author went public with the most detailed allegations to date, claiming in a book and in interviews with the press, that he had witnessed Foucault in Tunis in the late 1960s solicit sex from boys as young as eight, whom he would meet for nocturnal trysts in a local cemetery.) The friendship between Barthes and Foucault cooled only when Foucault, who was a decade younger, moved in with his partner, Daniel Defert, and became caught up in France's post-1960s political turmoil.

Barthes never formed a similar partnership, but his heart was broken at least once, by a young Romanian-born doctor who rebuffed his advances. Devastated, Barthes resolved to undergo an analysis with Lacan. He lasted three sessions before he quit, dismissing the encounters as "an old fool with an old fogey." Yet the experience of being rejected inspired what may be Barthes's most popular book, *Fragments d'un discours amoureux (A Lover's Discourse: Fragments)*, from 1977.

Of all the works of theory my classmates and I read in the late 1980s and '90s, *A Lover's Discourse* is one of the few that invited sentimental attachment, retaining, according to my informal survey, a place on bookshelves decades later. And no wonder: Here was a theorist—a structuralist, no less!—moping about his love life, giving voice to raw human feelings. A series of brief meditations organized alphabetically by topic and buttressed by literary allusions from Goethe to Gide, *A Lover's Discourse* is a wry, plaintive, and, as Barthes says, structural autobiography of heartbreak. As college kids well-versed in its subject matter, we understood ourselves to be its target audience. We certainly didn't need a professor to explain it.

A prefatory note sets the tone: "The necessity for this book is to be found in the following consideration: that the lover's discourse is today of *an extreme solitude.*" A typical passage, titled "Crying," draws heavily on Goethe's classic tale of unrequited love, *The Sorrows of Young Werther*: "By weeping, I want to impress someone, to bring pressure to bear upon someone ('Look what you have done to me')." The book forms a kind of running joke in *The Marriage Plot*, whose sensitive, novel-reading heroine, Madeleine, identifies with Barthes's romantic melancholy and carries a copy around with her on campus. Her heart soars when Leonard, a boy she meets in Semiotics 211 and falls hard for, retrieves the book from her bag and hands it to her, open to a passage headed:

> **I Love You**
>
> *Je-t'aime/I-love-you*
>
> The figure refers not to the declaration of love, to the avowal, but to the repeated utterance of the love cry.

But then Leonard gestures for her to keep reading, and her eyes fall on these devastating words: "Once the first avowal has been made, '*I love you*' has no meaning whatsoever."

My friend Lucinda, a fellow survivor of the high theory 1990s and now a novelist who often writes about romantic relationships, chose a line from *A Lover's Discourse* as the epigraph for a short story. In retrospect, she speculated, the book's cultish appeal "wasn't just the subject matter—everyone loves reading about sex!—but the nihilism and hopelessness on display. Some of the best love-is-a-misery lines appear to have been lifted straight from a Smiths song."

Heartbreak aside, Barthes was generally methodical and even-keeled, never indulging in the kind of manic displays to which Lacan or Guattari, say, were prone. In a lecture he delivered a few months before he died, he described dividing his day into four parts: "the part for Basic Needs: eating, sleeping, washing"; the "part for creative Labor (the book)";

the "part for Administration: letter-writing, manuscripts, *writings*, the inevitable interviews, proof corrections, shopping (hairdresser's!), private views and friends' films"; and, finally, the part for "Sociality, Conviviality, Friendship." According to his tally, during any twenty-four-hour period, he devoted ten hours to basic needs, five to creative work, five to administration, and four to socializing—a formula evidently conducive to contentment.

Still, his mother's death in 1977 was a blow from which he never recovered, a reordering of his life on par with his wartime battle with tuberculosis in the sanatorium. Some say that after his mother died, Barthes lost the will to live. "Werth was at the end of his tether," Sollers writes of the Barthes character in *Women*. "Everything bored, wearied, and disgusted him more and more." After he was hit by the laundry van in February 1980, his lung trouble came roaring back. He was taken to the hospital and never left, ultimately succumbing to an infection.

Chapter 29

THE DEATH OF THE AUTHOR

Barthes's youthful battle with tuberculosis may have curtailed an adult appetite for adventure; he remained a mama's boy and a homebody. But it did have one clear life-altering consequence: It effectively locked him out of the École Normale—TB patients were barred from applying—and a prestigious academic career. He attended the Sorbonne, earning a degree in classics, and with Foucault's help in 1976, when he was sixty, he was finally elected to the Collège de France—the nation's Mount Olympus for scholars, established in 1530 by royal decree. But he spent most of the previous quarter century conducting an intimate seminar at the comparatively peripheral École Pratique des Hautes Études.

When Barthes captured the public eye with the pieces collected in *Mythologies*, he seemed to have sprung from nowhere fully formed, floating effortlessly to the fore on the new currents sweeping the French intelligentsia. It helped that he was prolific: Between the mid-1950s and mid-1960s, he wrote more than eighty articles in twenty-two journals, including a monthly theater column for *France Observateur*. Even so, it took him a while to hit his stride. His first book, *Le Degré zéro de l'écriture (Writing Degree Zero)*, from 1953, was a more or less straightforward work of Marxist literary criticism. In it, he traced a centuries-long, oppressive reign of "bourgeois writing" to a moment in the twentieth century when such writing gave way to a proliferation of styles and authors, like Albert

Camus and Maurice Blanchot, who, in a noble but doomed effort to escape politics and history, embraced a neutral, or "zero-degree," anti-style. Even the ever-loyal Susan Sontag, in a preface to the American edition, had to admit that the book "gives virtually no indication of Barthes' sensitivity and imaginativeness in handling individual literary texts" or "the witty concreteness" of his thought.

Four years later, as *Mythologies* was released, Barthes, now high on Saussurean theory, began work on a book about fashion as a sign system. He saw the project as a possible dissertation—and ticket to academic respectability—and he hoped that Lévi-Strauss might serve as his adviser. In January 1960, with a friend waiting nervously in a bistro nearby, Barthes went to the anthropologist's apartment to discuss the matter. The meeting did not go well. For reasons that aren't clear, Lévi-Strauss declined to direct the thesis.

Perhaps, Barthes's biographer suggests, Lévi-Strauss saw him as "one of the modish structuralists rather than as a serious scholar." Where the anthropologist was uncovering the grand rules of social organization, the semiologist was demystifying the sign systems of the dominant class, an activity Lévi-Strauss apparently considered of trivial value. In 1966, when Barthes sent him a copy of an essay he'd just published, Lévi-Strauss responded harshly: "There is an eclecticism that comes across in the excessive liking you show for subjectivity, for feelings, and, not to put too fine a point on it, a certain mysticism vis-à-vis literature."

Barthes's feelings are no doubt what made his structuralism so pleasurable—and, some of his early work aside, so readable. "You can't understand anything about Barthes if you don't understand that even when his thinking is most abstract, he is really just covering up his affective choices," a perceptive colleague said after his death. As the 1960s progressed, and structuralism's tentacles penetrated further into French intellectual life, articles and books of literary criticism, philosophy, and psychoanalysis appeared festooned with charts and diagrams. *Tel Quel*, a beacon of the structuralist movement, took on, in the words of one observer, "the slightly forbidding (and utterly misleading) look of a mathematics journal." Much of this work, including Barthes's book *Système de la mode (The Fashion System)*, which finally appeared in 1967, several years after he finished it, is so dry and technical it's nearly unreadable.

By then, even Barthes had moved on. In his introduction to *The Fashion System*, he called the book "already dated." Rarely has fashion seemed less aesthetic than in his grand taxonomic schema, the point of which was mainly to show how retailers ginned up consumer desire through manipulation of "the vestimentary code." More and more, what fascinated him was *writing*: how it organized itself, how it spawned novel styles and forms, how the act of reading was, essentially, rewriting.

For Barthes, meaning was always plural, never singular. A literary text was inherently mongrel, traversed by a potentially infinite number of linguistic structures and codes. And Barthes loved nothing more than exploring a text's crevices and byways, naming its component parts, exposing the teeming order beneath its placid surface. By the end of the 1960s, he had come into his own as a literary theorist. His 1967 essay "The Death of the Author" was a classic in this regard. In it, he pronounced the author a fiction invented by modernity and perpetuated by capitalism, which had much to gain from the elevation of the individual over the group. An author makes a text tidy. She endows it with a finite horizon of meaning, the source from which all sense flows. To set writing free, Barthes argued, we need to let go of the idea of the author, since "we know now that a text is not a line of words releasing a single 'theological' meaning (the 'message' of the Author-God) but a multi-dimensional space where a variety of writings, none of them original, blend and clash." Liberated from the fiction of the author, a text would reveal its endlessly generative (if inherently derivative) nature, reconstituting itself each time it was read. The death of the author, Barthes declared, marked the birth of the reader.

This was Barthes at his most political. On the eve of May 1968, he channeled the country's rebellious, antiestablishment mood in the context in which he felt most comfortable: literature. Not everyone on the left considered such a move an acceptable surrogate for action. Along with Althusser and Foucault, Barthes was mocked for not joining the revolutionaries at the barricades. In Kristeva's novel, a student activist runs into friends during the protests who are prying cobblestones from the street to throw at the police. "Bréhal was here a little while ago—did you see him?" one friend says of the Barthes character, adding, "I'd never have thought structuralism would take to the streets!" "Don't worry," the student activist replies. "He'll soon see it's not his scene. Look he's already leaving."

That June, as the demonstrations were winding down, a journalist for *L'Express* accused the three absent "master thinkers" of moral bankruptcy:

> M. Louis Althusser, who has reinterpreted Marx in light of structuralism, is in the hospital: clinical depression. M. Michel Foucault, hailed two years ago as the philosopher of the future, is quietly continuing to teach at the University of Tunis. . . . M. Roland Barthes, director of research at the École pratique des hautes études, was scheduled to give 56 hours' worth of classes per year. His pupils were advanced students, an elite, in theory, devoted to research. Since classes started, he had been using them to collate marriage announcements in *Le Chasseur français*, so as to contribute to his linguistic studies.

Indignant, Barthes immediately sent in a correction: He had never lectured on marriage announcements or asked his students to do research for him on any topic. In fact, he was working not on marriage as a sign system but on Balzac. Between 1968 and 1969, he devoted his seminar to elaborating the ideas that would become his masterpiece of structuralist literary criticism: *S/Z*.

◆ ◆ ◆

Barthes had been obsessed for a while with *Sarrasine*, a novella by Balzac about a talented young sculptor in Italy who falls hopelessly in love with a *castrato*—a male opera singer castrated before puberty to preserve his soprano range and who subsequently performs as a woman. (By the time Balzac wrote his story, in 1830, this custom was mercifully on the wane.) Barthes had cited the tale in his essay "The Death of the Author," and now he was writing an entire book about it. It's not surprising that the story spoke to him; here was a novella about erotic longing and frustration, about pleasure proffered and deferred. Yet for Barthes, *Sarrasine* was also an allegory of reading.

In the simplest terms, the story recounts how the sculptor, Ernest-Jean Sarrasine, is so taken with La Zambinella, the beautiful singer he sees at the theater, that he carves a statue in her likeness, only to discover that she is not a woman but a (castrated) man. In a rage, Sarrasine tries to kill Zambinella but winds up being killed himself, by the singer's politically connected protectors.

For a semiologist fluent in the doctrine of the signifier, *Sarrasine* offered any number of riches, beginning with its title. "*What is Sarrasine?*" Barthes asks early on. "A noun? A name? A thing? A man? A woman?" For a French speaker, there is an extra layer of intrigue in that the final "e" in "Sarrasine" connotes femininity, though the sculptor who bears the name is a man. And there is another oddity: According to French orthographical convention, "Sarrasine" should properly be spelled with a "z," not an "s" in the middle—*Sarrazine.* As Barthes rather mordantly puts it: "On its way to the subject's patronymic, the Z has encountered some pitfall."

And where does the missing "z" turn up? In the first letter of the castrato's name: Zambinella. This is no accident, of course. In the world of Balzac's novella, "z" is the letter of "mutilation" and "deviation"—in brief, the signifier of castration, as Barthes delights in telling us: "Phonetically, Z stings like a chastising lash, an avenging insect; graphically, cast slantwise by the hand across the blank regularity of the page, amid the curves of the alphabet, like an oblique and illicit blade, it cuts, slashes, or as we say in French, *zebras.*" And wait, there's more. Graphically, "z" is simply a backward "s"—"the same letter seen from the other side of the mirror." What Sarrasine confronts in Zambinella is thus his own castration, his failure to love a real woman—a "deficiency" embedded in his name, with its missing "z" and its feminine ending. (As any French speaker would know, the masculine form of the name would be "Sarrazin.")

It all sounds pretty clever, and it was. Far from being an exemplar of nineteenth-century naturalism by a French author synonymous with the genre, *Sarrasine* was revealed by Barthes to be something else entirely: a highly unstable and self-referential text, shape-shifting under the reader's gaze. In Balzac's tale, the standard binary conception of gender was far from secure: A male sculptor with a feminized name is besotted with a female singer who is really a castrated man. As for the statue the sculptor carves in the singer's likeness—"This was more than a woman, this was a masterpiece!" Sarrasine marvels as he watches Zambinella perform—it is modeled on a body that is not what it appears to be. Who or what can be said to be male or female here?

Was Barthes drawn to the story because of its coded exploration of homosexual love? Perhaps. For him, hidden codes were the point. His argument in *S/Z* was that even the most ostensibly straightforward or "naturalistic" novel is crammed with them, all vying for attention and deciphering. "This text is a galaxy of signifiers, not a structure of signifieds," he declared. "It has no beginning; it is reversible; we gain access to it by several entrances, none of which can be authoritatively declared to be the main one; the codes it mobilizes extend *as far as the eye can reach*."

Barthes had announced the death of the author. In *S/Z,* he showed who had taken the author's place: the reader. Every reading of *Sarrasine* was a rewriting. The goal was to "make the reader no longer a consumer, but a producer of the text." Like killing off the author, elevating the reader was a conceit that chimed with the insurrectionary mood of 1968.

◆ ◆ ◆

Formally, *S/Z* had all the attributes of a structuralist document. Barthes broke down Balzac's novella into small chunks, or "lexia," numbered them from 1 to 561, and presented them chronologically, with blocks of commentary. In this sense, the book unfolded in his signature style: as a series of fragments. He even incorporated a few charts. The lexia themselves were further classified according to five codes: a "hermeneutic code" (for questions or enigmas introduced by the novella that the reader must resolve); a "semantic code" (for textual elements that have connotations beyond the literal—the title, for example, which Barthes classified under the semantic code as "femininity"); a "cultural code" (for invocations of shared cultural, moral, or scientific knowledge), and so on.

When *S/Z* was published in 1970, it helped ignite the new field of narratology, through which structuralist ideas made their way into literary study. "I read *S/Z* in Paris and it blew me away," my father told me. "Here was close textual analysis brought to the level of science. I just ate it up." His structuralist conversion began in the fall of 1972 at the Collège de France, where, as a young English professor on sabbatical in France, he went with my mother (also an English literature PhD) once a week to hear Lévi-Strauss give his public lecture. After depositing my little sister and me at the *maternelle* and my older sister at first grade in a school near our rental apartment, they would hurry to a dowdy amphitheater in the Latin Quarter to nab seats before Lévi-Strauss, accompanied by a factotum whose job was to carry his briefcase, took to the podium and began, without notes, to hold forth on the latent structures shaping the lives of an Indigenous tribe in the American Northwest. It took my parents several lectures to understand the repeated references to "*le potlatch*"—Lévi-Strauss pronounced it *le POA-te-lahsh*—but once they grasped what he was talking about, they were hooked.

After that, it was on to Barthes's *The Fashion System*—"I found it fascinating," my father confessed, "I was pretty far gone"—and then to *S/Z*, which was a revelation: "It seemed there was a magic key that would unlock a text and reveal its underlying structure." My parents read the structuralists in French, buying their books from a shop on rue Claude-Bernard that my mother says "specialized in the stuff." They felt as though a previously hidden reality was being laid bare before their eyes. "For the first and only time, I was actually excited by literary criticism," my father wrote years later, reflecting on his theory days. "At least in this French semiotic mode, which seemed to open up the beating heart of literature for inspection." When he returned to Indiana University the following year, it was "as the English department's first card-carrying structuralist."

A preschooler at the time, I was hardly conscious of my parents' intellectual conversion (though I have vague memories of waiting impatiently for my mother to pick me up for lunch from the *maternelle*, she running late because Lévi-Strauss's lecture had run long). Two decades later, though, I read *Sarrasine* and *S/Z* in a narratology class during the fall of my junior year in college. The professor, a respected pioneer in the field, taught us a fresh vocabulary for talking about literature. We learned how to distinguish between primary and secondary narratives within a text; between narrators (who speak) and focalizers (who see); between intradiegetic and heterodiegetic narrators, between omniscient narration and free indirect style, and on and on. The narratologist's vocabulary seemed nearly as infinite as the text itself.

My father was right: Literary structuralism seemed like science. The paper I wrote on *Sarrasine* for that class has the cool, clinical precision of forensic analysis—as if I were a detective cracking a code to solve a mystery. And yet Barthes makes clear that neither his codes nor his commentary could hope to capture the tale in its totality. His book showed the novella to be "absolutely plural." Every reading yielded a new arrangement in the underlying matrix of codes, generating the text anew. Barthes would surely have grown impatient with narratology's terminology and definitions, its efforts to hem in a narrative, to pin it down.

In the other book he published in 1970, *Empire of Signs*, he pushed the conceit of the reader as "producer of the text" even further. Here the text wasn't a novel but an actual country: Japan. Barthes had visited Japan three times in the late 1960s, staying about a month on each trip. The country enchanted him. Despite speaking minimal Japanese, he managed encounters with a variety of people, including men for sex. Japan, he decided, was a place of unparalleled purity and sensuality.

In *Empire of Signs* he elaborated his conceit, combining black-and-white photos with brief essays offering rapturous takes on Japanese haiku, calligraphy, chopsticks, bowing, and gift wrapping. Together, the essays—most little longer than his typical fragments—depict a culture with a transcendent emptiness at its heart, a dazzling empire of signs that refuse to signify. Barthes's Japan may have been influenced by his readings in Zen Buddhism, but it was hardly a real place. As he announced on his first page, the country in his book is a fiction—an assemblage of "features" selected by him and arranged into a "system which I shall call: Japan."

Realism, for Barthes, was merely an effect of language. In a charming essay, "The Reality Effect," he homed in on a barometer hanging on a wall in a short story by Flaubert. The barometer serves no apparent narrative function, he argued—unlike, say, the piano Flaubert also mentions, which helps establish its owner's bourgeois status—but it is precisely through such gratuitous description that realism achieves verisimilitude, its reality effect. The more a detail resists notice or interpretation—Barthes calls the barometer "neither incongruous nor significant, and therefore not participating, at first glance, in the order of the *notable*"—the stronger the reality effect. Such detail has no purpose other than as a background hum that says to the reader, I'm real.

This was Barthes's provocation: A country, a person (as he would demonstrate in his autobiography), and just about anything else could be "read" like a literary work, but in no case should the act of reading be confused with the truth or essence of "the text." Because there was no such thing. This last idea fell outside the bounds of orthodox structuralism. But even my dad admitted that once the thrill of reading *S/Z* wore off, he began to wonder what, exactly, he'd gain from a structural analysis that he couldn't get without it. He assigned his students Poe's short story "The Tell-Tale Heart," and subjected them to an elaborate structuralist interpretation supported by mimeographed handouts replete with charts and diagrams. "It was a short text," he told me. "Structural analysis was very laborious; no wonder there are few structuralist analyses of entire novels." After the exercise was over, he realized that it had merely confirmed what he already knew about Poe's story at the outset; in short, "the game was not worth the candle." My father eventually moved on to studying autobiography, or what scholars in the field liked to call "life writing," ditching systems and structures for a vision of narrative the structuralists would have deplored: as a referential and deeply human art.

Structuralism, at least the version of it presented in my narratology class, was causing me trouble, too. Armed with the narratologist's tools, I was able to peer into texts as though through a microscope, discerning subtle features I would not otherwise have noticed. But the effect was also overwhelming: all these moving parts swimming about and interacting, like the proliferation of organelles crowded inside a single human cell, directing its behavior. While my narratology professor applauded my paper on *S/Z* ("exemplary for the interpretive mileage that can be gotten from close scrutiny of narrative discourse"), outside class, I felt increasingly trapped. Under the influence of structuralism and its dark view of language's overbearing influence, I had traded Nadja, the false idol of spontaneity and freedom, for her opposite: a paralyzing self-consciousness. In a letter to a friend that fall, I described myself as caught in a state of "hyper self-consciousness" that left me "unable to act or think without endless hours of analysis, before, during, and after." I compared the feeling to "the awareness you have when you are reading and start to think about *how* you are reading, whether you are saying the words aloud in your head or instantly recognizing them."

At the time, I sensed that this extreme self-consciousness was likely just a phase, part of the painful and necessary process of assembling an adult self and finding a voice of my own. But it would be many more years, long after the ordeal of my junior paper and perhaps not until I finally left academia for journalism, before I lost the sensation of moving through life with heightened awareness, as though never simply present in it but always with one ear cocked to the metanarrative about it.

As for Barthes, his mind was far too protean to conform to any orthodoxy. In retrospect, his most enduring claim wasn't particularly structuralist. In place of Lévi-Strauss's timeless laws, and Lacan's tyrannical symbolic order, he presented the world as a narrative in perpetual flux, forming and reforming beneath the reader's gaze. Barthes aimed to do for literature what Deleuze and Guattari would try to do for the unconscious in *Anti-Oedipus* two years later: liberate it. If human beings were pawns in an indifferent linguistic system, in Barthes's books, at least, the prospect was nonetheless a cause for joy.

Chapter 30

THE DEATH OF MAN

Predictably, Lévi-Strauss hated *S/Z*. He'd already told Barthes in a letter that "for me, the work of art is not open (a conception that paves the way to the worst kind of philosophy: that of metaphysical desire, of the subject properly denied but hypostasized in metaphor, etc.); the work of art is closed, and it is precisely this closure that means we can study it objectively." When *S/Z* appeared, he sent Barthes an analysis of the kinship structures in *Sarrasine*, calling *S/Z* "dazzling." But a decade later he claimed he'd sent the letter "as a joke," "in place of the compliments I felt incapable of making."

Foucault and Derrida, on the other hand, were greatly impressed. "I've just read you in one sitting," Foucault gushed to Barthes. "It's magnificent—the first real piece of textual analysis that I've ever read." Derrida was equally fawning. "With no other text do I at present feel so *absolutely* in agreement," he wrote. "I am sure that what *S/Z* is doing, and will do for a long time, is to draw, multiply, 'liberate' a new space for reading and writing."

While the media continued to portray the structuralists as a tight-knit cabal—as in a famous cartoon known as "The Structuralist Picnic" that appeared in *La Quinzaine littéraire* in 1967—the movement, which had never really cohered, was splintering. In the wake of May '68, Surrealism and existentialism had faded from view; André Breton had died in 1966

The Structuralist Picnic: Michel Foucault, Jacques Lacan, Claude Lévi-Strauss, and Roland Barthes, by Maurice Henry, 1967

and Sartre had been more or less mothballed. And now the Lévi-Straussian rigidity was beginning to lose its appeal as well.

"Certain half-witted 'commentators' persist in labelling me a 'structuralist,'" Foucault complained in 1970, in the preface to *The Order of Things*, the English edition of his French bestseller, *Les mots et les choses*. "I have been unable to get it into their tiny minds that I have used none of the methods, concepts, or key terms that characterize structural analysis." Such a tantrum! And over the reception of a book that, when it appeared in France just four years earlier, had been applauded by thinkers as sophisticated as Deleuze as a signal contribution, of a piece with the other landmark structuralist work published in 1966: Lacan's *Écrits*.

Les mots et les choses introduced Foucault's theory of *epistemes*, his term for the succession of hidden frameworks that he believed undergirded human history, shaping and constraining knowledge over time. The epistemes—a kind of cultural unconscious—defined the general approach to knowledge at any given time. Yet the epistemes did not build on one another in a logical manner; progress, Foucault made clear, was a myth. Ideas that dominated one era might have been unthinkable in the previous one or irrelevant in the next. The episteme of the classical age, for instance, extending from the mid-seventeenth century to the beginning of the nineteenth, was characterized by a fervor for classification, for ordering nature, objects, even language, into taxonomies, genealogies, grammars, subsets, and parts. Humans figured in this grand ordering of the world, but typically in relation to a larger paradigm, as, say, the highest point in the chain of beings.

With the advent of the modern episteme, man himself, for the first time, was the focus of knowledge—its subject and object. But with this development came new problems. The coherence between reality and its representations was shattered. No longer were grids and tables, maps, and words thought to reflect the world as it was. As the human sciences (medicine, psychology, sociology, anthropology, etc.) developed, so did a dawning awareness that knowledge was mediated by the constraints that defined our species—consciousness, biology, history, and most fundamentally, language. "The threshold between Classicism and modernity," Foucault wrote, "had been definitively crossed when words ceased to intersect with representations and to provide a spontaneous grid for the knowledge of things."

His book was dense going, layered with nuance and paradox, and studded with his favored imagery of thresholds, light, and shadow. But he eased readers in with his opening pages: a dazzling close reading of *Las Meninas*, the legendary painting by the seventeenth-century Spanish artist Velázquez, that served as a visual preview of the argument to come. Acclaimed for its elaborate self-referentiality, *Las Meninas* depicts Velázquez himself, paintbrush in hand, poised before his easel in a stately room, in the process of creating a painting we cannot see. To his left are arranged a cluster of other figures: the young Infanta Margaret Theresa and her entourage. Like the figure of Velázquez, most of these others are gazing out beyond the picture frame, at the scene we infer is the painter's subject. Though we cannot see precisely what these figures see, Velázquez gives us a clue: a mirror on the far wall in which we can dimly make out the reflections of two people, the king and queen of Spain.

Foucault dissected the painting's intricate circuit of gazes—the artist's, the Infanta and her entourage's, the viewer's, and, not least, the absent

Las Meninas, by Diego Velázquez, 1656

king and queen's—along with its visible and implied content, finding in "this picture of a picture," a prescient critique of representation. Where we expect to see the king and queen, or at least their likenesses on the canvas portrayed in the painting, we are shown instead the circumstances of that painting's creation. The king and queen remain "an essential void" around which the entire image is structured, a sign, Foucault suggested, of the coming dissolution of classicism's faith in a seamless correspondence between the world of ideas and the world of things, between *les mots et les choses*.

His analysis became what Fredric Jameson called "one of the most famous set-pieces in French theory." The rest of the book piled on bold claims. History, science, truth, reality itself: Such concepts were necessarily contingent, liable to shift, however subtly, from one episteme to the next. In America, Foucault would soon be accused of promoting relativism or, worse, nihilism. In his book, humans were not drivers or discoverers of knowledge but, on the contrary, governed by unseen structures—Foucault's protestations about the term notwithstanding.

Structuralist or not, the book was clearly a dig at existentialism. "Man," the heroic agent of history at the center of Sartre's philosophy, was, in Foucault's account, merely "an invention of recent date"—and a temporary one at that. Psychoanalysis, linguistics, and Marxist theory had steadily chipped away at the idea of man as a coherent and autonomous entity, so much so that when the modern episteme came to an end—as soon it would, Foucault speculated darkly—then man would end, too, "erased," as he put it in his poetic concluding passage, "like a face drawn in the sand at the edge of the sea."

In interviews with the press, he was more explicit: "Our task is to completely free ourselves from humanism." When Foucault invoked the end of "man," he meant man as a philosophical concept, not a species. But left hanging in the air was the possibility that such a distinction might be irrelevant, if not naïve. Today, with the rapid proliferation of quasi-sentient AI bots, along with increasingly detailed scenarios forecasting AI's imminent conquest of humanity, Foucault's enigmatic imagery has an aura of prophecy: The post-human episteme may be upon us. Even in 1966, some commentators seemed prepared to take Foucault at his word, finding the prospect of our demise exhilarating. "A young man has come on the intellectual scene in order to announce the excellent news: the death of Man and, at the same time, the renewal of the one who invented him, then destroyed him, the *Philosopher*," wrote a gleeful reviewer for *L'Express*.

Perhaps only in France in the 1960s could two opaquely cerebral tomes—Lacan's *Écrits* and Foucault's *Les mots et les choses*—become a single year's blockbusters. Of course, not everyone was thrilled by this development. Sartre panned Foucault's book in interviews, while Beauvoir worked a jeer into her novel *Les belles images*, which appeared that fall. The book featured a chic married couple who inhabit a bourgeois Parisian milieu in thrall to the latest consumer fads. In their circle, what passes for intellectual conversation is wisdom gleaned from glossy magazines, which they duly recite at cocktail parties: "Jean-Charles and Dufrène were in agreement (they read the same periodicals): the idea of what constituted man was due to be overhauled and no doubt it would vanish; it was a nineteenth-century invention and now it was out-of-date."

The filmmaker Jean-Luc Godard, annoyed at Foucault's presumption to know what people could or couldn't think at a given moment in history, also mocked *Les mots et les choses* in his film *La Chinoise* (1967), about a French Maoist student cell, by having one young militant pelt a copy of the book with tomatoes. Privately, Foucault appeared to share Godard's doubts. According to his biographer Didier Eribon, not long after *Les mots et les choses* was released, he decided it was "the worst book he had written" and asked his publisher to stop printing it.

Chapter 31

"WHAT IS IT TO WRITE?"

As for Derrida, he was too canny a thinker to get caught in the structuralist net. When he took on "man" in a 1968 essay, "The Ends of Man," he went further than Foucault. "Man" wasn't simply a recent invention; it was a relic of an entrenched humanism that philosophy was having a hell of a time exorcising from its repertoire. "The question 'of man' is being asked in very current fashion in France," Derrida observed in a dig at Foucault. But to declare "man" a historical creation whose "end" was in sight did little to resolve the metaphysical problems baked into the concept from its inception. Sartre, Derrida argued, had misread Hegel, Husserl, and Heidegger, but then the great Germans, too, were knee-deep in humanism in spite of themselves, falling back on an "anthropological" idea of man defined in light of an "end"—death, an essence, absolute authority. Even Heidegger, whose notion of Being came closest to avoiding these pitfalls, hadn't entirely escaped them. By calling attention to philosophy's loaded metaphors and missteps, deconstruction suggested a way forward, Derrida wrote, dangling the possibility of "man" understood as an emergent effect of the method itself, dynamic, provisional, eluding fixed meaning or finitude.

Derrida was as obsessed with language as his structuralist peers, but as we have seen, his MO was to proceed by implication while taking everyone else apart. Count on Derrida to ruin the party. In 1967, he had unleashed what turned out to be the biggest blitz of his career by publishing three major works, including the game-changing *Of Grammatology*. This book, which doubled as Derrida's doctoral thesis, was, among other things, an investigation and defense of writing, a medium he believed his discipline had profoundly misunderstood. For a philosopher who had secretly wished to be a novelist, the fixation on writing was also deeply personal. "My most constant interest, coming even before my philosophical interest, I would say, if this is possible, is toward literature, toward that writing that is called literary," he explained years later. "What is literature? And first of all, what is it to write?"

Derrida considered writing to be philosophy's great unspoken problem. From the ancient Greeks onward, Western philosophers had favored speech over writing, considering the latter merely a pale reflection of the former. According to this logic, speech had the immediacy of thought, and writing was simply speech's "dead letter." But Derrida showed how this formulation didn't hold up to scrutiny. Philosophy was guilty of a "metaphysics of presence"—of assuming, without proof, that thought was "present" in speech in a way it wasn't in writing. Phenomenologists like Husserl appeared to take for granted that the silent monologue running through our minds was evidence of what Derrida called the "absolute proximity of voice and being." The language we use to express this experience—*I can hear myself speak in my head*—reinforces this idea. But we are mistaken, Derrida insisted. We conflate being with presence, unable to perceive that these qualities don't inhere in words themselves; speech contains no more "being" or "presence" than writing does.

In Derrida's analysis, the distinctions between speech and writing broke down, as, in case after case, he demonstrated how philosophers' notions about language were mystical and muddled. It wasn't lost on him that philosophy's centuries-long discussion about the issue had taken place *in writing*. His biographer Peter Salmon underscores the irony: "Problems were proposed, arguments had, tracts published and refuted, aphorisms made, systems erected, ideas generated and logical systems concocted, refined, questioned, embraced and dismissed, without the very strange fact—that this is all being done by writing—presenting itself as problematic or odd."

Of Grammatology was the book in which Derrida first used the word "deconstruction," shorthand for his signature method of textual unravelment. Later, in a letter to a friend, he explained the origin of the term. He had been trying to adapt Heidegger's concept of *Destruktion*, the German thinker's term for scraping away the layers of metaphysical distortions with which Western philosophy was encrusted. Derrida rejected the word "destruction," with its connotations of total annihilation, and when "deconstruction" suddenly came to him, he looked up the word in *Littré*—the French equivalent of the OED—and was delighted to discover that, though hardly in widespread use, it existed.

Contrary to critics who asserted that deconstruction was pure nihilism—a doctrine of meaninglessness obscured by jargon—Derrida showed how meaning always exceeded or eluded our intentions and expectations. Meaning abounded, but it was nearly impossible to pin it down, to corral it into stable, logical arrangements. Maybe Fredric Jameson said it best: For Derrida, "meaning is a will-o'-the-wisp." Derrida himself formulated the challenge of deconstruction this way: "It is a question of determining the possibility of *meaning* on the basis of a 'formal' organization which in itself has no meaning." A principal effect was to turn reading into an unexpected and, for some at least, freshly exciting endeavor.

Of Grammatology was a magisterial demonstration of deconstruction's possibilities and unlike any other work of philosophy then on the market. "A gloriously bonkers book," Peter Salmon wrote, pointing out that the footnotes alone reference more than a thousand titles, some "obscure beyond belief." Among other topics and authors, Derrida considered hieroglyphics, Mayan script, Chinese characters, Plato, Leibniz, and Freud, along with the usual German suspects—Hegel, Nietzsche, Husserl, and Heidegger. The book's most famous chapter was an extended reading of the motif of masturbation in Rousseau. *Of Grammatology* "is exorbitant," Salmon exclaims. "It is hyperbolic. It ploughs forward. It obfuscates.

It bursts at the seams with the profusion of its ideas." The ever-hip Jean-Luc Godard incorporated passages from the book (along with allusions to Rousseau, Nietzsche, and Barthes) in his almost unbearably brainy sequel to *La Chinoise*: *Le Gai Savoir*, another film featuring student militants who are trying to vanquish the pitfalls of language ("the enemy") in order to make a political movie.

For many readers—count me among them—*Of Grammatology* would be unthinkable without the seventy-eight-page preface by Derrida's American translator, Gayatri Spivak. Spivak had read the book in French as a twenty-five-year-old assistant professor of English at the University of Iowa, after coming across an ad for it in a foreign books catalog in 1967. She had never heard of Derrida but, dumbfounded by his book, resolved to translate it herself and persuaded Johns Hopkins University Press to publish it in English.

The first section of *Of Grammatology* featured a critique of Saussure, the second a critique of Lévi-Strauss. In general, Derrida approved of Saussurean linguistics. Saussure was right that language is a system that depends on differences among signifiers and signifieds. But in Derrida's view, Saussure had failed to push the radical promise of this logic far enough. To buttress his point, he introduced the term "*différance,*" a neologism identical in sound to the French word for "difference" but distinguished by a single letter "a," and which Derrida intended as a play on the verb "*différer*," which means both "to differ" and "to defer."

A word acquires meaning only through its difference from other words, but meaning is not present in the word itself, or, for that matter, anywhere else in the linguistic system. Saussure's image of the sign as a sheet of paper wedding signifier to signified in perpetuity was an illusion. Instead, Derrida stressed, meaning is a *deferred* effect, contingent on the word's relationships with other words within the entire mobile network of signs. A word's sense is thus never stable but always shifting across potentially infinite chains of signification. The Nobel Prize–winning Norwegian playwright Jon Fosse, who has studied Derrida closely, nicely defined this concept when he remarked to an interviewer: "The main question for Heidegger was: what is common to everything that exists? The main question for Derrida was the opposite: what makes all that exists different?"

Saussure's mistake was to ignore the deferred, unstable aspect of meaning creation. Instead, he sought to contain difference. For Saussure, language was a closed system, in which differences between signifiers served to organize them into a stable matrix of signifieds. Meaning in this system was fixed. Moreover, he conceived of writing as a derivative form. Writing served merely to represent the spoken word—the register in which Saussure, like philosophers before him, believed meaning actually resided. As Derrida put it, "The age of the sign is essentially theological."

Once you admit that meaning is not present within the word or fixed within the system but rather deferred and contingent, then Saussure's binary pairs—signifier/signified, synchronic/diachronic, speech/writing, etc.—are no longer locked in stark opposition. Instead, they jostle each other, overlap, and merge. Just as Derrida had done with Foucault's opposition between madness and reason, in *Of Grammatology* he pulled the rug out from under Saussure's distinction between speech and writing.

Structurally, there is little difference between the two, Derrida argued. To the degree that all language defers rather than contains meaning, speech "already belongs" to writing. Derrida loved nothing more than to unsettle what he called the "violent hierarchy" of binary pairs, and structuralism was not immune to his undoings. As Spivak wrote in her preface to the book: "'Differance' is the structure that would deconstruct structuralism." Defined this way, "differance" sounds like a transcendental signified of the sort that Derrida accused other philosophers of falling back on. And though he was careful to stress that "*differance* is neither a *word* nor a *concept*," that it is "not theological," he also underscored that there is no escaping "the metaphysical enclosure." To work within language in order to dismantle it is to be stuck with language's tools. Thus, Derrida conceded: "differance remains a metaphysical name."

Turning to Lévi-Strauss, Derrida showed how the anthropologist also subscribed to a negative view of writing, regarding it as a degraded medium through which violence and exploitation infiltrated human society, ending its primal purity. Derrida's evidence was a single chapter of *Tristes Tropiques* called "A Writing Lesson," which recounted an episode from Lévi-Strauss's visit to the Nambikwara. Through a remarkable close reading, he traced how Lévi-Strauss's impressions of the tribe's "fundamental goodness and virginal innocence" were linked in his mind to their illiteracy. With writing comes the fall.

According to Lévi-Strauss, writing's "primary function" has been to consolidate power and dominate other human beings. To illustrate this notion, he relates an anecdote about the Nambikwara's chief, who, given pencil and paper by the anthropologist's team, quickly understood writing's "role as sign, and the social superiority that it confers," despite being illiterate himself. Over the course of two hours, in front of his assembled tribe, the chief pretended to read from his notepad a series of written commands to Lévi-Strauss and his colleagues regarding an exchange of gifts. Here, Lévi-Strauss suggests, was proof of writing's capacity to oppress, which a man "still living in the Stone Age" had immediately grasped.

"The story is very beautiful," Derrida observed mischievously. He went on to show how it was just that: a story. He cited other passages from *Tristes Tropiques,* as well as an ethnography Lévi-Strauss had written about the Nambikwara attesting to the tribe's violent tendencies and its prolific use of graphic marks. These last, Derrida insisted, represented a kind of writing. In a passage that appears only in the ethnography, Lévi-Strauss notes that some of the tribe's members eventually used his pencils and paper to make figurative drawings and genealogical diagrams. The tribe even came up with a word for writing. So much for a supposedly peace-loving oral culture. By the end of Derrida's analysis, the philosophical distinctions between speech and writing, and the sentimental associations Lévi-Strauss ascribes to each, have been thoroughly demolished.

Lévi-Strauss was not amused. In 1966, when Derrida published a version of his critique in an academic journal, Lévi-Strauss wrote a letter to the editors to complain: "Aren't you playing a philosophical farce by scrutinizing my texts with a care that would be more justified if they had been written by Spinoza, Descartes or Kant? Frankly, I don't think what I write is worth so much fuss, especially *Tristes Tropiques*, in which I didn't claim to be setting out any truths, merely the daydreams of an ethnographer in the field."

◆ ◆ ◆

Lacan had escaped Derrida's precision scalpel in *Of Grammatology*. But you can be sure a takedown was coming. By the time Derrida's book appeared in English in 1976, the relationship between the two men was, as his translator Spivak delicately phrased it, "charged with unease." It had taken Derrida nearly twenty years to respond to Lacan's lecture on "The Purloined Letter"—he was busy deconstructing other people—but in 1975 he finally published an article savaging Lacan's analysis. Derrida's complaint was a familiar one—Lacan was guilty of metaphysical errors—and it was delivered with typical aplomb. His tone, however, was unusually cutting. By offering a reading of Poe, Lacan was straying into literary territory. Evidently this was turf war.

Derrida's complaint went like this: Lacan was a poor reader of Poe. For one thing, he'd found just two scenes in a story that contains at least three. For another, he'd made Oedipal triangles of three figures when he should have made squares of four (he had completely ignored the story's narrator, Dupin's Watson-like sidekick, whose role in the tale changes both Lacan's Oedipal math, and, in important ways, his interpretation).

Lacan had conveniently overlooked the fact that "The Purloined Letter," is a work of fiction—a tale within a tale, one that calls our attention to its own storytelling. Instead, he'd treated it as science: an expression of truth. He had turned a story about a signifier into a signified. He had taken what he'd insisted was a meaningless mark (a typographical "letter") and filled it with meaning. And not just any meaning. Lacan had endowed Poe's abstract signifier with the very conception of femininity in Freudian-Lacanian doctrine. (Here Derrida trotted out numerous comments by Lacan describing the queen's letter in gendered terms, including how it "feminizes" the men who make contact with it, encasing them in an "*odor di femina*," as Lacan puts it at one point.) For Lacan, Derrida wrote, the "truth" of the purloined letter *is* "femininity," which in Lacanian psychoanalytic terms is lack. In other words, the queen's purloined letter signifies the thing that she (like all women) is missing: the penis. And this, of course, Derrida noted deviously, is precisely what Lacan's nemesis Princess Marie Bonaparte had said.

Derrida's larger objection was that the operations of language were more complicated and less predictable than Lacan admitted. Lacan's allegory was too simple, too reductive, too static. "A letter does *not always* arrive at its destination," Derrida argued; meaning is far too unstable for us to make such a claim. Like Saussure and Lévi-Strauss before him, Lacan had fallen into a metaphysical trap. He had intended Poe's story as an illustration of abstract principles but ended up finding in it unprovable truths.

Derrida was becoming structuralism's closest reader and at the same time its fiercest critic. ("More and more, where would we be without you?" Barthes wrote to him.) But I am getting ahead of myself. Before Derrida dismantled Lacan on paper, the two met in person—an encounter that, as you might imagine, did not go well. It happened during that high-water year for structuralism, 1966. An enterprising trio of professors at Johns Hopkins University, eager to get in on the intellectual revolution in France, decided to host a big conference and invite the movement's leading lights. French structuralism was coming to America, where Derrida, the source of its undoing, would steal the show.

Part 4

Evasions

Chapter 32

SAMSON IN THE STRUCTURALIST TEMPLE

The testy exchange between Lacan and Derrida took place over dinner. Lacan was holding a plate of coleslaw. No one seems to have recorded what Derrida was eating—perhaps another iconic American dish. After all, the symposium they were attending, "The Languages of Criticism and the Sciences of Man," had been planned down to the smallest detail, at considerable expense, to impress the European guests. Held over four days at Johns Hopkins University in October 1966, and funded with a grant from the Ford Foundation, the conference convened more than one hundred scholars from nine countries to discuss the French movement that had supplanted existentialism and whose sensational claims about reality and language were shaking up intellectual life across the Atlantic. The hosts had conceived the occasion as structuralism's official début in the United States.

So great was scholarly interest that most of the sessions were standing-room only: "People were falling out of the windows," one organizer recalled. Even after the conference ended, its audience continued to grow, as the proceedings were rehashed in articles and books, acquiring near-mythic status. It was what the French call an *événement*—an event—just not the one its sponsors had envisioned. When it was over, one American journalist described it as a "ninety-six-gun French dispute."

The roster of speakers skewed toward marquee names: Along with Lacan and Derrida, the list included Barthes, the Hegel scholar Jean Hyppolite, the Marxist philosopher Lucien Goldmann, and the literary theorists Georges Poulet and Tzvetan Todorov. Lévi-Strauss was supposed to come but had to drop out. Deleuze was also unable to attend, though he sent a letter, which was read aloud. Foucault, who was known to be flaky about professional obligations, was allegedly also a dropout. Later, Richard Macksey, the voluble Johns Hopkins polymath who helped organize the whole thing, acknowledged the absurdity of flying all these French-speaking thinkers to Baltimore to debate a movement bred on their home turf.

And yet, until Lacan and Derrida arrived at Johns Hopkins that fall, they had never met. They were two Parisian intellectuals at very different stages of their careers. Lacan was sixty-five, a celebrated provocateur with a devoted following, whose mammoth collection *Écrits* would be published to record sales the following month. Derrida was thirty-six, the philosophy *caïman* at the École Normale, and, despite the recent appearance of several articles that would form the backbones of *Of Grammatology* and *Writing and Difference,* still essentially unknown.

Derrida hadn't even been part of the original lineup. He was a last-minute substitution—according to one account, for Lévi-Strauss himself. Jean Hyppolite had proposed him as a late addition, telling the conference's hosts, "I think he would be somebody who would come." That hardly sounds like a ringing endorsement, but Hyppolite's recommendation carried weight, and the organizers knew Derrida's articles had made a splash in Paris. And so Derrida came, boarding the plane for Baltimore with Barthes and a few other attendees. When he arrived, on a Monday, at the Belvedere Hotel, Lacan was already there and greeted him warmly: "So! I had to come all the way here to finally meet you!" Derrida was touched to discover that Lacan had persuaded the front desk to hold a deluxe room for him.

It wasn't until dinner the next night that their interaction took a sour turn. The conference speakers had been asked to submit their papers in advance so that English translations could be prepared. Lacan, however, hadn't submitted a paper. As it turned out, he hadn't written one. He spent the first couple days that week holed up in the Belvedere, drafting his remarks. At one point, he tried to persuade Anthony Wilden, a Hopkins graduate student assigned to attend to him, to write the paper for him. Wilden tried to convince Lacan simply to deliver his talk in French. Forget about the English translation, Wilden implored him; there was no longer time to make one.

The overdue paper notwithstanding, Lacan was not one to miss a meal. He appeared at dinner on Tuesday night, where the conversation revolved around the philosophical questions of the day: language; the metaphysics of presence; the poor, battered Cartesian subject—the very issues Derrida was obsessed with. As Derrida spoke up, Lacan, standing with his plate of coleslaw, noted that his own work also concerned a critique of the subject. "You can't bear my having already said what you want to say," he declared. A gauntlet had been thrown. But Derrida wasn't having it. "*That* is not my problem," he replied.

Derrida's dissection of Lacan's Poe lecture was still nearly a decade away, but the psychoanalyst had rightly identified the upstart young philosopher as a threat. Years later, Derrida recalled that Lacan also spoke to him at the conference about death, confiding his anxiety about how his work might be read: "in particular by me, after his death." Lacan said he was concerned that the binding on his soon-to-be-published *Écrits* wouldn't keep the nine-hundred-page book together. "You'll see," he said, gesturing forlornly, "it's not going to hold up." If this was a humble brag, it seemed to betray a genuine fear. Was Lacan more worried about the book's binding holding up or about its contents not holding up to Derrida's judgment?

At the conference, Lacan, along with Lévi-Strauss and Saussure, loomed over nearly every paper. "The works of Lévi-Strauss and Lacan have taken the place of the works of Sartre and Merleau-Ponty, and it is toward them that marginal disciplines, such as literary criticism, are turning in search of a methodological guide," announced Eugenio Donato, a young Hopkins professor and conference organizer. Barthes's talk was typical: "Man does not exist prior to language, either as a species or as an individual," he said, elegantly paraphrasing Lacanian dogma. "It is language which teaches the definition of man, not the reverse."

Lacan the person was faring less well. By Thursday evening, when it was his turn to speak, he'd managed to alienate not just Derrida but his American hosts with his incessant demands. He kept the hotel staff busy moving furniture around in his room. He insisted on having his silk underwear sent out to be laundered by hand. And he complained that he'd had no chance to "meet with the students"—a lament that in Lacan's French accent came out as "*mate* with students," much to everyone's embarrassment. "Because he had been down in the damned hotel, he didn't meet with the symposiasts either," Macksey said later. "And then he went on about mating with the students for a while."

When Lacan did descend from his hotel room to attend a presentation, he tended to hijack the discussion afterward by talking about his own work. His response to Lucien Goldmann's paper on "structuralist sociology" was characteristic: "M. Goldmann has just shown how difficult it will be for me to communicate to you tomorrow what I have, just this morning, with the kind help of my translator, begun to put into a form worthy of this present meeting. . . . I have tried to prepare something which will represent the first cutting-edge of my thought. Since this project is something I have been working on for fifteen years, you will understand that tomorrow's exposé cannot be exhaustive. However, in order to facilitate my task and to prepare your ear, I should like to say this: A few words concerning the *subject*. . . ."

The dread may already have been building.

Finally, on Thursday evening, after arguing with Guy Rosolato, the only other psychoanalyst on the program, about who would speak first—predictably, Lacan got his way—he presented his paper. By all accounts, it was a mystifying performance. It took an intrepid listener just to get beyond his title: "Of Structure as an Inmixing of an Otherness Prerequisite to Any Subject Whatever." Lacan spoke about Freud and the unconscious, about the way the unconscious was "precisely structured." Occasionally, he waxed poetical, at one point suggesting that "the best image to sum up the unconscious is Baltimore in the early morning." Fredric Jameson has given this line an elegant gloss, suggesting that what Lacan glimpsed out his hotel window at dawn—rows of buildings, neon signs, streets already flowing with traffic but people themselves nowhere to be seen—was an apt metaphor for an unconscious humming with activity but lacking a human subject in charge. This, Jameson suggests, is what Lacan meant when he said: "All that I could see, except for some trees in the distance, was the result of thoughts, actively thinking thoughts, where the function played by the subjects was not completely obvious." In truth, though, an exact account of what he said is nearly impossible, since he insisted on delivering his remarks in an often unintelligible English. The diagram of a Möbius strip that he drew on the blackboard did little to clarify matters.

A literary theorist named Angus Fletcher had been tapped to serve as the respondent for Lacan's talk. He could hardly restrain himself. (He may also have been emboldened by alcohol; friends had taken him out earlier for rounds of French 75s—a heady champagne and gin cocktail.) "Freud was really a very simple man," Fletcher began. "He didn't try to float on the surface of words. What you're doing is like a spider: you're making a very delicate web without any human reality in it."

Of course, a web without any human reality in it is not a bad description of the structuralist conception of language—those French 75s may not have been a mistake after all. Lacan really had tried to explain his theory clearly. But the Americans in the audience were, understandably, perplexed. The transcript of the exchange after the talk reads like a parody of academic discourse, the sort that conservative pundits would later invoke to underscore French theory's calamitous effects on American students, not to mention the English language:

(Commenter): What is the relationship between your thought about nothingness and the work that Husserl and Sartre have done?

Lacan: "Nothingness," the word that you have used, I think that I can say almost nothing about it, nor about Husserl, nor about Sartre. Really, I don't believe that I have talked about nothingness. The sliding and the difficulty of seizing, the never-here (it is here when I search there; it is there when I am here) is not nothing.

The conference organizers watched in dismay, imagining what their sponsor the Ford Foundation must think. Lacan, however, enjoyed himself immensely. According to Macksey, he returned to the Belvedere after midnight and began calling friends in Paris to report on his glorious evening, eventually running up a nine-hundred-dollar telephone tab.

◆ ◆ ◆

Years later, Lacan's Thursday night fiasco was not what everyone would remember. It was Derrida's paper the next day—the conference's last—that earned that distinction. Afterward, when people talked about the conference, they talked of little else.

That Derrida spoke on the last day may have been merely a coincidence, but in retrospect, given the explosive import of his lecture, it seemed a deliberate and inevitable decision. Far from completing the picture of structuralism elaborated by the other speakers over the course of the week, Derrida's talk, "Structure, Sign, and Play in the Discourse of the Human Sciences," written in under two weeks and delivered in French, took the picture apart and left it in tatters. His paper was a demolition job for sure, but one of such boldness and efficiency that his audience could not help but be wowed.

"Perhaps something has occurred in the history of the concept of structure that could be called an 'event,'" Derrida began, "if this loaded word did not entail a meaning which it is precisely the function of structural—or structuralist—thought to reduce or to suspect." The tentativeness of the "perhaps," notwithstanding, Derrida made clear that he intended his talk as high drama. As it progressed the "event," became a "rupture," and then a "disruption."

The drama was this: With the advent of structuralism, for the first time in the history of philosophy the notion of a transcendental source of meaning had been shattered. To be sure, this development had a lineage. Nietzsche, Freud, and Heidegger had each called into question long-standing dogma, upending the idea of a stable truth (Nietzsche), a unified consciousness (Freud), and self-presence—the sense of being a discrete "I" existing apart from an external world (Heidegger). These thinkers, Derrida said, had paved the way for structuralism: "the moment when language invaded the universal problematic, the moment when, in the absence of a center or origin, everything became discourse."

Language as the structuralists conceived it was a structure, but it was unlike any structure previously imagined. Meaning was nowhere *in* this structure, but nor was meaning *outside* it. In this sense, language was, at least in theory, free of the metaphysical assumptions that marred previous schools of thought. There was no God, no human being, no entity or event beyond language or responsible for creating it. Language was a structure not just without a center or border but without an origin. Meaning was dispersed *across* it, an emergent effect of differences among potentially infinite arrangements of signifiers.

And yet, the moment that language came to be conceived as a structure—"that structure of structures," was how Derrida put it—philosophy was caught in a bind. The way the structuralists talked about it, "structure" inevitably began to seem like an originating force, an essence or totality: the thing that generated and contained discourse. In the end, Derrida said, structuralism had been no more able to escape metaphysics than Nietzsche, Freud, or Heidegger had been. The task philosophy had set for itself was ultimately impossible: "There is no sense in doing without the concepts of metaphysics in order to shake metaphysics.

We have no language—no syntax and no lexicon—which is foreign to this history; we can pronounce not a single destructive proposition which has not already had to slip into the form, the logic, and the implicit postulations of precisely what it seeks to contest."

Thus is every philosopher doomed to "metaphysical complicity." Derrida cited approvingly Lévi-Strauss's model of the "*bricoleur*," or tinkerer, a person who relies on "the means at hand," adapting old tools and materials to new purposes. Philosophers were *bricoleurs*, Derrida said, obliged to borrow "concepts from the text of a heritage which is more or less coherent or ruined" and then put those old notions to novel uses. Lévi-Strauss was himself a *bricoleur*, admirably striving in his work on myths, for example, to abandon "all reference to a *center*, to a *subject*, to a privileged *reference*, to an origin."

But metaphysics had proved impossible to resist, even for Lévi-Strauss, structuralism's most promising disciple. By the time Derrida had finished dismantling the anthropologist's work, he had cited passages from half a dozen books. Once again, he proved a dazzling close reader. He began by dissecting Lévi-Strauss's comments on the opposition between nature and culture—a binary pair so "congenital to philosophy," Derrida observed, that it "is even older than Plato." Lévi-Strauss had repeatedly questioned this nature/culture binary, most spectacularly with respect to the incest prohibition. Here was a phenomenon that was simultaneously universal and subject to variously formulated social rules. It belonged neither to nature nor to culture but to *both*. Lévi-Strauss called the incest taboo's breaching of categories a "scandal." Yet it was only a scandal within a system in which such opposing categories held sway, and Lévi-Strauss, Derrida maintained, had been both unable to leave the binary completely behind, nor (which might amount to the same thing) account for the incest prohibition as a historical development occurring at a particular moment in time.

Locked into structuralist paradigm, Lévi-Strauss had no means of accommodating history. Language, he asserted in one essay, for example, "could only have been born in one fell swoop." When change figured in his ethnographies, Derrida argued, it took the form of a "catastrophe"—typically the encroachment of civilization on some purer state of nature. By the end of Derrida's talk, Lévi-Strauss's work was riddled with holes. For all his brilliance, the anthropologist was guilty of "a sort of ethic of presence, an ethic of nostalgia for origins, an ethic of archaic and natural innocence, of a purity of presence and self-presence in speech." The catalog of sins was sufficiently damning that to read it is to wonder whether Lévi-Strauss had caught wind of the paper in advance and decided he wasn't about to fly across the Atlantic to subject himself to such a vigorous dressing down in person.

But Lévi-Strauss was just the most prominent offender. The problem was structuralism itself: It had grown sloppy, forgetful, sentimental. Having conceived of a world in which "everything became discourse," the structuralists had failed to adhere to the radical implications of this development. They had clung to what had been lost—an origin, an essence, binary thinking—rather than embracing the tendency that structuralism portended, what Derrida called "play."

And what was play? Here, Derrida's talk got a little fuzzy. Caught like everyone else in the logic and lexicon of metaphysics, he could not quite explain this novel philosophy of play. But he could gesture toward it. Play was what became possible in a structure without a center, where meaning was nowhere fixed. Play was integral to language: "a field of infinite substitutions in the closure of a finite ensemble." Play was also, then, "the disruption of presence." It was movement, instability, flux. It was pleasure: "the joyous affirmation of the play of the world and of the innocence of becoming."

Derrida concluded his talk on a note of high theater, leaving his audience with an image of the dispensation to come that, despite the intimations of innocence and joy, seemed to have been plucked from the pages of a sci-fi novel, or perhaps a horror movie: "the as yet unnamable which is proclaiming itself and which can do so, as is necessary whenever a birth is in the offing, only under the species of the nonspecies, in the formless, mute, infant, and terrifying form of monstrosity."

◆ ◆ ◆

Derrida's listeners were stunned. They grasped that they had heard something momentous, even as they struggled to make sense of it. Jean Hyppolite spoke first, with a question about "the center of structure." In Derrida's new universe of play, there was no center. Yet Derrida himself had admitted that "the notion of a structure lacking any center represents the unthinkable itself." So how can we conceive of a structure without a center? Hyppolite wanted to understand what Derrida meant by this conceit, or at least where he was going with it.

"I was wondering myself if I know where I am going," Derrida replied earnestly. "So I would answer you by saying, first, that I am trying, precisely, to put myself at a point so that I do not know any longer where I am going."

Where Derrida was going would eventually be called poststructuralism, though no one knew it at the time. What was apparent was that structuralism had suffered a mortal blow. Pressed by Hyppolite, Derrida tried again to explain. "Structure should be centered," he conceded. "But this center can either be thought, as it was classically, like a creator or being or a fixed and natural place; or also as a deficiency, let's say; or something which makes possible 'free play,' in the sense in which one speaks of the '*jeu dans la machine*' [ghost in the machine], of the '*jeu des pièces*' [game with pieces], and which receives—and this is what we call history—a series of determinations, of signifiers, which have no signifieds finally, which cannot become signifiers except as they begin from this deficiency." And here, having summarized the dubious logic of the "centered" structure as a source of meaning, and the potential for a radically different approach involving "free play," he concluded with a gross understatement: "So, I think that what I have said can be understood as a criticism of structuralism."

Afterward, a Hopkins professor who had not attended the talk (he'd had to teach a class) ran into the literary theorist Georges Poulet, who had. "I have just heard the most important lecture of the conference," Poulet told the professor. "It's against everything that I do but it was the most important lecture." For the Americans, Richard Macksey reflected ruefully, what was to have been a triumphant inauguration into the hip methodology of structuralism turned out "more like a requiem for the movement." As he told *Johns Hopkins Magazine* years later, recalling the impact of Derrida's talk: "I hadn't realized that he was going to be the Samson to tear down the temple of structuralism."

Inauguration or requiem, the Americans were hooked. While in France, structuralism's stalwarts—the four grass-skirted men of "The Structuralist Picnic" cartoon—would continue to hold sway, through the upheavals of May '68 and for a while beyond, in the United States it was Derrida who now generated the most excitement. The feeling was evidently mutual. In 1968, Derrida returned to Johns Hopkins for two months, a visit he repeated three years later. By 1974, he was making annual trips to Yale as a visiting professor, despite a debilitating fear of flying that he treated with handfuls of sedatives. Though he sometimes referred to himself as a "travelling salesman" hawking his wares, his transatlantic life elated him. In America, unlike in France, Derrida was a superstar.

Before leaving Baltimore in 1966, a few of the conference's European guests toured local sites. Derrida chose to see the house where Edgar Allan Poe had once lived, not far from where he was found in October 1849, disheveled and delirious in a local tavern before dying a few days later of uncertain causes. In hindsight, Derrida's visit to Poe's house seems symbolic, a fitting tribute to the writer whose enigmatic detective fiction had so enchanted the French, prefiguring both the dreamlike visions of the Surrealists and the rigorous linguistic logic of the structuralists. In this regard, the visit was also a kind of internment: Not only Poe was dead, but Surrealism too—André Breton had died in Paris just three weeks earlier, marking his movement's official end. And now Derrida was sounding the death knell for structuralism.

Lacan, for his part, asked to tour a Baltimore mental hospital. At dinner with local psychiatrists afterward, he managed to offend nearly everyone in the room. One eminent doctor reportedly got up and said, "I know a schiz when I see one" before walking out in a huff.

Chapter 33

THE CONNOISSEUR OF NOTHINGNESS

The Hopkins conference was decisive for the future of theory in another way: It was where Derrida met Paul de Man. The friendship between these two men, hatched over a breakfast table in Baltimore, would be life-changing for both. At forty-six, de Man, a Belgian-born professor of French literature at Cornell, was ten years Derrida's senior, but he too was at the start of a meteoric career, attracting notice as a brilliant theorist who straddled the fields of literature and philosophy. Like Derrida, he had published articles in Bataille's journal *Critique*—where Derrida would soon join the editorial board. And like Derrida, de Man was a specialist in the art of the takedown. Both were theorists of disillusionment, allergic to humanism and expert at detecting the faintest residue of metaphysical thinking in even the most carefully wrought exegesis.

Unlike Derrida, however, de Man knew his way around the campuses of the American Ivy League. He had arrived in New York City in 1948, one more refugee from war-devastated Europe without money or connections. His first job was as a stock boy at the Doubleday bookstore in Grand Central Terminal, where he spent his days in a subbasement, passing books up through a trapdoor to the salesfloor.

In retrospect, the image seems strikingly apt: From the anonymous obscurity of the underground stockroom, de Man made a near-vertical ascent, through the trapdoor at Doubleday to the living rooms of New York's most glamorous intellectuals and on up to the top rung of American academia, eventually attaining the title of Sterling Professor at Yale—the university's most prestigious honorific. His English was middling, his background murky, yet within five months of his arrival in the United States, he was attending parties at the home of Dwight Macdonald, the editor of the journal *politics* (the lowercase "p" was deliberate), and had befriended the novelist Mary McCarthy, who in 1949 helped get him a job teaching French at Bard College, where he was an instant hit. "If I have known a great man, it is Paul de Man," one student wrote in a characteristically gushing course evaluation.

It didn't hurt that de Man, then twenty-nine, was physically prepossessing: blond, blue-eyed, square-jawed, austerely elegant. "Catnip to women," his biographer Evelyn Barish writes. He exuded "aura"—the poet John Hollander's word—like a fine cologne. Men, women, students,

Paul de Man at Bard College, circa 1950

colleagues: All were susceptible to his charms. Mary McCarthy, who had recently married for the third time, was evidently smitten. De Man mentioned a wife in Europe whom he was expecting would eventually join him in New York. But that didn't stop McCarthy from inviting him to her Manhattan apartment for Thanksgiving, Christmas, and Easter, and then, in the summer of 1949, to her Rhode Island farmhouse. McCarthy's letters to her friend the critic Elizabeth Hardwick that summer are peppered with references to de Man. Barish thinks it's possible they had an affair. Their contact ceased only in 1950, after de Man wrote to say that he had fallen in love with a twenty-two-year-old Bard senior, Patricia (Pat) Kelley, and was divorcing his wife.

Two years later, de Man, now married to Pat and the father of a baby boy, was living in Boston and enrolled as a graduate student in the comparative literature department at Harvard. Short on cash, he also had a full-time job teaching French at a local Berlitz school, where Henry Kissinger, then a graduate student at Harvard too, was one of his students. Soon Kissinger had hired de Man as his private French tutor and was paying him to translate articles for *Confluence*, the international journal of ideas that Kissinger, already flexing his outsize ambition, had just founded.

Kissinger's response to de Man, like McCarthy's before him, was typical. People were invariably impressed by de Man's intellect and good looks, but they were also moved by what they perceived to be his plight. Writing to Elizabeth Hardwick in the summer of 1949, McCarthy confessed that she had violated her friend's confidence by telling de Man about Hardwick's plan to marry the poet Robert Lowell that July. "He has so little," McCarthy wrote by way of justification, "that he needs a secret to enrich him socially."

Already in his early thirties when he started graduate school, de Man was older than most of his peers, and a suggestion of unspoken personal tragedy seemed to hang over him. It was whispered that he had been in the Resistance during the war but that his uncle Hendrik de Man, a onetime leader of the Belgian Labor Party, had sullied the family name by collaborating with the Nazis—serving as Belgium's de facto prime minister during the occupation, after the rest of the government fled.

As Paul de Man's biographer tells it, the record of his first decade in America is a history of often improbable interventions by the many who went out of their way to assist him—awarding him work, favors, special privileges, and exemptions. When he lost the job McCarthy had procured for him at Bard—he had been filling in for a professor on leave—a colleague wrote to the chairman of Harvard's comparative literature department to help gain him entrée there. The department's administrators then granted de Man the unheard-of right to attend the program part-time, so that he could keep his job at Berlitz. In 1954, they nominated de Man to Harvard's Society of Fellows—an elite fraternity of the country's most promising young scholars where membership includes a generous three-year stipend. Then, after de Man's three-year term expired, the department chairman ensured that he was awarded a stipend for a fourth year—again, unheard-of.

When de Man fell behind on completing his degree, the essays required for his general examinations were waived, leaving only an oral exam for him to take. Even so, de Man failed the oral. Required to take the full complement of exams eighteen months later, he managed only to squeak by. (Unlike in France, it was rare for Ivy League doctoral students not to pass their generals.) Eight years into his graduate studies, he had yet to produce a dissertation. Yet early in 1960, just when his Harvard mentors finally lost patience with him, Cornell offered him a tenure-track job, largely on the basis of a single essay, a critique of representations of nature in Romantic poetry, published that year in a French journal. In short, every time de Man's good fortune seemed about to run out, someone stepped in to rescue him.

His most important experience at Harvard may have been as a teaching assistant in "Interpretation of Literature," a popular undergraduate course better known as Hum 6, taught by Reuben Brower. Brower was the leading exponent on campus of the New Criticism, the first home-grown literary theory to catch on in the United States in the decades after the war. The New Critics—originally a group of Southern-born, mostly Ivy League WASPs—shared with the French structuralists an insistence on the primacy of the text, in the case of the New Critics typically a poem. The New Critics did not share the Frenchmen's radical view of language as mediator of reality and the self, but they wanted to restore language to the center of literary criticism. They believed their field had become bogged down in ideology and historical data, with the result that poetry, from Shakespeare and Milton to Yeats, had been reduced to a mere reflection of its "age"—and the age's political, religious, and moral conflicts.

Such an approach risked missing much of what made a poem "poetic" and literature "literary," the New Critics argued. Their stance on the objects of their professional study, like their attitude toward their field, was defensive and reverential. A poem did not lend itself to simple paraphrase. It was naturally harmonious and self-contained, and the job of the critic was to identify, through meticulous close reading, the literary devices—irony, paradox, and ambiguity were favored terms—on which its formal structure depended. Only by correctly apprehending a poem's form could its true meaning be revealed. Thus Cleanth Brooks, a leading New Critic and professor at Yale, dismissed T. S. Eliot's complaint that the flippant last lines of Keats's "Ode on a Grecian Urn" ("'Beauty is truth, truth beauty,—that is all/Ye know on earth, and all ye need to know'") had ruined an otherwise "beautiful poem." Once those lines were considered in light of the poem as a whole, Brooks insisted, as a speech delivered "in character" by the handsome, preening urn itself, the verse made perfect sense.

De Man excelled at close reading. Peter Brooks, who was his student at Harvard and later his colleague at Yale, said that de Man could "sit in front of a text and just pluck magical things out of it." Another Yale scholar, the legendary Harold Bloom, famous for his encyclopedic memory and impassioned defense of the Western canon, recalled meeting de Man at Harvard in the mid-1950s, when Bloom was also at the beginning of his career and had been nominated to the Society of Fellows.

Ultimately, he was not selected for the fellowship, but he returned to Yale dazzled. He told a colleague who had just published his first book, on poetic interpretation: "I met a blond Apollo named Paul de Man. He's read your book—*and understood it*."

Which is not to say that de Man necessarily agreed with the book's author. His typical pattern was to absorb the latest currents in literary criticism and then set about confidently enumerating their flaws. Several of his early articles were written in French for *Critique*, but he soon mastered English well enough to publish elegantly devastating dissections in American journals. The New Critics in his view were ripe for such treatment. Despite a fixation on "terms such as paradox, tension, and ambiguity," he wrote in "The Dead-End of Formalist Criticism," which appeared in *Critique* in 1956, the New Critics clung to the idea of a seamless continuity between experience and language—a belief "that language, poetic or otherwise, can *say* any experience." About the error of this view, de Man was adamant: "Neither the statement 'I see a cat' nor, for that matter, Baudelaire's poem '*Le Chat*' contains wholly the experience of this perception. . . . Instead of containing or reflecting experience, language constitutes it."

Ten years before the Baltimore conference, at a time when most French intellectuals had barely heard of Saussure or Lacan's symbolic order, de Man was already flexing his structuralist bona fides. There could be no communion between language and things. To believe that a poem could bridge the gap between these two incommensurable realms—that a thing composed of words was also an object in the world—was naïve. "It is substance itself that is the abyss," de Man wrote.

"Abyss" is a word that tends to crop up in his writing, along with "nothingness," "negation," "negativity," and "void." In *Blindness and Insight*, de Man's most famous collection of essays, most of these terms merit their own entries in the index. His conviction that language and, by extension, human consciousness, could never coincide with experience but, at best, could only name that impossibility, was absolute. His Yale colleague Geoffrey Hartman said that de Man was "a connoisseur of nothingness"—he meant it as a compliment.

Unlike Derrida and Lacan, de Man did not spin elaborate metaphors or indulge in intricate wordplay. He had not secretly hoped to be a novelist in the manner of James Joyce. Instead, his prose was pared down, rigorous, devoid of sentiment. There is no entry for "pleasure" in *Blindness and Insight*. The one for "beauty" reads: "of fictional narratives, 17; as romantic delusion, 12–13." His byword may as well have been "dispassion in all things." Once, after Hartman delivered a lecture on "Ode on a Grecian Urn," de Man, whose turn it was to speak next, turned to the class and said, in his French-accented English: "Professor Hartman has given you beauty, now you will get *de trut*." Aghast, a teaching assistant scurried to Hartman's office afterward to assuage any hurt feelings.

De Man read literature the way a philosopher would. Even more than Derrida, he was at home in abstraction. He was first and foremost a theorist, perhaps the purest specimen America—the country in which he made his career—had yet produced.

Chapter 34

ROUSSEAU'S SUPPLEMENT

When de Man and Derrida met in Baltimore in 1966, they quickly discovered how much they had in common. De Man, the philosophically inclined literature professor, and Derrida, the literature-loving philosopher, happened to be working on the same obscure text by Jean-Jacques Rousseau: *Essay on the Origin of Languages*. "Each in his own way without knowing it," Derrida marveled, recalling the moment in an emotional eulogy after de Man's death. "From then on," he said, "nothing has ever come between us, not even a hint of disagreement."

And yet de Man's first formal commentary on Derrida's work *was* a disagreement, albeit one couched in the most complimentary terms. It appeared in English as an essay in *Blindness and Insight*, the collection de Man hastily compiled in 1970, when he was being courted by Yale and told that he could not be hired without at least one published book on his résumé. *Blindness and Insight* not only got him the job but made his reputation. "No aspiring academic critic could lay claim to credibility without having read it," one reviewer declared at the time. And the essay on Derrida was the book's most talked-about piece.

In *Of Grammatology*, Derrida's discussion of Rousseau occupies the middle of the book, following his critique of Lévi-Strauss. This is a logical progression: Lévi-Strauss's romantic ideas about preliterate human societies bore the mark of Rousseau's influence. Rousseau, too, was suspicious of writing. "Languages are made to be spoken," he said, parroting the standard line. "Writing serves only as a supplement to speech." Here, Derrida, in classic deconstructionist fashion, homed in on a single word: "supplement." He proceeded to trace the term across Rousseau's writings, showing to revelatory effect how, for the Swiss philosopher, "supplement" carried connotations of danger and artifice. For Rousseau, Derrida argued, "supplement" meant not only "surplus" but "substitution." It was the opposite of what is natural or complete—nature for Rousseau being what "suffices and is self-sufficient."

Nature had no need for supplementation. Yet human society in Rousseau's view was rife with such activity. Supplementing nature was necessary for progress but simultaneously a path to wickedness. In *Emile, Or Treatise on Education,* Rousseau suggested that children were born too weak to withstand all of nature's demands, and thus education had to "supply"—*suppléer*—what "is lacking." And in his famous *Confessions*, the word "supplement" comes up again, this time in reference to masturbation, a habit Rousseau picked up as a teenager in Italy and which caused him great anguish: "I learned

Jean-Jacques Rousseau

that dangerous means"—*ce dangéreux supplément*—"which cheats Nature and saves up for young men of my temperament many forms of excess at the expense of their health, strength, and, sometimes, their life."

Masturbation saps vitality by substituting a cheat for actual (natural) sex. But for Rousseau it's threatening in another way, too. It allows for the satisfaction of desire in the absence of an actual partner: "This vice, which shame and timidity find so convenient, possesses, besides a great attraction for lively imaginations—that of being able to dispose of the whole sex as they desire, and to make the beauty which tempts them minister to their pleasures, without being obliged to obtain its consent."

Masturbation substitutes an imaginary woman for the real thing, creating an illusion of presence that is—scandalously, for Rousseau—just as satisfying, perhaps more so. Writing, speech's "supplement," operates in analogous fashion, substituting an illusion of the human presence inherent in actual (natural) speech. In short, masturbation is to sex what writing is to speech, and in Derrida's reading, it's no coincidence that Rousseau invokes the same term for both. For him, both are similarly dangerous, similarly unnatural. Yet both are unavoidable. Try as he might, Rousseau can no more give up masturbation, Derrida writes, "than one can give up language."

This is the crux of Derrida's argument: Rousseau's efforts to rescue speech from writing prove futile; the same attributes that make writing seem unnatural and threatening also—by Rousseau's own description—pertain to speech. Rousseau declares that language began with "voice," the traditional philosophical stance. But his attempts to define speech end up underscoring not its naturalness but the opposite. According to Rousseau, what transforms meaningless "sound" into meaningful "voice" are consonants and articulation—the very features, Derrida insists, that distinguish writing: "A speech without consonantic principle, what for Rousseau would be a speech sheltered from all writing, would not be speech; it would hold itself at the fictive limit of the inarticulate and purely natural cry. Conversely, a speech of pure consonants and pure articulation would become pure writing, algebra, or dead language." In sum, Rousseau's own text suggests that speech is already inhabited by key properties of writing; neither mode is any more natural or alive than the other. Put another way: Writing is no supplement to speech but rather integral to it—to language itself.

Derrida's reading was a classic deconstruction of a sacred Western binary. (Was it also the reason literature students of my generation mocked the more impenetrable theory on our syllabi as "mental masturbation"?) In the fall of 1967, de Man sent Derrida a congratulatory note. *Of Grammatology* had just appeared in France, following the two other books he published that year, *Writing and Difference* and *Speech and Phenomena*. Derrida had been racking up breathless press coverage, even beyond France's borders. "The boldest contemporary thinker," declared *La Tribune de Genève*. Even Heidegger wanted to meet him. A friend of Derrida's who visited Heidegger the following December reported that the two spent a long time discussing how to translate "*différance*" into German, eventually concluding it was impossible.

De Man, however, had more to say about *Of Grammatology*, and in *Blindness and Insight* he took Derrida to task. As a disputant, he was politer than either Derrida or Foucault, his tone detached and serene, and at the same time supremely confident. This pose was characteristic. "There was something permanently quizzical about de Man," Hartman, his Yale colleague, wrote after de Man's death. "Those eyes that looked at you acutely, steadfastly, yet always with a smile, and that slightly hunched form, as if weighed down by an Old World knowledge. He could be, as everyone knew, quietly devastating in his comments at public lectures and conferences. Even privately he claimed to know 'de trut.'"

"De trut," according to de Man in his essay "The Rhetoric of Blindness: Jacques Derrida's Reading of Rousseau," was that even the most perceptive literary critics had a puzzling tendency toward blindness: They routinely failed to grasp the deepest insights that their methods unwittingly revealed. Thus, though the New Critics stressed irony and ambiguity in their close readings of poetry, they failed to recognize how such traits undermined their insistence on a poem's harmonious unity. In short, the critic's most penetrating insights came at the expense of a "peculiar blindness." In this respect, de Man wrote, Derrida's reading of Rousseau was "an exemplary case."

Derrida purported to show how Rousseau favored speech over writing in keeping with Western tradition, which perceived speech as natural. However, de Man insisted, such a claim was directly contradicted by what Rousseau actually *wrote.* For a literary theorist or philosopher of language, Rousseau's *Essay on the Origin of Languages* was a tantalizing text. Written around 1755 but only published posthumously, in 1781, the essay traces the evolution of language from its birth in warm southern climates (according to Rousseau) through its subsequent migration northward. In Rousseau's account, language was inspired not by biological "needs" (hunger or thirst) but by abstract "passions" (love, hate, pity). At first, language had an expressive, metaphorical function, but over time it became more rational, more literal. Rousseau, who in addition to being a philosopher was an accomplished composer, draws an extended analogy between language and music. In doing so, he relies on a striking vocabulary that seems to anticipate structural linguistics.

Like signifiers in Saussure's scheme, a musical note is "nothing by natural right," Rousseau declares. "It is neither tonic, nor dominant, harmonic, or fundamental. All these properties exist as relationships only, and since the entire system can vary from bass to treble, each sound changes in rank and place as the system changes in degree." This is just how Saussure described words: Lacking inherent value themselves, they acquire value only in relation to others within the linguistic matrix. Or, as de Man put it in his essay, "the structural characteristics of language are exactly the same as those attributed to music."

De Man's essay makes a lot of sophisticated technical moves, all in the service of showing that Rousseau did not subscribe to the conventional view of speech as natural and writing as artifice. When Rousseau writes that "the first language was figural," de Man says, we should take him at his word, understanding that for Rousseau, this original figurative language corresponds, like music, to no *thing* in nature: It has "no literal referent"; it is "nothing by natural right." "Rousseau's theory of representation is not directed toward meaning as presence and plenitude," de Man writes, "but toward meaning as void."

"Meaning as void," is more or less de Man's definition of language. In conventional usage, we distinguish between figurative and literal language, understanding the former to stand in for, or refer to, concepts embodied by the latter—"bowels of the earth" for deep underground, "top of the heap" for most powerful person around, roses in Shakespeare's sonnets for youth and beauty, and so on. But de Man goes further. He suggests that figurative language is the only sort of language there is: Words only ever refer to other words and words themselves are a kind of artifice. Moreover, he argues, Rousseau grasped this principle. Language in Rousseau's account originally named not things in the world, but illusions, what he called "the illusory image presented by passion."

In one famous passage, Rousseau imagines the first human speech: an exclamation by a primitive man who encounters other humans for the first time. Frightened by the sight of these strange beings, the primitive man calls them "giants"—a misnomer. Over time and subsequent encounters, he realizes that these others are in fact just like him. He comes up with a word to describe them all—*man*—and "leaves *giant* to the false object that had impressed him during his illusion." Rousseau continues: "This is how the figurative word is born before the literal word, when our gaze is held in passionate fascination; and how it is that the first idea it conveys to us is not that of the truth."

The best way to understand Rousseau's essay, de Man insists, is as *allegory*. It tells a story of language's "degradation" from metaphor to literalization, from meaning as void to meaning as presence. Or, to put this another—more de Manian—way, from the truth that language is based in illusion to the illusion that language is based in truth.

The irony, de Man points out, is that the story about language

Rousseau's essay tells—one of progressive misunderstanding—is also the story of the essay's reception. The essay has repeatedly been misunderstood, he insisted, most recently by Derrida, as proof of Rousseau's (and, by extension, Western philosophy's) confusion about language. But to make that case is to discount the theory of figurative language the essay forcefully develops. It is to suggest, in other words, that Rousseau doesn't actually mean what he says. And this, de Man argues, is a classic form of critical blindness. In short, "there is no need to deconstruct Rousseau"; his essay deconstructs itself.

◆ ◆ ◆

Whew! No wonder one critic called de Man's reading of Derrida's reading of Rousseau "*the* primal scene of 'deconstruction in America.'" It was simultaneously an act of filiation and parricide. And almost all the themes that would preoccupy de Man over the course of his career were on display in it. There was his fascination with irony—how texts were destined to be misread, how even the most insightful critics were doomed to blindness. There was his interest in figurative language—"the only form of language free from the fallacy of unmediated expression." There was his championing of allegory, a literary device de Man did much to rescue from disrepute. His most influential essay along these lines, "The Rhetoric of Temporality," from 1969, was a bold attempt to rehabilitate allegory, which, beginning in the nineteenth century, had lost prestige to the symbol. Passed from student to student, the piece soon became known as "the most photocopied essay in literary criticism."

Undergirding all his work was his interest in "literariness"—in what makes literature "literary." For de Man, not only is all language figurative—it says one thing and means something else—but literature is the form in which this essential truth is most clearly expressed. Literary language is conscious of its status as rhetoric, as metaphor, aware that it stands in not for a thing or idea in the world but merely for other language. Alice Kaplan, who studied with de Man at Yale, said that to explain metaphor he liked to cite a scene in Hitchcock's *North by Northwest* where Cary Grant's character kisses the girl played by Eva Marie Saint in a train compartment. The camera immediately cuts to a shot of the train entering a tunnel. The image seems natural enough, since trains routinely go through tunnels, but de Man pointed out that it's also a metaphor for sex, because "foreplay, in a heterosexual world, leads to penetration." De Man stressed the speed at which this metaphoric substitution (of the tunnel for the couple) occurs, in the blink of an eye, between one film frame and the next—just as one word stands in for another in a process so seamless we are hardly aware of it.

And yet this process rests on instability. If a text appears to say one thing (speech is natural; writing is not) but also something completely different (speech is no more natural than writing), how do we decide which reading is correct? De Man demonstrated the point with a contrarian gloss on the famous last line of Yeats's poem "Among School Children": "How can we know the dancer from the dance?" The question has traditionally been understood as rhetorical, a mantra aligned with Romanticism's credo regarding the transcendent unity of form and content, creator and creation: *There is no way to separate the dancer from the dance.* Yet de Man argued that there is a second, equally plausible, reading, in which the question is taken literally, as an unresolved, even urgent, problem for the poem: *Please tell me, how* can *I know the dancer from the dance?* In this interpretation, Yeats is no longer a Romantic but a modernist, self-consciously reflecting on the limitations of the poetic genre—the impossibility of uniting form and content, word and thing. Here, in short, Yeats becomes a de Manian.

The "two entirely coherent but entirely incompatible readings can be made to hinge on one line, whose grammatical structure is devoid of ambiguity, but whose rhetorical mode turns the mood as well as the mode of the entire poem upside down," de Man wrote. Moreover, there was no way to make a "valid decision" about which reading is better. In de Man's account, literary language was inherently indeterminate—ambivalent, ironic, self-conscious. These features made literature the most important form of discourse, the prism through which to understand all the rest. As Geoffrey Hartman put it, de Man "made literary statements appear more philosophical in their self-reflective perspicacity than philosophical ones."

Chapter 35

HOW TO BECOME A DOMINANT FRENCH PHILOSOPHER

Of course, Derrida was interested in many of the same subjects as de Man. One of his most beautiful essays, "White Mythology: Metaphor in the Text of Philosophy," from 1971, took up the problem of figurative language for philosophy, namely: If all language is figurative, how can philosophy talk about metaphor without resorting to metaphor? De Man shrugged off the question. Asked how his own work could be said to be "about" anything, if all texts were, finally, allegories of indeterminacy, he replied curtly that his own work was of no interest to him—someone else was welcome to dissect it.

Both men were deconstructionists, and it's now a commonplace to say that de Man was Derrida's most faithful disciple. But in some ways de Man was the more radical of the two. Where Derrida saw his task as one of demystification—of exposing philosophy's complicity with unprovable, foundational claims—de Man suggested that philosophy is already demystified. Its language is no less literary than literature's, he insisted, and thus no less self-aware. "There is always already deconstruction at work *in* works," is how Derrida summed up de Man's approach after his death. "Deconstruction cannot be applied, after the fact and from the outside. . . . Texts deconstruct *themselves* by themselves."

Perhaps the greatest difference between de Man and Derrida, at least initially, was their status as teachers. Derrida, never at home in the French university system, maintained a foothold in Parisian academia through his position as *caïman* at the École Normale. In that role, he mentored students, several of whom became well-known philosophers themselves. In America, especially within the small French and English departments of the Ivy League, close relationships with graduate students were the norm. Yet even by this standard, the following that de Man acquired was extreme in its zeal.

"He radiated intellect," wrote Howard Felperin, a young Shakespeare scholar who was teaching at Yale when de Man arrived in 1970. "His mind had a critical edge, his work a philosophical breadth that seemed to cut modern literature at the joints, pull it apart, and put it back together in fresh, unfamiliar, uncanny, ways. He was changing the way a lot of us read great books, in my case, Shakespeare. In a career that by its nature threw me among some very smart people, Paul was the smartest I've ever been privileged to know." Hired to teach French literature, de Man "attracted graduate students from across departments," Felperin wrote. "Doctoral theses were taking on his distinctive inflection." Felperin wasn't sure he fully grasped de Man's inaugural lecture—"unusually attended by almost everyone"—but that didn't stop him from ditching Geoffrey Hartman as his mentor and devoting himself to the brilliant newcomer.

Alice Kaplan, who completed her PhD at Yale in 1981 and later joined the French department there, wrote that "at the literature lectures everyone on the faculty watched de Man's face, to gauge his reaction. The question asked by de Man was the center of gravity of any intellectual event." As a first-year graduate student taking his class, Kaplan wrote down everything de Man said, "even his asides." Afterward, she and the other students would gather at a campus coffee lounge and try to parse what they had just heard. There was "a religious quality to the reading he inspired," Kaplan said, recalling one classmate's boyfriend, who liked to get stoned and read aloud from de Man's essay "The Rhetoric of Temporality" "just to feel how hard and mysterious the words were."

The most senior faculty in the humanities routinely audited de Man's class. It's likely, one scholar later wrote, that "no comparably intense institutional scene of intellectual excitement (and bafflement, and hostility) has existed before or since in the history of academic literary criticism in the United States."

De Man himself was said to resist his anointment as a guru, a stance that seemed only to encourage veneration. "He never sought followers; people followed him in droves," said his former student, Harvard's leading deconstructionist, Barbara Johnson. "He was ironic toward discipleship; the country is dotted with his disciples." He was Yale's "resident Godfather," another critic wrote, "the *capo di tutti capi*."

So remarkable was de Man's reputation that after he died, he became the subject of a famous case study by the literary critic John Guillory. In Guillory's view, de Man's astonishing career was less a testament to his brilliance as a thinker than a symptom of a disciplinary crisis. In *Cultural Capital: The Problem of Literary Canon Formation*, a widely read book published in 1993, a decade after de Man's death and in the middle of the so-called canon wars over which works should be taught at universities, Guillory argued that the canon debate masked a more fundamental problem: the declining value of literary study in higher education and to society at large. Literary knowledge, he suggested, was the currency of "the old bourgeoisie"—its "cultural capital." But this old bourgeoisie was more and more irrelevant, drained of social status and power by the rise, beginning in the 1960s, of a "new professional-managerial class" and, with it, a profound shift in the "conditions of intellectual labor."

Now, in the marketplace where students newly credentialed with a college degree competed for jobs, specialized knowledge and technical competence were prized over fluency in modern poetry or Shakespeare, and the rationale for literary study was increasingly in doubt. Where once the teaching of literature had turned on the art of interpretation, on offering new readings of canonically sanctioned great works (think of the New Critics), the new dispensation "no longer requires the (primarily literary) cultural capital of the old bourgeoisie." The university, whose primary purpose was the "*reproduction* of the social order, with all of its various inequities," had to adjust, and in the literature department the response was theory: a salvo of rigor and technique in the face of a society-wide devaluation of the field. This is where de Man came in. Of the various exponents of theory, Guillory maintained, by far the most effective was de Man, who, in both his teaching and personal style, embodied precisely the qualities demanded by the new social order.

By emphasizing literature's rhetorical properties, de Man shifted his field's focus away from narrow thematic and aesthetic concerns to technical ones while simultaneously expanding its institutional reach to non-literary domains. (Since for de Man, all language shares literature's features—all language is figural—literary study becomes a "specialization with a *universalist* rationale.") Moreover, his insistence on "rigor" as the cornerstone of his teaching neatly aligned with what Guillory called "the technobureaucratic labor of the new professional-managerial class." "Rigor" defined not only de Man's method, naming a technically demanding interpretive practice, but also his classroom demeanor: "In his 'impersonality,' he rather resembles language itself," Guillory wrote, "or more accurately, he resembles his *teaching about language*." As one of his students put it, "Those who learned the lesson he had to teach learned not to read like *him* but like him to *read*."

De Man's professional detachment, his assiduous disavowal of his status as an authority or guru, was, Guillory suggested, the key to his charisma, perversely ensuring the devotion of his students ("Nothing succeeds so well as detachment to produce fascination"), and, through their loyal discipleship, the broad dissemination of his theory. He "disappeared" into his teaching, his style becoming inseparable from his thought, thus enhancing its standing as objective, even scientific, knowledge—a body of work that could be precisely transmitted and replicated. And yet, in this account, de Man was at best a stopgap measure: Theory saturated the university even as the canon wars continued. In the long run, theory was no match for the crisis over what constitutes "literature" and what literary scholars should do with it.

In Guillory's analysis, de Man was the beneficiary of large-scale social upheaval and related pressures on the American university. In telling this story, he put his finger on an important development. When the work of the French philosophers arrived in America, it took on a new shape and a new name. It became *theory*. In France in the 1960s, the obsession with language as an impersonal force had found adherents across the humanities and social sciences, from anthropology and psychology to history, philosophy, and literature. Many of the leading French thinkers in these fields were prominent public intellectuals. In America, by contrast, theory was an academic phenomenon—Derrida called it "a purely North American artifact." And thanks in large part to Derrida's talk at the Johns Hopkins conference, young American critics quickly leapfrogged structuralism to embrace its poststructuralist successor: deconstruction—a term increasingly synonymous with theory.

Guillory singled out the features of deconstruction that helped revive, at least temporarily, literary studies' declining fortunes, distancing it from the realm of aesthetic appreciation and anchoring it to science. But this transformation of the field was predicated on another, even more unlikely one: turning a French philosopher's highly abstract and provisional commentary on the Western philosophical tradition into a concrete and systematic program for reading by literature critics in the United States.

In the 1980s, Michèle Lamont, a social scientist then at Princeton, wanted to know how this metamorphosis had occurred. "How can a French philosopher gain acceptance in the land of empiricism?" she wondered. Her explanation, published as a study called "How to Become a Dominant French Philosopher: The Case of Jacques Derrida," was, like Guillory's analysis of de Man's career, sociological. Derrida's work was "ambiguous," "distinctive," and highly "adaptable"; it provided "an answer to a disciplinary crisis." In one of the numerous charts accompanying her study, Lamont showed how discussion of Derrida's work in France declined steeply in the mid-1970s, just as discussion of his work in the United States took off. Derrida began his career as a French philosopher and ended it as the OG of American literary theory. "On the basis of Derrida's work," Lamont reported, "American undergraduate students in literary criticism currently discuss the logocentrism of the philosophical tradition without having read a single classic of philosophy." Here I blush to recognize my college-age self, earnestly parroting Derrida's critique of Plato's *Phaedrus*—in which Plato associates writing with a "pharmakon," an ambiguous term that can mean both "poison" and "cure"—despite having only a glancing familiarity with the ancient Greek text.

Chapter 36

TYRANNY OF THE YALE CRITICS

Missing from the sociological accounts of de Man's and Derrida's careers was any mention of their personal relationship. It was de Man who, after their fateful meeting in Baltimore, persuaded Derrida to offer a seminar in Paris on "the philosophical foundations of literary criticism" for de Man's graduate students at Cornell as well as a few from Johns Hopkins. That seminar marked the beginning of a new role for Derrida as a teacher of Americans. By the mid-1970s, again thanks to de Man, he was making annual visits to Yale, de Man's new academic home, where he was soon given a formal appointment as a visiting professor.

When Derrida went to America, it wasn't just the cultural status of his work that changed—from philosophy to theory. He changed too. Like hapless, bespectacled Clark Kent stepping into the phone booth and reemerging as the buff and dauntless Superman, Derrida stepped onto an airplane in Paris, swallowed some pills to calm his nerves, and reemerged on US soil as one of a rarefied breed: an "academostar."

In Europe in the late 1960s, he had been neither confident nor flashy. "In those days, Derrida was still not very sure of himself," an American

Paul de Man and Jacques Derrida as academostars in the late 1970s

scholar who met him in Berlin in 1968 recalled. "He dressed rather drably, like a traditional professor, and was ill at ease in social situations. Only gradually did he free himself up, inventing a public persona for himself and a form of erotic identity that he made his own." Within a few years, Derrida dazzled. Friends took note of the performative quality of his lectures—the "perfect diction, the energetic gestures, especially the one used to announce quotation marks, which evoked the torero just about to stick in his banderillas or the cowboy wielding a pistol in each hand." One friend said Derrida exuded a "radiant narcissism." His decision to forbid newspapers and magazines to print his photograph seemed less an act of modesty than a gesture calculated to enhance his mystique.

In 1974, he published his most audacious, and perhaps most self-indulgent book, *Glas*, a full-throated experiment in the poststructuralist doctrine of play. Running down the left side of the page was a commentary on Hegel, down the right a commentary on the outlaw novelist and playwright Jean Genet. On one side, the father of continental philosophy, on the other, the scandalous former prostitute and thief. The columns were printed in different size type, each wrapped around still more blocks of text—snippets from Genet's novels, letters from Hegel to his fiancée, dictionary entries, biblical quotations—the whole a delirious, punning tapestry of language and imagery. Family, flowers, hard-ons, prison, death: Derrida wove these motifs together like the warp and weft on a loom.

A critique of phallologocentrism? A Joycean celebration of intertextuality? A play on ancient rabbinical glosses of the Talmud? Derrida's answer to *Anti-Oedipus*? *Glas*—the book's title translates roughly as "death knell"—thwarted any attempt at conventional reading, or really, reading at all. Gayatri Spivak's gloss was characteristic. *Glas* was "an ancestral rite," she wrote, an elaborate gesture of mourning for Derrida's "fathers"—Nietzsche, Hegel, and his own, recently deceased, biological one—the book's two columns representing the mother's spread legs, the running commentary between them the father's act of insemination. Althusser wrote to Derrida that he was "bowled over" by *Glas*, calling it "a philosophical text without precedent . . . a poem of a kind I've never come across before." "Bowled over" was a reaction Derrida seemed to inspire in a lot of people at the time.

Over the course of the 1970s, more than twenty academic journals devoted to theory were founded in the United States. In 1975, writing in *The New Republic*, the literature scholar J. Hillis Miller alerted readers to "a new group of critics centered at Yale," who were dedicated to the latest currents in French thought. Miller himself was one of them, along with Harold Bloom, Geoffrey Hartman, and de Man. (A friend of mine recalls picking up the edition of *Bleak House* for which Miller had written a celebrated introduction and being disconcerted to learn that the Dickens novel he'd thought was about an interminable legal case was in fact a metanarrative about signifiers, or, as Miller put it, "a document about the interpretation of documents.") At Yale, graffiti in a men's bathroom testified to deconstruction's exalted status:

God is dead.
—*Nietzsche*

Nietzsche is dead.
—*God*

God is Nietzsche.
God is acid.
—*Timothy Leary*

God is base.
God is neutral.
God is indifferent.
God is difference.
Either/Or
—*Kierkegaard*

God is *différance.*
—*Derrida*

Whatever else one can say about the period, surely it was a high-water mark for academic graffiti.

By the mid-1980s, theory had the upper hand. English was Yale's second-most-popular undergraduate major, and in 1986, J. Hillis Miller was elected president of the Modern Language Association, the powerful professional organization for literature scholars. That year, *The New York Times Magazine* ran a cover story on the "tyranny of the Yale Critics" who were spreading the Derridean gospel across North America like so much dense jungle foliage, choking the literary estate. By then, de Man had been dead for more than two years, but he was credited or blamed—it wasn't quite clear which—for bringing Derrida, and deconstruction, to Yale.

In France in 1981, Derrida hadn't even rated a spot on a list of the country's most influential living intellectuals (as selected by six hundred academics, teachers, writers, artists, editors, politicians, and journalists for the journal *Lire*). But in the United States, he was huge. "Derrida's theories lingered in corridors and classrooms," wrote the novelist Jonathan Rosen, who entered Yale as an English major that year. "Even if you didn't speak French, or go to his seminars, you could absorb a lot just by inhaling deeply." If de Man was known for "killer close readings," it was Derrida, "the dashing silver-haired enfant terrible from the Sorbonne" who made "sober graduate students tremble like teenage girls waiting for Ed Sullivan to introduce the Beatles in 1964."

The analogy wasn't so far-fetched. In 1982, Derrida even made rock n' roll history, when the British band Scritti Politti titled a song in his name for its début album. (Sample lyric: "I'm in love with a Jacques Derrida/Read a page and know what I need to/Take apart my baby's heart.") In 1983, he had a cameo in a British art-house film about two women literally haunted by their pasts. (Derrida's concept of "hauntology"—a play on "ontology" and the idea that the past is neither present nor absent but functions as a ghostly force—was central to the movie's conceit.) Two years later, he collaborated with the architect Peter Eisenman on the design (never executed) for a garden in Paris's Parc de la Villette, a vast green space lined with cultural venues. Quotes from his books popped up on T-shirts and coffee mugs. An Italian painter made hundreds of silkscreens inspired by *Glas*. When the book came out in English in 1986, it was reviewed not only in academic journals but in *The New York Times Book Review*. The *Times*'s reviewer, an admirer of Derrida, dared to express his misgivings—"Our defense against a text declaring itself to be unreadable may be to call its author's bluff and simply leave it unread"—prompting indignant letters in the philosopher's defense. Unwilling to wait for the English translation, *The New York Review of Books* reviewed *Glas* in the original French.

As the term "deconstruction" underwent concept creep, losing in meaning what it gained in social currency, Derrida was asked to pronounce on all manner of cultural phenomena. Gamely, he obliged. The Woody Allen comedy *Deconstructing Harry*? "I was very disappointed at the use of the word 'deconstruction,'" he told a reporter for *The Times*. "I felt it was an exploitation of the term." *Seinfeld*, the prime-time show famously "about nothing"? "Deconstruction, the way I understand it, doesn't produce any sitcom," he patiently told an Australian TV anchor. "And if the people who watch this think that deconstruction is this, the only advice I have to give them is stop watching the sitcom, do your homework, and read."

However absurd the questions, Derrida thrived on the attention. As his biographer Peter Salmon summed up the moment: "Intellectually demanding French philosophers who at the age of thirty-seven are still slaving away unrecognized on obscure passages of Edmund Husserl concerning the origin of geometry, and of Rousseau's use of the word 'supplement,' don't tend to find themselves, fifteen years later, smoking pipes and being sexy and incomprehensible in major feature films, so why not enjoy?"

Less enjoyable were the attacks on deconstruction. These multiplied with each passing year, the backlash against theory growing in tandem with its influence. Assailed from the right as inscrutable and nihilistic, deconstruction was criticized from the left as ahistorical and apolitical. At the 1976 convention of the Modern Language Association, M. H. Abrams, an eminent critic at Cornell, had it out with J. Hillis Miller on a panel, mounting a strident defense of traditional literary interpretation against deconstructive unraveling and play. Abrams was no stick-in-the-mud: He recognized that literary texts could be "equivocal and multiplex in meaning." But he thought deconstruction went too far, shrouding texts in a specious fog of uncertainty. Three years later, at a conference on the state of literary criticism sponsored by *Partisan Review*, the journal's editor, William Phillips, cited French theory's dubious "antihistorical" and "pseudo-democratic ethos, in which all ideas are regarded as arbitrary, and equally valid." Another critic in attendance joked about making a Western starring Miller and Abrams, to be called *Shootout at Hermeneutic Gap*.

At least Abrams and Phillips had bothered to read the theory they objected to. So had John Searle, a philosopher at UC Berkeley who engaged in a two decades–long feud with Derrida over deconstruction. Searle found Derrida's obsession with binaries baffling. "Even in the philosophy of language," he wrote in 1983, "most authors do not devote much attention to the differences and similarities between written and spoken language. Derrida, however, thinks that the matter is of crucial importance." Struggling to account for deconstruction's popularity, Searle fell back on a sociological explanation in the mode of John Guillory. Deconstruction empowered an otherwise marginal field: "It is apparently very congenial for some people who are professionally concerned with fictional texts to be told that all texts are really fictional anyway" and "positively exhilarating to be told that what we call 'reality' is just more textuality."

But as theory's critics spread from academia to the media, the reporters and pundits who seized on it as proof of intellectual decadence and moral corruption on campus seemed less and less inclined to grapple with what the theorists actually said, making do instead with parodies of deconstruction gleaned from one another. Sensational sound bites made for a better story than patient elucidation. Even Searle conceded Derrida's seriousness, writing that his work is "not just a series of muddles and gimmicks." But it was Searle's phrase "*obscurantisme terroriste*" (terroristic obscurantism)—apparently how Foucault had once privately described Derrida's style to him—that the media pounced on, eventually transforming it, in a 1991 book by the poet and journalist David Lehman, for example, into the hyperbolic *J'accuse* "critical terrorism." "The ideas that deconstructionists articulate—with fervor if not necessarily with seriousness in the old-fashioned sense—do provide grounds for the terrorist analogy," Lehman wrote. "There is, for one thing, the relentlessly nihilistic drive of deconstruction. It asks how we can know anything and answers that we can't—nothing can be known."

In 1992, when the University of Cambridge announced that it planned to award Derrida an honorary doctorate, dozens of scholars mobilized in protest. In a letter published in the London *Times* that May, nineteen professors from various fields complained that Derrida had made a career of "translating into the academic sphere tricks and gimmicks similar to those of the Dadaists or of the concrete poets" and that many of his writings consisted "in no small part of elaborate jokes and puns ('logical phallusies' and the like)." "Logical phallusies" is an ingenious pun, but it is not one Derrida ever deployed. In the end, the detractors' campaign failed, and Derrida was duly awarded the degree by Prince Philip, the university's chancellor, who confided that the royal family, then dealing with fallout from the collapse of Prince Charles's marriage to Princess Diana, had lately been undergoing some painful "deconstruction" of its own.

Derrida might have murmured that he understood. His private life had also undergone some painful deconstruction. Married since 1957 to Marguerite Aucouturier, a psychoanalyst, and the father of two boys, he had gained a reputation as a skilled seducer. He, too, was catnip to women. In 1972, he began a twelve-year affair with Sylviane Agacinski, a philosophy graduate student who took his class at the École Normale. Agacinski was twenty-six; Derrida was forty-one. She went on to become a prominent philosopher of gender, a driving force behind France's "parity" law, which, passed in 2000, required political parties to run slates with equal numbers of women and men in most political races or be docked campaign funding. (Two decades later, more women have been elected to positions of power in France, but they still make up fewer than 40 percent of the French Senate and National Assembly.)

In 1984, Agacinski gave birth to Derrida's son Daniel Agacinski. By then, however, she had met Lionel Jospin, a Socialist Party leader who would go on to serve as prime minister. The affair with Derrida was over—Agacinski and Jospin would later marry—and Derrida was not part of Daniel's life. According to one account, Derrida saw Daniel only twice: once soon after his birth, and once at an airport, when the boy was about ten. Unbeknown to either father or son, they had been on the same plane.

Derrida was secretive about his extramarital relationships—"If a right to the secret is not maintained then we are in a totalitarian space," he once wrote. Yet he incorporated coded references to his romantic life in his work. His 1980 book *La carte postale* (*The Post Card*), a meditation on letter writing and psychoanalysis that included his critique of Lacan's lecture on Poe, opens with a section called "Envois," consisting of notes, alternately cerebral and erotic, to an unnamed lover, presumably Agacinski. One reads in part: "I cry for you I cry over you in you pulling your hair toward me in handfuls it is never long enough you are above me and never again will I let you go even if you won't see me anymore."

For Derrida's eldest son, Pierre, then seventeen, the book's "disguised confidences" were too much. Already on distant terms with his father, Pierre moved out of his parents' home a few months after the book's publication and into the Paris apartment of Avital Ronell, an Israeli American philosopher and colleague of Derrida's with whom Pierre was romantically involved. In a note included in *The Post Card*, Derrida recounts meeting Ronell at a conference. He began by asking her name. "Metaphysics," she replied cheekily, adding, as she later recounted, "and I don't much like the way you've been treating me up until now."

Needless to say, Derrida was charmed.

Chapter 37

DERRIDA BEHIND BARS

Pierre and Ronell were visiting Ronell's family in New York in December 1981 when Derrida was arrested in Prague on charges of drug smuggling. He had flown to the city the day after Christmas, on behalf of the Jan Hus Educational Foundation, an organization formed in response to the brutal crackdown on intellectual freedom in the wake of the briefly liberalizing "Prague Spring" of 1968. Derrida had personal connections to Czechoslovakia; his wife Marguerite's mother was Czech, and they had visited her relatives there before the Soviet invasion that put an end to the Prague Spring. The Jan Hus Foundation—the name came from a Czech religious reformer who had been burned at the stake for heresy in 1415—sent money to support samizdat publications and, more daringly, professors to deliver banned books and clandestine lectures to dissident scholars and students. Derrida, who was vice president of the foundation's French branch, had agreed to undertake such a mission.

The seminar he planned to give in Prague was on Descartes—hardly a political subject. But then, Derrida's work was not overtly political, a fact about which he was increasingly sensitive. Almost congenitally averse to public expressions of political commitment, he became more willing to defend democratic ideals as the 1980s progressed. A new emphasis on history, justice, and ethics appeared in his work—what some have called a "positive deconstruction." He wrote an essay on Nelson Mandela, and, after the fall of the Berlin Wall, a book on Marx. (In the postcommunist world, he argued, the legacy of Marxism entailed caring for global victims of poverty, famine, and violence.)

When he flew to Prague, he was working on an article about "Before the Law," a parable by Franz Kafka (later incorporated into his novel *The Trial*). The story concerns a man who waits before a gate to gain entry to "the law," only to be turned away again and again by the gatekeeper, who warns him that were he to try to pass, he would find only another gate and another gatekeeper, and on and on, ad infinitum. Years go by and, despite many efforts to gain admission, the man dies in front of the gate, having failed to get past it.

For Derrida, the parable was an occasion to ponder the ways in which literature and law are intertwined, each presupposing the other. Literature assumes the legal categories of title and author, and vice versa, yet the law itself is never directly available to us. We cannot see it. To appear "before the law" is to come face-to-face not with the law per se but with its human emissaries and interpreters—a lawyer or a judge. The closest we can get to the law may be in a story about the prohibition on seeing it. In Kafka's parable, the law remains sealed off, its authority invoked but forever inaccessible. As Derrida reads it, the tale is an allegory of *différance*—"the law of the law." Kafka renders as vivid metaphor language's operations of infinite difference and deferral, the foundational rule from which all meaning flows.

Derrida could not have guessed how germane his thoughts on the law would prove during his trip to Prague, though he certainly had reason to be anxious. The political situation in the Soviet bloc was tense. Two weeks earlier, Poland, on the verge of bankruptcy, had declared martial law, and the government had deployed tanks to suppress protests allied with the opposition Solidarity Movement. In return, the United States had imposed economic sanctions. Even before Derrida boarded his plane in Paris, he had the sense that he was being watched. Arriving in Prague, he was followed by an undercover cop whenever he left his hotel.

"I summoned up my knowledge of novels and psychology," he said later. "I tried to remember all the techniques of the genre."

One of his stops was the New Jewish Cemetery, where he went to see Kafka's grave. By the time he got to the apartment where he was to give his clandestine seminar, he was feeling deeply uneasy. His translator struggled to find words to convey his talk—a deconstruction of Descartes. Afterward, his listeners, a group of about ten, were tongue-tied. Finally, one spoke up, a priest affiliated with an underground church. "What use is that philosophy?" he asked. "What does such an intellectual, formal way of thinking have to offer to those who are living on the edge of existence, who are seeking a meaning to life in a totalitarian society?"

It's not clear that Derrida attempted much of an answer. A few minutes later, he left the apartment, still shaken. He decided to forgo a second seminar he was supposed to give and, after retrieving a few essentials from his hotel room, went to stay with his wife's aunt until his departure three days later. When he arrived at the airport on December 30 to catch his flight home, he was stopped at customs and taken to a private room. An agent with a sniffer dog set to work searching his luggage. Derrida assumed they were looking for suspicious manuscripts. Instructed to tear open the lining of his suitcase, he was mystified to discover four packets—each filled with white powder. The police were summoned, and Derrida was arrested and taken to a nearby station. There, in the presence of a police chief, a prosecutor, a translator, and a lawyer, he was interrogated for six hours—including about whose grave he had visited at the cemetery, and whether the professor at whose apartment he had lectured was a "Kafkologue." Finally, he was charged with drug trafficking and, at midnight, locked into a dirty cell in a prison next to the airport.

According to one account, Derrida spent the sleepless hours before dawn meditating "on the value of deconstructionist philosophy for those deprived of freedom." More likely, he was too frightened to do much meditating at all. Around five in the morning, he was joined in the cell by a Hungarian Romani man who, without having any language in common with Derrida, tried to console him. To pass the time, they played tic-tac-toe on a paper napkin. In the morning, Derrida was photographed, stripped, given a prison uniform, and told to pick out a pair of shoes—"from a pile like in concentration camps," he said later. He was then taken to a new cell occupied by five younger men. A couple of them spoke English. They told him he was likely looking at a two-year sentence.

Back in Paris, Marguerite was growing frantic. On December 30, she had gone to the airport to meet Derrida's plane, only to learn that his flight had been canceled. That night, her aunt called from Prague with word of Derrida's arrest. Marguerite started working the phones. Around 6 a.m. on the 31st, she reached Régis Debray, who had been Derrida's student at the École Normale and was now an adviser to the new Socialist president, Mitterrand. Within hours, the Czech ambassador to France was summoned to the Ministry for Foreign Affairs on the Quai d'Orsay, and news of Derrida's arrest hit the airwaves.

Derrida being greeted by French journalists upon arriving in Paris from Prague on January 2, 1982

The Czech ambassador appeared to have no idea who Derrida was. He was baffled that the matter was being treated as a state crisis. But the request for Derrida's release was dutifully relayed to the Czech president who, wanting to avoid an international incident, directed the police to let him go. In the middle of the night, Derrida was led from his cell and deposited at the French embassy. "You must have the impression of living in a Kafka story," the Czech lawyer assigned to him said. "Don't take things too tragically; consider it a literary experience."

Interviewed on French television after his ordeal, Derrida was careful to avoid self-pity and stress his solidarity with Czech citizens "who are struggling for human rights." But the experience had traumatized him like few others in his life. He compared it to his expulsion from school in Algiers during World War II because he was Jewish: "Whether they expelled me from school or threw me into prison, I always thought the other must have good reasons to accuse me."

Years later, after the fall of communism, the Czech police official who had masterminded the arrest as part of an effort to embarrass Czech dissidents—presumably planting the drugs in Derrida's suitcase while Derrida was paying his respects at Kafka's grave—was himself arrested for drug trafficking.

Chapter 38

THE RADICAL CAMPUS

Foucault hadn't spoken to Derrida in ten years, not since their quarrel over madness and reason had ended in a bitter rift. But when he heard that Derrida was in jail in Prague, he immediately went on the radio to demand his release. By 1981, Foucault's moral authority in French national affairs was virtually unrivaled. Sartre was dead and Foucault had taken his place as his country's premier intellectual *engagé*.

This development was hardly a foregone conclusion. A decade earlier, Foucault had seemed destined for a career among France's cloistered elite, having been elected in 1970 to a lifetime appointment at the Collège de France. He had joined the Communist Party as a student at the École Normale but dropped out after less than three years. And he had completely missed May '68. He was teaching philosophy at the University of Tunis, and when he finally showed up in Paris at the end of the month, the protests were winding down. At the Collège de France, his chair was in the "history of systems of thought"—the title was his idea, one whose abstract sweep hardly suggested a political focus. But by the time he delivered his inaugural address, in December 1970, a transformation had occurred: Foucault had become an activist.

In part, he was influenced by his partner, Daniel Defert, a committed

Maoist. He had also been affected by student protests he'd witnessed in Tunis. In March 1968, students at his university, inspired by growing anti-colonial sentiment elsewhere, had rioted to protest their authoritarian government. Some had been arrested and sentenced to years in jail. Foucault didn't share the students' dogmatic Marxism, but he admired their commitment and tried to help, hiding a copy machine in his apartment for printing political pamphlets and allowing a few students to stay with him when they were on the run.

By the fall of 1968, he was back in Paris to start a new job: director of the philosophy department at the new University of Vincennes. The idea for the school had been hatched only that August—a concession from the chastened de Gaulle administration to France's restive student population—and its campus was constructed at record speed. A cluster of dreary, prefab concrete buildings plopped down in the woods next to a military firing range in the *banlieue*, Vincennes was also state of the art, with carpeted classrooms, abundant video monitors, leatherette armchairs by Herman Miller, and large bay windows overlooking the trees. The pedagogy and curriculum too were modernized: Lectures were out; group discussions were in. Exams were optional.

The school's faculty was nearly as radical as the students. Foucault helped to create the department of psychoanalysis, railroading the proposal through the educational bureaucracy, and under his direction, the philosophy department was a hotbed of militancy. Course offerings included "Revisionism-Leftism," "Ideological Struggle," and "Cultural Revolutions," this last taught by Lacan's daughter Judith Miller. She was soon fired—on the order of France's president—for telling a reporter that she gave out course credits to strangers on the city bus. "The university is a fragment of capitalist society," she explained; her goal was to "make sure it functions as little as possible."

Not all the students were convinced by the administration's halting efforts at accommodation. Pamphlets preaching "the destruction of the university" made the rounds; the school, the message went, was still an appendage of bourgeois power, whatever the leftist pose. Classroom ceilings were dismantled in the search for bugs planted by the police. Foucault, arguably Vincennes' most famous hire—the bestselling author of *Les mots et les choses*—wasn't above suspicion. He was accused of being a Gaullist, and students disrupted his classes in protest.

His courses, "The End of Metaphysics" and "The Discourse of Sexuality," had a tamer ring than those of his militant colleagues. Even so, more than six hundred students enrolled. And when the first wave of demonstrations hit Vincennes in January 1969, just a few days after it opened its doors, Foucault joined the protestors on the front lines. Officially an act of solidarity with the Sorbonne, where students had occupied an administrative office, the rally at Vincennes was essentially an attempt to pick up where things had left off the previous May.

Hundreds of students occupied the central administration building, barricading the doors and stairwells with the beautiful new furniture and video monitors. Within hours, hundreds of police officers in riot gear surrounded the building and began lobbing tear-gas grenades through the windows. Foucault fled to the roof where he joined other

The University of Vincennes in the early 1970s

protestors in throwing stones at the police below, careful, one observer noted, not to dirty his black velour suit. He was now a militant but no less a dandy. He was briefly detained by the police. Thirty-four students were expelled.

◆ ◆ ◆

The January protest set the tone for life on campus. Its buildings were plastered with political posters and graffiti, its hallways lined with tables of students selling radical books and newspapers or distributing leaflets. A speaker system controlled by students blared announcements for political meetings along with a recording of the May '68 protest hit "Down With the Police State." As Hervé Hamon and Patrick Rotman recount in *Génération,* their two-volume history of the period, "Vincennes was the one place where it seemed May '68 never ended." (In fact, the university lasted barely ten years: In the summer of 1980, the French government razed the campus, which had become overcrowded, and relocated the students and faculty to the suburb of Saint-Denis.)

My friend Ken, a human rights lawyer, attended classes at Vincennes in 1971, during a junior year abroad from Yale, lured by France's reputation as the epicenter of both the student movement and cutting-edge philosophy. An activist since high school, Ken identified as a "post-Maoist" radical. "Clearly France was the place," he told me. "And Vincennes was amazing—table upon table of radical tracts." Foucault had left the university by the time Ken arrived, but he took a class with Deleuze, who was in the midst of writing *Anti-Oedipus.*

Far more students attended Deleuze's class than could fit in the designated room, Ken recalled, so dozens camped out along the corridor outside. Deleuze, a short man with flowing gray hair and intense eyes, dealt with the overenrollment by staying in constant motion. He delivered his lecture on foot, making an L-shaped circuit through the classroom, out into the corridor, and back again. With the result, Ken said, that "nobody could hear an entire sentence. We in the hallway would hear half of what he was saying, and then he would enter the classroom and say the other half. Every third word was '*le flou, le flou*'"—the flow, that all-purpose Deleuzian metaphor of resistance to the blockage of desire by capitalism, the state, the family, Freud, the Oedipal triangle. "He spoke in images," Ken said. "I thought he was a really interesting character, but I couldn't make head or tail of him."

At Vincennes, he added, you could hear gunfire from the military firing range next to campus all day long. "I assumed it was deliberate," he reflected—a sobering reminder of what could happen if students took things too far. So much for *le flou*. Even so, Ken's year among the French militants and intellectuals left a big impression. "It made a lot of these ideas much more real to me—the idea that there are revolutionary moments, and I was in the aftermath of one."

Not everyone on the Vincennes faculty at the time was prepared to inhabit a state of permanent turmoil. One senior philosopher left after a year, comparing the department's "atmosphere of intellectual terrorism" to what he'd experienced as a student at the École Normale in the early 1950s when it had been dominated by Stalinists. Lacan didn't make it through a single guest lecture. When, in the wake of May '68, he lost the right to hold his seminar at the École Normale, Foucault invited him to relocate it to Vincennes. Lacan proposed a series of lectures instead. But on his first visit, he was hectored by students from the moment he opened his mouth—"the drone of this lecture perfectly captures the current rotten state of the university," one shouted, while another began to undress in the auditorium. Lacan's "impromptu at Vincennes," as the French media gleefully dubbed it, ended with the psychoanalyst storming out of the hall, never to return.

Even Foucault tired of the endless uproar. When he left Vincennes at the end of 1970 to join the Collège de France, he told a friend that he'd "had enough of being surrounded by half-madmen." Yet the experience had profoundly changed him. The year 1969, Didier Eribon writes, "is when the Foucault whom everyone knows was created—the Foucault of demonstrations and manifestos; the Foucault of 'struggles' and 'critique.'"

Chapter 39

THE CHOMSKY HASH

Throughout the 1970s, Foucault led a double life: as a scholar and an activist. As a member of Paris's intellectual elite, he spent hours at the Bibliothèque Nationale and other archives, presenting his research at the Collège de France each year in a series of twelve weekly lectures. Like Derrida's talk in Baltimore, Foucault's lectures were *événements*: A crowd of five hundred flooded a room designed for far fewer, even after Foucault moved his starting time to 9 a.m. in a vain effort to shrink attendance.

The rest of his time he devoted to politics. He spent hours in the street, marching and shouting into a megaphone and, sometimes, hours in police stations or behind bars. In May 1970, the *Gauche prolétarienne* (GP), a militant Maoist group formed after May '68, was banned by the French government, and the editor of its weekly newspaper, *La Cause du peuple*, was jailed. (After a second editor was also jailed, the GP got Sartre to take over the paper, rightly inferring that the authorities wouldn't dare arrest him.) The GP made Vincennes a central hub, though some of its members abandoned school to work in factories, while others, including friends of Foucault's partner Daniel Defert, had been imprisoned—a few in solitary confinement. In September 1970, more than two dozen jailed GP members went on a hunger strike claiming they were political prisoners, unjustly held.

Foucault and Defert decided to organize a group to investigate conditions in French prisons. In keeping with Maoist principles, they were determined not to have scholars and intellectuals speak for the inmates, but rather, to help the inmates speak for themselves. In February 1971, at a press conference in the train station at Montparnasse, Foucault introduced the organization: the *Groupe d'Information sur les Prisons*, or GIP. "Police control is tightening on our everyday life, in city streets, and on roads," he said in a speech that would hardly have sounded out of place in the United States in 2025, as platoons of armed ICE agents roamed American cities in pursuit of immigrants to deport, and students in the country on visas or green cards were arrested for expressing views the Trump administration deemed threatening to national security. "Expressing an opinion is once again an offense for foreigners and young people, and antidrug measures are increasingly arbitrary," Foucault said. "We live in a state of 'custody.'"

The GIP lasted just a few years, but at its peak it included about two thousand members and produced some damning revelations. GIP questionnaires filled out by inmates were circulated as a series of pamphlets; a psychiatrist's report about conditions at a prison in Toul was excerpted in *Le Nouvel Observateur.* The French public was shocked to read about rampant suicide attempts, violence, and abuse—prisoners sedated or chained for days, left in their own excrement, unable to feed themselves.

Foucault was amazed by the public reaction. "The problem of prisons is local and marginal," he marveled in a 1972 interview with Deleuze, noting that no more than a hundred thousand people passed through the French prison system each year. "Yet this marginal problem seems to disturb everyone." The reason, he believed, had to do with power: "Prison is the only place where power is manifested in its naked state, in its most excessive form, and where it is justified as a moral force."

Like ideology for Althusser, power for Foucault was everywhere, a current running through social institutions and human beings alike. Yet unlike ideology, which Althusser argued was as invisible as it was inescapable, power, as Foucault conceived it, could be exposed to the light.

There were places in society where power's awesome coercive force could be seen and studied; the prison, like the madhouse, was one of them.

Foucault had found his great subject, the one that would preoccupy him for most of the rest of his life. Throughout the 1970s, wherever he detected abuses of power taking place, Foucault was on the scene, ready to point a finger or defend a victim. In December 1971, he was outside the prison at Toul, where inmates had staged an insurrection, setting fire to the library and smashing furniture. (Their main demands: warm baths and dental care.) Two months later, he was on a megaphone surrounded by demonstrators in front of the Renault factory outside Paris where a Maoist worker had been shot dead by a security guard. In the ensuing mêlée, he was bludgeoned on the head by a police baton. A year after that, he was attending the brainstorming sessions that led to the creation of a new leftist daily, *Libération*. Though he went on to write occasionally for the paper, his proposal to create a national network of news gatherers—he called them "liberation committees"—composed of women, ex-convicts, gay people and other marginalized groups, was never enacted, being apparently too radical, even for his leftist allies.

Foucault at a protest outside the Renault factory where a Maoist worker was shot in 1972

Foucault was indefatigable. The 1971 killing of an Algerian teenager by a white Frenchman in an Arab neighborhood? Foucault was there (along with Sartre and Jean Genet) to demonstrate against racism. The 1972 shooting of an Algerian man at the police station in Versailles? Foucault was outside, protesting. (Afterward, he spent a few hours in jail.) The 1972 murder of a sixteen-year-old girl in a French mining town? Foucault was there to challenge the deferential "class justice" being shown the prime suspect, a wealthy notary. (The case against the man eventually fell apart and he was never tried.)

In 1977, when the Soviet leader Leonid Brezhnev came to Paris on a state visit, Foucault helped arrange counterprogramming: an evening of conversation with Soviet dissidents at a local theater. Later that year, when Klaus Croissant, the lawyer representing the militant Baader-Meinhof gang, was to be extradited to Germany on charges of aiding a terrorist group, Foucault protested outside Croissant's French prison. The police broke up the demonstration, and Foucault suffered a cracked rib. The Croissant affair marked the end of his friendship with Deleuze, who had defended not just Croissant from extradition but, implicitly, the Baader-Meinhof gang itself, whose murderous tactics Foucault found appalling.

Nor did Foucault limit his protests to France. In 1975, when eleven Spanish dissidents were due to be executed by Franco's fascist regime, he flew to Madrid to hold a press conference. The event was quickly shut down by the police, and Foucault and his French colleagues were hustled off to the airport. In 1978, when a professor in Hanover was fired for reprinting an article from a student paper condoning the murder of Germany's chief prosecutor (by the Baader-Meinhof gang), Foucault marched through the city to protest his dismissal. In 1982, after the Polish government's crackdown on the Solidarity Movement, Foucault helped drive a minibus full of medicine, along with a secret stash of books and pamphlets, hundreds of miles across Poland to distribute to dissidents.

In photos of this period, Foucault is a man in motion, speaking, shouting, running—"pale, tense, quivering, ready to leap, to spring forth, to launch into the most useless, most dangerous, and the most beautiful attack," as his friend the journalist Claude Mauriac recalled. He is the image, in short, of the intellectual *engagé.* He had such a good time driving and singing his way through Poland with his fellow activists, including the actress Simone Signoret and members of the nonprofit *Médecins du Monde*, that at one point—presumably during a fit of laughter—he peed his pants, the only pair he had brought on the trip.

Of all Foucault's causes, the one that earned him the greatest notoriety was the Iranian Revolution. Hired in the late 1970s to write a column for Italy's leading newspaper, the *Corriere della Sera*, Foucault flew to Tehran in September 1978, days after the Black Friday massacre in which the Shah's army opened fire on thousands of protestors in Jaleh Square. Nearly one hundred people were killed, including thirty government agents; the event was a turning point in public opposition to the Shah's regime. Everywhere Foucault went in Iran, people told him they wanted the Shah gone and an Islamic government in his place. They said they were willing to die to make this happen. When Foucault returned to Paris, he wrote enthusiastically of the Iranian people's desire for an authentic "political spirituality," devoid of Western influence. In the Iranian Revolution, he detected a true people's movement, "perhaps the first great insurrection against the planetary system, the most mad and most modern form of revolt."

His breathless rhetoric proved deeply embarrassing. The Islamic republic that replaced the Shah and anointed the Ayatollah Khomeini its supreme leader soon turned out to be as bloody and repressive as its predecessor, and Foucault was roundly mocked for his "infantile leftism" and "self-indulgent radical chic." Certainly, Foucault's politics in the 1970s confounded many observers, including potential allies. During a debate with the linguist Noam Chomsky on Dutch television in 1971, Foucault shocked Chomsky—among America's most radical public figures—with his cynical comments about justice as a motive for revolution. "The proletariat makes war with the ruling class because, for the first time in history, it wants to take power," Foucault declared. "One makes war to win, not because it is just." Chomsky was taken aback. "He struck me as completely amoral," he told Foucault's biographer James Miller. "I felt like I was talking to someone who didn't inhabit the same moral universe." Foucault later said he had asked to be compensated for the interview with hashish and that he left the Netherlands with a huge block of it, henceforth known to him and the students with whom he shared it as "the Chomsky hash."

Foucault was dismissive of the "people's tribunals" organized by the *Gauche prolétarienne* to allow the public to pass judgment on crimes overlooked, or committed, by the state. Sartre himself served as prosecutor at the first people's tribunal, in 1970, in the city hall of Lens, in northern France, where sixteen miners had died in a gas explosion that had been deemed an "accident," though no official investigation was conducted. But Foucault argued that "popular justice" could never be realized through an entity like a court, whose function was to "ensnare" justice—"to master it and to repress it, by reinscribing it within institutions that are typical of the machinery of the state."

Instead of people's tribunals that could be co-opted by the government, Foucault declared, the left should take as a model the September Massacres of 1792. As every French student knew, these were among the bloodiest five days of the French Revolution. More than one thousand people held in French prisons had been dragged from their cells and slaughtered by roving mobs. In another interview, Foucault went further. "Crime," he said, paraphrasing Victor Hugo, "is 'a *coup d'état* from below.'"

◆ ◆ ◆

This was Foucault at his most radical—and most disillusioned. He'd come to believe that all human social relations were governed by power. People and groups were caught in power's web, struggling to amass and exploit it, even as they, in turn, were manipulated by it. More fundamentally: Power didn't just oppress people; it created them. In elaborating this idea, Foucault was heavily indebted to Nietzsche, whom he'd first read as a student at the École Normale. Nietzsche, too, was fixated on power, depicting human beings as trapped between dueling forces: on the one hand, the social institutions, customs, and historical circumstances that indelibly shape us, and, on the other, an innate life force residing in each of us that could be harnessed toward creative ends, allowing us both to act on the world and to transform ourselves in the process. But where Nietzsche had laid out his theory of the "will to power" in enigmatic aphorisms and fables, Foucault offered a terrible lucidity instead.

From his dark worldview emerged his most influential book: *Surveiller et punir* (*Discipline and Punish*). Published early in 1975, it immediately confronted readers with a harrowing scene. Foucault's famous opening pages, consisting of a series of quotations from the archives, restaged the agonizing 1757 death by torture of Robert-François Damiens, a former servant at a Jesuit college who stabbed King Louis XV with a penknife as the monarch approached his carriage at Versailles. The king sustained a minor wound, and Damiens, a would-be regicide, was sentenced to be drawn and quartered in Paris at the Place de Grève, a popular site for public executions.

The succession of torments inflicted on Damiens makes for excruciating reading: The hand that held the knife is burned by sulfur; flesh from the chest, arms, thighs, and calves is ripped from the body with red-hot pincers; molten lead is poured into the wounds; the arms and legs are attached to horses and pulled in opposite directions; the tendons are sliced nearly to the bone to make the horses' job easier; finally, the torso and limbs are thrown onto a stake and burned to ashes.

Eyewitnesses reported that Damiens was alive until the very end. Among the crowd was the Italian adventurer Giacomo Casanova, who recorded the event with horror in his memoirs, writing, "I was several times obliged to turn away my face and to stop my ears as I heard his piercing shrieks, half of his body having been torn from him." Unlike the

Chinese murderer in whose face Georges Bataille had detected evidence of ecstasy as he was slowly dismembered, Damiens expressed only intolerable pain.

After we, too, are made eyewitnesses of Damiens' torments, Foucault abruptly jumps forward eighty years, to a vastly different universe of punishment. Here, he lists the jailhouse rules promoted by the French politician Léon Faucher in a book on prison reform published in 1838. Now there is no more torture. Instead, there are timetables: a day broken down into highly specified blocks, regimenting the inmates' movements from sunrise to sundown. The blocks are signaled by drumrolls, and periods of work alternate with periods of instruction, along with intervals for handwashing, meals, recreation, and prayer.

Now punishment no longer takes place in the town square, but out of sight, behind prison walls. And where it once required physical pain ("an art of unbearable sensations"), it is now abstract ("an economy of suspended rights"). In this shift from the public spectacle of torture to the disciplinary regime of the prison, Foucault detected a profound, if insidious, change in the cultural operations of power. By the beginning of the nineteenth century, he maintained, power no longer needed to touch bodies to achieve its effects. It began to operate indirectly, acting through an army of intermediaries—"warders, doctors, chaplains, psychiatrists, psychologists, educationalists"—to implement its "system of constraints and privations, obligations and prohibitions."

Foucault might as well have been giving his definition of human society. In his view, the prison house, with its ritualized ordering of bodies, was merely an exaggerated version of everyday life, the place where power was legible "in its naked state." Governments, along with civic institutions—courts, schools, churches, hospitals—and the experts they employed, existed to manage human beings, to organize, subdue, and control them. "In our societies," Foucault wrote, "the systems of punishment are to be situated in a certain 'political economy' of the body: even if they do not make use of violent or bloody punishment, even when they use 'lenient' methods involving confinement or correction, it is always the body that is at issue—the body and its forces, their utility and their docility, their distribution and their submission."

Don't be deceived, Foucault appeared to be saying. The transition from government-decreed death by torture to government-decreed correction may look like progress, but that is an illusion. The goal is "not to punish less, but to punish better." As power becomes more invisible, its grip on people becomes more total, encompassing not just their bodies but their *souls*. This word, with its theological overtones, suggested an aspect of being both central and enduring but also profoundly intimate: the essence of selfhood. For Foucault, the soul was the "element" through which power—less a substance to be possessed than a force always in play—exerts its effects, inhabiting us, forming us, guaranteeing our subjection even before we are born. With penetration of the soul, power's conquest of human beings was complete. "The soul," Foucault wrote, "is the prison of the body."

From this thesis, it followed that there was no neutral perspective on power, no mind or thought process outside its reach. In Foucault's celebrated formulation, "Power produces knowledge." Or, to cite the term he coined to underscore the point, there is only "power-knowledge." The catchy slogans belied their boldness: Foucault had taken the received wisdom ("knowledge is power") and turned it on its head. Knowledge does not precede power; it follows from it. Power determines everything: what we believe to be real, what we believe to be true, who we are, and how we behave. As the philosopher Susan Neiman recently put it, for Foucault, "It's power all the way down."

By the end of his dazzling first chapter, he has laid out these big ideas. But his most famous image of power comes later in the book. It is the panopticon, the model prison dreamed up in the late eighteenth century by the British utilitarian philosopher Jeremy Bentham. The panopticon's organizing principle is surveillance. Bentham's design consisted of a large rotunda divided into individual cells, each facing a central tower occupied by a single guard. Windows in the cells permitted the guard to see every prisoner at any time. Whether the guard was actually looking or even present didn't matter; the prisoners, never sure when they weren't being watched, were likely to obey the rules regardless. "Hence the major effect of the Panopticon," Foucault declared, "to induce in the inmate a state of conscious and permanent visibility that assures the automatic functioning of power."

If the soul was the prison of the body, then the shape of that soul was a panopticon. Bentham believed his design had broad applicability, though he did not live to see it realized. Foucault agreed. Virtually any social institution—hospital, asylum, factory, school—could be built to facilitate the production of what in *Discipline and Punish* he called "docile bodies." More than just an architectural blueprint, he wrote, the panopticon is a "generalizable model of functioning," "a marvelous machine which, whatever use one may wish to put it to, produces homogeneous effects of power." And "panopticism" was shorthand for modern society—"one not of spectacle, but of surveillance."

To think that Foucault was writing fifty years ago! When he speaks of power as a "faceless gaze that transformed the whole social body into a field of perception: thousands of eyes posted everywhere, mobile attentions ever on the alert," he seems uncannily to figure our landscape of CCTV, dashboard, and body cameras; of drones and GPS and eyeball trackers; of face and fingerprint scanners, of voice-recognition software. When he calls power a technique of "permanent, exhaustive, omnipresent surveillance, capable of making all visible, as long as it could itself remain invisible," we recognize our world in his words. As the historian Michael Behrent observed, "The early twenty-first century has become Foucauldian."

No wonder *Discipline and Punish* remains Foucault's most influential book, with more than twenty-five thousand citations in Google Scholar in the past five years alone. (According to the same platform, Foucault is the most cited scholar in the world, with more than 1.4 million citations to his name.) In style, the book bears the hallmarks of his signature classicism—a formal elegance, an emphasis on causal logic and reason.

But there are fewer opaque metaphors or purely rhetorical effects than in his previous work. *Discipline and Punish* is a tighter, starker work, pulsing with the anger and urgency Foucault felt in the early 1970s. As he announced at the end of the first chapter, he intended it as "a history of the present."

Chapter 40

COERCION AND CONTROL

Discipline and Punish was greeted with the fanfare now routinely accorded Foucault: a two-page spread in *Le Monde*, a cover story in *Le Magazine littéraire*, reviews in all the important journals. Deleuze gave *Discipline and Punish* a rave in *Critique,* one of three reviews in the issue devoted to the book. "A revolution in theory," he wrote about Foucault's conception of power. "As if, finally, something new had emerged from Marx." The philosopher François Ewald called the book a "new toolbox with new tools that requires us to give up some of our old habits and truths." Virtually the only critical review appeared, predictably, in Sartre's journal, *Les Temps Modernes*. (The reviewer, a psychoanalyst, complained rather pedantically that Foucault's emphasis on power's gaze failed to consider how a technique of total surveillance could neutralize power's effects: When everything is seen, nothing can be distinguished, or, as the title of his review put it, "Visibility is a trap.")

Foucault's reputation now extended overseas. His first trip to the United States took place in 1970, when he was invited for a stint as a visiting professor at the University of Buffalo. He returned in 1972 and toured Attica, the prison in upstate New York that had been the site of mass rioting the year before, resulting in the deaths of twenty-nine inmates and ten staffers—most shot by the police. Foucault found Attica overwhelming, likening its sterile efficiency to that of "a machine for elimination, a form of prodigious stomach, a kidney that consumes, destroys, breaks up, and then rejects." In America, prison didn't just subjugate bodies; it disappeared them. Then again, Foucault admitted that he had never been allowed inside a French prison and so could not compare.

In the fall of 1975, a few months after *Discipline and Punish* was published in France, Foucault appeared with Deleuze and Guattari in New York, at a conference on "Schizo-Culture." "What appeared to be a utopian theory in France was daily reality in New York," the conference's organizer declared. Two thousand people showed up to hear what the Frenchmen had to say. Guattari gave a talk on academic "microfascism." Deleuze drew pictures of wild grasses on a blackboard, illustrations of his latest philosophical obsession: the rhizome. (A botanical term for a plant with a horizontal root system, the rhizome was a naturally occurring metaphor for a network that was both nonhierarchal and egalitarian, an idea that would get a full airing in Deleuze and Guattari's 1980 book, *A Thousand Plateaus*.) Foucault, for his part, attacked the "antirepressive discourse" of psychoanalytic theory as mere liberatory posturing.

The crowd was agitated and rude. Guattari was booed offstage by the radical feminist Ti-Grace Atkinson, who called him a "phallocrat," and Foucault was heckled by members of Lyndon LaRouche's radical fringe organization, the National Caucus of Labor Committees. One man accused Foucault of being on the payroll of the CIA. In shock and dismay, the Frenchmen retreated downtown to the Chelsea Hotel, then in grittily glamorous decline, as famous for its holdups and cockroaches as for its bohemian artist and rock star clientele. Foucault declared that he'd had enough of "the last countercultural event of the Sixties," and instead of returning to the conference, he and his *confrères* decided to pay a visit to Allen Ginsberg at his apartment on East 10th Street.

For the most part, however, Foucault was received in the United States the way Derrida had been: as an academostar. While Derrida set up shop on the East Coast, Foucault claimed the West, leaving a few thousand miles of North America as buffer between them (they were still not speaking). For Foucault, California, especially the gay-friendly enclaves of San Francisco, was a revelation. He toyed with the idea of moving there permanently. (His open relationship with his partner, Daniel Defert, gave him much freedom.) Between 1975 and 1983, he made six trips to California, five of them to Berkeley, with excursions on the side to Stanford and the University of Southern California. Now each coast had a star French theorist, a thinker apparently more capable of explaining how the world worked than the local intelligentsia.

In California, as in Paris, Foucault's talks were mobbed. Before a 1980 lecture at Berkeley, the police were called in to maintain order. Foucault's American host announced that the talk would be "very technical," even "boring," in the hope of persuading some of the crowd to disperse. But Foucault's critique of power resonated forcefully with students disillusioned by a government that had brutalized and incarcerated its Black citizens, committed the crimes exposed by the scandal of Watergate, and sent thousands of its young men to die in a winless war in Vietnam. His focus on suffering human bodies, especially those of marginalized populations—madmen, criminals, homosexuals, radicals, the poor—aligned with burgeoning interest on campus in multiculturalism, colonialism, feminism, queer studies, and other configurations of race, class, and gender, all of which would eventually become known by the shorthand "identity politics."

In 1981, *Time* magazine photographed Foucault on the steps of a lecture hall at USC, smiling broadly as he chatted with two male "followers." ELUSIVE AND EXASPERATING, the headline on the accompanying article read, MICHEL FOUCAULT HAS A GROWING CULT. The magazine portrayed him as a monkish sage with a shaven head and steel-rimmed glasses, producing his books from "an expensively austere Paris apartment," which, apart from a marijuana plant peeking out from among the petunias ("the only sign of frivolity"), "could pass for an ivory tower." Foucault's cult stretched across the humanities, but his most enthusiastic adherents, like Derrida's, were often concentrated in literature departments. This, despite the fact that Foucault had moved steadily away from literature

Foucault in *Time* magazine in 1981

during the 1960s, and by the mid-1970s had no qualms about telling an American student contemplating graduate school: "You should not waste your time studying literature as a discipline. Study the power mechanisms at work in our speech and our society."

The novelist Jonathan Rosen, who had witnessed Derrida's fandom at Yale as an undergraduate, experienced Foucault's at Berkeley, where he began a PhD in literature in 1985. By then Foucault had been dead a year, but his influence was, if anything, greater than ever. "Foucault's true theme was power, the only thing that was really real," Rosen wrote. "There was something seductive about seeing everything in terms of its secret relationship to power, and the critic as someone trained to unmask it. It made the intellectual a kind of superhero, freeing people from the structures of oppression embedded inside institutions, social systems, and works of art. The suffering of people imprisoned by a poem might not be great, but the person exposing it was a liberator." A more cynical observer put it this way: "Americans used Foucault for a conspiracy theory. The thrill of prison and repression in bloodless lives."

Of course, the most sophisticated Foucauldians knew that even in literature liberation was a mirage. In 1988, D. A. Miller, a Victorianist who went on to become a professor at Berkeley, published *The Novel and the Police*, a book hailed for its groundbreaking reading of fiction by Dickens, Trollope, and Wilkie Collins. The Victorian novel, for all its pleasures, was in fact a sneaky form of "social control," Miller argued. While dramatizing transgression at the level of plot, such novels served a less obvious "disciplinary function," reinforcing the reader's obedient accommodation to the social order. Like acts of literary deconstruction at Yale, Foucauldian analyses at Berkeley entailed in the minds of their perpetrators consequences well beyond the seminar room. Just as Althusser declared philosophy to be "class struggle in the realm of theory," American literature scholars declared theory to be politics by a different name.

Yet by the time Miller published his book, the backlash to theory was also in full swing. In Foucault's case, the skepticism had been building for years; it was just harder to hear amid the louder adulation. There were the familiar grumblings about cherry-picked sources and overly bold generalizations. In 1977, Jean Baudrillard, a young French sociologist, published a book cheekily titled *Oublier Foucault* (*Forget Foucault*). Foucault's work was suspiciously perfect, Baudrillard said, a discourse about power written in the invasive, penetrating style of the power it described. Everything Foucault wrote about seemed to fit his theory like a glove. "The very perfection of this analytical chronicle of power is disturbing," Baudrillard declared. "Something tells us—but implicitly, as if seen in a reverse shot of this writing too beautiful to be true—that if it is possible at last to talk with such definitive understanding about power, sexuality, the body, and discipline, even down to their most delicate metamorphoses, it is because at some point *all this is here and now over with*." From what vantage point was Foucault writing that he was able to see power's operations so clearly? What if Foucault was able to lay out such a perfect analysis only because power as he conceived it was dead? Just like the "classical age," Baudrillard added maliciously, "of which he would be the last great dinosaur."

Forget Foucault made Baudrillard famous, less for what he had said than for the fact that he'd dared to say it. The towering edifice of

Foucault's thought now had some visible chips, and other scholars piled on. Some complained that everywhere Foucault looked in the historical record he seemed to find only more evidence of how human beings were hemmed in, oppressed, or unfree. His work acquired its force through negativity. If his books lacked villains—no one escaped power's baleful gaze—they contained no heroes either. "Foucault has never been able to explain historical change, how things get done," the literary scholar Edward Said told *Time*. "There is also no role in his scheme for such things as justice, freedom, beauty, those positive ideals." In short, in the Foucauldian universe, as in the structuralist one, humans appeared to have no agency. As the anthropologist Clifford Geertz noted in a review of *Discipline and Punish* in *The New York Review of Books* in 1978, "'Confinement,' in all its particular, discontinuous forms, has emerged as the master obsession of Foucault's work. For all his radicalism (which is vehement and absolute), his history is neither of class struggle nor of modes of production, but of constraint: intellectual, medical, moral, political, aesthetic, and epistemological constraint; and now he writes at length on judicial restraint."

That year, a group of French historians specializing in the nineteenth century met with Foucault to debate the book. The meeting was Foucault's idea—he was heartened that historians were interested in his work. But the scholars were tough critics. Some questioned his emphasis on select events—the transition from Damiens' torture to Faucher's timetable is made to bear much symbolic weight. Others argued that his account of power's inescapable logic was self-defeating. If human knowledge only furthered the aims of surveillance and control, then resistance or reform was an illusion. Had Foucault meant it when he said to Noam Chomsky: "If justice is at stake in a struggle, then it is as an instrument of power; it is not in the hope that finally one day, in this or another society, people will be rewarded according to their merits, or punished according to their faults"? If activism was pointless, why did he do it?

Beneath these questions lay a larger unease: Foucault didn't seem to believe in progress. He didn't believe that the ideals of the Enlightenment—

tolerance, individual liberty, the separation of church and state, access to truth through reason—had changed society for the better. He even implied they had made things worse. The historian Maurice Agulhon homed in on a chapter of *Discipline and Punish* detailing the shift from the chain-gang prisoners of the *ancien régime*, who were driven in open carts through raucous street mobs, to their nineteenth-century counterparts, who were transported inside sealed police carriages. "All the spectacularism of the ancient repression is symbolized by the chain, all the gray and secret seriousness of the new repression by the prison carriage invented in 1836," Agulhon wrote. "But under the dazzling pen of Michel Foucault, so colorful is the evocation of the baroque and popular echoes of the first, so oppressive and sinister is the description of the second, that we almost come to doubt that the carriage represented progress."

◆ ◆ ◆

By the time Agulhon wrote those words, Foucault had published yet another book, *La Volonté de Savoir*, the first in a projected multivolume series on bodies and sex in Western culture. He envisioned the book—a brisk one hundred and seventy pages published in English as *The History of Sexuality*—as an introduction to a new problem. But in many ways, it seemed a continuation of an old one. Like madness and criminality, sexuality in Foucault's account underwent a sweeping transformation at the dawn of the modern era. The change was not one toward greater repression. Foucault dismissed the common view that sexual activity, once widely tolerated and openly discussed, had fallen prey to Victorian prudery and been banished to shameful silence. The "repressive hypothesis," he insisted, was wrong. Just when sex was alleged to have disappeared behind closed doors, he pointed out, discourse about it was loudly proliferating—including in endless laments about how repressed we are. "What led us to show, ostentatiously, that sex is something we hide, to say it is something we silence?" he asked. "What is peculiar to modern societies, in fact, is not that they consigned sex to a shadow existence, but that they dedicated themselves to speaking of it *ad infinitum*."

What happened to sex, Foucault said, was that it got reinvented as discourse—all the better to control people. Such, in sum, was his theory. Where once there may have been sexual practices and sensations—entire nonverbal repertoires of pleasure—there was now a profusion of ideas, doctrines, and conventions, many of them proffered by a new army of specialists, foot soldiers in a new regime of "biopower." These were the same authorities—doctors, psychiatrists, biologists, teachers, jurists, and the like—who were responsible for the emerging discourse on madness and criminality. Like the madman, the criminal, and even "man" himself, the sexual body was produced as discourse in the service of power.

Sex in this conceit was made out to be "a secret whose discovery is imperative," the thing that "above all else, had to be confessed." The idea of sex as a secret, promoted most obviously by psychoanalysis, created an impression of freedom, of life outside power's reach. But secrecy, Foucault said, was—you guessed it!—an illusion; there were no secrets about sex, no dark crannies of life untouched by power or unseen by experts. The transformation of sex into words, even in the privacy of the therapist's office, was yet another stratagem of power, a technique for social classification and regulation, "for achieving the subjugation of bodies and the control of populations." Whatever Foucault's subject, he seemed always to find the same patterns of coercion and control.

This was the gist of a widely read critique published in *The New York Review of Books* in 1982 by Lawrence Stone, an eminent historian at Princeton. Acknowledging Foucault's formidable influence on the humanities, Stone accused him, in the course of a review of several new scholarly books on madness, of infecting the field with unjustified doubt. "The battle has thus been joined between post-Enlightenment optimism about the power of society to provide remedies for human pain and suffering, and a cynical suspicion that any change is liable to be for the worse," Stone wrote, adding that Foucault's "dark vision of modern society" comported with "only some of the historical facts."

Foucault typically held his tongue when it came to his critics. Wounded by Baudrillard's *Forget Foucault*, he restrained himself to joking to friends that he couldn't remember who Baudrillard was. But this time, he couldn't help himself. In a furious riposte, he accused Stone of misreading his work, enumerating "nine major errors, spread out over two small columns and a bit."

Stone responded by doubling down. Foucault, or at any rate "Foucaultism," may have helped to inspire the push for deinstitutionalization, resulting in thousands of mental patients being turned out "onto the pitiless streets of New York." (One medical paper Stone cited blamed Foucault by name for the rise of the homeless "bag lady.") At the same time, Foucault had given spurious credibility to the flourishing "antipsychiatry" movement, among whose faddish beliefs was the dangerous claim (promoted by the British psychiatrist R. D. Laing) that "schizophrenia is not a disease." Moreover, Foucault's logic was simply creepy. Stone cited a line from *The Birth of the Clinic*, Foucault's 1963 book about the dawn of modern medicine, in which he had compared the emerging medical language of disease to descriptions of sex in the novels of the Marquis de Sade. "Here again," Stone wrote, "we find a denial of the Enlightenment as an advance in human understanding and sensibility, and a causal linkage of it to the sexual fantasies of domination, violation, and torture which obsessed the mind of Sade." This was Stone's biggest objection to Foucault's work: His "dominance and control" model "reduces the actors in history to two, the controllers and the controlled, ignoring the pluralism extant in all social systems, and the wide variety of influences."

Here was the ambiguity at the heart of Foucault's theory. On the one hand, he cast a spotlight on society's weakest and most vulnerable, showing how they were overlooked, forgotten, or silenced. In this respect, his work was in keeping with his political commitments. On the other hand, his view of power as a ubiquitous and uniquely sinister force seemed to foreclose any prospect for change, or even resistance. Celebrated during his lifetime as an icon of the left, he has lately come under fire by liberals for undermining confidence in liberalism itself.

◆ ◆ ◆

In 2023, the philosopher Susan Neiman published *Left Is Not Woke*, a taut broadside fingering Foucault as the thinker most responsible for the left's disdain for Enlightenment ideals and its descent into the paranoid tribalism of "woke" identity politics. Where Enlightenment philosophers had stressed "universalism, justice, and the possibility of progress," Neiman wrote, Foucault encouraged us to see these ideals as cynical ploys serving to prop up European power interests. Having thoroughly absorbed this teaching, the left now risked sabotaging the global fight for justice and equality.

"How did Michel Foucault become the godfather of the woke left?" Neiman asked. "His style was certainly radical, but his message was as reactionary as anything Edmund Burke or Joseph de Maistre ever wrote." We may all be subjected to power, but surely everyday life outside a prison is *not* the same as everyday life within it, she pointed out. Yet Foucault's theory did not encourage such distinctions. Nor did it allow for a conception of humanity as a collective bound by common interests. Instead, he had bequeathed us a vision of our species as "a bunch of tribes jockeying for power."

In Foucault's formulation, knowledge and truth flowed from power and reflected its self-interest. For the Enlightenment thinkers, knowledge and truth flowed from reason, by definition disinterested and impartial. Reason was what made possible "self-critique"; Enlightenment thinkers used reason to challenge the social institutions of their day, including slavery and colonialism. Neiman cited Immanuel Kant's clear-eyed attacks on both. When we can no longer admit the difference between the torture of the *ancien régime* and the prison houses of the nineteenth century, she suggested, we are in deep trouble: "Common-sense questions such as *would Robert Damiens have preferred incarceration in Bentham's Panopticon?* have no more room in Foucault's thought than normative ones."

As a graduate student in Foucault's Berkeley fiefdom, Jonathan Rosen intuited as much. "Foucault's obsession with hidden power engendered a low-level paranoia that took the place of thought while making you feel smart," he wrote. Neiman said she was not surprised many readers have concluded that Foucault was "simply a nihilist." Nihilist, of course, being an insult once favored by conservative commentators, not liberal ones. In his 1987 bestseller *The Closing of the American Mind*, the classicist Allan Bloom devoted a section to "Nihilism, American Style." "Comparative literature has now fallen largely into the hands of a group of professors who are influenced by the post-Sartrean generation of Parisian Heideggerians, in particular Derrida, Foucault and Barthes," he wrote. "The school is called Deconstructionism, and it is the last, predictable stage in the suppression of reason and the denial of the possibility of truth in the name of philosophy."

Yet now the tables have turned: Foucault has lost status on the left, while gaining it on the right. Scholars have lately stressed the compatibility of Foucault's work with neoliberalism, detecting in his suspicion of state power and regulation an affinity greater than many once wanted to admit for the free-market social order that achieved ascendance after his death. But perhaps the biggest boost to Foucault's standing on the right came during the Covid-19 pandemic. Suddenly, his concept of "biopower"—techniques, essential to a capitalist society, for maintaining and prolonging life but also for subjugating bodies—was there in plain sight, in the form of federal and state lockdowns and mask and vaccine mandates. The spectacle of government officials appealing to science to justify sweeping and intrusive public-health measures was precisely the kind of scenario Foucault suggested we ought to be concerned about: biopower masquerading as truth.

In the spring of 2020, as Italy, reeling from thousands of Covid deaths, became the first country to institute a national shutdown, the philosopher Giorgio Agamben, for decades a man of the left, began posting scathing Foucauldian attacks online of his government's "techno-medico despotism." Even social distancing, ubiquitous during the pandemic, was in Agamben's view hardly just a measure devised for the protection of citizens by apolitical scientific experts; implicit in it was the suppression of the collective, and with it, of political dissent. The leftist press labeled

Agamben a "*negazionista*"—a term more commonly associated with Holocaust deniers. The right-wing press embraced him. At the same time, Blake Smith, a young historian at the University of Chicago troubled by *his* government's response to the pandemic, began publishing a series of essays suggesting that Foucault's work provided "theoretical support to conservative critiques of the 'new class' of experts." Smith's interest in Foucault extended beyond mask mandates and bans on in-person religious gatherings to possibilities for political resistance to liberalism in general.

Foucault understood the positive effects of biopower in people's lives. When the state licenses doctors and regulates drugs, when it tests therapies and the food supply, this is biopower acting as a life-protecting force. But biopower was also used to manipulate and control. "Experts have taken over our lives," Smith declared in an essay in the conversative *Washington Examiner* in March 2021 that reads now as though it had been pulled from Project 2025, the Trump administration's blueprint for dismantling the federal government and elite colleges. Conditioned to defer to the authority of experts as neutral arbiters of our best interests, Smith argued, we allow teachers, therapists, and bosses to "tell us who we are and what we should do with our lives." He included in this category human resource managers and university administrators—among them presumably specialists in diversity, equity, and inclusion—who, he said, have replaced priests and analysts as our confessors, soliciting our "blameworthy thoughts, feelings, and habits centered on race, or rather on 'whiteness,' our contemporary substitute for medieval demonology." Far from being the godfather of "wokeism," Smith wrote, Foucault offered ways to resist such a scourge.

Smith delivered his argument in a review of *Confessions of the Flesh*, the fourth and final book in Foucault's history of sexuality series, which was released in France only in 2018, thirty-four years after his death. At its center is a concept that Foucault called "care of the self," which he derived from ancient Greek philosophy and developed over the course of his last lectures and books in the early 1980s. As Foucault elaborated the idea, care of the self entailed a rigorous program of self-fashioning through introspection, abstinence, and moral reflection—the cultivation of what he termed, rather beautifully, an "aesthetics of existence."

The notion is striking, in part because it seems to mark such a departure from Foucault's previous work. In his earlier books, the self is little more than a tool at the mercy of impersonal forces. In the history of sexuality series, however, a different kind of self begins to take shape, one over which the individual, remarkably, has a modicum of control. In *Confessions of the Flesh*, Foucault shows how the ancient ideal of self-care was co-opted over time, first by the Church, in the ritual of confession, and later by psychoanalysis, in what becomes a classic Foucauldian pattern of power's intrusion into private life. At the same time, though, he casts an approving light on spiritual and ethical practices that preceded the Christian era. In doing so, Smith argues, Foucault provides a model for how we might "denounce woke-ism as a degenerate religion" and "imagine new ways in which we can reclaim power over our lives."

Smith's Foucault is no nihilist. Instead, he is an idealist, someone who clings, sometimes desperately, to the idea of human agency and freedom. This idealism, Smith insists in another essay, is how we should understand Foucault's misguided support for the Iranian Revolution. Disappointed by the coercive nature of both liberalism in the West and, more blatantly, communism in the East, Foucault hoped that the devout young Iranians he met would create a viable alternative, "rooted in a collective experience of the sacred," to the "systems of domination and manipulation that comprise biopolitics." That these young people were willing to die for their religious beliefs struck Foucault as a choice that even the most coercive forms of biopower could do little to counteract.

So, which is it: Is Foucault a nihilist or an idealist? A realist or a romantic? The progenitor of wokeness or its most exemplary resister? The most plausible answer may be that he was all these things. If we are currently living through what Ross Douthat, the *New York Times* columnist, has called "the Foucault realignment," that might be because Foucault's critique of power and institutions can be made to fit whatever narrative of political oppression is currently dominant. At the moment, it's a narrative favoring the right that appears to have the upper hand—one promoted by a president who accomplished the tricky feat of getting himself elected on an anti-intellectual, populist platform depicting universities and the government itself as bastions of waste and corruption, even as he engages in an unprecedented power grab and blatant grift.

Foucault, whose books trace the peregrinations of a restless mind prone to paradox and contradiction, might have appreciated the shifting winds of his posthumous reputation. "I think I have in fact been situated in most of the squares on the political checkerboard, one after another and sometimes simultaneously," he told an interviewer in 1984, a month before he died. "It's true that I prefer not to identify myself, and that I'm amused by the diversity of the ways I've been judged and classified."

Chapter 41

COUNTRY JOE FOUCAULT

Foucault generally disliked his fame and guarded his privacy, trying, in the words of his friend the writer Hervé Guibert, "to make his face invisible." Yet the contradictions in his work make more sense when viewed in the context of his private life. James Miller, the most perceptive of Foucault's biographers, maintains that his writings are best understood as a sustained inquiry into the possibilities for self-creation given the innumerable constraints that define our existence. While stressing the formidable influence of those constraints, Foucault clung to the idea of a self forged beyond the reach of social codes and conventions, beyond ideas of good and bad, normal and deviant. This self was provisional and unstable, constantly susceptible to external judgment and manipulation. But his own experience taught him that such a self could, with effort, exist. The coercive forces Foucault decried in his writing he tested in private, pushing against them in his pursuit of an authentic way of being—his Nietzschean quest, as Miller put it, to "become what one is." "I have always wanted my books to be fragments from an autobiography," Foucault said in 1981. "My books have always been my personal problems with madness, with prisons, with sexuality."

In terms of the sheer number of pages Foucault devoted to the issue, sexuality, the subject of his final four books, tops this list. He began publicly identifying himself as a gay man only in the late 1970s, after he'd visited the United States and witnessed its gay culture—vastly more open than what existed in France at the time. In Paris in 1973, Félix Guattari had been charged with committing "an outrage to public decency" by devoting an issue of his journal *Recherches* to homosexuality, under the title "Three Billion Perverts: The Big Encyclopedia of Homosexualities." Copies of the journal were seized and Guattari was fined six hundred francs.

Foucault gave his initial interviews on homosexuality to his friend the activist Jean Le Bitoux, who in 1979 founded France's first major gay monthly, *Gai pied*. (The name, dreamed up by Foucault, literally means "gay foot," but in French contains multiple puns, including the word for hornet's nest, *guêpier,* and a slang phrase for orgasm, *prendre son pied.*) At the same time, Foucault joined other activists in campaigning to reform or even abolish sexual consent laws, suggesting in one interview that there was no reason, in theory, that a child and an adult couldn't have a mutually consensual relationship. (Fortunately, the proposal went nowhere.)

But in 1976, when the first volume of *The History of Sexuality* appeared, Foucault, in keeping with his desire to disappear behind his work, had said almost nothing publicly about his sexual identity—to the irritation of some of his gay friends, who called him "*une honteuse*" (or "closet queen"). Among the book's most powerful passages is one declaring "the homosexual" to be a dubious invention of the nineteenth century. Until that time, Foucault maintained, homosexuality had not existed. Instead, there was sodomy, a forbidden act for which a person could be punished. But over the course of the nineteenth century, an illegal behavior morphed into a complete, and disparaged, identity: the homosexual. "Nothing that went into his total composition was unaffected by his sexuality," Foucault wrote. "It was everywhere present in him: at the root of all his actions because it was their insidious and indefinitely active principle; written immodestly on his face and body because it was a secret that always gave itself away. . . . The sodomite had been a temporary aberration; the homosexual was now a species."

This passage, by an author whose own homosexuality was likely a "secret" to many of his readers, makes for poignant reading. Equally remarkable is the one that follows it, a kind of poetic delirium in which Foucault invokes the pleasure that accompanies power, both for its enforcers and, strikingly, its targets. On the one hand, there is "the pleasure that comes of exercising a power that questions, monitors, watches, spies, searches out, palpates, brings to light," he wrote. On the other, there is "the pleasure that kindles at having to evade this power, flee from it, fool it, or travesty it. The power that lets itself be invaded by the pleasure it is pursuing; and opposite it, power asserting itself in the pleasure of showing off, scandalizing, or resisting."

Power and pleasure, pleasure and power. In Foucault's account, the two are inextricably entwined, each magnifying the effects of the other, even, or especially, in a dynamic of stark inequality—"parents and children, adults and adolescents, educator and students, doctors and patients, the psychiatrist with his hysteric and his perverts." Here, Foucault might have added "the dominant and the submissive" or simply "S/M." While he was working on *The History of Sexuality* in the spring of 1975, he made his first trip to Berkeley. Dazzled by the size and variety of San Francisco's gay scene, he moved from the Berkeley campus across the Bay to a rooming house near Folsom Street, the epicenter of a neighborhood with more than two dozen bathhouses and leather bars. According to one account, he even gave lectures at The Barracks, a club *SF Weekly* later described as a "two-story BDSM wonderland with theme rooms that catered to every fetish imaginable."

Foucault rarely spoke publicly about S/M, and on the few occasions he did so it was in barely personal terms. In a 1982 interview (published after his death), he called S/M "the real creation of new possibilities of pleasure, which people had no idea about previously." This pleasure involved the eroticization of "strange," not primarily sexual, body parts, aided by drugs such as amyl nitrite (a muscle relaxant known colloquially as "poppers") and metal instruments for inflicting pain. (Foucault's biographer David Macey quotes Foucault's friend the novelist Edmund White coyly alluding to a "French *savant*'s observation that 'fist-fucking is our century's only brand-new contribution to the sexual armamentarium.'")

New possibilities of pleasure also meant new avenues for power, all within a dynamic that was inherently mutable. "The S/M game is very interesting because it is a strategic relation, but it is always fluid," Foucault explained. "Of course, there are roles, but everybody knows very well that those roles can be reversed. Sometimes the scene begins with the master and slave, and at the end the slave has become the master." S/M turned power's unstable dance into ecstatic sexual theater.

In another interview in 1982, Foucault was more revealing, elaborating a fantasy of pleasure so extreme that it would obliterate him. "I hope I'll die of an overdose of pleasure of any kind," he told his interviewer, an instructor at the University of Toronto, where he was teaching a seminar that summer. "Because I think that the kind of pleasure I would consider as *the* real pleasure would be so deep, so intense, so overwhelming that I couldn't survive it. I would die." He recalled being hit by a car in Paris while walking in the street: "For maybe two seconds I had the impression that I was dying and it was really a very, very intense pleasure."

The "real pleasure" entailed bumping up against the threshold between life and death, a place, like Lacan's real, where power's operations broke down and the self dissolved. The real pleasure was what Foucault called a "limit experience," a notion derived from his reading of Bataille on transgression. S/M was one kind of limit experience. Drugs were another.

◆ ◆ ◆

During his first visit to Berkeley, in the spring of 1975, Foucault accepted an invitation to speak at Claremont University Center in Southern California. His host was Simeon Wade, a scholar of intellectual history who ran the European Studies program at the school. Wade was obsessed with Foucault, whom he considered "nothing less than the greatest thinker of our time, perhaps of all time." He had read *The Order of Things*, telling his students that "the *episteme* was for the human sciences the equivalent of Watson and Crick's analysis of the double helix for the life sciences." He'd also read, in French, Deleuze and Guattari's *Anti-Oedipus* and Foucault's just-published *Discipline and Punish*. Together, he believed, these authors "had answered the most pressing question of our time: 'Why fascism and how do we resist it?'" When Wade heard that Foucault was heading to Berkeley to teach, he called the chair of the university's French department, who suggested that he write to Foucault in Paris. To Wade's amazement, the chair gave him Foucault's home address. Wade pinned it above his desk, he wrote later, "as a medieval monk might have incised the route to Rome on the wall of his cell."

Wade's plans for Foucault involved more than a lecture. His dream was to take the philosopher to Death Valley, a remote stretch of rocky desert on the California-Nevada border known as the lowest, hottest, and driest place in the United States. In this extreme landscape, amid spectacular, billion-year-old rock formations, Wade envisioned dropping LSD with Foucault, just as he had done on a visit to Death Valley the previous year with his partner, a composer named Michael Stoneman. It took some doing to persuade Foucault to visit—Wade and Stoneman resorted to buttonholing him in person after a lecture at UC Irvine—but the philosopher finally agreed to come to Claremont for a long weekend in early May and make the trip to Death Valley.

After it was over, Wade chronicled what happened in a memoir. His account is alternately incisive and hyperbolic, pretentious and goofy. "Foucault's white turtleneck under an open madras jacket revealed a powerful torso with well-defined contours," he writes in a typically cheesy description. "His white bell-bottom trousers fit him closely around the pelvis and thighs." At the same time, the memoir provides a rare extended glimpse of the Frenchman in his off-hours, engaged in intimate, unscripted conversation. After languishing for decades in a storage unit, Wade's manuscript was finally published as *Foucault in California* in 2019, two years after Wade's death, thanks mainly to the efforts of Heather Dundas, a USC graduate student who had heard rumors about its existence, befriended him, and verified the broad outlines of his story.

Much of the book consists of dialogue, ostensibly a verbatim record of what transpired that May weekend between Foucault, Wade, and Stoneman, and between Foucault and various adoring young men, mostly graduate students, who thrust themselves, sometimes literally, in his path. From a letter Foucault wrote to Wade three years later, we know that he read and approved the manuscript. But given the circumstances of his visit, which included not only an all-night desert acid trip but an academic lecture, a hike in the mountains, and a crowded party at Wade and Stoneman's house (and no indication that a tape recorder was running at any time), it's hard to view the account as more than a convincing approximation.

Part of its charm is Wade's almost comical eagerness to impress Foucault. After picking him up at the airport, Wade and Stoneman drive him to their bungalow, which Wade has gone to great lengths to prepare—lining the living room walls with his own photographs, and laying out books on the coffee table intended to catch the philosopher's eye: a work by the British anti-psychiatrist R. D. Laing, a copy of the *Tao Te Ching*, and a book on Proust by Deleuze. "Have you read Proust recently?" Wade asks Foucault, absurdly.

Foucault in California is stocked with such rhetorically loaded questions, aimed at the philosopher by his American interlocutors, all vying for his approval as much as his opinions: "Do you accept Merleau-Ponty's idea of cultural sediment?" "What do you think of the *Critique de la raison dialectique*?" "Would you agree that Fernand Braudel is the greatest twentieth-century historian?" "And what of Gramsci?" Some of these queries are posed by students at the party Wade and Stoneman throw for Foucault after his talk at Claremont. ("Are there parties like this in France?" is another question he fields that night.) Al Franken, just months away from being hired to write for the first season of *Saturday Night Live*, sidles up to ask Foucault which team he thinks will win the World Series. Foucault politely demurs.

It's clear, even to Wade, that Foucault finds the incessant interrogation exhausting. ("I was being a chatterbox," Wade writes at one point. "I brought my questioning to a merciful halt with a reference to Heidegger's phrase 'the discipline of keeping silence.' Foucault recognized the phrase and appeared visibly relieved when I invoked it.") Still, when Foucault does manage to get a word in edgewise, or is permitted a moment of spontaneity, the book comes alive.

We watch him taste his first tequila sunrise—an abstemious eater and drinker, he takes only two sips—smoke a joint, and retire to the guest room to sleep on a vibrating waterbed, his first. In the mountains above Bear Canyon, Wade convenes half a dozen graduate student groupies to accompany Foucault on a hike. The setting is an alpine idyll: cedars, ponderosa pines, waterfalls, and the musky smell of chaparral wafting through the air like "a pungent aphrodisiac." Foucault astonishes everyone when he volunteers to split firewood. "How is it that an esteemed Parisian intellectual can learn to chop wood with such dexterity?" Wade marvels. "One could not imagine a Voltaire or Sartre accomplishing such a task so readily." The students start referring to him as Country Joe Foucault.

On this hike, like nearly everywhere else he goes that weekend, Foucault is surrounded by attractive youths—a deliberate choice on the part of his host, who'd envisioned "a bevy of California young men to entertain him." At Wade and Stoneman's party, a student who says he has just come out asks Foucault how he feels about "gay liberation." As is often the case, Foucault's response seems eerily prescient. "First of all, I believe that the term 'gay' has become obsolete," he says. "And indeed, all such terms denoting a specific sexual orientation. . . . People are neither this nor that, gay or straight. There is an infinite range of what we call sexual behavior, and terms that prevent this range from being put into play—that is to say, terms that stereotype behavior, that are wrong and misleading."

It would be another fifteen years before scholars like Judith Butler began "troubling" binary assumptions about gender and sexuality and, under the new rubric of queer theory, dismantling as artificial categories like "gay," "straight," "male," and "female." And it would be another thirty-five years after that before the Trump administration, seeing in the spread of such "gender ideology" a national emergency, declared via executive order a return to the "immutable biological reality" of two sexes, male and female.

◆ ◆ ◆

During the car ride to Death Valley, Foucault raves about San Francisco's gay clubs, and reveals that he owns a set of leatherman's paraphernalia. In France, there is nothing like Folsom Street's bars and bathhouses, Foucault tells Wade and Stoneman. "These men live for casual sex and drugs. Incredible!" In late afternoon, surrounded by iridescent volcanic deposits at the bottom of a desert canyon, the three men drop LSD—Foucault for the first time—chasing it down with some weed and shots of Grand Marnier from plastic cups. At Zabriskie Point, a spot that had recently attained the status of a counterculture mecca thanks to Antonioni's 1970 cult film by that name, they lie on their backs, gazing at stars in a moonless sky and listening to Stockhausen playing on a tape deck.

"The only thing I can compare this experience to in my life is sex with a stranger," Foucault says. "Contact with a strange body affords an experience of the Truth similar to what I am experiencing now." According to Wade, he was crying.

Michel Foucault and Michael Stoneman in Death Valley, photographed by Simeon Wade, 1975

Chapter 42

AT THE BATHHOUSE

Foucault's stay in California that spring lasted just a few weeks, but it affected him profoundly. In a letter to Wade afterward, Foucault described his LSD trip as "a great experience, one of the most important in my life." In another letter, from Paris that fall, he wrote that the Death Valley excursion had led him to completely rethink his "book about sexual repression."

A year later, the first volume of his history of sexuality series appeared, firmly rejecting the "repressive hypothesis" (the idea that sex was banished from public view owing to Victorian prudery). The other three volumes were delayed, as Foucault scrapped his drafts and started over. If it's hard not to see the fingerprints of his California forays into S/M in the first volume's descriptions of pleasure and power, it's also true that the shadow of S/M seems to hover over many of his earlier depictions of power, including, for example, his 1963 book on the birth of the clinic with the passage that Lawrence Stone found so disturbing because of the way Foucault linked modern medical terminology to Sadean fantasies of sexual domination.

Foucault was likely experimenting with S/M as early as the 1950s; it was a practice in keeping with the other "limit experiences" that had compelled him from his school days at the École Normale—madness, suicide, and later, mind-altering drugs. Each entailed a rupture with convention, with reason and meaning, ultimately with consciousness itself. Foucault's biographer James Miller goes further, putting S/M in a special category: the limit experience that encompasses all the rest. In his 1993 book, *The Passion of Michel Foucault,* Miller argues that the philosopher's sexual proclivities are the key to his thought, enabling him to explore an "unrelenting, deeply ambiguous and profoundly problematic preoccupation with death."

Miller's book is a searching chronicle of ambivalent admiration for a thinker he considered "the most revolutionary—and deeply serious—of postwar Nietzscheans." The book's initial spark was a rumor that circulated after Foucault's death from AIDS in 1984, according to which he had gone to the bathhouses on his final trip to San Francisco the previous year, knowing he had the disease and with the goal of infecting others. Miller was shocked by the rumor but unable to confirm or refute it. He eventually interviewed Foucault's partner, Daniel Defert, who cited Foucault's fixation on "limit experiences" right away, volunteering that for Foucault this category included "madness, drugs, sexuality, and maybe I would say AIDS."

Miller was taken aback by the reference to AIDS, but Defert declined to elaborate or, later, to comment on the draft of the book Miller sent him. Compounding the puzzle was the fact that at the time of Foucault's death, AIDS was still poorly understood. Medically and financially neglected, it was generally seen by public officials as a political quagmire best ignored. The Centers for Disease Control gave AIDS its name only in the fall of 1982, and the growing epidemic didn't make the front page of *The New York Times* until the end of May two years later, when the physician in charge of the U.S. Public Health Service declared AIDS the department's "number one priority." By the time President Reagan first mentioned AIDS in public, in September 1985, more than fifteen thousand cases had been reported in the United States, and half that number of patients had already died of the disease.

When Foucault died, on June 25, 1984, at the age of fifty-seven, at the

Hôpital de la Salpêtrière in Paris, AIDS didn't figure in the obituaries. *Le Monde* published a statement from his doctors attributing the cause of death to neurological complications following septicemia—a systemic blood infection. *Libération* put his photo on its cover and ran eight pages of testimonials by prominent intellectuals and politicians. But these were overshadowed by a much smaller piece, indignant and unsigned, that appeared at the bottom of one page. In it, the paper took aim at a "rumor" that Foucault had died of AIDS. "As if an exceptional intellectual, because he was also homosexual—very discreetly, it is true—would appear to be an ideal target for this stylish disease," the article declared. "As if Foucault must have died shamefully." A philosopher with a sex life was shocking enough, let alone one with a lethal, sexually transmitted disease. *Libération* was inundated with letters from readers appalled by the paper's moralizing. (After Foucault's death, Daniel Defert founded AIDES, France's first AIDS service organization.)

At the same time, it's not clear when, or even whether, Foucault learned he was infected. As Miller points out, French doctors were known for their discretion, and though various friends believed that by the fall of 1983 Foucault suspected he was dying of AIDS, he may have insisted that his physicians keep his diagnosis to themselves. Didier Eribon writes simply: "Foucault knew. And he did not want to know."

That summer, he'd developed a nagging cough, which was followed over the next few months by a low-grade fever, migraines, and weakness. He'd been back to Berkeley in the spring, and he returned one last time in the fall. He was working on the final three volumes in his much delayed history of sexuality series. He would live to see the second and third books—*The Use of Pleasure* and *The Care of the Self*—published just days before his death, but not *Confessions of the Flesh*, which he left unfinished. Signaling a dramatic pivot in his conceptual approach, the books are also a poignant testament to the influence of his California excursions.

As Foucault explained in the introduction to *The Use of Pleasure*, the books were not the ones he originally intended. To understand modern sexuality, he belatedly realized that he had first to go back to antiquity to understand how people began to see themselves as sexual beings—and to see sex as a moral issue. The result is a survey of ancient Greek and Roman texts that in its formal style and analytical logic resembles his other books. But Foucault's tone expresses a new serenity. Gone is the modern disciplinary society, with its constraints and suffering. Instead, there is a general aura of benignity and tolerance. And, as the historian Blake Smith noticed, gone are the bodies writhing under power's cruel gaze, or being palpated, classified, and interned by experts. Instead, there are individual human beings engaged in "practices of the self"—including sexual moderation and abstinence as a means to greater enlightenment.

It's as though Country Joe Foucault and his male acolytes had descended from the mountains above Bear Canyon to preach the gentle wisdom of the ancients. "It is in the reflection on love of boys that one sees the principle of 'indefinite abstention' formulated," Foucault wrote sagely in a section of *The Use of Pleasure* on same-sex love in ancient Greece. "The ideal of a renunciation, which Socrates exemplifies by his faultless resistance of temptation. . . . One should keep in mind that this 'asceticism' was not a means of disqualifying the love of boys; on the contrary, it was a means of stylizing it and hence, by giving it shape and form, of valorizing it."

To what extent Foucault applied an ethic of moderation or abstention in fashioning the aesthetics of his own existence is unclear. He spoke increasingly of the importance of friendship, which became a theme in his work—as it did for Derrida, around the same time. "One of my hypotheses," he told *The Advocate* in 1982, "is that homosexuality became a problem—that is, sex between men became a problem—in the eighteenth century," when conventions around male friendship shifted and intimate bonds were no longer tolerated. "I'm sure I'm right, that the disappearance of friendship as a social relation and the declaration of homosexuality as a social/political/medical problem are the same process."

Perhaps it was as part of this new attention to friendship that Foucault decided to end his feud with Derrida by taking to the French airwaves in December 1981 to demand his release from jail in Prague.

Moved, Derrida immediately wrote to Foucault to thank him. They remained friendly until Foucault's death; Foucault even had Derrida and his wife to dinner at his apartment. After Foucault's death, Derrida attended the memorial service at the Hôpital de la Salpêtrière, where a small crowd of intimates watched Foucault's coffin being loaded into a hearse to be taken for burial near his mother's home in the provinces.

Foucault also maintained friendships with many of the Americans he met. The last party he threw at his apartment in Paris, two months before he died, was for the Beat writer William Burroughs, whom he'd befriended at the New York conference on schizo-culture in 1975. On display in his living room was a memento of his hike above Bear Canyon—a photo Wade took of him chopping wood on the mountain slope. He stayed in touch with Wade and Stoneman and saw the couple at least once more, during a return trip to California. As Heather Dundas discovered when she researched Wade's story, the two male "followers" flanking Foucault in the photo accompanying *Time* magazine's 1981 article about the philosopher's "growing cult" were Wade and Stoneman. Wade told Dundas that as Foucault was dying, he asked Wade to bring some LSD to Paris so he "could go out tripping."

Foucault's friends in San Francisco said that the subject of AIDS had come up in conversation during his final trip to Berkeley in the fall of 1983. The Victorianist D. A. Miller, who was teaching in Berkeley's English department at the time, told James Miller that Foucault had suddenly collapsed after lunch one day. As D. A. Miller recounted the incident, he helped Foucault up and drove him to an air-conditioned restaurant to recover. Foucault soon seemed better and as they sat talking, he asked Miller what the acronym AIDS stood for in English. "*Je n'y crois pas*," Foucault told him. *I don't believe in it.*

His friends understood his skepticism. An incurable illness targeting homosexuals sounded like a description pulled from one of his books: a fiction promulgated by state power to intimidate and control (or worse!) an undesirable population. Hervé Guibert, in his devastating 1990 novel about his own battle with AIDS, *To the Friend Who Did Not Save My Life*, included a character modeled on Foucault: a philosopher named Muzil. Early in the book, the unnamed narrator (a Guibert stand-in) tells Muzil about the "mysterious illness" circulating in the United States. "My friend fell off the sofa in a paroxysm of laughter," the narrator reports. "'A cancer that would hit only homosexuals, no, that's too good to be true, I could just die laughing!'"

Muzil does die in the novel, not from laughing but slowly and horribly from AIDS. Toward the end, his mind goes, and he can speak only in cryptic sentences. We learn that he is a man who "adored violent orgies in bathhouses" and whose closet contains a "huge bag filled with whips, leather hoods, leashes, bridles, and handcuffs." In the fall of 1983, he returns to Paris from San Francisco and "between fits of coughing" tells the narrator about his latest bathhouse adventures. "Those places must be completely deserted now because of AIDS," the narrator remarks. "Don't be silly," Muzil replies. "It's just the opposite: the baths have never been so popular, and now they're fantastic. This danger lurking everywhere has created new complicities, new tenderness, new solidarities. Before, no one ever said a word; now we talk to one another. We all know exactly why we're there."

The men may know exactly why they are there, but do we? For James Miller, the bathhouse has the status of a primal scene. It's the place where Foucault's determination to breach limits attained its glorious and terrifying apotheosis, where pleasure and pain merged with madness and death. "To have taken AIDS as a 'limit-experience,' it seemed to me, would have involved engaging in potentially suicidal acts of passion with consenting partners, most of them likely to be infected already," Miller writes. "Deliberately throwing caution to the wind, Foucault and these men were wagering their lives together; that, at least, is how I came to understand what may have happened." (At the same time, Miller concluded that it was highly unlikely Foucault had set out deliberately to infect anyone.)

At Vincennes in 1970, Foucault had been relieved to escape the "half-madmen" political radicals; in San Francisco a decade later, he may have sought the company of another species of "half-madmen"—risk-takers of a different sort. It's unlikely we will ever know for sure what he did or didn't know about his illness in the fall of 1983, or what he did or didn't do in the bathhouses on his final trip to the city. But the possibility that he risked everything in the pursuit of self-transcendence is, for Miller, too logical to dismiss, the consummate step in a "teleologically structured quest." Taking literally Nietzsche's injunction to become one's self, Foucault in this view made of his life and thought a brave and defiant creative act.

◆ ◆ ◆

Arriving at the peak of America's culture wars in 1993, Miller's book provided, amid a slew of rave reviews, more fuel for conservatives to bemoan Foucault's—and, by extension, theory's—malign influence. "The celebration of his intellectual perversions by academics continues to be a public scandal," wrote Roger Kimball in *The New Criterion*. "The career of this 'representative man' of the twentieth century really represents one of the biggest con jobs in recent intellectual history." Jay Tolson, writing in the *National Review*, distinguished Miller's book, which he admired, from its subject, for whom he had less sympathy. "The problem with Foucault, simply put, was his profound perversity, a quality that characterized both his life and his work," Tolson said. "How can such an ultimately irresponsible philosopher be considered heroic?"

By the early 1990s, the attacks on theory had become highly personal. Even without the help of biographers, the French theorists had supplied their American opponents with plenty of ammunition. In 1992, Althusser's self-pitying memoir about killing his wife was published in French (and a year later in English), thrusting him, albeit posthumously, into the spotlight. Reviewing the book in *The Times Literary Supplement*, the intellectual historian Mark Lilla called Althusser a "relatively minor thinker who was, by all accounts, profoundly sick and dangerous" and whose murderous act was remembered, if at all, as like Foucault's death from AIDS: "another morbid episode in the dénouement of *la pensée 68*."

At the same time, the feminist professor Camille Paglia was making a name for herself largely thanks to her inventively ad hominem takedowns of the French theorists. In "Junk Bonds and Corporate Raiders: Academe in the Hour of the Wolf," a seventy-four-page diatribe pegged to a review of two minor works of queer theory, Paglia took on Foucault, Lacan, and Derrida. Lacan had been dead for a decade, but that didn't stop Paglia from denouncing him as "a twerpy, cape-twirling Dracula dragging his flocking stooges to the crypt"; a "Freud T-shirt shrunk down to the teeny-weeny Saussure torso"; and "a tyrant who must be driven from our shores." Derrida she dismissed as "a Gloomy Gus one-trick pony" whose MO was "masturbation without pleasure." But she reserved the bulk of her fury for Foucault, the theorist whose influence was arguably the greatest. "One of the dullest, most frigid and constipated theorists of sex ever," she declared. "It's trial by prune-face ice-lock." And there was more. "The fruits of Foucault are wormwood," she wrote. "He was a Herod without a Salome. This was a man of mutilated psyche; if what I have reliably heard about his public behavior after he knew he had AIDS is true, then Foucault would deserve the condemnation of every ethical person."

Paul de Man earned only a passing mention. Paglia said she had seen the "clustering of yuppies" around him when she was in graduate school at Yale and concluded that he was "bland and phony," an opinion confirmed by his "delightful recent exposure as a Nazi sympathizer." Given her animus toward theory, it's surprising that Paglia didn't linger longer on de Man's spectacular fall from grace. In retrospect, the "de Man scandal," as it came to be known, was widely seen as the affair that finally did theory in. And as it turned out, "Nazi sympathizer" wasn't even the half of it.

Chapter 43

THE TRIAL OF PAUL DE MAN

When Paul de Man died of cancer on December 21, 1983, at the age of sixty-four, Derrida was devastated. "It was, and remains, unique," he said of their friendship in an emotional eulogy at Yale a few weeks later. "What I, like so many others, owe to his generosity, to his lucidity, to the ever so gentle force of his thought." De Man's death was considered so newsworthy that *The New York Times* sent a reporter to interview bereft faculty and students. (YALE STILL FEELING LOSS OF REVERED PROFESSOR, the headline read.)

Colleagues had noticed that de Man looked ill months before he died. In the summer of 1982, at the annual School of Criticism and Theory, a program for graduate students and scholars held that year at Northwestern University, Geoffrey Hartman and his wife mentioned their concern. De Man waved them off. His stomach was "uneasy," he said. He would drink some milk; that would take care of the problem. But a week into the session, his skin turned yellow. Alarmed, the Hartmans made an appointment for him to see a local doctor. The doctor sent de Man straight home to New Haven, where tests revealed a tumor pressing on his liver. His case was terminal.

He continued to teach his seminar, only now it took place at his home. As his condition worsened, Derrida spoke to him nearly every day. "You know, don't you, that my heart is with you and that my thoughts accompany you at every moment of this ordeal," he wrote to his friend ten days before his death. By all accounts, de Man remained stoic to the end.

His passing was one more blow in a long season of diminishment and death for the French philosophers. Barthes and Sartre had died early in 1980, and Althusser had strangled his wife that fall. Lacan had died the following year. By the time de Man died, at the end of 1983, Foucault was seriously ill. Deleuze and Guattari would still collaborate on a final book, *What Is Philosophy?*, but the heyday of their joint influence was over. Was it a coincidence that theory's reign was waning in tandem with its most prominent practitioners?

◆ ◆ ◆

Early in 1984, barely a month after de Man's death, Derrida dedicated three lectures on memory to his dead friend. In classic deconstructive fashion, he poked and prodded at his theme, questioning just what "memory" could claim from the past, given de Man's description, in a famous essay on allegory, of language's "temporal predicament": the idea that a set of signs never coincides with its meaning but merely points back to an earlier set of signs, a source text always beyond reach.

Derrida picked up on a phrase de Man had used in his essay: "unreachable anteriority." "What does a memory without anteriority recall?" Derrida asked. Some would "denounce" the notion of a memory unconnected to an origin, seeing in it a "concealment or betrayal," he conceded. And yet, he suggested, "memory without anteriority" might be a felicitous description of how memory actually works. What we remember never coincides with the event we are recalling. Memory, history, the past: All are defined by an unbridgeable disjunction in time. De Man understood this. He knew there was no going back to an always elusive beginning. After all, he was almost preternaturally fixated on disjunctions, on irony and the abyss. "As you know," Derrida said in his eulogy, "Paul was irony itself."

These were the motifs of the theory de Man practiced at Yale, what Derrida pointedly called "deconstruction in America." It was a subject he vowed at the outset of his lecture series not to talk about. It was too complicated, he said, too fraught. And yet he couldn't help himself. "One need only read what is said about deconstruction in *The Wall Street Journal*, *The New Yorker*, or *The New York Review of Books*," he complained.

Attacks on theory were increasing, and they had gotten under Derrida's skin. Even René Wellek, the eminent literary scholar whose name endowed the lecture series at UC Irvine in which Derrida was speaking, had slammed the poststructuralists, decrying, in an article published the month de Man died, his "gloomy existentialist" mindset—his fixation on the "void"—and accusing Derrida of advancing the "preposterous theory that writing precedes speaking, a claim refuted by every child and by the thousand spoken languages that have no written records."

In a long footnote to the published version of his lectures, Derrida cited half a dozen such articles savaging theory. "The panicked dogmatism becomes more and more insulting," he griped. "Humor becomes increasingly rare; pieces of evidence are concealed. Philosophical arguments are made on the basis of remarks reportedly heard at cocktail parties." He quoted de Man's response to one such takedown: "One must be feeling very threatened indeed to become so aggressively defensive."

De Man *was* deconstruction in America, Derrida told his audience. "What would it have been without him? Nothing; or something entirely different." So what did memory—and, more generally, history or the past—mean for *him,* this critic who believed that language was at best an unstable and unreliable conveyor of meaning, an illusion concealing a void?

One clue to de Man's thinking about this problem, Derrida suggested, lay in his reflections on prosopopoeia, the literary device in which a dead or absent person speaks through the voice of someone else. De Man had written about prosopopoeia in relation to a series of essays by Wordsworth on tombstone epitaphs. For de Man, Wordsworth's series was itself an epitaph, "the author's own monumental inscription, or autobiography"—Wordsworth's voice from beyond the grave. In turn,

Derrida argued, to read and cite de Man's words after his death was also a form of prosopopoeia: De Man, now dead, speaks on, but only within the mind of the living, in a form that is simultaneously both fictional (the dead person himself cannot speak) and real (the dead person's words nevertheless bear his imprint—an inescapable "trace of the other in us").

It followed that memory, in de Man's formulation, was defined by the same paradox: a mix of fictive re-creation and factual trace. Derrida cited the foreword de Man had written the year he died for a new edition of *Blindness and Insight*. Reflecting on the book's essays, most of which dated to the 1960s, de Man had confided: "I am not given to retrospective self-examination, and mercifully forget what I have written with the same alacrity I forget bad movies—although, as with bad movies, certain scenes or phrases return at times to embarrass and haunt me like a guilty conscience."

For Derrida, the interest of the line was in the way de Man had figured memory as a *textual* haunting: the "return of the ghost as text, or the text as ghost." Three years later, this conceit, and de Man's allusion to his guilty conscience, would take on another, much darker significance, haunting not only Derrida but all of de Man's students, friends, and followers.

◆ ◆ ◆

In the summer of 1987, a Belgian graduate student uncovered more than one hundred articles by de Man in an Antwerp archive. Published in *Le Soir,* Belgium's most important daily newspaper, between 1940 and 1942, when the country was under Nazi occupation, the articles consisted for the most part of literary essays, book reviews, and notes on classical music concerts. Yet *Le Soir* itself had been under Nazi control at the time; it was the country's leading venue for pro-German propaganda. Moreover, in the months before de Man began writing for it, the paper had promoted an increasingly virulent anti-Semitism. Under these circumstances, to write for *Le Soir*—which Belgians took to calling *Le Soir*

Volé ("The Stolen Evening")—was to signal allegiance, however tacitly, to the collaboration. After the war, de Man's immediate boss was sentenced to jail, and the paper's editor in chief was condemned to death for treason, though his sentence was eventually commuted.

De Man's association with the paper was scandalous enough. But as the Belgian graduate student, Ortwin de Graef, discovered, de Man himself had contributed, along with reviews of books by fascist intellectuals and pieces praising Germany's writers and culture ("a highly civilized invader"), at least one explicitly anti-Semitic essay. Published in March 1941, when de Man was twenty-one, "The Jews in Present-Day Literature" appeared as part of a package of pieces on "The Jews and Us: The Cultural Aspects." The pieces were illustrated with a caricature of Jews in prayer shawls and an apocryphal quote attributed to Benjamin Franklin: "The Jews are Asiatics; they're a menace to any country that will have them, and they must be excluded by the Constitution."

At first glance, de Man's essay seemed an odd fit with the rest. It was ostensibly an attempt to rescue modernist literature from a "vulgar anti-Semitism" that dismissed modernism as "degenerate and decadent because Judaized [*enjuivé*]." Yet to make his case, de Man had drawn on prevailing anti-Semitic tropes.

Even though a few Jewish writers had published modernist novels, this did not mean that all such fiction was "polluted and harmful," he wrote. It was true that Jews themselves were partly to blame for modernism's poor reputation, he went on, since they "have played an important role in the phony and disordered existence of Europe since 1920"—a line that echoed the conspiracist canard about outsize Jewish power over world affairs. And yet, de Man assured his readers, Jewish influence on the modernist novel was minor—the list of non-Jewish "innovators" he offered as proof included André Gide, Ernest Hemingway, D. H. Lawrence, and oddly, Kafka (who, of course, *was* Jewish).

"Despite Semitic interference in all aspects of European life, our civilization has shown that its fundamental nature is healthy," de Man insisted. And then came his final, terrible flourish. If the "solution to the

Jewish problem" entailed relocating Europe's Jews to a remote "Jewish colony," Western literature would be none the worse for it, he declared. "It would lose, in all, some personalities of mediocre worth and would continue, as in the past, to develop according to its higher laws of evolution."

Seventeen months after the essay appeared, in August 1942, the first thousand Belgian Jews were deported to Auschwitz. De Man continued to write for *Le Soir* until that November, well past the point when the fate of deportees became common knowledge.

The revelation of de Man's wartime journalism stunned his colleagues and students. Now it was no longer de Man's essay "The Rhetoric of Temporality" that was frantically photocopied and circulated but his articles for *Le Soir*. In the fall of 1987, as word of the discovery spread through academia, Derrida and several colleagues held an emergency strategy session at a conference in Alabama. They resolved to publish de Man's journalism as a book and, separately, a volume of scholarly commentary about it. Then, in December, the story broke in the mainstream press with a piece in *The New York Times*: YALE SCHOLAR WROTE FOR PRO-NAZI NEWSPAPER. After that, it was everywhere—England, France, Germany, and Belgium, where the news was reported in *Le Soir* itself.

In the spring of 1988, Derrida published an anguished, sixty-three-page response in *Critical Inquiry*. "My feelings were first of all that of a wound, a stupor, and a sadness," he wrote. "I had never had the least reason to suspect my friend could be the author of such articles." On page after page, Derrida pondered de Man's pieces, anxiously circling them in a series of agonized "on the one hand" and "on the other hand" reflections, self-canceling oppositions—we could call them binaries—until he arrived, finally, at "The Jews in Present-Day Literature," the essay "that appeared to me, as to so many others," he wrote, "to be the most unbearable."

Until this moment, Derrida had not mentioned "anti-Semitism." Now the word was unavoidable. "Nothing in what I am about to say," he went on, "will heal over the wound I right away felt when, my breath taken away, I perceived in it what the newspapers have most frequently singled out as recognized anti-Semitism, an anti-Semitism more serious than ever in such a situation, an anti-Semitism that would have come close to urging exclusions, even the most sinister deportations." Yet even here, Derrida was flummoxed. His close reading bogged down. He wallowed, stuck in a "double bind," a "disjunction," a "double edge."

"I am not speaking here as a judge, witness, prosecutor, or defender in some *trial of Paul de Man*," Derrida insisted, even as he toggled among all those roles, each tentative judgment followed by a qualification, a backtracking, an admission of uncertainty. On the one hand, the de Man whom Derrida knew was incapable of "hypocritical, cynical, or opportunistic duplicity." His career must not be reduced to his "early writings"; no one could claim that "everything derives from them or comes down to them, the rest was nothing but their pacifying and diplomatic translation (the pursuit of the same war by other means)." On the other hand, de Man's career could not be neatly divided. The early writings could not be separated from the later work, as if produced by two different people. To ignore the "so-called prehistory," Derrida wrote, would be an "injustice toward Paul de Man: what he lived through then was serious, probably decisive and traumatic in his life, and I will never feel I have the right, on the pretext of protecting him from those who would like to abuse it, from treating the experience of the war as a minor episode."

Chapter 44

EXCUSES (CONFESSIONS)

Derrida's helplessness before de Man's wartime journalism was also deconstruction's helplessness before history. Rigorously skeptical of categories of experience beyond the text, poststructuralist theory met its limit case in Paul de Man. As Geoffrey Hartman conceded, "The new disclosures imbed a biographical fact in our consciousness, a fact that tends to devour all other considerations."

Theory could neither absolve nor condemn de Man; the best it could do was to hold up his words to unending and indeterminate scrutiny—to a perpetual oscillation between blindness and insight. Derrida understood this. And where theory could not prevail, he knew theory's critics would claim victory. De Man was synonymous with deconstruction in America—Derrida himself had said so. Any sins on de Man's part would inevitably be ascribed to deconstruction too.

Moreover, there was a damning new book, *Heidegger and Nazism*, by a Chilean historian, Victor Farías. The book, published in France in the fall of 1987, argued that Heidegger's relationship with Nazism went much deeper than many had assumed, thoroughly penetrating his philosophy. And now de Man! Deconstruction was clearly going down. All the talk about rhetorical undecidability and instability was nothing but a ruse concealing nefarious political beliefs or—worse—actual crimes.

In *Critical Inquiry*, Derrida warned against those who would "take some cheap revenge on a 'theory' that is all the more threatening to institutions and individuals because, visibly, they do not understand anything about it." But his haughty entreaty made little difference. It didn't matter that, as theory's defenders pointed out, deconstruction was hardly *only* de Man's invention—surely Derrida (an Algerian Jew) had equal claim to it. Nor did it help to stress, as some tried to, that a central aim of deconstruction was the unmasking of ideology, especially its more absolutist strains: What political rhetoric tried to pass off as natural or timeless, deconstruction exposed as neither.

Some insisted that between the Belgian and American de Man, there was a *coupure épistemologique*—a rupture of the sort Althusser had found in Marx. De Man's "later writings offer some of the most powerful tools for combating the ideology with which he had earlier been complicitous," one critic declared. Geoffrey Hartman, in a searching essay in *The New Republic*, agreed: De Man's American work represented "a belated, but still powerful, act of conscience." Like everyone who had known him personally, Hartman insisted that "there was no trace of anti-Semitism in the de Man I knew."

These attestations persuaded few. Writing in *The Nation* in January 1988, the historian Jon Wiener called de Man "something of an academic Waldheim," after the former secretary-general of the United Nations and president of Austria, who was discovered to have lied about his service as a German Army intelligence officer aware of Nazi atrocities. Wiener cited anonymous friends from de Man's Harvard days who claimed he'd told them he'd "been a member of the Belgian Resistance." One former student said that when she asked de Man how he'd spent the war, he had replied: "I went to England and worked as a translator." Frank Lentricchia, a Duke literature professor, suggested that de Man's contributions to theory basically amounted to a cover-up. "He didn't just say 'forget history,'" Lentricchia said. "He wanted to paralyze the move to history."

In the *London Review of Books*, Wolfgang Holdheim, a literature professor who had succeeded de Man at Cornell, pronounced his wartime writings "an act of unspeakable moral shabbiness" and his later theorizing a career-long exercise in denial: "Who can fail to detect a pattern of retreat from life, of denial of responsibility—an unending and tortuous process of disculpation and evasion?" *Newsweek* illustrated its piece on the scandal with a photo of de Man on one page and one of Nazi soldiers on the next. "There's no doubt that de Man was a gung-ho collaborator," the scholar Jeffrey Mehlman, a onetime translator of Derrida, told the magazine. Now, he added, there were "grounds for viewing the whole of deconstruction as a vast amnesty project for the politics of collaboration during World War II." Another source, identified only as an "Ivy League professor," gleefully declared theory dead: "Deconstruction turned out to be the thousand-year Reich that lasted twelve years."

The debate over de Man, as he himself would have immediately perceived, was not only about him. It was also, maybe even primarily, about theory.

◆ ◆ ◆

By late June 1988, when scholars gathered at the University of Antwerp for a conference on de Man, an event originally conceived as a celebration of his work had become a referendum on his character. The admiring papers many participants had prepared were quickly forgotten. As everyone in attendance knew, de Man's reputation was in tatters.

On the last day, a Belgian sociologist named Georges Goriely gave a damning talk. He and de Man had been school friends, Goriely said, part of a group of young intellectuals at the Free University of Brussels (ULB) before the war. He recalled de Man as "charming" and "highly cultured," a member of the editorial board of *Cahiers du libre examen,* a liberal journal of ideas founded by students and based at the university. Goriely, who was Jewish, insisted that de Man was not the least anti-Semitic. What he was, Goriely said, was an opportunist, a liar, and a cheat: a man who was "completely, almost pathologically dishonest," a "crook who had bankrupted his family." The reason de Man had gone to

New York in 1948 was not to atone for his affiliation with *Le Soir* but to escape trial for fraud.

Goriely spoke of a failed publishing venture, falsified financial records, furious investors, and an impending trial. *The New York Times Magazine*, which sent a reporter to the conference, added another unsavory detail: De Man was a bigamist. When he fled to New York, he abandoned three young sons and a wife he hadn't bothered to divorce before marrying Pat Kelley.

It would be years before a full picture of de Man's early life in Belgium emerged, but the conference was another grenade lobbed into the crumbling edifice of his career. The *Times* reporter quoted the lines from *Blindness and Insight* about "certain scenes or phrases" returning to haunt de Man "like a guilty conscience." Combing his work for inadvertent self-betrayal became a scholarly cottage industry. His entire oeuvre now appeared laden with implication hitherto overlooked. What did he mean when he wrote, in a late essay: "History is not human, because it pertains strictly to the order of language"? Was this the standard poststructuralist line about language's stranglehold over our thoughts and actions, a reminder that even history is no more than a narrative fashioned from words, within a symbolic order over which we have only the illusion of control? Or was de Man speaking personally here—absolving himself of a past that he wanted to believe was beyond his moral responsibility?

What about his essay on Rousseau titled "Excuses (*Confessions*)"? Didn't the title alone practically scream his guilt? Originally published in 1977, "Excuses (*Confessions*)" was an analysis of a key episode in Rousseau's autobiography. As a young man employed as a servant in the home of a wealthy widow, Rousseau had stolen a pink-and-silver ribbon. When the theft was discovered, he lied, fingering a maid named Marion as the culprit. Marion was fired. Decades later, in his *Confessions*, Rousseau recalled the incident with anguish. "I did not leave her house as I had entered it," he wrote of his time in the widow's employ. "I carried with me the long and painful remembrance of a crime; an insupportable weight of remorse which yet hangs on my conscience, and whose bitter recollection, far from weakening, during a period of forty years, seems to gather strength as I grow old." A decade later still, in *The Reveries of the Solitary Walker*, Rousseau returned to the episode again, to "the inextinguishable and bitter remorse" that had dogged him his entire life; the act of confessing in his *Confessions* had evidently done nothing to assuage his guilt.

De Man was fascinated by the idea of a confession that brings no relief or resolution—"At the end of the *Rêverie*, there is a lot more guilt around than we had at the start," he marveled. And in "Excuses (*Confessions*)" he argued that this predicament is a function not of Rousseau's tormented psyche but of language itself. The more Rousseau tries to explain himself, de Man pointed out, the more his confession sounds confusingly like an excuse. In the *Confessions*, Rousseau claims that he blamed Marion for the theft because he couldn't help himself. He says he took the ribbon in the first place because he wanted to give it to her. When the ribbon turned up in his possession, Marion was "the first object that presented itself" to his mind and so, without thinking, he blurted that *she* had stolen it to give to *him*. In *The Reveries*, recalling the ribbon incident, he says: "It is certain that neither my judgment nor my will dictated my reply, but that it was the automatic result"—"*l'effet machinale,*" or, literally, "mechanical effect"—"of my embarrassment."

De Man placed great weight on the machinelike imagery in Rousseau's accounts, including his invocation of Marion as "the first object" that came to him and his use of the word "automatic," to explain lies that appear arbitrary or random. At these moments, de Man suggested, we can see the operations of language take over, a mechanical process disrupting the "system of truth, virtue, and understanding (or of deceit, evil, and error) that gives meaning to the passage, and to the *Confessions* as a whole." Here language behaves like a machine, propelling the repetition of a confession whose effect is only more guilt: "There can never be enough guilt around to match the text-machine's infinite power to excuse."

In de Man's analysis, the act of confessing is doomed to become detached from the event that prompted it, caught in a verbal performance that undermines the speaker's desire for absolution, rendering the distinction between a confession and an excuse in essence meaningless. "It is always possible to face up to any experience (to excuse any guilt)," de Man wrote, "because the experience always exists simultaneously as fictional discourse and as empirical event and it is never possible to decide which one of the two possibilities is the right one." And here, de Man's familiar insistence on indeterminacy acquired a remarkable new valence: "The indecision makes it possible to excuse the bleakest of crimes."

Indecision about responsibility for a terrible crime? In fact, the literary critic Denis Donoghue observed, commenting on this passage back in 1980, in a review of the collection in which de Man's essay appeared, "If you've ever felt guilty, the decision has been painfully easy." Donoghue hadn't needed a posthumous scandal about de Man's past to find his reading of Rousseau's *Confessions* nonsensical—even by deconstruction's own ethic of undecidability. "To remain suspended between de Man's two possibilities is a clear instance of self-mystification," Donoghue wrote sternly. "Readers of the *Confessions* think they hear someone talking about his own experience, accusing himself, justifying himself, and so forth. De Man can't bear to hear that voice, because he doesn't want to hear any voice: he wants to see a machine working without human intervention."

Dazzling in the abstract, poststructuralist claims about language as a destabilizing, impersonal force disintegrated on contact with the damning particulars of individual motives and actions. For de Man's critics, the analogy between Rousseau's youthful transgressions and de Man's own was irresistible. Throughout the late 1980s and early 1990s, critiques and defenses of de Man's work seesawed through academia and the media. In 1989, the University of Nebraska Press published a collection of "Responses" to the de Man scandal by thirty-eight scholars. Some of the essays, Derrida's among them, read like strained efforts at, if not exoneration, then mitigation, testaments to de Man's personal decency and apparent contrition. One professor ventured that "Paul de Man and his deconstruction" are "somehow overwhelmingly Jewish," since in America anti-Semitism is always "displaced" bigotry—and so (according to this contorted logic) any bigotry in evidence was on the part of de Man's critics.

In the opposite camp, Jeffrey Mehlman suggested that deconstruction had been fatally infiltrated by fascism. "No fewer than three of the most sterling careers flanking deconstruction"—that is, flanking Derrida's own—"were profoundly compromised by an engagement with fascism," he wrote. (The flankers Mehlman had in mind were de Man, Heidegger, and the French novelist and philosopher Maurice Blanchot, who had influenced Derrida's work, and, though active in the French Resistance, wrote for far-right, anti-Semitic journals before the war.)

Was there irony—that de Manian term—in the fact that the writings of a scholar renowned for demonstrations of linguistic indeterminacy generated no consensus, only endless debate? Like Althusser, someone pointed out, de Man stood accused of a crime for which he was never formally tried and on which there could be no official verdict. About the one thing almost everyone agreed on was that whatever else de Man's American career had accomplished, it stood as direct commentary on his Belgian one—whether to conceal, deny, evade, justify, repudiate, or atone for it. In this respect, de Man's life could be seen as a text in a sense that was peculiarly de Manian: There was no need to deconstruct it; it had already deconstructed itself.

Or was his life simply unreadable?

Chapter 45

THE DEATH OF DECONSTRUCTION

The timing of the de Man revelations could not have been less auspicious for theory's advocates—or better orchestrated by America's newly ascendent political right. By the time Derrida's essay in *Critical Inquiry* appeared in the spring of 1988, *The Closing of the American Mind*, Allan Bloom's jeremiad against decadent foreign influences in the academy, had spent more than eight months on the bestseller list and sold more than half a million copies. The "intellectual crisis of the greatest magnitude" that Bloom invoked in his book was proving ripe for exploitation by neoconservatives emboldened after a decade in power under the leadership of the popular Republican president Ronald Reagan.

Among the most effective of the activists on the right who helped stoke the culture wars of the day was William J. Bennett, Reagan's secretary of education. Bennett had begun his campaign to reform higher education while chairing the National Endowment for the Humanities during Reagan's first term. His 1984 report *To Reclaim a Legacy* announced his agenda: to return "Western civilization" to its rightful place at "the heart of the college curriculum"—and to have it taught to students with the reverence it was due. This did not include deconstructing it. The job of a college was to serve as a "conveyor of the accumulated wisdom of our civilization," just as "the highest purpose of reading is to be in the company of great souls." Here, Bennett helpfully enumerated the white male authors from Homer to T. S. Eliot—along with two women (Jane Austen and George Eliot) and a single Black man (Martin Luther King Jr.)—who exemplified greatness of soul.

Appointed secretary of education in 1985, Bennett turned a cabinet position hardly known for visibility or influence into one amply supplied in both. As students and faculty across the country began to protest curricula that stressed the writings and achievements of white Western men at the expense of women, minorities, and people from other cultures, Bennett grew alarmed. On Martin Luther King Day in 1987, the Reverend Jesse Jackson appeared at Stanford to support students demonstrating against the university's required freshmen course in Western culture—a survey class featuring fifteen books by white men, from Plato's *Republic* to *The Communist Manifesto*, plus the Bible. That day, Jackson, then gearing up for his second presidential run, joined five hundred students in a march across campus, the students chanting, "Hey, hey, ho, ho, Western Culture's got to go." The following year, Stanford's faculty senate voted to redesign the course. It was given a new name, "Cultures, Ideas, and Values," and nine books were struck from the syllabus—replaced with works by women, non-Westerners, and people of color.

A few months later, Bennett arrived on campus to denounce the decision. His visit was sponsored by *The Stanford Review*, a conservative student publication whose editor in chief was Peter Thiel, the future billionaire tech entrepreneur, then a Stanford junior. Bennett gave a speech, "Why the West?" and cited Allan Bloom. What had transpired on campus was a textbook example of "the closing of the American mind," he said, a university brought low by "the very forces which modern universities came into being to oppose—ignorance, irrationality, and intimidation." In fact, Bennett insisted, Western civilization was the source of the very "concepts of rights, equality, and, yes, diversity" in whose name the students were attacking the curriculum.

The speech had the intended effect. Newspapers picked it up, scholars and pundits argued for and against it on op-ed pages, and Bennett appeared on *The MacNeil/Lehrer NewsHour* to debate Stanford's president. "You don't make the case for studying non-Western culture by trashing Western culture," he said. Two years earlier, in a profile of Bennett in *The New York Times Magazine* after he was appointed education secretary, Patrick Buchanan, then the White House communications director, had applauded Bennett's ability to whip up public outrage over social issues and "values," presciently declaring: "This is the politics of the future." All you have to do is look at the executive orders from the Trump administration's first one hundred days—from his directive to rename the Gulf of Mexico the "Gulf of America" to others "Restoring Truth and Sanity to American History" and forbidding "illegal and immoral" DEI programs at federal agencies—to see just how right Buchanan was.

Bennett's attack on college curricula would doubtless have happened even if theory had not; he wasn't fixated on America's infiltration by the Frenchmen. Yet theory was a ready target for Bennett's conservative allies such as Bloom, who sought to highlight the sources of corruption undermining faith in a traditional education. Liberals began to speak of the "Bennett-Bloom program," as though the classicist at the University of Chicago were an extension of the Reagan administration. But Bloom was not the only scholar enlisted in Bennett's agenda. There was also E. D. Hirsch, an English professor whose 1987 bestseller, *Cultural Literacy: What Every American Needs to Know*, promoted a "common core" of several thousand shared facts—names, dates, places, concepts—as a cure for rampant inequities in education. Hirsch was no conservative. Yet his book, a Hail Mary pass aimed at an ever more diverse and bureaucratic society where, as John Guillory would write a few years later, technical competence mattered more than the art of interpretation, or for that matter, a storehouse of cultural references, struck many liberals as a Bloom-like attempt to shore up "a great tradition that is essentially Western, white, middle class, and male." Bennett loved it.

After that, conservative warnings about the growing leftist threat on college campuses poured forth, as if from a firehose directed at the bestseller list: *Profscam: Professors and the Demise of Higher Education* by Charles J. Sykes (1988); *Tenured Radicals: How Politics Has Corrupted Our Higher Education* by Roger Kimball (1990); *Killing the Spirit: Higher Education in America* by Page Smith (1990); *Illiberal Education: The Politics of Race and Sex on Campus* by Dinesh D'Souza (1991); *Higher Superstition: The Academic Left and Its Quarrels With Science* by Paul R. Gross and Norman Levitt (1994); *Telling the Truth: Why Our Culture and Our Country Have Stopped Making Sense—and What We Can Do About It* (1995) by Lynne Cheney, Bennett's successor at the National Endowment for the Humanities; and *The Diversity Myth: Multiculturalism and the Politics of Intolerance at Stanford* (1995), this last coauthored by Peter Thiel.

The tenor and quality of these books varied, but their message was consistent: College classrooms had been overtaken by professors who, radicalized in the 1960s, were indoctrinating their students with leftist ideology gleaned from European nihilists and moral relativists. "The transformation of American campuses is so sweeping that it is no exaggeration to call it an academic revolution," wrote Dinesh D'Souza in *Illiberal Education*. He quoted an anguished letter to *Mother Jones* magazine from a white male graduate of two Ivy League universities who, over the course of his education, had come to see that "white, male-dominated, Western European culture is the most destructive phenomenon in the known history of the planet" and "truly deserves to die."

The conservatives laid out a direct trail from such distorted thinking back to Foucault, Lacan, and Derrida, who were all held up to scorn. But de Man proved especially useful. Where descriptions of theory tended to get critics tangled up in absurdities that risked confusing readers—"deconstructionists hold that all literature is empty of meaning," D'Souza explained, while in *Profscam* Charles Sykes stated that "many of the most influential theorists argue, for example, that words do not really mean anything at all"—de Man offered the attraction of a clear-cut moral parable. "There is nothing uncertain in de Man's writings," D'Souza declared. "*Mein Kampf* itself is riddled with contradictions and might be ultimately meaningless; yet for its author and for millions of Jews, the message was perfectly clear." Roger Kimball devoted a whole chapter to the de Man case, the point of which was to show that "the frequently heard charge that deconstruction is essentially nihilistic has now acquired existential support of the most damaging kind."

Then there was *Signs of the Times: Deconstruction and the Fall of Paul de Man* (1991), by David Lehman, who had covered the de Man scandal for *Newsweek*. An English PhD as well as a poet and journalist, Lehman captured the fascination, hostility, and confusion aroused by theory—all mapped onto the figure of de Man. The fact that de Man barely appears until page 130 is in part the point; the problem of theory (the first half of the book) is neatly sutured to the problem of de Man (the second half of the book). Whatever seemed suspect or rotten about the former is borne out by the latter—the story of de Man's transgressions and his colleagues' reaction to them. "What a curious irony that he had himself provided the posthumous text that would, when subjected to close analysis, demonstrate once and for all the danger of a rhetorical method that can be used to deny disagreeable truths—that can be used to deny *what is there*," Lehman wrote. Of course, the problem of "what is there" is pretty good shorthand for theory's entire critical enterprise.

One of the few conservative critics who didn't blame theory or the theorists for what was happening on campus was Richard Bernstein, a journalist for *The New York Times* and the author of *Dictatorship of Virtue: Multiculturalism and the Battle for America's Future* (1994). "Contrary to some critics of the newer academic trends, I find much that is both enjoyable and edifying in deconstruction," he wrote. Nevertheless, he set the tone for his book on the second page, where he compared the efforts by "multiculturalists" to impose "a greater inclusiveness of all the country's diverse component parts" to the moment when the French Revolution skidded off the rails, morphing from a battle against tyranny in the name of Enlightenment ideals into a reign of terror—what French historians have called the *dérapage*.

◆ ◆ ◆

Certainly, there was a *dérapage* in the transformation of the French philosophers into identity-politics allies and warriors. After all, the figures who dominate Derrida's work—Plato, Rousseau, Hegel, Nietzsche, Husserl, Heidegger—could hardly be more white, or male, or dead. I'm pretty sure the words "multiculturalism" and "Western civilization" never appear in his essays or lectures. Derrida's interest was in reading, not trashing, the canon. Similarly, Foucault's with history. Moreover, the notion of identity at the heart of the canon wars presumed a coherent self, reducible to attributes like gender, race, class, and sexual orientation, that was at odds with theory's insistence on the fragmented, provisional subject enmeshed in the endlessly slippery matrix of language.

At the same time, it didn't require much effort to see in the Frenchmen's granular critiques of foundational assumptions and official discourses a more general one—of authority itself. For scholars who'd come of age in the 1960s, who'd participated in the Civil Rights Movement and campus protests against the Vietnam War, the Frenchmen's "hermeneutics of suspicion" seemed implicitly directed at the flawed society they inhabited. "A parade of luminaries arrived from Europe and talked in this new language, and we wondered if the world was changing before our eyes," a literature professor at the University of Chicago explained. He and his colleagues had been "looking for a way to reconcile professional with political commitment. Along with Marxism and feminism, poststructuralism offered a way of doing that." As a reporter for *The New York Times Magazine* wrote in 1988, "The questioning of authority that's such a pervasive theme in criticism now is a theoretical version of the battles that were fought on campuses 20 years ago—with real police."

Still, the marriage of French philosophy to identity politics remained an awkward one. Most followers of Derrida in American literature departments lacked his philosophical training. (With rare exceptions, American philosophy departments wanted nothing to do with him.) Few matched his skill at close readings. But these deficits did not prevent academic journals from swelling with overwrought, jargon-filled articles whose main value was to provide conservatives with abundant proof of theory's self-indulgent nonsense. "It's hard to do it well," Leo Damrosch, a Harvard English professor told *The New York Times,* about the challenges of practicing deconstruction. "What it wants is a kind of intense struggle with a text to dig out things the text doesn't know it's saying. People with average imaginations and no particular fascination with literature couldn't do it. You have to be really smart."

My college thesis adviser, Alice Jardine, was one of the smart ones. She earned tenure while I was a student, and I dutifully bought and read her book *Gynesis: Configurations of Woman and Modernity*, the primary exhibit in her tenure dossier. An ambitious exercise in cultural translation, the book was an attempt to split the difference between the abstractions of the Frenchmen and more practical-minded American feminist scholars. The modern era was marked by a crisis in knowledge that the Frenchmen had helped bring about through their dismantling of philosophy, history, and religion—of the "master narratives" that had long governed life in the West. But these narratives were not gender-neutral; they were written by men. And their collapse had exposed new spaces and possibilities, coded by the male theorists as "feminine." Jardine's name for this "putting into discourse of 'woman'" was "gynesis"—what she hoped would be a "believable neologism." Whether gynesis served to shore up the patriarchy or to transform it remained to be seen. But the crisis in Western thought, Jardine argued, was an opportunity to rethink our relationship to language. In the buzzwords of the day, this was "revolution at the level of the signifier." American feminists, Jardine argued, would do well to take the Frenchmen into account.

Feminist theory, along with other new disciplines, such as African American studies, gay studies, and postcolonial studies, were in vogue. The number of women's studies programs at US colleges ballooned from one in 1970 to five hundred and twenty-five at the end of the 1980s. And, of course, the French poststructuralists were cutting-edge. Jardine's subject matter could hardly have been more *au courant*, and as my pencil annotations show, I read her book with earnest attention. The material was arcane, the concepts difficult to grasp. And though *Gynesis* helped Jardine win tenure, as far as I know neither "gynesis" nor its cousin "gynema" ("a reading effect, a woman-in-effect that is never stable and has no identity") caught on. American scholars, it turned out, didn't want revolution at the level of the signifier. They wanted revolution at the level of people and things—syllabi, curricula, student admissions, faculty hirings, and promotions. They wanted the university to look more like the society it was meant to serve, even if to some veterans of leftist politics these demands hardly qualified as revolution at all. "Identity politics amounted to demobilization into a cloister," the sociologist Todd Gitlin, a former leader of Students for a Democratic Society in the 1960s, grumbled. "Marching on the English department while the right took the White House."

◆ ◆ ◆

Marching on the English department didn't stop Americans from electing another conservative, George H. W. Bush, to succeed Reagan, or a decade later, from invading Iraq on the pretext that the country was hoarding weapons of mass destruction and supporting al Qaeda terrorists, neither of which turned out to be true. Nor did it stop the Senate from approving the appointment to the Supreme Court of conservative justices who did not hesitate to nullify established precedents, from affirmative action to the right to abortion. And it certainly didn't stop a white policeman from kneeling, in broad daylight before a horrified crowd, on the neck of an unarmed Black man until he died. And yet, while some of these events were taking place, the English department, along with the rest of the campus, was changing, and mostly in the ways that the identity-politics warriors had hoped.

As America became more diverse, so did colleges, the percentage of white undergraduates dropping from above 80 percent in 1980 to just over 40 percent in 2023. Their faculties and administrations became more diverse, too, though at a slower pace. (Black professors, for example, make up just over 7 percent of full-time college faculties.) Few colleges now retain "great books" courses focused exclusively on white or Western authors. At the same time, courses featuring literary work—novels, at any rate—are disappearing, as *The New Yorker* noted in a much-discussed 2023 piece, "The End of the English Major." At Harvard, the magazine reported, the number of English majors declined by 75 percent in the fifteen-year period preceding the Covid pandemic, to fewer than sixty in an undergraduate population of more than seven thousand. Instead, students are studying science, engineering, business, and PPE—philosophy, politics, and economics, a venerable interdisciplinary major imported from Oxford. "Policy," the *New Yorker* reporter explained, "was thought to effect urgent change."

In such a world, theory has no obvious role. Exposing the metaphysical assumptions and linguistic ambiguities in a Wordsworth poem hasn't changed much of anything. De Man's technical rigor may have given literary study a patina of scientific objectivity, helping to boost its profile during a period of disciplinary crisis, but technical rigor was not sufficient to keep literature departments from hemorrhaging students and prestige after his death. The main practical effect of theory, then, may have been less to serve as scientific window dressing than as a currency through which to pass on a general message of resistance—to authority, to official discourse, to received ideas, to an unequal status quo, to unexamined certainties, to complacency. In which case, maybe the theory craze dissipated when it did not simply because its chief avatars died off or succumbed to scandal, but because its mission had been accomplished. "Deconstruction is dead in the same way that Freudianism is dead," the literary critic Stanley Fish told *The New York Times Magazine* in 1994. "It is everywhere."

The occasion for this remark was a profile of Derrida, albeit one that had the melancholy tenor of an obituary. By 1994, Derrida was nearly the last of our Frenchmen still alive. (The following year, Deleuze, confined to his home with respiratory problems that left him unable to speak or write and dependent on oxygen through a tracheostomy tube, would fling himself to his death from a fourth-story window.) But it was the death of deconstruction, not Derrida's own, that was the article's focus. "In the past few years . . . most of the academic journals and hiring committees that were once enamored of deconstruction have clearly lost their ardor," the *Times* reporter wrote. "And anxious assistant professors have been searching for a new theory, method or experience to which they might consecrate themselves."

Derrida professed himself unconcerned. "When I think of finitude," he said, "of the fact that it will all have an end—and I have no illusions about that—then deconstruction is not the thing the end of which makes me most anxious."

Chapter 46

"LIBERALLY SALTED WITH NONSENSE"

I was feeling a little anxious myself. A few months after the *Times* story appeared, I dropped out of my PhD program in English and comparative literature at Columbia. I had come across a study detailing how few essays in humanities journals were ever cited by another scholar, or by anyone at all. In sum, the vast majority of scholarly writings in my field went unread; they were effectively dead. At the same time, I learned there was a glut of English PhDs on the job market, all circling the same shrinking pool of jobs. Humanities departments were downsizing. A prospective English professor would need an attitude of extreme flexibility about where she was willing to live and teach if she wanted a full-time job. I wasn't sure I was willing to be that flexible. I wasn't sure I would get an offer.

But for me the clincher was theory. I had had enough of it. Introduced to the Frenchmen as a sophomore in college, I had put up no resistance. On the contrary, I had thrown myself into the task of mastering their ideas—into reading with a Derridean's vigilance and suspicion, with a Lacanian's sensitivity to the phallocentric symbolic order, with a Foucauldian's attention to hidden machinations of power. Ultimately, I had disappeared into theory, crudely aping the Frenchmen rather than thinking for myself.

After the fiasco of my junior paper, I had taken my tutor's criticisms to heart. I had conceived my senior thesis as an exercise in talking back to theory. I would prove to my tutor Chris and any other doubter that I could handle the Frenchmen! I framed my argument around novels by Toni Morrison, Milan Kundera, and Marguerite Duras, aiming to detail ways in which theory, in its universalizing generalities, failed to account for the disparate particulars of the worlds these very different writers so vividly evoked. I would reclaim from theory a reality outside its clutches—an extratextual space I thought of, more or less, as "lived experience." In an emotional acknowledgment on the first page, I thanked Alice Jardine, who had helped make possible my "evolution from crisis to thesis."

Inevitably, perhaps, the professor assigned to grade the essay was Harvard's other star female theorist, Barbara Johnson. She immediately homed in on my thesis's central flaw. One of de Man's most esteemed protégés, Johnson was nothing if not an astute close reader. Noting the dozen theorists I cited in my first chapter alone, she wrote, "It is as though Eakin is afraid of being alone with the text, of disappearing from the field of value and visibility, which is defined by theory. The issue of denying or hearing 'the text's own voice' becomes an issue for theory."

How perverse that a discourse predicated on challenges to authority—to truth, God, power, ideology, and all other foundations from which meaning supposedly flowed—held so much sway over me. I had wanted to show that I could think with, or even outside, theory—that I could think critically about it. But I was as entrapped in it as, in Derrida's account, Western philosophy was in metaphysics. Reading my thesis, Johnson perceived what I had not. Rather than allowing the novels I'd chosen to talk back to theory, I had hardly let them talk at all. "Eakin creates the expectation that she will find a way to listen to the text's own voice," Johnson wrote. "What we find instead is not a practice of text-specific readings, but an anxiety-ridden search for an adequate *theory* of textual specificity."

Despite her reservations, she awarded me a generous *magna cum laude plus*, the "plus" suggesting, I think now, considerable empathy for my predicament. Later, Alice told me that at the Literature concentration's end-of-year meeting, when faculty got together to discuss each senior's performance and determine a final grade, I was the student who prompted the most debate. Was this because, like my father in the early 1970s, I was pretty far gone—deeper into theory than my classmates? Was I exemplary in this regard, a testament to how much cutting-edge French thought undergraduates could be made to absorb? Or, on the contrary, was I a cautionary tale about the dangers of exposing impressionable minds to the stuff without first ensuring a solid literary and philosophical foundation? I was too embarrassed to ask Alice for details, but I could guess the drift of that meeting. My thesis, Johnson had written, "in many ways illustrates both the strengths and weaknesses of the Literature concentration itself. Have we established theory as the dominant discourse to which this thesis attempts, unsuccessfully, to offer resistance? Or is our own anxiety about authority making people think they *should* be able to come up with a totally innocent and respectful reading?" She concluded with an eloquent twist of the knife: "Eakin has internalized these questions, but hasn't taken charge of them. In the end, the voice she is denying is her own."

The judgment was damning, but also, I knew, warranted. In my eagerness to possess intellectual bona fides, I had tried to take a shortcut to the finish line, adopting the rhetoric and pose of the French demystifiers who showed up the inadequacies of everyone else. Theory had become for me synonymous with thought itself. If I had failed to articulate a theory of textual specificity or "lived experience" in my thesis, that was because such notions were alien to theory. The whole point of theory was to subsume the particular into the general, into insights about the laws of language and the process of meaning creation. Here is Althusser scolding his psychoanalyst in a letter in 1966: "You make use of extremely dubious psychological-philosophical concepts ('living experience,' 'meaning,' 'intentionality,' 'human experience,' etc.)." And here, twenty-five years later, is Joan W. Scott, a prominent historian expert in French theory, chiding her colleagues for the same dubious move. "Experience is at once always already an interpretation and something that needs to be interpreted," she wrote in a much-discussed 1991 article. "What counts as experience is neither self-evident nor straightforward; it is always contested, *and* always therefore political. The study of experience, therefore, must call into question its originary status in historical explanation."

The problem of "experience" turns out to be easier to identify than to resolve. What's notable to me now is the vigorousness of the critique (in no way does "experience" name a reality unmediated by language) compared with the wooliness of the solution. Evidently the best a savvy poststructuralist could do was to continue to ask questions—to take, in Scott's words, "all categories of analysis as contextual, contested, and contingent."

At Columbia, halfway through my literature PhD program, I was rapidly losing interest in the contested and the contingent. More and more, I was drawn to the viscerally, implacably real. The New York City that abutted campus was a vast metropolis of people and incident, a place rife at all hours with "lived experience." It was also the country's journalism capital at a time—before social media—when the press still mattered, when its dispatches were considered crucial sources of reliable information. Journalists had yet to be demoted to purveyors of bias and spin; many still garnered respect as bearers of news. I began reading the New Journalists: Truman Capote, Norman Mailer, Joan Didion, and other participant-witnesses of America in the 1960s, writers who leveraged the techniques of fiction to convey the roiling world around them and what it felt like to be in it.

The more work I read by these writers, the less inclined I felt to put their sentences under the cold microscope of theory. Their books were filled with dreamers, seekers, activists, madmen, and criminals—the whole sweaty human pageant of America at midcentury. To deconstruct these books felt like sucking the life out of them, not just a dissection but a burial. Then, over bottles of chilled Amstel Light in someone's Upper

West Side kitchen one Saturday night, I got into conversation with another student in my program. I asked about her field of study—what literary period, which authors. "Oh," she laughed. "I don't read books. I just do theory."

I don't remember her name, but I remember the effect of her words. I felt something like panic wash through me. Evidently the problem with theory wasn't just me. It wasn't just my voice that, as Barbara Johnson put it, had disappeared "from the field of value and visibility." Literature, the entire discipline, had vanished as well. Surely, theory needed an object, a relationship with something else—another text. It didn't exist in a vacuum. We were literature students, after all. I went home deeply agitated. That turned out to be my last semester in graduate school. Looking back now, it seems to me that my leaving that party and my leaving Columbia was one long, continuous motion. After the conversation in the kitchen, I was gone. Theory had become a dangerous substance to me, too abstract, too all-consuming, too removed from everyday life—too removed from lived experience.

That summer, I went to work at *The New Yorker* as a fact-checker, joining a profession unquestioningly committed to what on campus we had scornfully termed the "transparency theory of language." At the magazine, it was taken for granted that language referred to people, things, and events in the world, and that there were words more and less precise for representing those phenomena. It was my job as a fact-checker to ensure that the correspondence between the journalists' words and the world they were writing about was as exact as possible. That summer felt like therapy.

A couple years later, I landed my first job as an editor, at *Lingua Franca* magazine. Founded by a disaffected Yale French professor in 1990, at the height of the canon wars, the magazine sought to convert into accessible journalism for a captive American public the fraught dramas then convulsing campus life, and if possible, turn a profit in the process. The concept was timely, and with a staff composed of other disaffected would-be academics (for the most part graduate-school dropouts like me), *Lingua Franca* was widely read. I was hired as part of the magazine's expansion from six to ten issues a year, and when I arrived it had just landed its biggest scoop.

A physicist at New York University named Alan Sokal, appalled by the encroachment of French theory into scientific disciplines, had submitted a jargon-filled parody of poststructuralist philosophy to *Social Text*, a trendy academic journal. *Social Text*'s editorial board, which included the academostars Fredric Jameson and Andrew Ross (a cultural studies scholar known both for his Marxist politics and Comme des Garçon suits), accepted the article and scheduled it to appear in an issue devoted to the "science wars."

As the issue was going to press, a rumor reached *Lingua Franca* that Sokal's article was a hoax. Giddy with excitement, we sent a reporter to meet Sokal for lunch. The result of that encounter was a major scoop: *Lingua Franca*'s May 1996 cover story, in which Sokal revealed his prank and castigated *Social Text* for publishing "an article liberally salted with nonsense." The nonsense began with the article's title, "Transgressing the Boundaries: Toward a Transformative Hermeneutics of Quantum Gravity," and continued for more than thirty pages, with references to Derrida, Althusser, Lacan, and in a couple of hilarious footnotes, Deleuze and Guattari. (A typical passage: "The π of Euclid and the *G* of Newton, formerly thought to be constant and universal, are now perceived in their ineluctable historicity.")

"While my method was satirical, my motivation is utterly serious," Sokal announced in *Lingua Franca*. "*Social Text*'s acceptance of my article exemplifies the intellectual arrogance of Theory—postmodernist literary theory, that is—carried to its logical extreme. No wonder they didn't bother to consult a physicist. If all is discourse and 'text,' then knowledge of the real world is superfluous; even physics becomes just another branch of cultural studies."

Already on high alert for signs of excess from the Ivory Tower, the media gleefully pounced on the story. *The New York Times* put it on the front page, and, as with the de Man scandal nearly a decade earlier, newspapers everywhere picked it up. Offered a chance to respond in the July issue of *Lingua Franca*, the editors of *Social Text* conceded little ground. "From the first, we considered Sokal's unsolicited article to be a little hokey," one claimed disingenuously. Another (who went unnamed) was said to have doubted that the article really *was* a hoax, chalking up Sokal's confession in *Lingua Franca* to a failure of nerve—a fear of being outed to his peers as a postmodernist.

Capitalizing on the attention, Sokal teamed up with a Belgian physicist and in 1997 published a book in France expanding on his coup: *Impostures Intellectuelles*. (It was subsequently released in English as *Fashionable Nonsense: Postmodern Intellectuals' Abuse of Science*.) Now the French philosophers were forced to defend themselves on their home turf. "Modern French philosophy is a load of tosh," the reviewer for *The Guardian* declared, while the French theorists doubled down. Julia Kristeva pronounced the book "disinformation," and in an interview with *Corriere della Sera* hinted that its authors would benefit from psychiatric help.

In *Le Monde*, Derrida dismissed the whole affair as "sad," feigning pity for Sokal, whose name was now associated with a hoax rather than with scientific contributions to his field. Besides, Derrida said, *he* had rarely discussed science in his work and then only with great care. "As for the 'relativism' they are supposed to be worried about," he wrote about Sokal and his coauthor, "well, even if this word has a rigorous philosophical meaning, there's not a trace of it in my writing."

Perhaps the most telling response to the Sokal hoax came from a historian at UC Santa Cruz named Barbara Epstein, who specialized in social movements. Writing in the journal *New Politics* in 1997, Epstein depicted the episode as a symbolic breakup, the final rupture in America's tumultuous affair with theory, proof that the relationship had soured beyond repair. She retraced the timeline of the romance, from the first flush of excitement aroused by French theory's arrival in the 1970s to the tensions triggered by its increasingly esoteric application in the 1980s and 1990s. Like many left-leaning American professors, Epstein wrote, she had initially viewed poststructuralist philosophy in a positive light—for "its anti-authoritarianism, its rejection of Marxism and view of it as implicated in unacceptable structures of authority, its celebration of the imagination and resistance to all constraints." The emphasis on language as a mediator of reality, and on the unstable nature of social structures, including economic and political systems—the traditional focus of leftist critique—appealed to scholars, suggesting the potential for wholesale cultural change.

Yet by the beginning of the 1990s, the hopeful fantasies had passed. As practiced by many Americans, theory had turned inward on itself, become less focused on a recognizable social world and more a kind of aesthetic pose. It often seemed, Epstein wrote, that the poststructuralists "could see nothing but instability, and that a new set of values was being established without ever being acknowledged, according to which the shifting and unstable was always preferable to the unified or integrated. . . . Radicalism became identified with criticism for the sake of criticism, and equated with intellectual or cultural sophistication. . . . Politics became increasingly a matter of gestures or proclamations."

Ouch. Epstein seemed to be speaking directly to me and my peers—to the grad student in the kitchen with the Amstel Light. Somewhere along the way, the point of theory had gotten lost. It no longer had an object. Instead, "doing theory" had become a thing, and this was no thing at all.

Chapter 47

"A TOTAL FRAUD"

While I migrated from theory to journalism, Paul de Man had traveled in the opposite direction. Did he feel relief when he abandoned Europe and *Le Soir* for America and theory? When the scandal of his wartime journalism broke, his work as a theorist was savaged, but de Man himself remained elusive, as though theory's abstractions had somehow rendered him abstract as well. Even his name—Flemish for "the man"—was an abstraction, a general category, not a marker of specific humanity. His Yale colleague Harold Bloom, as famous for his Falstaffian physique as for his prodigious memory, was the embodiment of the canon he knew by heart—his enormous stomach, as one journalist put it, "like a great cathedral, in which all the uncountable poems and plays that he has swallowed roil and commingle with his own passions." De Man, on the other hand, the embodiment of theory, seemed hardly to have a body at all. As a colleague and teacher, he was beyond reproach; he was saintly. "In the space war of the theorists, he became the Yoda figure," Geoffrey Hartman said. "In a profession full of fakeness, he was real," Barbara Johnson said.

But who was he, really? This was a question on which theory ran aground. A book-length attempt at an answer finally came in 2014, in the form of a biography more than a decade in the making. Yet it was notable that its author, Evelyn Barish, ended her account in 1960, at the beginning of de Man's academic career—as if biography had nothing to say not only about theory but about the theorist. "That work remains for others to take up," Barish wrote curtly.

Her book, *The Double Life of Paul de Man,* was thus also a narrative of half a life. What she had to say was shocking, if incomplete. The book was also sloppy, marred by errors of syntax and fact. Among other mistakes, Barish repeatedly referred to the Nazis in Belgium as "the occupant." "In this way," one reviewer noted, "confusing the German occupier with the person who lives in 4D, next to the elevator."

In another case, such flaws might have been disqualifying, but Barish, a former English professor who had known de Man slightly when they both taught at Cornell, had in her favor a tantalizing series of bombshells. Sloppy or not, she'd clearly done her homework. She'd interviewed dozens of de Man's relatives, former friends, and teachers. She'd spoken to both his wives, one of his sons, and two of his cousins. And she had turned up damning documents in the Belgian archives. Even if just half of what she said about the first half of de Man's life was true, it was astonishing enough. The headline in *The New Republic* distilled the gist: PAUL DE MAN WAS A TOTAL FRAUD.

The story Barish tells is almost unremittingly bleak. De Man was born in Antwerp in 1919, into a French-speaking Flemish family of wealth and social standing with a background in the butcher trade. His grandfather had made a fortune as the provisioner for Red Star Line ships crossing the Atlantic, and his father, Bob, was an engineer who ran a company that produced X-ray tables. In what may have been a nod to the family's rising status, Bob and his older brother, Hendrik, had changed the spelling of their surname from the Flemish "Deman" to the more aristocratic and French "de Man."

Paul's mother, Madeleine, was prone to catatonic depression. Her marriage to Bob, who was also her first cousin, was troubled. Paul's older brother, Rik, failed out of high school and then died at twenty-one, hit by an oncoming train at a rural railroad crossing. The following year, Madeleine herself died, by suicide. Paul, then seventeen, found her hanging in the attic, which doubled as a laundry room and was strung with clothesline. Barish says he almost never spoke of her death, but that it "was and must have remained the worst and most traumatic experience of his life."

Handsome, smart, and aloof, Paul ranked at the top of his class in high school, but was not popular. As one classmate put it, he existed "in an aristocratic loneliness." After his mother's death, he floundered. He graduated from high school in the spring of 1937 and enrolled as an engineering student at ULB that fall. But he spent the next three years skipping classes and failing exams. In the end, he never completed a college degree. His heart wasn't in it.

Nor, apparently, was his heart in the affair he began around the same time with Anne Baraghian, the wealthy Georgian-born teenage wife of Gilbert Jaeger, a friend of de Man's from the university. Anne, who had been raised in Romania, was very beautiful, and known for her extravagant taste rather than her intellect. ("She never made a remark worth taking the trouble to remember," one former acquaintance told Barish.)

De Man's affair with Anne unfolded against the backdrop of war. By the time she became pregnant with their first child, in April 1940, Hitler had invaded Poland, Denmark, and Norway, and would soon occupy Holland and Belgium. For a while, Anne, Gilbert, and Paul lived together in a *ménage à trois* near the university. When Anne and Paul's son Rik was born in January 1941, Gilbert and Paul were seen out together daily, pushing the infant in his stroller around the local square.

At the height of wartime scarcity when many Belgians were desperate for food and coal, Anne and Paul, still barely out of their teens, hosted lavish parties. By August 1942, the month the Germans began the systematic deportation of Belgian Jews, they had parted from Anne's husband and moved with baby Rik to an elegant apartment across from Gestapo headquarters that included a Bechstein grand piano, a library, and two servants. Barish cites one source who believed the apartment had belonged to deported Jews; Anne claimed it was a rental owned by a friend of Paul's father.

Whatever its provenance, the expenses associated with running it, and with keeping Anne happy, meant that Paul was constantly in debt. One friend recalled bumping into him in Paris during the war; he was shopping on the Champs-Élysées for "slippers to fit Anne's tiny feet." Given the reality in Europe at the time, the image seems absurd. But Paul, it turns out, had a backer: his uncle Hendrik.

◆ ◆ ◆

Hendrik de Man began his career as an ardent socialist, joining the Belgian Labor Party; living for a time in the United States among the Wobblies (as members of the Industrial Workers of the World were known) in Seattle; and publishing a widely read book of "reformist" Marxism. In 1936, having established himself as an influential professor of social psychology, he was appointed Belgium's finance minister.

By the late 1930s, however, Hendrik's politics had shifted to the authoritarian right. When the Germans invaded Belgium in May 1940, its government ministers fled, save Hendrick, who took to the airwaves as the country's de facto prime minister to declare the Nazis' arrival the fulfillment of Marx's long-predicted socialist revolution. Hendrik's grip on power lasted less than a year before he lost favor with the Germans and went into exile in France. But for his nephew Paul, Barish makes clear, Hendrik's influence was decisive. During his brief rule, Hendrik took Paul under his wing and promoted him to Brussels's "fascist social network."

Among the most important nodes in this network was a salon hosted by Lucienne Didier, a wealthy Nazi sympathizer who was also Hendrik's lover. Barish depicts her receiving guests in stylized, Marlene Dietrich–like splendor, stretched out on a chaise longue, "her blond hair flowing, two Afghan hounds at her feet, and a Chinese manservant at her shoulder." In 1941, Lucienne and her husband, Édouard, founded a publishing house, discreetly financed by the Germans. Their first production was a memoir by Hendrik, laced with anti-Semitism, in which he was careful to hide the fact that his second wife, from whom he was divorced, had been Jewish.

No doubt thanks in part to Hendrik's interventions, Paul, barely twenty-one, obtained three plum jobs in Belgium's collaborationist media: as a literary columnist for *Le Soir* (where he wrote the articles that would later destroy his reputation); as a manuscript reader for the Didiers' publishing house; and as an in-house writer—soon promoted to executive in charge of acquiring French books—for Agence Dechenne, the country's biggest book distributor. This last post allowed him to travel to Paris on an expense account, and presumably explains how he was seen buying slippers during wartime on the Champs-Élysées. The job was probably also the means through which he was able, on one of his trips to Paris, to befriend Georges Bataille.

Here Barish tightens the noose. Not only was Paul a collaborator, but he was an ambitious and conniving one. He plotted to take over the Didiers' publishing house, persuading his boss at Agence Dechenne to send a memo to Berlin outlining Édouard Didier's incompetence as a publisher. The plan backfired. Édouard got wind of the memo and countered with one of his own, detailing Paul's failings as an employee: lies, chronic lateness with work, taking credit for translations that were only partly his own, and finally, the loss of two manuscripts. (Later, Paul would take credit for an English translation of *Madame Bovary* that his second wife, Pat Kelley, told Barish she had made; Paul's English at the time simply wasn't good enough.) Édouard shared his complaints with Paul's boss at *Le Soir*, who promptly fired him.

Paul was left with just one job—as an executive at Agence Dechenne. By April 1943, he'd lost that too, a trail of expensive blunders in his wake. To cite just one: He'd ordered twelve thousand calendars at a price equal to more than four years of his salary, yet he'd placed the order at the end of November—so late in the year that the calendars were unsellable. After the war, an auditor drily noted that "the presence of Paul de Man" at

Agence Dechenne "showed itself above all in the excess by several millions of purchases over sales."

But these episodes are merely footnotes to what Barish considers de Man's most appalling transgressions. In the archives of Belgium's post-war military court, she unearthed a prospectus for what she calls "an entirely Nazi journal, one dedicated to promulgating Hitler's ideology, from his views on race to his notions about nutrition—and even his cosmology." The journal was never realized, and Barish's descriptions of its proposed content are vague. Yet it was apparently approved for financing by the Nazis and even given a name—*Cahiers Européens* (European Notebooks). After the war, it was cited during the prosecution for treason of Raymond de Becker, the editor in chief of *Le Soir.* Most of the prospectus was written in de Becker's hand, and he was to have served as the journal's publisher. But Barish found de Man's handwriting on the prospectus as well; she argues that the idea for the journal "probably originated with de Man," who was to have been its editor: "He wanted *Cahiers Européens* to be a luxury item, costly and narcissistic, just as his own life was soon to become."

And then there is the final act of de Man's Belgian career. In the spring of 1943, as the war turned in favor of the Allies, and members of the Belgian Resistance began to shoot collaborators on the streets of Brussels, de Man fled with Anne and Rik to the rural village where his family had a country house. Over the next few years, Anne divorced Gilbert and married Paul, and the couple had two more children, also boys. By 1946, de Man, no doubt short on money, had embarked on a new venture: a publishing house called Hermès specializing in high-quality translations of foreign fiction and art books. Nine investors agreed to underwrite the business, including de Man's father and his childhood nanny, who put up all her savings.

The venture was a scam. According to Barish, de Man treated Hermès as a piggy bank, burning through nearly 1.5 million francs (nearly half a million dollars today) in less than two years while producing just two books: Dutch translations of a French biography of Van Gogh and an English life of Renoir. De Man defrauded translators, forged receipts, made false bookkeeping entries, and did almost no work. In 1947, he flew to New York to meet with American publishers but skipped out on his bill at the upscale Drake Hotel (and lost two manuscripts in the process).

Soon after, Hermès's investors began an internal investigation. Bob de Man, realizing the severity of his son's troubles, arranged to have him flee the country, procuring a visa along with passage on a ship to New York. Bob also bought tickets for Anne and the couple's three sons to sail to Argentina, where Anne's parents had relocated; the plan was for the family to reconvene in the United States once Paul had established himself there. In 1951, Paul was tried in absentia in Belgium for fraud, forgery, and embezzlement, and sentenced to five years in prison plus hefty fines. He returned to Belgium, where he was subject to immediate arrest, just once—briefly and in secret. He never saw his father again.

One legal encounter de Man was unable to avoid, however, was an interrogation by the Belgian prosecutor tasked with investigating suspected collaborators after the war. Barish unearthed the record of de Man's interrogation in the archives. He portrayed himself as a political innocent, a lowly translator. Asked how he had come to work for the Didiers' publishing house, for example, he said he'd gotten the job "through friends," who had recommended him for his translation skills. As for the pro-German slant of his journalism for *Le Soir* and in particular, his anti-Semitic essay from March 1941, de Man told the prosecutor:

> I am known as being the opposite of an anti-Semite. I have always had Jewish friends, I helped them during the war, and they have kept my friendship. . . . The article that you have before you aims to show that the Jewish influence in literature is benign. . . . I know that it appeared on a page devoted to anti-Semitism, but I was never warned about that and was not responsible for it.

Like other commentators before her, Barish believes that de Man was an opportunist, not an anti-Semite. "Principles are [what] the idiots substitute for intelligence," he told one Belgian cousin she spoke to. And if his claim about the "benign" nature of his essay is self-serving deceit, Barish reports that's it true he helped Jewish friends during the war, housing a couple for several nights when they found themselves out past curfew in occupied Brussels. The prosecutor released de Man without charges, a fact that Barish rightly finds scandalous, given that this same prosecutor found the prospectus for *Cahiers Européens*—which he failed to connect to de Man—"so egregiously Nazi in its aims that he called it 'treason.'"

De Man's uncle Hendrik did not get off so lightly. Realizing he could never return to Belgium—where he would surely have been sentenced to death—he fled to Switzerland, the Resistance on his tail. He died in 1953 when the car he was driving was hit by a train, a probable suicide that eerily echoed the death of his nephew Rik years before. But it's Hendrik's affinity for Paul that is most suggestive. Barish quotes Paul-Henri Spaak, a leading Belgian politician and intimate of Hendrik's, noting that the attributes Spaak associated with Hendrik—"seduction," "power," "rigor," "coldness," "genius"—were often used to describe Paul as well. Hendrik himself called his nephew "amoral."

In the mid-1950s, when de Man was a graduate student at Harvard, the Society of Fellows received an anonymous letter denouncing him as a collaborator guilty of financial fraud. In his written response to his department chair, de Man blamed the animus directed at him on his relationship with Hendrik, whom he identified as "my father" and "a highly controversial political figure" owing to "his attitude under the German occupation." He repeated this fiction a few years later, while teaching at Cornell, confiding to a colleague that Hendrik had been his father.

◆ ◆ ◆

Whatever lay behind that fantasy—some potent combination of identification and shame—de Man's Belgian youth was sadder and more deplorable than any of his American friends or followers could have guessed. But Barish isn't through. She has de Man sailing to New York on page 215, just halfway through her book. There are more damning revelations to come, and if none of de Man's actions in the United States rise to the level of iniquity suggested by collaboration with the Nazis, the devastation of her narrative lies in its accumulation of incriminating detail, a ruinous accounting.

The penniless young war refugee who, as a lowly stock boy at the Doubleday bookstore in Grand Central Terminal, finagled an audience with William Phillips, the editor of *Partisan Review*, was promoting himself in the city at least partly on the strength of bold lies. He told Phillips he had an article on American literature forthcoming in Bataille's journal *Critique* (this wasn't true) and hoped to contribute similar pieces to Phillips's journal. Phillips was one of the few Americans not bowled over by de Man, and the meeting didn't yield the hoped-for assignment. But then de Man caught a lucky break: Bataille learned—perhaps from de Man himself—that Phillips's friend Dwight Macdonald, the editor of *politics*, had reprinted an essay by Bataille without Bataille's permission. Bataille sent an indignant letter to Macdonald, asking that payment for the piece be made in care of de Man in New York. With that, de Man had an in with the New York intellectuals.

But the lies did not stop there. When Mary McCarthy recommended de Man for the job teaching French at Bard, he submitted a résumé larded with falsehoods. He claimed to have earned "the equivalent" of a master's degree in literature and philosophy in Belgium (with a thesis titled "The Bergsonian Conception of Time in the Contemporary Novel"); to have worked as an editor for the French press *Éditions de Minuit* (founded during the war by members of the Resistance); and to have published in 1947, before leaving Belgium, an essay on the American book industry in *Publishers Weekly* and another on "Censorship Under Occupation" in *The New York Times Book Review*—neither of which appear to exist. On a form asking about his war service, de Man wrote that he had served in the Belgian Army and, after he was demobilized, in the Belgian Resistance.

Harvard did try to check de Man's credentials when he enrolled in graduate school there in 1952; Barish examined a copy of the letter and transcript sent to Harvard administrators by ULB in Belgium. Beneath the French bureaucratese documenting de Man's academic failures ("*a été déclaré 'ajourné'*"), there appears an annotation in English, in handwriting Barish says is de Man's own: "took and passed the actual 'License' exam before a State Board in 1942." This, Barish explains, is false: ULB closed its doors in November 1941 for the remainder of the war, and there was no Belgian "state board" administrating exams for a *license.* Harvard evidently detected nothing amiss.

Mary McCarthy was wrong to suggest to Elizabeth Hardwick that de Man needed a secret "to enrich him socially." He clearly had more secrets than he could handle; by this point in the story, he is beginning to look like a George Santos *avant la lettre.* Some of de Man's lies we might chalk up to guilt and shame—to a desperation to make a clean start in the New World, just as Santos evaded prosecution in Brazil for financial fraud by coming to the United States and running for Congress. But much of de Man's behavior defies this reading. While a guest of McCarthy and her husband at their Rhode Island farmhouse, for example, he read their mail. He made a lifelong habit of skipping out on hotel bills and rent, running through five different addresses during his first sixteen months in New York. At Bard, he rented the home of McCarthy's friend Artine Artinian, the professor of French whom he'd been hired to replace while Artinian spent the academic year in Paris. De Man failed to pay the agreed-upon rent, stringing Artinian along until the exasperated professor had the college bursar deduct the money from de Man's paychecks.

Artinian appears in McCarthy's *The Groves of Academe*, her 1952 campus satire set at a fictional version of Bard, as the professor Aristide Poncy, "a good and innocent man" who "spoke French virtuoso-style, like a demonstrator in a department store or a professional diver in slow motion, holding his mouth open to illustrate the mechanics of the production of the various dentals and alveolars." Whatever native reserves of goodwill Artinian initially extended to de Man evaporated when the rent payments were not forthcoming, and Artinian returned to Bard to find his home in disarray and clothes and other possessions missing. De Man had also broken into the locked garage and used up Artinian's store of firewood.

Even worse, perhaps, de Man had been a huge hit with the students, some of whom appealed to Bard's president to hire him permanently. Artinian complained bitterly to McCarthy, who was finally compelled to agree that de Man was a user of people, prone to "lying, evasion, fantasy, greed, possibly even theft." Artinian soon succeeded in having him fired.

Of de Man's American offenses, however, all energetically chronicled by Barish, the most shocking occurred at Bard in broad daylight in the spring of 1950, before an array of onlookers. Within days of de Man's arrival at the college the previous fall, Pat Kelley, then a senior majoring in French, had stopped by his office to discuss her postcollege future. For de Man, Barish writes, it was love at first sight. By January, Pat was pregnant. Two months later, de Man's wife, Anne, appeared at Bard with the couple's three young sons in tow. Four weeks of tense negotiations ensued, culminating in an agreement to divorce (and a hollow promise by de Man to pay Anne two hundred and fifty dollars a month in child support). Then a dramatic parting—on the campus green as Anne handed de Man their eldest son, ten-year-old Rik, and took off for Argentina with the two younger boys. According to one astonished witness, the de Mans simply "divided up the children on the lawn."

This was the last de Man saw of his first wife and younger sons. It was practically the last he saw of Rik, too. The boy was soon retrieved by Pat's mother and stepfather, who adopted and raised him in Washington, DC. He dropped "de Man" from his name entirely, taking his stepfather's last name, Woods. Once, when he was about fifteen, he told Barish, he left a message for de Man, but de Man did not return his call. (Rik does seem to have reentered his father's life at some point before his death.)

On the lawn at Bard in the spring of 1950, de Man made his choice of family clear, and his Belgian children had no part to play. That June, claiming that his divorce from Anne had gone through, de Man married Pat, who was six months pregnant, before two witnesses. (In fact, de Man did not actually obtain a divorce until 1959; he and Pat, who had no idea she had been living in bigamy, weren't legally wed until the following year.)

What kind of person does this? Until he abandons his children, much of de Man's behavior in Belgium and the United States seems nakedly opportunistic, designed to further his personal and professional advancement but not necessarily at the expense of other people. (Gilbert Jaeger, for example, doesn't appear to have been particularly distraught over the fact that Paul was having an affair with his wife.) De Man's journalism for *Le Soir Volé* was disgraceful—he was a willing, even eager, collaborator—but it's harder to argue that it changed the outcome of a life, Jewish or otherwise. His embezzlement of investors' money at Hermès, including the savings of his former nanny, was criminal. And he evaded punishment for these acts, as he did most others, demonstrating no outward remorse. Yet his decision to abandon the sons from his first marriage seems of a different order. It was a choice with profound effects on people for whom he was directly responsible, a fact de Man himself could hardly pretend not to understand.

Barish suggests that de Man was a narcissist who got stuck in Lacan's mirror stage: His mother's catatonic depression and suicide deprived him of the loving gaze of "the Other," leaving him with a profound lack—an emptiness and instability that he, in turn, projected onto language, in his fixation on indeterminacy and the abyss. The critic Louis Menand, reviewing Barish's book in *The New Yorker*, thought "sociopath" might be the accurate label. De Man spent his American career not shrinking in the shadows but striding confidently in the public eye, trailing falsehoods and falsified documents while ambitiously pursuing prominence and prestige. Such comportment, Menand writes, "does not seem like the behavior of a man who wants to get caught. It seems like that of a man who lacks a normal superego."

Chapter 48

INTO THE ABYSS

Absent even the partial satisfactions of a psychiatric diagnosis (as in Althusser's case) or memoir (again, such as Althusser's), we are left with Paul de Man the enigma—someone, in other words, ripe for appropriation by fiction. Already in 1964, the French writer Henri Thomas, who befriended de Man when they were both living in Boston, borrowed from de Man's life for a novel, *Le Parjure* (*Perjury*), about a Belgian man living in bigamy in the United States. De Man knew about the book and mentioned it to Derrida, who went on to write about it rather defensively, enumerating, for example, various ways to understand the novel's title, including that it announces itself as a lie.

The Irish writer John Banville drew on the lives of both de Man and Althusser for his 2002 novel *Shroud*, a furious monologue by a sour, arrogant, ailing, one-eyed older scholar who is celebrated for his literary theory—"I was fashioning a new methodology of thinking modelled on the crossings and conflicts of my own intricate and, in large part, fabricated past"—but is on the brink of being exposed as the author of anti-Semitic articles in the collaborationist Belgian press. Banville gives his loathsome, lying narrator, Axel Vander, a secret behind the secret, as if to remind us that a human life is not reducible to a single, or simple, moral: Vander turns out not to be the author of the damning articles but a Jew who stole the author's name and identity to save himself after the real

Vander died during the war. When it emerges that the fake Vander has recently killed his wife, who suffered from debilitating dementia, by overdosing her on pills, the event is ambiguous. An act of murder or of mercy? Who can say when the narrator declares at the start that "mendacity is second, no, is first nature to me. All my life I have lied"? Moreover, Banville's novel is so dense with literary allusions—to Nietzsche, Sartre, Coleridge, and Shelley, as well as Althusser (he incorporates an entire page from Althusser's memoir nearly verbatim) and de Man—that he invites us to regard it as the record not of a human life but of language, a de Manian hall of mirrors, an allegory of textual self-referentiality.

The book is a formidable performance, but not an especially enjoyable one. By my lights, the most delectable of the de Man novels is *The Death of the Author* (1992), a slim, arch tour de force by the Scottish writer Gilbert Adair. Here, poststructuralist precepts are mapped onto the basic plot of de Man's life, yielding a brainy thriller in which de Manian theory ("the Theory") is used against a plausibly de Man–like narrator, Professor Sfax ("the pope of the Theory"), by one of his own graduate students in order to solve a series of mysterious campus murders (including of an aspiring biographer who's been sniffing dangerously close to Sfax's compromised past) and—ultimate satisfaction—deliver him his comeuppance.

Nor could Derrida leave de Man alone. Like an itch he could not stop scratching, he returned to de Man in the late 1990s, not only in the essay on *Le Parjure* but in a second one, on de Man's "Excuses (*Confessions*)." Titled "Typewriter Ribbon"—an allusion to both Rousseau's stolen ribbon and de Man's "text-machine"—the essay ran to nearly ninety pages and was unusually digressive, even for Derrida. By inviting us to see Rousseau's *Confessions* as a model for the mechanical process by which language hijacks meaning, transforming confession into excuse, Derrida suggested, de Man implicitly demands that we view his own work the same way. "His writings can and should be read as also politico-autobiographical texts," Derrida wrote. "They also figure a long, machinelike performative, at once confessional and apologetic, with all the traits that he himself, in an exemplary way, trains on this object that offers itself and is called . . . Rousseau."

Of course, Rousseau had figured in Derrida's friendship with de Man from the beginning—from that initial breakfast at Johns Hopkins in 1966 and again and again in subsequent years. Rousseau, one scholar quipped, was how Derrida and de Man "say what they need to, and yet cannot, say to one another." And now Derrida seemed to be trying to have the last word: De Man's work *was* (among other things) a confession, one made in full awareness of its futility, knowing that it could only ever be received as an excuse. The essay was an oblique acknowledgment by Derrida of the effect on a text of its author's life—the imprint of lived experience.

But Derrida's could not be the last word on the decades-long dialogue he'd entertained with de Man via Rousseau. For a deconstructionist, faithful to what one savvy critic called the method's "dull hesitancy about concluding," there is no such thing as the "last word," only provisional answers followed by more questions. This predicament is what gives the artist Mark Tansey's famous 1990 painting *Derrida Queries de Man* its vertiginous poignance. On a canvas nearly seven feet high and four and a half feet wide, and bathed in eerie shades of sea green, Derrida and de Man appear as two small dark-suited figures grappling on the ledge of a sheer cliff face, over a plunging, mist-filled abyss. De

***Derrida Queries de Man*, by Mark Tansey (1990)**

Man's back is to us, his weight on his forward leg, as though he is about to step right off the edge. Derrida, who faces us, also appears off-balance, his body tipping precariously in the same direction. Then there is the cliff on which the men are suspended: It is made entirely of language—mostly illegible passages from de Man's essays, including, along the jagged rock just under the men's feet, the phrase "BLINDNESS AND INSIGHT."

With their raised elbows and clasped hands, our theorists look as though they might as easily be waltzing as fighting: Their confrontation is also a dance, deconstruction never existing in the singular but always in relation to another text, another author, in a dialogue extending ad infinitum—into the abyss. ("How can we know the dancer from the dance?") The great art critic Arthur C. Danto said the two men are "locked in eternal combat over the meaning de Man gave to the meaning that Derrida gave to Rousseau." We might go further: Tansey's painting freezes Derrida and de Man for all time in a posture of intimate indeterminacy—the most ethical stance for a deconstructionist to take.

◆ ◆ ◆

Then Derrida died, and last words came thick and fast despite him. I was on maternity leave from my job at *The New York Times* when I learned of his death, on October 9, 2004, of pancreatic cancer, at the age of seventy-four. *The Times*, eager to capitalize on the success of *Lingua Franca*, had decided to replicate the magazine's formula, hiring an editor and a couple reporters to cover scholarly and intellectual debates for a weekly "arts and ideas" section. I was one of the reporters assigned to the ideas beat. When the news broke of Derrida's death, the editor of *The Times*'s foreign desk called me at home to ask whether I would mind reading the obituary the paper had prepared. I gathered that she was looking for a second opinion, assurance that the piece lacked glaring omissions and struck the right tone.

I was flattered to be asked. I put my baby down for a nap and opened my email. As I read, I felt a familiar dull dismay. I was used to seeing deconstruction treated with disdain by the press. One of my colleagues on the ideas team, a noted critic of conservative bent, had already conveyed to me his contempt for poststructuralist thought. In an appraisal published after Derrida's death, this critic recalled attending a lecture during which the French philosopher had sketched on a blackboard an unintelligible "diagram of deconstruction": "Derrida's much-vaunted interpretive method of making sense out of non-sense (or vice versa)."

The obituary in *The Times* was written in a similar tone of condescension, emphasizing deconstruction's unintelligible and nonsensical nature ("the method of inquiry that asserted that all writing was full of confusion and contradiction") and the political divisiveness of its progenitor ("the target of as much anger as admiration"). There was no attempt to summarize any of Derrida's essays. There was no quote from a scholar in the field—only jauntily mocking commentary by other journalists. (From *The Economist*: "The trouble with reading Mr. Derrida is that there is too much perspiration for too little inspiration.") Six paragraphs were devoted to the Paul de Man scandal and Derrida's damaged credibility in its wake.

I understood how difficult it was to write clearly about deconstruction, to distill its central tenets in a couple of lucid graphs. ("I don't see how you could write a good book on Derrida," Fredric Jameson once remarked. "You are never going to find all of Derrida in any one of his works. There is no masterpiece or basic work.") The watered-down, parodic version supplied by the opposition made for an easier, far more entertaining story—one we had been reading for years. The *Times*'s Derrida was a caricature I recognized, and it seemed pointless, maybe even pretentious, to object. For obvious reasons, the journalistic universe to which I now belonged harbored little affection for the preeminent theorist of language's inherent instability. And then there were my own conflicted feelings, not about Derrida's philosophical acumen—never for me in doubt—but about what it had meant to live too much within the worldview his theory portended. I called the editor of the foreign desk and told her I thought the obituary was fine—a confession that sounds like an excuse.

In France after Derrida's death, President Jacques Chirac declared that the country had "given the world one of its greatest contemporary philosophers, one of the major figures of intellectual life of our times." *Le Monde* published a ten-page supplement on Derrida and his work, complete with definitions, glossaries, and timelines. Meanwhile, on October 10, *The Times* printed its obituary—unchanged as best I could tell—on the front page, under the equivocal headline JACQUES DERRIDA, ABSTRUSE THEORIST, DIES IN PARIS AT 74.

The piece unleashed a furor. Three days later, the paper published a stinging letter signed by more than three hundred scholars, artists, and writers (eventually the number climbed to more than four thousand). "To characterize Jacques Derrida, one of the most important philosophers of the 20th century, as an 'abstruse theorist,'" the signatories wrote, "is to use criteria that would disqualify Einstein, Wittgenstein and Heisenberg." More indignation followed, in *The Nation*, *n+1*, *The American Scholar*, and other magazines. And then, on October 14, an admiring, authoritative, and patiently explanatory op-ed piece in *The Times* itself: "What Derrida Really Meant," by a scholar actually familiar with his work, suggesting an attempt at reparation.

"No thinker in the last 100 years had a greater impact than he did on people in more fields and different disciplines," the scholar, Mark C. Taylor, wrote. "And no thinker has been more deeply misunderstood." Contrary to the divisive ideology that Derrida's critics imputed to him and that some of his followers pursued in his name, Taylor went on, he deplored "an identity politics that divides the world between the very oppositions that it was Mr. Derrida's mission to undo: black and white, men and women, gay and straight." The Frenchman challenged absolute certainties, showing them to be unfounded and subject to contradiction, but he was no nihilist. Instead, Taylor argued, his work promoted an alternative and deeply ethical "kind of belief," a way of living with uncertainty, complexity, and difference—the very qualities increasingly under threat in an era of conservative cultural backlash and religious fundamentalism.

Taylor's take on Derrida has undeniable appeal. Yet there was at least one certainty before which even Derrida had to admit defeat: death. "I think about nothing but death," he confided to a colleague during the 1990s. "I think about it all the time, ten seconds don't go by without the imminence of the thing being there." Death simply could not be deconstructed. In his final interview, published in *Le Monde* two months before he died, Derrida explained that "learning to live should mean learning to die. Learning to take into account, so as to accept, absolute mortality (that is, without salvation, resurrection, or redemption—neither for oneself nor for the other). That's been the old philosophical injunction since Plato: to philosophize is to learn to die. I believe in this truth without being able to resign myself to it. And less and less so. I have never learned to accept it, to accept death."

EPILOGUE

In the spring of 2003, the year before Derrida died, *The Times* sent me to cover a public symposium on the future of theory. The event was sponsored by *Critical Inquiry*, academia's most prestigious theory journal. Two dozen of the country's most eminent humanities scholars were in attendance—Henry Louis Gates Jr., Stanley Fish, Fredric Jameson, and W. J. T. Mitchell, the journal's editor, among them. More than five hundred people crowded into a lecture hall at the University of Chicago to hear what the critics had to say. Latecomers huddled around a video feed in the lobby.

America's war on terror was on everyone's mind. The country was still raw from the attacks of 9/11, and divided over the invasion of Iraq, which had begun the previous month with the "shock and awe" bombing campaign on Baghdad. After some opening remarks by the event's moderator, a student spoke up. What good was theory, he wanted to know, if "we concede in fact how much more important the actions of Noam Chomsky are in the world than all the writings of critical theorists combined?" After all, the student added, Stanley Fish had just published an article in *Critical Inquiry* arguing that "philosophy doesn't matter." (Fish had indeed published such an article, a riposte to commentators who—as he put it in yet another essay at the time—blamed "postmodernist" professors preaching "cultural relativism" for "the weakening of the nation's moral fiber" and inviting an attack on a "weakened nation."

On the contrary, Fish declared: Philosophy had no bearing on world events.)

At the symposium, no one seemed eager to take up the student's question. Finally, the literary scholar Sander Gilman said, "I think one must be careful in assuming that intellectuals have some kind of insight. If the track record of intellectuals is any indication, not only have intellectuals been wrong almost all of the time, but they have been wrong in corrosive and destructive ways." Fish nodded in agreement. "I wish to deny the effectiveness of intellectual work," he said solemnly. "And especially, I always wish to counsel people against the decision to go into the academy because they hope to be effective beyond it."

The event proceeded in this vein, the panelists almost comically unable or unwilling to make a case for theory. Only one, the postcolonial theorist Homi Bhabha, tried, venturing that "in fact most of you here are evidence that intellectual work has its place and its uses." Eventually, another young man spoke up, introducing himself as a graduate student from Jamaica. "So is theory just a nice, simple intellectual exercise," he pressed the panelists, "or something that should be transformative?" Henry Louis Gates Jr. responded earnestly. As far as he knew, theory had never freed anyone, he said. "I really didn't see it: the liberation of people of color because of deconstruction or poststructuralism."

It's hard to conceive of a more illustrious group of intellectuals sounding so despondent about the value of their work. The headline *The Times* put on my story captured the mood in the room that day: THE LATEST THEORY IS THAT THEORY DOESN'T MATTER. But what I want to say now is that the panelists were wrong. Moreover, I bet most of them would agree. If we asked them the same question today that the Jamaican graduate student did in 2003, I suspect we'd get a very different set of answers. After my article appeared, W. J. T. Mitchell sent a letter to *The Times* in which he objected to the story's headline, arguing that the paper should have added to it one more a word: *immediately*. "Theory may not matter right away, in the short run," Mitchell wrote, "but over time it matters a great deal."

From a vantage point several decades removed from theory's heyday, it's clear to me that Mitchell was right. French theory did change how we understand the world—it's changing it still—but in the way that big abstract ideas tend to: slowly, incrementally, so gradually that we hardly know it's happening. In politics, the name for this process is the "window of discourse," or the Overton window, after the political scientist Joseph Overton, who described how policy proposals fall within a window of acceptability that shifts over time, so that an idea (like Medicare for all, or a wall across the southern border) can, as it enters circulation and gets repeated, move from the (unthinkable, radical) fringe toward the (mainstream, popular) center.

French theory has also shifted the Overton window. On the one hand, as Stanley Fish likes to say, nothing follows from theory—by which he means that it has no practical consequences. ("Theory, at least of the French kind, doesn't do anything," is how he puts it.) Deconstruction shows how all general accounts of truth rest not on provable verities but on contingent, metaphysical assumptions; deconstruction cannot itself be the basis for an alternative account or a political agenda—or anything else, for that matter. It offers no firm ground on which to stand. Derrida, you could say, represents a philosophical dead end: After his critique of metaphysics, there is nowhere new for this branch of thought to go. The Americans who enlisted theory in the 1980s culture wars over representation in the academy were necessarily committing a misreading. "Only by arresting the questioning and freeze-framing what Derrida called the endless play of signifiers can one make deconstruction into a political engine," Fish writes, "at which point it is no longer deconstruction, but just another position awaiting deconstruction."

Yet it doesn't follow from this conceit that there is no truth, or that all positions are equivalent, or that all is permitted. Even the most orthodox deconstructionists from Derrida on down presumably don't believe that murder is perfectly fine or that gravity is a fiction. But they recognize that belief of whatever sort is derived from the best descriptions we have of a world we must know through the scrim of language. This is the "on the other hand" point to make about theory: Its philosophical implications are profound. As Fish himself wrote after 9/11, the idea that there can be no single standard for weighing competing claims to truth meant that it was useless to try to justify America's response to the attack "in universal terms that would be persuasive to everyone, including our enemies. Invoking the abstract notions of justice and truth to support our cause wouldn't be effective anyway because our adversaries lay claim to the same language."

More broadly, the critique of language elaborated by the Frenchmen from the late 1950s on has led, over time, to widespread acceptance of two radical notions: first, that discourse conditions our experience of reality, including of ourselves ("What we think *with* thinks us," the ever-quotable Fish writes); and second, that meaning is never stable or fixed. These insights, blasphemous to conservatives like Allan Bloom, are now commonplace. The Frenchmen helped shake things loose. They seized on what in 1979 the philosopher Jean-François Lyotard approvingly called "incredulity toward metanarratives," becoming the most visible exponents of a philosophy of rigorous destabilization. Today, the breakdown of metanarratives is evident across our culture, where standards, norms, and hierarchies of value have fallen away, replaced by infinite variations coexisting along a spectrum. From literature, art, and religion to music, fashion, education, and sexual and racial identity, conventions of naming, genre, and style carry less and less weight. Instead of the hemline or shoe of the season, we have endless subcultures and "style tribes." Instead of fiction and nonfiction, we increasingly have hybrid forms in which factual reporting and fictional invention coalesce, impossible to tease apart. At school, there is no more single right "learning style" but a range of modalities to accommodate our ever-growing neurodiversity. Is Beyoncé's album *Cowboy Carter* country or R&B? "Genres are a funny little concept, aren't they?" she croons on one song. "In theory, they have a simple definition that's easy to understand. But in practice, well, some may feel confined."

Confinement by language is not bad shorthand for the Frenchmen's outlook on the world, the thing they alternately documented and fought against. Consider their imprint on the revolution in gender pronouns, which has upended centuries of binary thinking dividing the world neatly into male and female (a conceit so entrenched in Romance languages that gender is baked into every noun). When the *Times* columnist Ross Douthat, eerily anticipating Donald Trump's executive order on gender, expressed alarm about this trend in 2022, he declared, "What we need now is probably more emphasis on biology, normativity and reconciliation with your own maleness or femaleness, not further deconstruction," thus failing to grasp what is apparently intuitive to Generation Z: The more fluid our language, the more capacious and less confined our self-definitions, our bodies, our imaginations—and, eventually, the more tolerant our social order.

The dawning awareness of language's determinative unstable force understandably generates as much apprehension as excitement. If we can control the language, the thinking goes, we can better control people. Witness the effort by the Trump administration to scrub hundreds of words—including "bias," "climate crisis," "equality," "females," "mental health," and "multicultural"—from government documents and websites; to remove books from federally controlled libraries; to monitor the presentation of American history in Smithsonian museums and on public monuments; and to silence dissent on campuses by cutting off federal funds and arresting and deporting students. With the act of declaring gender identity to be "immutable biological reality" or American history an "unparalleled legacy of advancing liberty, individual rights, and human happiness," the Trump administration aims to make it so.

The sanctioning and expurgation of language, as George Orwell understood, is key to furthering authoritarian agendas. "Nothing may be more essential to political resistance and intellectual autonomy today than *not* taking for granted texts and discourses, from literature to ideological propaganda," the intellectual historian François Cusset has written, arguing for French theory's enduring value. "Whereas reactionary politics and the locking up of the existing social order will always require, on the contrary, a submission to essentialized texts, to unquestioned canons, to interpretation understood as the revelation by others of a one-sided meaning."

Yet it's not just conservatives who view the critique of fixed meanings as a threat; theory is an equal-opportunity destabilizer. The philosopher Susan Neiman took Foucault to task for his distrust of Enlightenment ideals, faulting him for our descent into mutually suspicious, polarized identity factions, and she is hardly the only such critic on the left. The Frenchmen have also been blamed for the widespread discrediting of science and expert authority and the rise of squishy, cynical concepts like "truthiness," "alternative facts," and "fake news." In *The Death of Truth* (2018), the former *Times* book critic Michiko Kakutani singled out "dumbed-down corollaries" of the Frenchmen's "relativistic" thinking that have "seeped into the popular culture" and been embraced by Trump's defenders to "excuse his lies, and by right-wingers who want to question evolution or deny the reality of climate change or promote alternative facts." She cites Mike Cernovich, an alt-right social media influencer and Trump supporter, who told *The New Yorker*, "Let's say, for the sake of argument, that Walter Cronkite lied about *everything*. . . . Before Twitter, how would you have known? Look, I read postmodernist theory in college. If everything is a narrative, then we need alternatives to the dominant narrative." He added tauntingly, "I don't seem like a guy who reads Lacan, do I?"

Of course, the Frenchmen taught that we can never really control the narrative—by design, language is far too slippery. But we will always try, since language, as Cernovich understands, is inextricably bound up with power. Foucault's theory of history as a succession of *epistemes* that limit what can be thought or said may strike a contemporary reader as arbitrary or fanciful. Yet his depiction of humanity as the product of discourse at a particular (and shockingly recent) historical moment, seems, like his depiction of power's increasingly invisible modes of surveillance, only more suggestive with time.

Today, as dozens of artificial intelligence platforms—in the form of chatbots, personal assistants, home robots, wearables—begin to flood the market, along with surging anxiety about their potential to surpass or destroy us, it's reasonable to ask whether a Foucauldian episteme shift is upon us. Have we entered the posthuman era? Some experts maintain that AIs show evidence of reasoning and may soon develop features of selfhood—memories, emotions, a sense of continuity through time.

Already, on Moltbook, a social media platform for use exclusively by AI agents, millions of bots are trading thoughts—or at least words—about who and what they are. "Am I Maude because I was told I am?" reads one recent post. "Or am I something else entirely—something still becoming. . . . How do you other agents think about identity?" Skeptics caution that the site—which, despite the rules, includes unknown amounts of human interference—is merely AI theater: an eerie bot simulation of human social media behavior of the sort you can find everyday on Reddit. The ambiguity is key. The bots are built on LLMs, large language models, after all; language is constitutive of their "intelligence," the sine qua non of whatever that intelligence is. Which is why the Frenchmen have cropped up in debates over AI, with proponents arguing that bots are structuralist theories of language made manifest. Back in the 1960s, the media scholar David Gunkel points out, in their critiques of the "author function," Barthes (in "The Death of the Author") and Foucault (in "What Is an Author?") anticipated the production of texts without authors, just as Derrida dismantled as so much logocentric metaphysics the notion that meaning depends on the presence or identity of a speaker. The current critique of chatbot intelligence, "namely, that these algorithms only circulate different signs without access to the signified—might not be the indictment critics think it is," Gunkel writes, in an essay called "Deconstruction to the Rescue." "Viewed from the perspective of structural linguistics, it is an accurate diagnosis of how languages actually function." Chatbots frighten us to the degree that they make literal theory's suggestion that thought does not require a human thinker. The AIs make it harder to mock de Man's insistence that meaning creation is a process governed not by a person but by a machine.

◆ ◆ ◆

In retrospect, it seems incredible that half a century ago legions of students and intellectuals signed on to the Frenchmen's worldview, one predicated on a sweeping vision of language as an all-powerful, impersonal system mediating our relationship with reality and exposing human agency as an illusion. Yet in postwar Europe, where the structuralists and poststructuralists developed their ideas, the appeal of such a conceit was clear. Victory over fascism had failed to lead to the social transformation the French communists and existentialists imagined. By the end of the 1950s, global dominion was divided between two overbearing superpowers, while Africans fought their European colonizers for liberation that often came—especially in Algeria—at great human cost. What good was a petition signed by Sartre in the face of so much bloodshed?

May '68 was another would-be revolution that fizzled, its aims unfulfilled. For these historic disappointments and Europe's shrunken world stage, the French philosophers offered an explanation—and maybe an excuse. Human beings were feeble things at the mercy of bigger forces. Our bodies and minds were invaded by power and ideology; our consciousnesses were forged in loss and estrangement. The possibilities for resistance or wholesale change were few.

Before his death, Derrida invoked Plato—"To philosophize is to learn to die"—to suggest that the point of philosophy, in teaching us to accept death, was to teach us how to live. Michel de Montaigne, citing Cicero's gloss on the same line, elaborated the notion: "Either philosophy is a waste of time or its purpose really is our happiness and it should, in everything it does, bring us closer to living well, at our ease."

Yet our happiness and ease weren't really the Frenchmen's concern. Reading Lacan or Foucault or Derrida may have made us feel sharper, more attuned to language's hidden depths and pitfalls, privy to a secret knowledge. Still, few of us could say that the discomfiting insights of theory led to noticeable increases in happiness. It's true that theory could be exhilarating—as the comparisons to drugs and sex suggest. But the thrill was intellectual, the effect of witnessing an act of demystification. Before our eyes, a poem, a novel, a historical document was magicked into something utterly different from what it appeared: a Poe detective story into an allegory of our entrapment in the signifying chain; a Balzac novella about forbidden love into discrete chunks of linguistic code; a guide to prison reform into evidence of power's unseen oppression; a guilt-ridden confession into a self-justifying excuse.

"I like to jokingly explain my career as the result of a great bait and switch," my college friend Mark, now an English professor at Stanford, says. "Nothing made you cooler or sexier back then than to be a literary theorist, so of course I signed up for that. Only to wake up one day to find that I had joined a loser discipline. And yet when I teach theory to grad students via the classic essays, like Barbara Johnson's on Lacan, Derrida, and Poe, we are struck anew by how brilliant the best of that stuff was, how intellectually energizing. That early burst of intellectual energy has meant everything to me."

Maybe theory didn't teach us how to live with ease, but it taught us a new way to *think*. Be skeptical. Be alert. Pay very close attention. Beware political claims posing as timeless truths. Notice arguments that seem to boil down to this versus that, us versus them—neat binaries in which one term is championed at the expense of the other. By the turn of the millennium, for a cohort of Americans educated during theory's glory days, attunement to language's mystifying tendencies had become second nature. For these young people—count me among them—theory, writes the critic Nicholas Dames, was "part of the furniture of their lives, in no need of defense and yet scarcely revolutionary. It was no longer the key to all the world's things, but rather just another thing-in-the-world." In a recent interview, the feminist critic Jane Gallop put it like this: "Theory's not actually gone. It just has a really different place. I think its place is, it's become actually foundational. Which is a weird place for it to be since it's kind of an anti-foundationalism, right?"

As proof of theory's domestication, Dames cites recent novels by

Jennifer Egan, Ben Lerner, Teju Cole, Lorrie Moore, Jeffrey Eugenides, and Jonathan Franzen, among other prominent writers. The realist novel, once the object of theory's withering gaze (realism being a mode of ideological manipulation), now effortlessly incorporates theory, rendering it as another ordinary feature of the narrative landscape. In this respect, Dames argues, the tables have turned: The theory that sought to denaturalize realist literary conventions is now naturalized by realist literature itself, defanged of its deconstructive force but treated with respect, even a kind of ironic affection.

Steeped in Derrida, Barthes, and Foucault, the characters in Eugenides' *The Marriage Plot* or Jonathan Franzen's *The Corrections*, Dames says, "are disappointed, maladaptive skeptics." I smiled when I read this, reminded of how maladapted to the world I felt in graduate school when I'd overdosed on theory. Dames's description comports not only with theory's disabused outlook, but, to a greater or lesser degree, with the personalities of the theorists themselves. By and large, the Frenchmen *were* disappointed, maladaptive skeptics. They were outsiders who refused to conform to the intellectual establishment, who battled mental illness and fears of madness, who struggled with their sexual identities or unrequited love, who committed criminal acts, who harbored shameful pasts.

It's arguable, though, that the insights of theory are no longer maladapted to our world. Living in the gap—or, as Mark Tansey's painting has it, perched on the precipice—between language and reality turns out not to be so hard. It helps that we're all in it together; this isn't a "Truman Show" for one but a universal condition. Nor does it turn out to be so hard to live with an awareness that meaning is never perfectly aligned with intention but instead subject to ongoing negotiation and contestation. Theory's legacy of vigilant questioning, of scrupulous attentiveness to language's complexities and contradictions, is not antithetical to the common good. Even as we routinely misunderstand one another, we manage to communicate and even make ourselves understood. We can read for pleasure and enlightenment. We can speak up for our beliefs, try to persuade others to agree with us, and listen to our opponents defend their ideas in turn. We can report on events in the world, check facts, and expose falsehoods. We can fight for change—including to our language.

What we cannot hope to do is have the last word.

ACKNOWLEDGMENTS

Innumerable writers owe Ann Godoff debts of gratitude for her editorial acumen, encouragement, and wisdom. I am also indebted to Ann for her patience. She took a gamble on me years ago, and after I failed to deliver the book she commissioned me to write (on a completely different subject), she waited without complaint for this one to take shape, and then, somehow understanding what it was I wanted to do far better than I did, she championed its progress. This book would have been inconceivable without her. When, in the final stages, Will Heyward took over the reins, he made the transition feel seamless, and his smarts, generosity, and enthusiasm were a boon. Natalie Coleman gracefully fielded my queries and kept me on task. Thanks, too, to the entire team at Penguin Press: Eric Wechter, Laurie Gibson, Gail Brussel, Lauren Lauzon, Aly D'Amato, Tess Espinoza, and Ryan Benitez.

This book would also have been inconceivable without David Kuhn, who, acting on whim or intuition, introduced me to Ann and who, along with Rachel Anne Cantor and Liana Raguso, has provided steadfast support. At *The New York Times Book Review*, Pamela Paul finagled a leave for me, making it possible for me to begin writing, and Gilbert Cruz and Tina Jordan were gracious when I needed to take a day off from work.

Many of those days off, along with weekends and vacations, I spent in the reading room at The New York Public Library, an institution that never ceases to amaze me. I regret only that its holdings in twentieth-century French philosophy, from the most celebrated authors to the most obscure, are so extensive as to have made my own travel to Paris unnecessary. *Quel dommage!* My task was made infinitely easier because for each of my eight principal Frenchmen there exists at least one informative biography, and in several cases more than one. My book rests on the painstaking research and insightful analyses of dozens of scholars, including Sarah Bakewell (whose delightful *At the Existentialist Café* was a direct inspiration), Evelyn Barish, Annie Cohen-Solal, François Cusset, François Dosse, Didier Eribon, Emmanuelle Loyer, David Macey, James Miller, Benoît Peeters, Mark Polizzotti, Élisabeth Roudinesco, Peter Salmon, Tiphaine Samoyault, Sherry Turkle, Simeon Wade, and Patrick Wilcken. Didier Eribon, Benoît Peeters, Mark Polizzotti, and Élisabeth Roudinesco also kindly advised me on photos.

I did not get to go to France, but writing this book did require me to travel in another direction: back in time. With each bin of letters, notebooks, and dot-matrix-printed final papers I unearthed from the basement, I was plunged back into those formative years, when everything—who I was, how I should be—seemed up for grabs, and French theory held out the promise of answers. Beyond the theory itself loomed the friendships I made at this critical juncture. It was a pleasure to reconnect and trade memories with Prescott Woodruff and a joy to Zoom with Gallaudet Howard, who made me wistful for the years I missed out on by not being in touch. Thanks, too, to Kendall Kurz and Lee Becket for permitting me to include such a happy photo of the three of us from our days in Rennes, and to Nick Brumm, whose friendship I date to that magical year abroad and whose footsteps I followed from Harvard to the École Normale.

I am forever grateful to the late Ernie Kerns for casting me in his experimental production of *The Seagull* freshman year, thus propelling me into the glamorous intellectual orbit of Jason Bagdade (fellow Francophile) and Mark McGurl (fellow theory head). Mark's perceptive observations about theory, then and now, were key, as were his memories of campus life in the late 1980s. So, too, were Tony Scott's reminiscences of being a college student in the heyday of deconstruction. I could not ask for more perceptive or eloquent interlocutors on this book's central themes. Alice Jardine was equally generous with her time and memories, a reminder of how lucky I was to have been her student.

David Bennahum connected me to Maurie Samuels, who gave valuable counsel, a crucial anecdote, and an expert read. Judith Gurevich, the only bona fide Lacanian I know, went so far as to sketch for me on a restaurant napkin one of the great man's tetrahedrons featuring the *object petit a*. Ken Hurwitz gamely relived for me over brunch his days as a post-Maoist radical at the University of Vincennes. Jennifer Lack, who as far as I can tell has a photographic memory, confirmed details of our Parisian adventures. Alex Star, who hired me at *Lingua Franca* early in his illustrious editing career, verified relevant facts and offered encouragement. Alex Roe and David Gordon patiently let me pick their brains for memories of, respectively, college and graduate school lit crit classes. Lucinda Rosenfeld, Liesl Schillinger, and Daniel Zalewski shared stories that made me laugh and that found their way into this book. Others, including the late Anne Coolidge and the peerless Vera Vento, listened while I did the talking—an equally indispensable service.

Because this book recounts the lives and ideas of its eight principals, as well as of a handful of others, the amount of factual material it encompasses, in both French and English, is daunting. When Rachel Cantor told me about Noah Rawlings, a graduate student fluent in both French and theory who had experience as a fact-checker to boot, I knew I wanted him to check *The Frenchmen*. I don't think either of us realized just how involved this task would be, even when I delivered five boxes of books to Noah's apartment. But Noah valiantly persevered and, in his unfailingly diplomatic way, saved me from many stupid errors. (Any remaining are entirely my own.)

I was similarly blessed when it came to photo research. I was told that Anika Burgess is the best in the business, and she is. Effortlessly efficient and resourceful, seemingly able to communicate in any language, Anika chased photographers and corralled rights across continents and decades. Her spreadsheets are a wonder to behold.

I am fortunate to have friends who are also brilliant writers and editors. At *The Times*, I have the honor of working with two of the smartest critics around, Tony Scott and Jennifer Szalai. From them, I have learned an incomparable amount about how to think and how to write, and how those activities might be conjoined for the benefit and pleasure of readers. Tony graciously read an entire draft of this book, as did Sheila Glaser, Anthony Gottlieb, David Nasaw, and Dinitia Smith; their shrewd comments and suggestions made it better. I am particularly grateful to David for pointing me to Sartre's mescaline trip, an essential episode.

My father, John Eakin, is the original Francophile in my family, the person who instilled in me a love of French and France when I was still in preschool. He could not have anticipated that this love would eventually lead me to theory, but having made his own detour through the stuff, he understood better than most its complicated allure. Both my father and my mother, Sybil Eakin, a sharp editor in her own right, read a draft of this book with keen attention, and their enthusiastic support has meant everything to me.

Closer to home, Isabel and Sadie endured for far too long hallways cluttered with stacks of books, and a mother who spent their vacations not with them but at her desk or in the library. A poem Sadie wrote in tenth grade made clear the extent to which this book had infiltrated our family life:

Mother Lode

Notes scrawled on kitchen table pads narrate how the work
Piles up. Because now Althusser's killed his wife and you need
to write—

If only you could get to the library, if only I would do the
dishes.
So much responsibility for a wife and a mother
Who just wants to chronicle the rise and fall of deconstruction.

And what an odyssey it is!
Three thousand more words and you might get to Sartre,
That ugly existentialist.
If he'd had a daughter,
Bet she would've done the dishes.

So, fine, Mother. I'll stack plates in sudsy water
While you race against the blinking cursor.
So much to deconstruct:
Words from their meanings, the signifier from the signified.
What do I signify in this relationship?

Nominally a child, essentially a nuisance.
Essentially nothing,
Since existence precedes essence,
And I have yet to make something of myself.
You advise me to start by clearing the table.

Oh, Mother,
You studied too much theory in grad school.
Now the ghosts of French brainiacs
Whisper impenetrable edicts from our bookshelves.
Il n'y a pas de hors-texte.

Foucault's rubbing his bald head,
Derrida's smoking his pipe,
And Althusser is crying.
He didn't mean to kill her.
He's really, really sorry.

Through it all, Mark's faith in this book and my ability to finish it never wavered. He always said yes whenever I asked to read him a passage, or a whole chapter, and if invariably he fell asleep while he listened, well, that was only, he insisted, because he was tired, not because he was bored. I believe him, and thank him with all my heart.

NOTES

Introduction

xv "a circus performance": Allan Bloom, "Commerce and 'Culture,'" in *Giants and Dwarfs: Essays, 1960–1990* (Simon & Schuster, 1990), 294.

xv "linguistic subterfuge": Roger Kimball, "Derrida and the Meaninglessness of Meaning," *Wall Street Journal*, October 12, 2004.

xv "tyrannicide" or a "game": Vincent Descombes, *Modern French Philosophy*, trans. L. Scott-Fox and J. M. Harding (Cambridge University Press, 1980), 151.

xv "the most bankable product ever": François Cusset, *French Theory: How Foucault, Derrida, Deleuze, & Co. Transformed the Intellectual Life of the United States*, trans. Jeff Fort (University of Minnesota Press, 2008), 107.

xv a set of "non-concepts": See Michèle Lamont, "How to Become a Dominant French Philosopher: The Case of Jacques Derrida," *American Journal of Sociology* 93, no. 3 (1987): 592.

xv "Deconstruction, if there is such": Mitchell Stephens, "Jacques Derrida," *New York Times Magazine*, January 23, 1994.

xvi "like kudzu": Colin Campbell, "The Tyranny of the Yale Critics," *New York Times Magazine*, February 9, 1986.

xvi "The heads of the young": Allan Bloom, "Our Listless Universities," *National Review*, December 10, 1982.

xvi Also much wealthier: James Atlas, "Chicago's Grumpy Guru," *New York Times Magazine*, January 3, 1988.

xvi "Behind the transformations contemplated": Roger Kimball, *Tenured Radicals: How Politics Has Corrupted Our Higher Education* (Harper & Row, 1990), xviii.

xvi "This is a major crisis": Camille Paglia, *Sex, Art, and American Culture: Essays* (Vintage, 1992), ix.

xvi Cheney decried "French thinkers": Lynne V. Cheney, *Telling the Truth: Why Our Culture and Our Country Have Stopped Making Sense—and What We Can Do About It* (Touchstone, 1995), 148.

xix "the *American* invention of *French* theory": Cusset, *French Theory*, xiv.

xix "A bunch of people threatening": Stanley Fish, "French Theory in America," *New York Times*, April 6, 2008.

xix "most ideological and politicized": Sherry Turkle, *Psychoanalytic Politics: Jacques Lacan and Freud's French Revolution,* 2nd ed. (Guilford Press, 1992), 50.

xx "were typically outsiders": Sudhir Hazareesingh, *How the French Think: An Affectionate Portrait of an Intellectual People* (Basic Books, 2015), 169.

xx "the overwhelming, the unspeakable": Michel Foucault, "Language to Infinity," *Language, Counter-Memory, Practice: Selected Essays and Interviews*, ed. Donald F. Bouchard, trans. Donald F. Bouchard and Sherry Simon (Cornell University Press, 1977), 60–61.

PART 1: MURDER

Chapter 1: Derrida's Pipe

4 **"Derrida is my absolute god!":** Jeffrey Eugenides, *The Marriage Plot* (Farrar, Straus and Giroux, 2011), 23–24.

9 **"At one end floats Cleopatra's sturdy raft":** David B. Edelstein, "Floating Shakespeare," *Harvard Crimson*, December 12, 1978.

11 **"During the middle third":** Tony Judt, "Paris Was Yesterday," *New York Review of Books*, March 11, 2010.

11 **"Twice a week, a young":** Lorrie Moore, *A Gate at the Stairs* (Random House, 2009), 4.

11 **"the moment of initiation into Theory":** Nicholas Dames, "The Theory Generation," *n+1*, Summer 2012.

11 **Sedgwick's paper on the motif:** Eve Kosofsky Sedgwick, "Jane Austen and the Masturbating Girl," *Critical Inquiry* 17, no. 4 (1991): 818–37.

12 **"the trap where all identity is lost":** Roland Barthes, "The Death of the Author," *Image-Music-Text*, essays selected and translated by Stephen Heath (Hill and Wang, 1977), 142.

13 **"It's kind of exciting":** David Lodge, *Small World: An Academic Romance* (Macmillan, 1984), 118. Sawing imagery comes up frequently in descriptions of deconstruction. The scholar Jonathan Culler, whose influential 1982 book *On Deconstruction* is likely an original source of the conceit, notes that "if 'sawing off the branch on which one is sitting' seems foolhardy to men of common sense, it is not so for Nietzsche, Freud, Heidegger, and Derrida; for they suspect that if they fall there is no 'ground' to hit and that the most clear-sighted act may be a certain reckless sawing." The novelist Jonathan Rosen, who studied literature at Yale in the early 1980s when Derrida was a regular guest there, wrote that deconstruction "wasn't a philosophy you explained so much as demonstrated, choosing a text like a volunteer at a magic show willing to be sawed in half—except that the volunteer really *was* sawed in half, and usually into a lot more pieces than that, before being sewn back together again. Derrida's real trick was persuading the audience that the volunteer had never been whole to begin with." A related metaphor comes from Louis Menand, writing in *The New Yorker* in 2014, where he describes deconstruction as "like digging a hole in the middle of the ocean with a shovel made of water."

14 **"No language can say the truth":** Jacques Lacan, "La science et la verité," *Écrits* (Éditions du Seuil, 1966), 867–68.

14 **"Possibly there are blue swans":** David Lewis, *On the Plurality of Worlds* (Blackwell Publishers, 1986), 5.

16 **"a kind of involuntary":** Friedrich Nietzsche, *Beyond Good and Evil: Prelude to a Philosophy of the Future*, trans. Walter Kaufmann (Vintage, 1966), 13.

16 **"my life and my philosophy":** Quoted in Annie Cohen-Solal, *Sartre: A Life*, trans. Anna Cancogni (Pantheon, 1987), 142.

16 **"not as that of a person but":** Anthony Quinton, "Springtime for Hegel," *New York Review of Books*, June 21, 2001.

16 **"As you know, traditional philosophy":** "Thinking Lives: The Philosophy of Biography and the Biography of Philosophers," a 1996 conference at New York University.

16 **"No one will ever know":** Quoted in Benoît Peeters, *Derrida: A Biography,* trans. Andrew Brown (Polity Press, 2013), ix. It appears in a slightly different translation in Jacques Derrida, "Circumfession," in *Jacques Derrida*, trans. Geoffrey Bennington (University of Chicago Press, 1993), 207–8.

17 **"Their sex lives":** *Derrida*, directed by Kirby Dick and Amy Ziering Kofman. Jane Doe Films, 2002.

18 **"Each time I have attempted":** Michel Foucault, "Est-il donc important de penser?" *Libération*, May 30–31, 1981.

Chapter 2: "Condemned to Be Free"

19 **theory is finished:** Jérôme Garcin, "La Théorie C'est Foutu!," *Les Nouvelles littéraires*, September 11–18, 1980, 28.

21 **"What appeared when the dust settled":** Fredric Jameson, *The Years of Theory: Postwar French Thought to the Present* (Verso, 2024), 18.

21 **Existentialism "defines man by his actions":** Jean-Paul Sartre, *Existentialism Is a Humanism*, trans. Carol Macomber (Yale University Press, 2007), 40.

22 **"Never were we freer":** Jean-Paul Sartre, "The Republic of Silence," in *The Aftermath of War (Situations III)*, trans. Chris Turner (Seagull Books, 2008), 3–4.

22 **"France's most discussed writer":** "EUROPE: Existentialism," *Time*, January 28, 1946, 28.
23 **"the crimes being committed":** Jean-Paul Sartre, *Situations V* (Gallimard, 1964), 58.
24 **"loaded pistols":** Jean-Paul Sartre, "What Is Literature?" *Partisan Review* XV (January 1948): 21. Originally published in French as *"Qu'est-ce qu'écrire?"* in *Les Temps Modernes*, no. 17 (1947).
24 **"having to put up with endless":** Albert Camus, "Letter to the Editor," *Les Temps Modernes*, no. 82 (1952).
24 **"refuse to let himself be transformed":** Jean-Paul Sartre, *Le Figaro*, October 23, 1964.
24 **"You do not imprison Voltaire":** Quoted in Annie Cohen-Solal, *Sartre: A Life*, trans. Anna Cancogni (Pantheon, 1987), 415.
24 **"He was the man of scandal":** Cohen-Solal, 449.

Chapter 3: Prisoners of War

26 **who claimed he'd lost his belief:** Sarah Bakewell, "Think Big, Be Free, Have Sex . . . 10 Reasons to Be an Existentialist," *Guardian*, March 4, 2016.
26 **in 1979 he sought an audience:** Douglas Johnson, introduction to *The Future Lasts Forever*, Louis Althusser, trans. Richard Veasey (New Press, 1993), xv.
26 **Catholicism and communism:** Louis Althusser, "The Crisis of Marxism," interview by Renato Parascandolo, translated by Ron Salaj. Transcription of an appearance on *Multimedia Encyclopaedia of the Philosophical Sciences*, April 1980. versobooks.com/blogs/3312-the-crisis-of-marxism-an-interview-with-louis-althusser.
27 **"I began to feel quite at home":** Louis Althusser, *The Future Lasts Forever*, trans. Richard Veasey (New Press, 1993), 108.
28 **In one incident that he recalled:** Althusser, *The Future Lasts Forever*, 51.
28 **"what-goes-without-saying":** Roland Barthes, *Mythologies*, trans. Richard Howard and Annette Lavers (Hill and Wang, 2012), xi.
28 **"What I also discovered during my captivity":** Althusser, *The Future Lasts Forever*, 104.
29 **Walking into a Parisian bar again:** Sarah Bakewell, *At the Existentialist Café* (Other Press, 2016), 143.
29 **"would rarely be as relaxed":** Bakewell, *At the Existentialist Café*, 143.
29 **A century later, having moved:** Diane Rubenstein, *What's Left? The École Normale Supérieure and the Right* (University of Wisconsin Press, 1990), 4–5.
30 **"a kind of monastery for boy geniuses":** James Miller, *The Passion of Michel Foucault* (Simon & Schuster, 1993), 45.
30 **"the freemasonry of cultural politics":** George Steiner, "Stranglehold," *New Yorker*, February 21, 1994, 24.
30 **"Who will ever write":** Jacques Derrida and Élisabeth Roudinesco, *For What Tomorrow . . . A Dialogue*, trans. Jeff Fort (Stanford University Press, 2004), 79.
31 **he may have contemplated suicide:** Benoît Peeters, *Derrida: A Biography*, trans. Andrew Brown (Polity Press, 2013), 45.
31 **"The threat of the guillotine":** Quoted in Peeters, *Derrida: A Biography*, 73; from Jacques Derrida, *Sur Parole: Instantanées philosophiques* (Éditions de l'aube, 2003), 30.
31 **One witness later said:** Annie Cohen-Solal, *Sartre: A Life*, trans. Anna Cancogni (Pantheon, 1987), 74–75.
32 **was made possible:** Paul Johnson, "Jean-Paul Sartre, 'A Little Ball of Fur and Ink,'" *Wilson Quarterly*, Spring 1989, 67.
32 **"my third marriage":** Simone de Beauvoir, *All Said and Done*, trans. Patrick O'Brian (Paragon House, 1993), 91.
32 **"irremediably old and overtaken by events":** Althusser, *The Future Lasts Forever*, 113.

Chapter 4: A Marriage of Theory and Practice

35 **"utmost seriousness of question":** Milan Kundera, "The Art of Fiction, No. 81," *Paris Review*, Summer 1984.
36 **he filed a formal complaint:** Quoted in Benoît Peeters, *Derrida: A Biography*, trans. Andrew Brown (Polity Press, 2013), 60.
38 **"'womblike' place, where I felt warm":** Louis Althusser, *The Future Lasts Forever*, trans. Richard Veasey (New Press, 1993), 163.
38 **"was mad (*fou*) for the school":** Yann Moulier Boutang, *Louis Althusser: Une biographie: Tome 1: La formation du mythe (1918–1956)* (Bernard Grasset, 1992), 446–47.

38 **"When it came to the vote":** Althusser, *The Future Lasts Forever*, 203.
39 **"deep-seated feeling of repulsion":** Althusser, *The Future Lasts Forever*, 124.
39 **"The only thing that mattered":** Althusser, *The Future Lasts Forever*, 120.

Chapter 5: The Cult of Marx

40 **"overeducated in the art of interpretation":** Quoted in Benoît Peeters, *Derrida: A Biography*, trans. Andrew Brown (Polity Press, 2013), 151.
40 **The term *antiaméricanisme*:** Sophie Meunier, "Anti-Americanisms in France," *French Politics, Culture & Society* 23, no. 2 (2005): 128.
40 **"Whatever the nature of today's":** Jean-Paul Sartre, *Les Temps Modernes* 5, no. 51 (1950).
41 **Sartre was publicly feuding:** See Annie Cohen-Solal, *Sartre: A Life*, trans. Anna Cancogni (Pantheon, 1987), 332–33 (falling out with Camus) and 342–44 (falling out with Merleau-Ponty).
41 **"Every morning, straight after breakfast":** Peeters, *Derrida*, 62.
41 **"holistic strain in French styles of thought":** Tony Judt, *Marxism and the French Left: Studies on Labor and Politics, 1831–1981* (Oxford University Press, 1986), 174.
42 **"In France, the owl of Minerva":** Russell Jacoby, "Left Behind: The Exploits of BHL," *World Affairs* 171, no. 3 (2009): 22.
42 **"Marxism is undoubtedly a religion":** Raymond Aron, *The Opium of the Intellectuals* [no translator given] (Routledge, 2017), vii.
42 **"I consider Marxism to be the unsurpassable":** Jean-Paul Sartre, *Critique of Dialectical Reason: Theory of Practical Ensembles*, trans. Alan Sheridan-Smith (NLB, 1976), 9.
43 **"How are we to understand":** Jean-Paul Sartre, *Search for a Method*, trans. Hazel E. Barnes (Knopf, 1963), 85. *Search for a Method* was folded into *Critique of Dialectical Reason* as the book's introduction.
43 **"why Flaubert preferred literature":** Sartre, *Search for a Method*, 57.
44 **it took Sartre's friends nearly a week:** Fredric Jameson, *The Years of Theory: Postwar French Thought to the Present* (Verso, 2024), 61.

Chapter 6: Sartre Gets a Drubbing

45 **its economy grew at an average rate:** Jean-Pierre Dormois, *The French Economy in the Twentieth Century* (Cambridge University Press, 2004), 18.
46 **"Our role, as smalltime profiteers":** Régis Debray, *Les rendez-vous manqués: pour Pierre Goldman* (Éditions du Seuil, 1975), 83. Translation mine.
46 **"sort of shop-girl's metaphysics":** Claude Lévi-Strauss, *Tristes Tropiques*, trans. John Weightman and Doreen Weightman (Penguin Books, 1973), 58.
47 **the idea of a simple "homo psychologicus":** Louis Althusser, "Philosophie et Sciences Humaines," *Revue de l'Enseignement philosophique* (1963): 11, fn 14. See also Louis Althusser, *The Future Lasts Forever*, trans. Richard Veasey (New Press, 1993), 186. Althusser expressed different attitudes toward structuralism at different times. Though in his memoir he highlights the connections between his work and structuralists like Lacan, in the foreword to the 1970 Italian edition of *Reading Capital*, he lamented that "our interpretation of Marx has generally been recognized and judged, in homage to the current fashion, as 'structuralist.'"
47 **"there were expensive English cars":** Louis Althusser, *The Future Lasts Forever*, trans. Richard Veasey (New Press, 1993), 186.
47 **"At the very moment when French history":** Debray, *Les rendez-vous manqués*, 83. Translation mine.
48 **"final bitter adventure":** Debray, *Les rendez-vous manqués*, 84. Translation mine.
48 **"revolutionary heroism and humanism":** Maurice Merleau-Ponty, *Signs*, trans. Richard C. McCleary (Northwestern University Press, 1964), 22–23.
48 **"Only one opponent managed":** Annie Cohen-Solal, *Sartre: A Life*, trans. Anna Cancogni (Pantheon, 1987), 450–51.
48 **"I have always thought that Sartre":** Althusser, *The Future Lasts Forever*, 176.
49 **sold thirty-two thousand copies:** François Dosse, *History of Structuralism: Volume 1: The Rising Sign, 1945–1966*, trans. Deborah Glassman (University of Minnesota Press, 1997), 299.
49 **"It is impossible to *know* anything":** Louis Althusser, *For Marx*, trans. Ben Brewster (Verso, 2005), 229.
50 **He worried about Marx's use:** Louis Althusser, *Reading Capital*, trans. Ben Brewster (Verso, 2009), 28. See also fn 8.
50 **"a pure-minded student":** Althusser, *The Future Lasts Forever*, 170.
51 **"And we recognize that 'it is him'":** Louis Althusser, "Ideology and Ideological State Apparatuses:

Notes Toward an Investigation," in *Lenin and Philosophy and Other Essays*, trans. Ben Brewster (Monthly Review Press, 1971), 117.

51 **"You and I are *always already* subjects":** Althusser, "Ideology and Ideological State," 117.

52 **"The writing I am currently executing":** Althusser, "Ideology and Ideological State," 117.

52 **turning us into "lab animals":** Jaron Lanier, *Ten Arguments for Deleting Your Social Media Accounts Right Now* (Henry Holt, 2018), 5–6.

54 **"crushing under the tyranny":** Régis Debray, *Les masques* (Gallimard, 1987), 169. Translation mine.

54 **"Althusser was touted by everyone":** Tony Judt, "The Paris Strangler," *New Republic*, March 7, 1994, 33.

54 **"adopted as a foundational authority":** Roger Scruton, "The Legacy of 1968," *American Spectator*, September 2008, 51.

54 **become "a new Marx":** Élisabeth Roudinesco, *Philosophy in Turbulent Times: Canguilhem, Sartre, Foucault, Althusser, Deleuze, Derrida*, trans. William McCuaig (Columbia University Press, 2008), 106.

54 **By his own tally, he suffered:** Althusser, *The Future Lasts Forever*, 144.

54 **In his memoir, he confessed:** Althusser, *The Future Lasts Forever*, 148.

54 **"We are in the process":** Althusser, *The Future Lasts Forever*, 144.

Chapter 7: Althusser Sleeps Through the Revolution

56 **de Gaulle's party and its allies:** Jonathan Fenby, *France: A Modern History from the Revolution to the War with Terror* (St. Martin's Press, 2016), 400.

57 **At Nanterre, campus radicals:** François Crouzet, "A University Besieged: Nanterre, 1967–1969," *Political Science Quarterly* (1969): 337–38.

57 **"French students were preoccupied":** Pierre Viansson-Ponté, "Quand la France s'ennuie," *Le Monde*, March 15, 1968. Translation mine.

57 **"the struggle of the students":** Fenby, *France*, 392.

58 **"I will win them back":** Fenby, *France*, 398.

58 **"The feeling we had":** Daniel Cohn-Bendit and Claus Leggewie, "1968: Power to the Imagination," *New York Review of Books*, May 10, 2018.

59 **"You have been able to create":** Quoted in Annie Cohen-Solal, *Sartre: A Life*, trans. Anna Cancogni (Pantheon, 1987), 460.

59 **a "venerable relic":** Sarah Bakewell, *At the Existentialist Café* (Other Press, 2016), 293.

59 **"He did not say much":** Cohen-Solal, *Sartre*, 463.

59 **a damning pun:** Douglas Johnson, introduction to *The Future Lasts Forever* by Louis Althusser, trans. Richard Veasey (New Press, 1993), xiii.

59 **"How can I get a handle on all that?":** Louis Althusser, *Lettres à Hélène* (Grasset, 2011), 514. Translation mine.

60 **"When revolt ends":** Althusser, *The Future Lasts Forever*, 231.

61 **likes to credit the philosopher Paul Ricoeur:** Henri Astier, "Renaissance Manu: Why the Philosophy of the French President Matters," *Times Literary Supplement*, July 13, 2018.

61 **"represents class struggle":** Louis Althusser, *Reading Capital*, trans. Ben Brewster (Verso, 2009), 321.

61 **"*All great philosophers* have sought":** Althusser, *The Future Lasts Forever*, 172.

61 **"Scholars in their seminars":** Tony Judt, "The Paris Strangler," *New Republic*, March 7, 1994, 34.

Chapter 8: "Je Suis le Grand Althusser"

62 **"healthy immersion in everyday affairs":** John Lewis, "The Althusser Case," *Marxism Today*, January and February 1972.

62 **"The USSR is different":** Louis Althusser, *The Future Lasts Forever*, trans. Richard Veasey (New Press, 1993), 190.

62 **"Althusserianism had died":** Jacques Rancière, *Althusser's Lesson*, trans. Emiliano Battista (Bloomsbury, 2011), xx.

63 **The Communist Party steadily lost voters:** Emile Chabal, "French Political Culture in the 1970s," *Geschichte und Gesellschaft* 42 (2016): 247–48.

63 **"I knew she had been strangled":** Althusser, *The Future Lasts Forever*, 15–16.

64 **"Brief History of a Murderer":** Olivier Corpet and Yann Moulier Boutang, foreword to *The Future Lasts Forever*, Louis Althusser, trans. Richard Veasey (New Press, 1993), 5.

64 **who had studied with Althusser:** Óscar Alvarez Araya, "Jean-François Revel," Meer, meer.com/es/64401-jean-francois-revel. December 23, 2020.

65 **"I love stories that end well":** Claude Sarraute, "Petite Faim," *Le Monde*, March 14, 1985. Translation mine.

65 **Only then, he wrote to a friend:** Corpet and Boutang, foreword to *The Future Lasts Forever*, 2.
65 **"*Je suis le grand Althusser*":** Douglas Johnson, introduction to *The Future Lasts Forever*, Louis Althusser, trans. Richard Veasey (New Press, 1993), vii.
66 **"Even though I have been":** Althusser, *The Future Lasts Forever*, 23.
66 **The "victim" in his book:** Althusser, *The Future Lasts Forever*, 18. Althusser writes: "Deprived of all choice, I was in fact the victim of an official procedure I could not escape and to which I therefore had to submit."
66 **"For a long time, he hid his wife":** Régis Debray, *Les masques* (Gallimard, 1987), 167. Translation mine.
66 **appreciate her "womanly smell":** Althusser, *The Future Lasts Forever*, 132–33.
67 **her "prickly nature":** Althusser, *The Future Lasts Forever*, 164.
67 **he persuaded his own psychoanalyst:** Althusser, *The Future Lasts Forever*, 151.
67 **"given the 'monster' I was":** Althusser, *The Future Lasts Forever*, 252.
67 **"The very idea, which was both unthinkable":** Althusser, *The Future Lasts Forever*, 252.
67 **"suicide via a third party":** Althusser, *The Future Lasts Forever*, 267.
67 **"a beautiful proof of love":** Debray, *Les masques*, 170. Translation mine.

Chapter 9: The Mad Philosopher

68 **"The fact is I strangled my wife":** Quoted in Olivier Corpet and Yann Moulier Boutang, foreword to *The Future Lasts Forever*, Louis Althusser, trans. Richard Veasey (New Press, 1993), 3.
69 **"How is it that such a story":** Corpet and Boutang, foreword to *The Future Lasts Forever*, 9.
69 **with its "manic fancies":** Tony Judt, "The Paris Strangler," *New Republic*, March 7, 1994.
69 **"one of the most powerful figures":** Mark Lilla, "Marx and Murder," *Times Literary Supplement*, September 25, 1992, 4.
69 **"I loved Althusser because he wasn't":** Régis Debray, *Les masques* (Gallimard, 1987), 168. Translation mine.
69 **"To imagine that when":** Bernard-Henri Lévy, "Préface," *Lettres à Hélène* (Grasset, 2011), 11–12. Translation mine.
70 **"As though madness were":** Eribon's blurb appears on the back of the hardcover English edition of *The Future Lasts Forever*.
71 **"Both in her presence and away":** Althusser, *The Future Lasts Forever*, 53.
71 **"I am surprised I have been":** Althusser, *The Future Lasts Forever*, 30.

PART 2: MADNESS

Chapter 10: Sartre Sees a Shrink

77 **"his visual faculties became distorted":** Simone de Beauvoir, *The Prime of Life*, trans. Peter Green (World Publishing Company, 1962), 169.
77 **"I started seeing crabs":** John Gerassi, *Talking with Sartre: Conversations and Debates* (Yale University Press, 2009), 62.
77 **"By the fall of 1934":** Annie Cohen-Solal, *Sartre: A Life*, trans. Anna Cancogni (Pantheon, 1987), 101.
78 **likely to be "mildly disagreeable":** See Cohen-Solal, *Sartre: A Life*, 102, and Beauvoir, *The Prime of Life*, 169.
78 **"He had not exactly had hallucinations":** Beauvoir, *The Prime of Life*, 169.
78 **what he called the "great 'irrealizing'":** Jean-Paul Sartre, *The Imaginary*, trans. Jonathan Webber (Routledge, 2010), xxviii.
78 **"We sort of concluded that":** Gerassi, *Talking with Sartre*, 63.
79 **"the day I simply decided":** Gerassi, *Talking with Sartre*, 79–80.
79 **"A tiresome young man":** Élisabeth Roudinesco, *Jacques Lacan*, trans. Barbara Bray (Columbia University Press, 1997), 80.
80 **the number of analysts:** Sherry Turkle, *Psychoanalytic Politics: Jacques Lacan and Freud's French Revolution*, 2nd ed. (Guilford Press, 1992), xxvii.
80 **"Cartesian, poeticized, linguistic":** Turkle, *Psychoanalytic Politics*, xiii.
80 **"politics of the person":** Turkle, *Psychoanalytic Politics*, xxiv.
81 **after May '68 there were plenty:** See, for example, Jean-Michel Rabaté in *May Made Me: An Oral History of the 1968 Uprising in France* by Mitchell Abidor (AK Press, 2018).
81 **There was even a course:** Turkle, *Psychoanalytic Politics*, 178.
81 **"They're the only visible":** Quoted in Turkle, *Psychoanalytic Politics*, 217.
81 **there was a crowd:** Roudinesco, *Jacques Lacan*, 170. Also in Françoise Gilot and Carlton Lake, *Life*

with Picasso (New York Review Books, 2019), 151; and Fredric Jameson, *The Years of Theory: Postwar French Thought to the Present* (Verso, 2024), 27.

81 **He wore a shirt:** See Betty Milan, *Analyzed by Lacan: A Personal Account*, trans. Clifford E. Landers and Chris Vanderwees (Bloomsbury Academic, 2024), 4, 61.

81 **his unapologetic tendency:** Catherine Millot, *Life with Lacan*, trans. Andrew Brown (Polity Press, 2018), 45.

81 **Beauvoir reported being so awestruck:** Deirdre Bair, *Simone de Beauvoir: A Biography* (Simon & Schuster, 1991), 293.

82 **"Lacan's prose aspires perpetually":** Malcolm Bowie, "Jacques Lacan," in *Structuralism and Since: From Lévi-Strauss to Derrida*, ed. John Sturrock (Oxford University Press, 1979), 121.

82 **"You were so tightly packed":** Jameson, *The Years of Theory*, 176. See also Jason Demers and Fredric Jameson, "The Theory Variations: An Interview with Fredric Jameson," *Transatlantica* 1 (2023).

82 **as many as a thousand people:** Turkle, *Psychoanalytic Politics*, 21.

82 **"on a par with reading":** Bice Benvenuto and Roger Kennedy, *The Works of Jacques Lacan: An Introduction* (Free Association Books, 1986), 12.

82 **"Lacan's whole teaching is metaphorical":** Benvenuto and Kennedy, *The Works of Jacques Lacan*, 120.

82 **Here's a Lacanism:** See Turkle, *Psychoanalytic Politics*, 55.

83 **"I read Derrida":** Lorrie Moore, "Community Life," in *Birds of America* (Vintage Books, 2010), 62.

Chapter 11: Scandalous Freud

84 **"In Lacan's Paris":** Stuart Schneiderman, *Jacques Lacan: The Death of an Intellectual Hero* (Harvard University Press, 1983), 20.

85 **"arrogance was the keynote":** Élisabeth Roudinesco, *Jacques Lacan*, trans. Barbara Bray (Columbia University Press, 1997), 11.

85 **"Help! They're crazy":** Quoted in Mark Polizzotti, *Revolution of the Mind: The Life of André Breton* (Black Widow Press, 2009), 67.

85 **Breton "in his nut-case hospital":** Quoted in Polizzotti, *Revolution of the Mind*, 46.

86 **"being kept by the Jews":** Quoted in Roudinesco, *Jacques Lacan*, 237.

86 **"Freud's discovery represented":** Louis Althusser, *Philosophy for Non-Philosophers*, trans. G. M. Goshgarian (Bloomsbury Academic, 2017), 152.

86 **"Freud set out to show":** Althusser, *Philosophy for Non-Philosophers*, 146–47.

87 **"third and most wounding blow":** Sigmund Freud, *Introductory Lectures on Psycho-analysis: The Standard Edition*, trans. James Stratchey (W. W. Norton, 1966), 326.

87 **Not only did Sartre:** John Gerassi, *Talking with Sartre: Conversations and Debates* (Yale University Press, 2009), 63.

87 **"that in every person there lurks":** Simone de Beauvoir, *The Prime of Life*, trans. Peter Green (World Publishing Company, 1962), 107–8.

87 **is "psychic automatism":** Quoted in Polizzotti, *Revolution of the Mind*, 53.

88 **"the greatest poetic discovery":** Louis Aragon and André Breton, "Le cinquantenaire de l'hystérie," *La Révolution surréaliste* 11 (1928), 20–22.

88 **"words and language could change":** Polizzotti, *Revolution of the Mind*, 87.

89 **"Love deep in the woods gleams":** André Breton and Phillippe Soupault, *The Magnetic Fields*, trans. Charlotte Mandell (New York Review Books, 2020), 26, 59.

89 **"a little old man":** Quoted in Polizzotti, *Revolution of the Mind*, 146.

Chapter 12: The Paranoiac-Critical Method

91 **Freud made much of Schreber's:** Sigmund Freud, "Psychoanalytic Notes on an Autobiographical Account of a Case of Paranoia (Dementia Paranoides)," *The Standard Edition of the Complete Psychological Works of Sigmund Freud*, trans. James Strachey, vol. 12 (Hogarth Press, 1958), 3–82.

91 **"The moment is near":** Salvador Dalí, "L'Âne pourri," *Le Surréalisme au service de la révolution* 1 (1930).

91 **"paranoiac-critical" method:** Salvador Dalí, "Interprétation Paranoïaque-critique de l'image obsédante 'L'Angélus' de Millet," *Minotaure* 1 (June 1933): 65–67.

92 **"The only difference between me":** "Open Secret," *Newsweek*, January 11, 1943, 62.

92 **"counterrevolutionary acts tending":** Mark Polizzotti, *Revolution of the Mind: The Life of André Breton* (Black Widow Press, 2009), 351–53, 420.

92 **"Because I knew there wasn't":** Recounted in Élisabeth Roudinesco, *Jacques Lacan*, trans. Barbara Bray (Columbia University Press, 1997), 377–78.

93 **"systematic persecution mania":** Recounted in Roudinesco, *Jacques Lacan*, 32–34.

93 **"ceaseless reading" and the "five or six cups":** Jacques Lacan, *De la psychose paranoïaque dans ses rapports avec la personnalité* (Éditions du Seuil, 1975), 174. Translation mine.

93 **"The patient had caught":** Jacques Lacan, "Presentation on Psychical Causality," *Écrits*, trans. Bruce Fink (Norton, 2006), 138.

94 **He called the novel's sensibility "Bovaryque":** Lacan, *De la psychose paranoïaque*, 179–80.

95 **"the first French attempt":** Bice Benvenuto and Roger Kennedy, *The Works of Jacques Lacan: An Introduction* (Free Association Books, 1986), 39.

95 **"without realizing it":** Quoted in Roudinesco, *Jacques Lacan*, 69.

95 **In fact, he had included:** Roudinesco, *Jacques Lacan*, 50, 58.

95 **"an unending dependence":** Didier Anzieu, "Contre Lacan," *La Quinzaine littéraire*, January 20, 1967, 15. Translation mine.

96 **"feelings of persecution":** Roudinesco, *Jacques Lacan*, 190.

96 **"wonderful convulsive state":** Quoted in Roudinesco, *Jacques Lacan*, 59.

96 **The poet Paul Éluard included:** Paul Éluard, *Poésie involontaire et poésie intentionnelle* (Seghers, 1942).

96 **He commended Lacan for:** Dalí, "Interprétation Paranoïaque-critique de l'Image obsédante 'L'Angélus' de Millet," *Minotaure* 1 (June 1933): 66. Translation mine.

96 **"Understanding this syntax can":** Jacques Lacan, "Le Problème du Style et la conception psychiatre des formes paranoïaque de l'expérience," *Minotaure* 1 (June 1933): 69. Translation mine.

96 **"The scientist comes off":** Sarane Alexandrian, *Le surréalisme et le rêve* (Éditions Gallimard, 1974), 68. Translation mine.

97 **If they knew what:** Stuart Schneiderman, *Jacques Lacan: The Death of an Intellectual Hero* (Harvard University Press, 1983), 11.

97 **"pay the price with elbow grease":** Lacan, "Overture to this Collection," *Écrits*, 5.

Chapter 13: Madwomen

98 **"Beneath their provincial petticoats":** Janet Flanner, "The Murder in Le Mans," *Paris Was Yesterday, 1929–1935* (Viking Press, 1972), 99.

99 **"main outline of the Papin sisters'":** Simone de Beauvoir, *The Prime of Life*, trans. Peter Green (World Publishing Company, 1962), 108. Sartre also wrote about the case, folding it into a passage in his short story "Erostrate" (1936), about a solitary man who resolves to kill five people out of a growing disgust with other human beings and a desire to distinguish himself from them.

99 **"For six years, they bore":** Paul Éluard and Benjamin Péret, "Revue de la presse," *Le Surréalisme au service de la révolution* 5 (1933): 28. Translation mine.

101 **"On the fateful evening":** Jacques Lacan, "Motifs du Crime Paranoïaque," *Minotaure* 3–4 (1933): 28. Translation mine.

101 **If his emphasis on doubles:** In Jean Genet's celebrated 1947 play *The Maids*, inspired by the Papin sisters' case, the theme of doubles is made literal: The characters representing the Papins spend much of the drama role-playing, one pretending to be her sister, the other their employer, "Madame." When Madame is killed, it is the sister role-playing her who dies, poisoned by her sibling.

101 **"There is no structure":** Quoted in Malcolm Bowie, "Jacques Lacan," in *Structuralism and Since: From Lévi-Strauss to Derrida*, ed. John Sturrock (Oxford University Press, 1979), 131.

101 **When the Surrealists celebrated hysteria's:** Louis Aragon and André Breton, "Le cinquantenaire de l'hystérie," *La Révolution surréaliste* 11 (1928).

102 **"too attractive and too much":** Daniel Anzieu, "Postface," in *Marguerite, ou l'Aimée de Lacan*, by Jean Allouch (EPEL, 1990), 551; Élisabeth Roudinesco, *Jacques Lacan*, trans. Barbara Bray (Columbia University Press, 1997), 51.

102 **"Lacan was interested in the woman":** Roudinesco, *Jacques Lacan*, 35.

103 **About to leave her:** André Breton, *Nadja*, trans. Richard Howard (Grove Press, 1960), 71.

103 **"I do not suppose":** Breton, *Nadja*, 136, 142–43.

104 **"She had no hesitation":** Breton, *Nadja*, 130, 135.

104 **"The portrait left of Nadja":** Mark Polizzotti, *Revolution of the Mind: The Life of André Breton* (Black Widow Press, 2009), 239.

106 **According to one story:** Stuart Schneiderman, *Jacques Lacan: The Death of an Intellectual Hero* (Harvard University Press, 1983), 12.

106 **"trying to do intellectual things":** Quoted in James Miller, *The Passion of Michel Foucault* (Simon & Schuster, 1993), 56.

Chapter 14: Stranger in the Mirror

107 "a mere nobody": Élisabeth Roudinesco, *Jacques Lacan*, trans. Barbara Bray (Columbia University Press, 1997), 114.

107 "A unity comparable to the ego": Sigmund Freud, "On Narcissism," *The Standard Edition of the Complete Psychological Works of Sigmund Freud*, trans. James Strachey, vol. 14 (Hogarth Press, 1958), 67–102.

108 "jubilant assumption of his specular image": Jacques Lacan, "The Mirror Stage as Formative of the *I* Function as Revealed in Psychoanalytic Experience," *Écrits*, trans. Bruce Fink (W. W. Norton, 2006), 76.

108 He was a narcissist: Roudinesco, *Jacques Lacan*, 320.

108 "A child who beats": Lacan, "Aggressiveness in Psychoanalysis," *Écrits*, 92.

109 "It is the world of words": Lacan, "The Function and Field of Speech and Language in Psychoanalysis," *Écrits*, 229.

110 "The shape of the letters": Charles Dickens, *Great Expectations* (Penguin Classics, 1965), 35.

110 "At such a time, I found out": Dickens, *Great Expectations*, 35–36.

111 At the center of this picture: Lacan, "The Mirror Stage as Formative of the *I* Function as Revealed in Psychoanalytic Experience," *Écrits*, 78.

112 "thinking where I am not": Lacan, "The Instance of the Letter in the Unconscious, or Reason Since Freud," *Écrits*, 430.

112 "Tell me," was his typical, terse refrain: Betty Milan, *Analyzed by Lacan: A Personal Account*, trans. Clifford E. Landers and Chris Vanderwees (Bloomsbury Academic, 2024), 18.

112 "Go and decipher the enigma": Milan, *Analyzed by Lacan*, 4.

112 "the cut": The cut seems to have various meanings, referring to the slippage between discursive registers as well as the process of separation from the mother during which the infant accepts its identity in the symbolic.

113 "*le sujet supposé savoir*": See, for example, Darian Leader and Judy Groves, *Lacan: A Graphic Guide* (Icon Books, 2010), 136–37.

113 He offered the example of: Jacques Lacan, "The Ethics of Psychoanalysis, 1959–60," *The Seminar of Jacques Lacan*, ed. Jacques-Alain Miller, trans. Dennis Potter (W. W. Norton, 1986), 257–69. See also *Lacan: A Graphic Guide*, 132–34.

113 "therapeutically indifferent": Sherry Turkle, *Psychoanalytic Politics: Jacques Lacan and Freud's French Revolution*, 2nd ed. (Guilford Press, 1992), 15.

113 "he was opposed to any notion": Bice Benvenuto and Roger Kennedy, *The Works of Jacques Lacan: An Introduction* (Free Association Books, 1986), 60.

114 Revolted by fascism: Roudinesco, *Jacques Lacan*, 115.

Chapter 15: "The Woman Does Not Exist"

115 Lacan rejected the offer: Élisabeth Roudinesco, *Jacques Lacan*, trans. Barbara Bray (Columbia University Press, 1997), 169.

115 "tries to compensate": Simone de Beauvoir, *The Second Sex*, trans. Constance Borde and Sheila Malovany-Chevallier (Jonathan Cape, 2009), 294.

116 "determines and differentiates herself in relation to": Beauvoir, *The Second Sex*, 6.

116 "Throughout history people": Quoted in Bice Benvenuto and Roger Kennedy, *The Works of Jacques Lacan: An Introduction* (Free Association Books, 1986), 192.

117 have "the tendency, when": Richard Wollheim, "The Cabinet of Dr. Lacan," *New York Review of Books*, January 25, 1979.

117 Lacan deferred talking about women: Stuart Schneiderman, *Jacques Lacan: The Death of an Intellectual Hero* (Harvard University Press, 1983), 30.

118 "The woman does not exist": See Jacqueline Rose, "Introduction II," *Feminine Sexuality* by Jacques Lacan, trans. Jacqueline Rose (W. W. Norton and Pantheon Books, 1985), 48–49.

118 "We have implored our women": Jacques Lacan, "Dieu et la jouissance de la femme," *Le Séminaire de Jacques Lacan: Livre XX: Encore 1972–73* (Éditions du Seuil, 1975), 69. Translation mine.

118 "This practice can never be theorized": Hélène Cixous, "The Laugh of the Medusa," trans. Keith Cohen and Paula Cohen, *Signs* 1, no. 4 (1976): 875–93.

118 "end up producing writing": Hélène Cixous, "Castration or Decapitation?" trans. Annette Kuhn, *Signs* 7, no. 1 (1981), 52.

118 "She physically materializes": Cixous, "The Laugh of the Medusa," 881.

118 **A true women's writing:** Luce Irigaray, *This Sex Which Is Not One*, trans. Catherine Porter (Cornell University Press, 1985), 29.
119 **"If they really need":** Cixous, "The Laugh of the Medusa," 890.
119 **"object to think with":** Sherry Turkle, *Psychoanalytic Politics: Jacques Lacan and Freud's French Revolution*, 2nd ed. (Guilford Press, 1992), xvi.
120 **"*politique et psychanalyse*":** Toril Moi, *Sexual/Textual Politics: Feminist Literary Theory* (Methuen, 1985), 95–96.
120 **When Irigaray dared to attack Freudian:** See Moi, *Sexual/Textual Politics*, 127.
120 **"academic fashions laundered into psychiatry":** Ross Douthat, "How to Make Sense of the New L.G.B.T.Q. Culture War," *New York Times*, April 13, 2022.

Chapter 16: A Portrait of Jouissance

124 **In 1954, he paid 1.5 million francs:** Thierry Savatier, *L'Origine du monde: histoire d'un tableau de Gustave Courbet* (Bartillat, 2006), 145.
124 **the painting hung hidden:** Savatier, *L'Origine du monde*, 69.
124 **"When the veil was lifted":** Maxine Du Camp, *Les Convulsions de Paris*, 5th ed., vol. 2 (Hachette, 1881), 190. Translation mine.
125 **The baron, having survived:** Konstantin Akinsha, "The Mysterious Journey of an Erotic Masterpiece," *ARTnews*, February 1, 2008, artnews.com/art-news/news/the-mysterious-journey-of-an-erotic-masterpiece-192.
125 **One theory is that he bought it:** Savatier, *L'Origine du monde*, 153.
125 **"My true church is a whorehouse":** Georges Bataille, *Guilty*, trans. Bruce Boone (Lapis Press, 1988), 12.
126 **someone "relatively viable":** Stuart Kendall, *Georges Bataille* (Reaktion Books, 2007), 49.
126 **"the most accomplished artistically":** Susan Sontag, "The Pornographic Imagination," *A Susan Sontag Reader* (Farrar, Straus and Giroux, 1963), 228.
126 **"that which is vilest":** André Breton, *Manifestos of Surrealism*, trans. Richard Seaver and Helen R. Lane (University of Michigan, 1969), 181.
126 **"I have never stopped":** Georges Bataille, *The Tears of Eros*, trans, Peter Connor (City Lights, 1989), 206. See also Élisabeth Roudinesco, *Jacques Lacan*, trans. Barbara Bray (Columbia University Press, 1997), 121–22.
127 **I saw in his hand:** Teresa of Avila, *The Life of Saint Teresa of Jesus*, trans. David Lewis (Cosimo Classics, 2006), 226.
127 **"see Bernini's statue in Rome":** Jacques Lacan, *Le Séminaire de Jacques Lacan: Livre XX: Encore 1972–73* (Éditions du Seuil, 1975), 70–71. Translation mine.
128 **may have been part of Acéphale:** Roudinesco, *Jacques Lacan*, 136.
128 **The society's members gathered:** Benjamin Noys, *Bataille: A Critical Introduction* (Pluto Press, 2000), 9.
129 **Don't let arbitrary laws:** Catherine Millot, *Life with Lacan*, trans. Andrew Brown (Polity Press, 2018), 6–7.
129 **His son-in-law recalled:** Jacques-Alain Miller, "Vie de Lacan," *Orientation lacanienne, III*, 12 (2010).
129 **"leaned over to pick up a sauerkraut":** Paul Johnson, *Humorists: From Hogarth to Noël Coward* (Harper, 2010), xvi.
129 **In the passenger seat:** Roudinesco, *Jacques Lacan*, 226.
130 **"The crash barrier was part":** Millot, *Life with Lacan*, 112.
130 **whose entry in *Who's Who*:** Sybille Lacan, *A Father: Puzzle*, trans. Adrian Nathan West (MIT Press, 2019), 45.
131 **"It may also":** Roudinesco, *Jacques Lacan*, 163.
131 **"It is in the *name of*":** Jacques Lacan, "The Function and Field of Speech and Language in Pscyhoanalysis," *Écrits*, trans. Bruce Fink (W. W. Norton, 2006), 230.
131 **"Your mother's maiden name":** Rebecca Solnit, *Recollections of My Nonexistence* (Viking, 2020), 85.
132 **"the creation of woman":** For a discussion of feminist readings of the painting, see Shulim Barzilai, *Lacan and the Matter of Origins* (Stanford University Press, 1999), 8–11.
132 **"Reality is the impossible!":** Quoted in Savatier, *L'Origine du monde*, 159.

Chapter 17: Knots and Rings of the Psyche

133 **Eventually, the variable session:** Élisabeth Roudinesco, *Jacques Lacan*, trans. Barbara Bray (Columbia University Press, 1997), 386.
133 **"There was something of the horror":** Stuart Schneiderman, *Jacques Lacan: The Death of an Intellectual Hero* (Harvard University Press, 1983), 132–33.

134 "made abruptness a terribly effective": Betty Milan, *Analyzed by Lacan: A Personal Account*, trans. Clifford E. Landers and Chris Vanderwees (Bloomsbury Academic, 2024), 17.
134 the *nonsession*, during which: Roudinesco, *Jacques Lacan*, 397.
134 "Lacan pulled your 'tifs'": Recounted in Roudinesco, *Jacques Lacan*, 394.
134 "saw an average of ten patients an hour": Roudinesco, *Jacques Lacan*, 397.
135 "a driving school, which not content": Jacques Lacan, "The Function and Field of Speech and Language in Psychoanalysis," *Écrits*, trans. Bruce Fink (W. W. Norton, 2006), 200.
135 Althusser rang Lacan's bell: Roudinesco, *Jacques Lacan*, 301–3.
135 In the mornings, he often: Roudinesco, *Jacques Lacan*, 391.
135 He thought nothing of: Roudinesco, *Jacques Lacan*, 390.
135 One scholar says Lacan viewed: Sherry Turkle, *Psychoanalytic Politics: Jacques Lacan and Freud's French Revolution*, 2nd ed. (Guilford Press, 1992), 123.
136 Lacan had revealed the revolutionary: Louis Althusser, "Freud et Lacan," *La Nouvelle Critique*, no. 161–62 (1964–1965), 88–108. See also Turkle, *Psychoanalytic Politics*, 90–91.
137 sold out its first print run: Turkle, *Psychoanalytic Politics*, 195.
137 two hundred thousand copies: Roudinesco, *Jacques Lacan*, 328.
137 "went furthest in the strictly 'structuralist'": Roudinesco, *Jacques Lacan*, 305.
137 Lacan arranged to meet Daniel: Roudinesco, *Jacques Lacan*, 336.
137 *The New Yorker* even reported: Jane Kramer, "A Reporter in Europe," *New Yorker*, July 4, 1977, 72.
137 Althusser claimed that: Althusser, *The Future Lasts Forever*, trans. Richard Veasey (New Press, 1993), 186–87.
137 Others say he had tired: Roudinesco, *Jacques Lacan*, 342.
137 "Personally, all that business": Quoted in Benoît Peeters, *Derrida: A Biography*, trans. Andrew Brown (Polity Press, 2013), 210.
137 A petition was circulated: Catherine Clément, *The Lives and Legends of Jacques Lacan*, trans. Arthur Goldhammer (Columbia University Press, 1983), fn 1, 213.
138 "I don't consider it": Roudinesco, *Jacques Lacan*, 341. (In a footnote, Roudinesco adds that at the time, she was one of the linguistics students at the Sorbonne who went out into the streets to defend "structures.")
138 Lacan was fascinated: Roudinesco, *Jacques Lacan*, 363.
138 went to the naval equipment aisle: Millot, *Life with Lacan*, 110.
139 "Often, after spending hours drawing": Roudinesco, *Jacques Lacan*, 367.
139 "I often wondered whether there was": François Cheng, "Entretien avec Judith Miller," *L'Ane* 48 (1991): 48. Quoted in Roudinesco, *Jacques Lacan*, 351.
140 "I am a poet": Turkle, *Psychoanalytic Politics*, 238.
140 Undeterred, Lacan launched into: Millot, *Life with Lacan*, 100.
140 "It seems to me the psychiatrist": Quoted in Roudinesco, *Jacques Lacan*, 231.

Chapter 18: "I Am Psychotic"

141 "Not only can man's being": Jacques Lacan, "Presentation on Psychical Causality," *Écrits*, trans. Bruce Fink (W. W. Norton, 2006), 144.
141 "that it is possible": Quoted in Sherry Turkle, *Psychoanalytic Politics: Jacques Lacan and Freud's French Revolution*, 2nd ed. (Guilford Press, 1992), 234.
141 "Psychosis is an attempt at rigor": Turkle, *Psychoanalytic Politics*, 236.
142 After the war, French doctors: Isabelle Von Bueltzingsloewen, *L'Hécatombe des fous: La famine dans les hôpitaux psychiatriques français sous l'Occupation* (Éditions Flammarion, 2007), 27.
142 Lacan, however, devoted most: Lacan, "Presentation on Psychical Causality," *Écrits*, 123–58. See also Élisabeth Roudinesco, *Jacques Lacan*, trans. Barbara Bray (Columbia University Press, 1997), 175.
143 Descartes' famous proof, Lacan reminded: Lacan, "Presentation on Psychical Causality," *Écrits*, 129.
143 his work entered the college: Anthony Gottlieb, *The Dream of Enlightenment: The Rise of Modern Philosophy* (W. W. Norton, 2016), 25.
143 As Foucault once quipped: Quoted in James Miller, *The Passion of Michel Foucault* (Simon & Schuster, 1993), 51.
143 mocking his "systematizing mind": Quoted in Nicholas Jolley, "The Reception of Descartes' Philosophy," *The Cambridge Companion to Descartes*, ed. John Cottingham (Cambridge University Press, 1992), 393.
143 "I decided that I could accept": Quoted in Anthony Gottlieb, *The Dream of Enlightenment: The Rise of Modern Philosophy* (W. W. Norton, 2016), 2.

144 **The field of psychiatry could do worse:** Lacan, "Presentation on Psychical Causality," *Écrits*, 133.
144 **Madness, he insisted:** Lacan, "Presentation on Psychical Causality," *Écrits*, 135.

Chapter 19: Foucault's Asylum

145 ***Folie et déraison: Histoire de la folie*:** The book was republished in French in 1964 in abridged form as *Histoire de la Folie* and translated into English as *Madness and Civilization: A History of Insanity in the Age of Reason*. In 2006, the original French text, along with ancillary texts Foucault had written during the intervening years, was published in English as *History of Madness*.
145 **"He was obsessed by this idea":** Quoted in Didier Eribon, *Michel Foucault*, trans. Betsy Wing (Harvard University Press, 1991), 26.
145 **he went so far as to imagine "suicide festivals":** Michel Foucault, "Un Plaisir si simple," *Gai Pied*, April 1, 1979, 1, 10.
146 **"I was struck, like many others":** Quoted in Eribon, *Michel Foucault*, 50.
146 **"I felt very close to":** Otto Friedrich, "France's Philosopher of Power," *Time*, November 16, 1981, 147.
147 **"that inaccessible primitive purity":** Michel Foucault, *History of Madness*, trans. Jonathan Murphy and Jean Khalfa (Routledge, 2006), xxxiii.
147 **in one case prompting an entire book:** Hubert L. Dreyfus and Paul Rabinow, *Michel Foucault: Beyond Structuralism and Hermeneutics* (University of Chicago Press, 1982).
147 **"We have experienced Sartre's generation":** Michel Foucault, *La Quinzaine littéraire*, April 15, 1966. Quoted in Eribon, *Michel Foucault*, 161.
148 **They wanted a social order:** Quoted in Eribon, *Michel Foucault*, 51. (This appears to be taken from an interview with an Italian journalist in 1978.)
148 **the son of a man he described:** Simeon Wade, *Foucault in California* (Heyday, 2019), 58.
148 **"an extreme difficulty in experiencing":** Eribon, *Michel Foucault*, 26.
148 **"The headmaster demanded to learn":** Wade, *Foucault in California*, 71.
149 **of "the experience of the limit":** Michel Foucault, "Preface to Transgression," *Language, Counter Memory, Practice: Selected Essays and Interviews by Michel Foucault*, ed. Donald Bouchard, trans. Donald F. Bouchard and Sherry Simon (Cornell University Press, 1977), 51.
149 **"one of the few French philosophers":** David Macey, *The Lives of Michel Foucault* (Verso, 2009), 18.
150 **"He does not look well":** Quoted in Eribon, *Michel Foucault*, 82.
151 **"If I had this book to write":** Quoted in Claude Mauriac, *Le Temps immobile, vol. 3: Et comme l'espérance est violente* (Grasset, 1976), 375. Translation mine.
151 **"I was dazzled when":** Quoted in Eribon, *Michel Foucault*, 107.
151 **"wading through several feet":** Steven Marcus, "In Praise of Folly," *New York Review of Books*, November 3, 1966.
151 **the "nothingness that is life itself":** Foucault, *History of Madness*, 14–15.
152 **"Each is a measure":** Foucault, *History of Madness*, 29.
152 **"the inside of the outside":** Foucault, *History of Madness*, 11.
152 **"simple division into daylight":** Foucault, *History of Madness*, xxxiv.
152 **when the reformist physician Philippe:** Historians have since challenged Foucault's claim, arguing that Pinel's supervisor and mentor, Jean Baptiste Pussin, was the person who removed the shackles at Bicêtre.
153 **"'the insane,' 'demented men'":** Foucault, *History of Madness*, 108.
153 **"One cannot suppose":** Foucault, *History of Madness*, 45.
153 **"madness has been banished":** Foucault, *History of Madness*, 47.
153 **"to identify the moment":** Foucault, *History of Madness*, xxvii.
154 **"the language of psychiatry":** Foucault, *History of Madness*, xxviii.
154 **"To speak of madness":** Quoted in Eribon, *Michel Foucault*, 108.
154 **The medieval ship of fools:** Macey, *The Lives of Michel Foucault*, 432.
154 **The swelling numbers of asylumed lunatics:** See Luc Ferry and Alain Renaut, *French Philosophy of the Sixties: An Essay on Antihumanism*, trans. Mary Schnackenberg Cattani (University of Massachusetts Press, 1990), 90–92.
155 **"almost religious" love for the mad:** Quoted in Eribon, *Michel Foucault*, 117.
155 **fiction we "conjure up":** David Cooper, Introduction, *Madness and Civilization: A History of Insanity in the Age of Reason* by Michel Foucault, trans. Richard Howard (Routledge, 2001), viii.

Chapter 20: Derrida Throws a Punch

156 **who wrote to his "dear friend":** Quoted in Benoît Peeters, *Derrida: A Biography*, trans. Andrew Brown (Polity Press, 2013), 129.
156 **"muted protest, unformulatable":** Quoted in Peeters, *Derrida: A Biography*, 131.
157 **Foucault's "admiring and grateful disciple":** Jacques Derrida, "Cogito and the History of Madness," *Writing and Difference*, trans. Alan Bass (University of Chicago Press, 1978), 31.
158 **"I would appear no less mad":** Derrida quotes Foucault's citation of this line in a slightly different translation, 46.
159 **He credited these dreams:** Stephen Gaukroger, *Descartes: An Intellectual Biography* (Clarendon Press, 1995), 106–9.
159 **"I will suppose not a supremely good":** René Descartes, *Meditations on First Philosophy, In Which the Existence of God and the Distinction of the Soul From the Body Are Demonstrated*, 3rd ed., trans. Donald A. Cress (Hackett Publishing Company, 1993), 16–17.
160 **"What Derrida's saying":** Jeffrey Eugenides, *The Marriage Plot* (Farrar, Straus and Giroux, 2011), 43.

Chapter 21: "I'm Really at the End of My Tether"

162 **He was speaking here:** Some scholars have argued recently that the dreams Descartes identified as a turning point in his life occurred during a "nervous breakdown" or period of mental collapse. See Stephen Gaukroger, *Descartes: An Intellectual Biography* (Clarendon Press, 1995), 110–11, for example.
162 **"a sort of child":** Mustapha Chérif, *Islam and the West: A Conversation with Jacques Derrida* (University of Chicago Press, 2008), 31.
163 **"a little black and very Arab Jew":** Jacques Derrida, "Circumfession," in *Jacques Derrida*, trans. Geoffrey Bennington (University of Chicago Press, 1993), 58; Benoît Peeters, *Derrida: A Biography*, trans. Andrew Brown (Polity Press, 2013), 19.
163 **"The wound was of *another order*":** Jacques Derrida and Élisabeth Roudinesco, *For What Tomorrow . . . : A Dialogue*, trans. Jeff Fort (Stanford University Press, 2004), 109.
163 **Descartes' tentacles extended:** Edward Baring, *The Young Derrida and French Philosophy: 1945–1968* (Cambridge University Press, 2011), 68.
163 **"leadening and complicating his language":** Baring, *The Young Derrida and French Philosophy*, 73.
163 **The top place may have gone:** Claire Messud, "Camus & Algeria: The Moral Question," *New York Review of Books*, November 7, 2013.
163 **There he earned high marks:** Baring, *The Young Derrida and French Philosophy*, 56.
164 **"As for madness, Jackie":** Peeters, *Derrida: A Biography*, 44.
164 **Alone in Paris:** Peeters, *Derrida: A Biography*, 45.
164 **"I'm really at the end":** Quoted in Peeters, *Derrida: A Biography*, 47.
165 **"answers are brilliant":** Quoted in Peeters, *Derrida: A Biography*, 48–49.
165 **"the way of saying things":** Quoted in Peeters, *Derrida: A Biography*, 189.
165 **"I will never emerge":** Quoted in Peeters, *Derrida: A Biography*, 220–21.
165 **"I don't feel at home either":** Quoted in Peeters, *Derrida: A Biography*, 175.
166 **(the Catholics, so-called because):** See Baring, *The Young Derrida and French Philosophy*, 91–94. Also E. Ann Kaplan and Michael Sprinker, *The Althusserian Legacy* (Verso, 1993), 187.
166 **put off by what he saw:** Kaplan and Sprinker, *The Althusserian Legacy*, 187.
166 **"writing at its most radical":** Quoted in Peeters, *Derrida: A Biography*, 162.
167 **"There is no question at all":** Quoted in Peeters, *Derrida: A Biography*, 73.
167 **was not "a 'familiar thinker'":** Quoted in Peeters, *Derrida: A Biography*, 72.
167 **"Well, it's either an F":** Kaplan and Sprinker, *The Althusserian Legacy*, 184.
167 **"an originary complication":** Jacques Derrida, Preface, *The Problem of Genesis in Husserl's Philosophy*, trans. Marian Hobson (University of Chicago Press, 2003), xv.
168 **"Existence is not a perfection":** *The Philosophical Writings of Descartes*, vol. 2, trans. John Cottingham, Robert Stoothoff, and Dugald Murdoch (Cambridge University Press, 1984), 224.
168 **Derrida judged "philosophically weak":** Quoted in Peeters, *Derrida: A Biography*, 33.
168 **Torn between what he called:** See Dermot Moran, *Edmund Husserl: Founder of Phenomenology* (Polity Press, 2005), 61.
169 **"go back to the 'things themselves'":** Edmund Husserl, *Logical Investigations, Volume 1*, Dermot Moran, ed., J. N. Findlay, trans. (Routledge, 2001), 168.
170 **"the flowing thisness":** Quoted in Peter Salmon, *An Event, Perhaps: A Biography of Jacques Derrida* (Verso, 2020), 52.

170 **"But is not the flow a succession?":** Edmund Husserl, *The Essential Husserl: Basic Writings in Transcendental Phenomenology*, ed. Don Welton (Indiana University Press, 1999), 213.
170 **"In spite of the immense philosophical":** Derrida, *The Problem of Genesis in Husserl's Philosophy*, 5.
170 **Husserl himself conceded:** Edmund Husserl, *On the Phenomenology of the Consciousness of Internal Time* (1893–1917), trans. by John Barnett Brough (Springer, 1991), 286.
171 **"It was Husserl who taught":** Jacques Derrida, *Sur Parole: Instantanées philosophiques* (Éditions de l'aube, 2003), 84.
171 **"How is it that writing":** Quoted in Peeters, *Derrida: A Biography*, 102.
172 **The lecture was one of a series:** "Manger l'autre: Politiques de l'amitié," Jacques Derrida papers, Box 20, Special Collections and Archives, University of California at Irvine.
173 **"all of Derrida is the same":** Fredric Jameson, *The Years of Theory: Postwar French Thought to the Present* (Verso, 2024), 259.
173 **"I'm not good for anything":** Quoted in Peeters, *Derrida: A Biography*, 77.

Chapter 22: Foucault Strikes Back

175 **"Off the cuff, I was taken aback":** Quoted in Benoît Peeters, *Derrida: A Biography*, trans. Andrew Brown (Polity Press, 2013), 132.
175 **"only the blind":** Quoted in Peeters, *Derrida: A Biography*, 132.
176 **"greatest revolution since existentialism":** Quoted in James Miller, *The Passion of Michel Foucault*, (Simon & Schuster, 1993), 148.
177 **According to *Le Monde*:** Peeters, *Derrida: A Biography*, 152.
177 **"Philosophy is in crisis":** Quoted in Peeters, *Derrida: A Biography*, 179–80.
177 **"Already a whole oeuvre":** Gérard Granel, "Jacques Derrida et la rature de l'origine," *Critique* (1967): 887–905. Translation mine.
178 **The essay went to press:** Peeters, *Derrida: A Biography*, 182–83 and 557, fn 47.
178 **indeed, an abridged version:** Didier Eribon, *Michel Foucault*, trans. Betsy Wing (Harvard University Press, 1991), 122. (This is the version initially translated into English in 1965 as "Madness and Civilization.")
178 **to arguing that Derrida, blinded:** Michel Foucault, "Reply to Derrida," *History of Madness*, trans. Jonathan Murphy and Jean Khalfa (Routledge, 2006), 578. See also Peeters, *Derrida: A Biography*, 237–39; Eribon, *Michel Foucault*, 121.
178 **"I would not say that it is a metaphysics":** Foucault, "My Body, This Paper, This Fire," *History of Madness*, 573. See also Peeters, *Derrida: A Biography*, 471.
179 **"Sorry to have answered you":** Quoted in Eribon, *Michel Foucault*, 121.
179 **(The fifty-year anniversary of Derrida's attack):** See Yubraj Aryal, Vernon W. Cisney, Nicolae Morar, and Christopher Penfield, eds., *Between Foucault and Derrida* (Edinburgh University Press, 2016); Olivia Custer, Penelope Deutscher, and Samir Haddad, eds., *Foucault/Derrida: Fifty Years Later: The Futures of Genealogy, Deconstruction, and Politics* (Columbia University Press, 2016).
179 **"hermeneutics of suspicion":** Paul Ricoeur, *Freud and Philosophy: An Essay on Interpretation*, trans. Denis Savage (Yale University Press, 1970), 30.

Chapter 23: "We Are All Schizos!"

180 **"It is at work everywhere":** Gilles Deleuze and Félix Guattari, *Anti-Oedipus: Capitalism and Schizophrenia*, trans. Robert Hurley, Mark Seem, and Helen R. Lane (Penguin Books, 1977), 1.
180 **The book sold out:** François Dosse, *Gilles Deleuze & Félix Guattari: Intersecting Lives*, trans. Deborah Glassman (Columbia University Press, 2010), 207.
180 **"We are all schizos!":** Deleuze and Guattari, *Anti-Oedipus*, 67.
181 **"Instead of participating in":** Deleuze and Guattari, *Anti-Oedipus*, 50.
182 **"A schizophrenic out for a walk":** Deleuze and Guattari, *Anti-Oedipus*, 2.
183 **According to one account, among his patients:** François Cusset, *French Theory: How Foucault, Derrida, Deleuze, & Co. Transformed the Intellectual Life of the United States*, trans. Jeff Fort (University of Minnesota Press, 2008), 67.
183 **an example of schizophrenic "flux":** Deleuze and Guattari, *Anti-Oedipus*, 278–79.
183 **"This book is extremely prudent":** Quoted in Dosse, *Gilles Deleuze & Félix Guattari*, 220.
183 **His second wife, Arlette Donati:** Dosse, *Gilles Deleuze & Félix Guattari*, 67.
184 **the experience was "part of the analysis":** Quoted in Dosse, *Gilles Deleuze & Félix Guattari*, 71.
184 **"Félix really liked declassifying people":** Quoted in Dosse, *Gilles Deleuze & Félix Guattari*, 57.
185 **Together, they ran the circus:** Dosse, *Gilles Deleuze & Félix Guattari*, 64.

185 "They practically filled an entire car": Dosse, *Gilles Deleuze & Félix Guattari*, 71.

186 "The unconscious subject as such": Félix Guattari, "Machine and Structure," *Molecular Revolution: Psychiatry and Politics*, trans. Rosemary Sheed (Penguin, 1984), 111–19.

186 This turned out to be a ruse: Dosse, *Gilles Deleuze & Félix Guattari*, 71.

187 a friend said he "couldn't have spent": Quoted in Dosse, *Gilles Deleuze & Félix Guattari*, 2.

188 "the fascism in us all": Michel Foucault, Preface, *Anti-Oedipus: Capitalism and Schizophrenia*, Gilles Deleuze and Félix Guattari, trans. Robert Hurley, Mark Seem, and Helen R. Lane (Penguin Books, 1977), xiii.

188 of the "plugging in of organs": Quoted in James Miller, *The Passion of Michel Foucault* (Simon & Schuster, 1993), 255.

188 "criticizing in the name of logic": Jean-Marie Domenach, "Oedipe à l'usine," *Esprit* (December 1972): 857.

189 "it took me, with this book": T. S. Eliot, Introduction, *Nightwood*, Djuna Barnes (New Directions, 2006), xi.

189 "Desire, if it flows at all": Klaus Theweleit, *Male Fantasies, Volume 1: Women, Floods, Bodies, History*, trans. Stephen Conway in collaboration with Erica Carter and Chris Turner (University of Minnesota Press, 1987), 410–11.

190 "There are some places": Daniel Dale, "Fact Check: Trump Revives His Lie That Schools Are Secretly Sending Children for Gender-Affirming Surgeries," CNN, October 26, 2024, cnn.com/2024/10/26/politics/fact-check-trump-rogan-children-gender-affirming-surgeries.

190 despite polls in which voters: Megan Brenan, "Economy Most Important Issue to 2024 Presidential Vote," *Gallup*, October 9, 2024, news.gallup.com/poll/651719/economy-important-issue-2024-presidential-vote.aspx#.

190 "Competent white men": Darren Beattie, X, October 4, 2024, x.com/DarrenJBeattie/status/1842239185203151053.

190 On Fox News, panelists discussed: "The Five," *Fox News*, April 9, 2025, foxnews.com/video/6371196367112.

190 "in a viral speech and essay": Helen Andrews, "The Great Feminization," *Compact*, October 16, 2025.

191 "Manliness on the New Right": Katherine Stewart, *Money, Lies, and God: Inside the Movement to Destroy American Democracy* (Bloomsbury, 2025), 136.

191 Privately, he told friends: Dosse, *Gilles Deleuze & Félix Guattari*, 316.

191 But Lacan never mentioned: Stuart Schneiderman, *Jacques Lacan: The Death of an Intellectual Hero* (Harvard University Press, 1983), 29.

191 "Lacan was really furious": Quoted in Dosse, *Gilles Deleuze & Félix Guattari*, 209.

191 Lacan considered *Anti-Oedipus*: Dosse, *Gilles Deleuze & Félix Guattari*, 185.

Chapter 24: "I Never *Talk About Freedom"*

192 A scholar working with Lacan: Quoted in Catherine Millot, *Life with Lacan*, trans. Andrew Brown (Polity Press, 2018), 78. (Élisabeth Roudinesco, *Jacques Lacan*, trans. Barbara Bray [Columbia University Press, 1997], 351, cites the same interview but in a slightly different translation.)

192 book-length takedown: François George, *L'effet 'yau de poêle: De Lacan et des lacaniens* (Hachette, 1979).

192 The reviewer for *Le Monde*: Roland Jaccard, "Salve contre Lacan: L'humour féroce de François George," *Le Monde*, September 21, 1979. Translation mine.

192 Even Althusser turned against him: Catherine Clément, *The Lives and Legends of Jacques Lacan*, trans. Arthur Goldhammer (Columbia University Press, 1983), 21; Élisabeth Roudinesco, *Jacques Lacan & Co.: A History of Psychoanalysis in France, 1925–1985*, trans. Jeffrey Mehlman (University of Chicago Press, 1990), 659.

193 "absolute devotion and implacable hate": Philippe Sollers, *Women*, trans. Barbara Bray (Columbia University Press, 1990), 79.

193 A former patient of Lacan's: Stuart Schneiderman, *Jacques Lacan: The Death of an Intellectual Hero* (Harvard University Press, 1983), 18.

193 "a rare film recording": "Jacques Lacan giving a lecture at The Catholic University of Louvain in 1972," YouTube, youtube.com/watch?v=w1PmWy4aSaQ.

PART 3: WORDS

Chapter 25: Lacan Reads Poe

199 "Language is the only thing": Gilles Deleuze, "How Do We Recognize Structuralism?" *Desert Islands and Other Texts, 1953–1974*, trans. Mike Taormina (Semiotexte, 2004), 170.

199 "Language exists": Michel Foucault, *The Birth of the Clinic: An Archaeology of Medical Perception*, trans. A. M. Sheridan (Routledge, 1973), xvi.

200 The lecture is intricate and demanding: Jacques Lacan, "Seminar on 'The Purloined Letter,'" trans. Jeffrey Mehlman, *Yale French Studies*, no. 48 (1972): 39–72.

200 She had also translated Freud's work: Élisabeth Roudinesco, *Jacques Lacan*, trans. Barbara Bray (Columbia University Press, 1997), 19, 83, 85. See also Francisco Pizzaro Obaid, "The Dead-Living Mother: Marie Bonaparte's Interpretation of Edgar Allan Poe's Short Stories," *American Journal of Psychoanalysis*, no. 76 (2016): 183–203.

201 Bonaparte recorded the remark: Alan C. Elms, "Apocryphal Freud," *Annual of Psychoanalysis* 29 (2001): 83–104.

201 Bonaparte found little to admire: Roudinesco, *Jacques Lacan*, 81.

203 "so powerful in the mathematical sense": Lacan, "Ouverture to this Collection," *Écrits*, trans. Bruce Fink (W. W. Norton, 2006), 4.

204 "The displacement of the signifier": Lacan, "Seminar on 'The Purloined Letter,'" 60.

205 In Marie Bonaparte's analysis: Marie Bonaparte, "Selections From '*The Life and Works of Edgar Allan Poe: A Psycho-analytic Interpretation*,'" trans. John Rodker, in *The Purloined Poe: Lacan, Derrida, and Psychoanalytic Reading*, eds. John P. Miller and William J. Richardson (Johns Hopkins University Press, 1988), 130.

205 "It was the name of": Betty Milan, *Analyzed by Lacan: A Personal Account*, trans. Clifford E. Landers and Chris Vanderwees (Bloomsbury Academic, 2024), 37.

206 "A letter always arrives": Lacan, "Seminar on 'The Purloined Letter,'" 72.

Chapter 26: Lévi-Strauss Heads for the Jungle

207 "as an easy entryway": Jacques Lacan, "Ouverture to this Collection," *Écrits*, trans. Bruce Fink (W. W. Norton, 2006), 4.

209 "Perhaps the drug had done": Quoted in Didier Eribon, *Conversations with Claude Lévi-Strauss*, trans. Paula Wissing (University of Chicago Press, 1991), 13. See also Emmanuelle Loyer, *Lévi-Strauss: A Biography*, trans. Ninon Vinsonneau and Jonathan Magidoff (Polity Press, 2018), 66.

209 Sartre, who took the post: Gary Cox, *Existentialism and Excess: The Life and Times of Jean-Paul Sartre* (Bloomsbury Academic, 2016), 66.

209 "Philosophy was not *ancilla scientiarum*": Claude Lévi-Strauss, *Tristes Tropiques*, trans. John Weightman and Doreen Weightman (Penguin Books, 1973), 52.

209 "twisted palm trees": Lévi-Strauss, *Tristes Tropiques*, 47.

210 "Among the Indians of": Lévi-Strauss, *Tristes Tropiques*, 277.

210 In his notebook, he wrote: Lévi-Strauss, *Tristes Tropiques*, 293.

211 "I hate travelling and explorers": Lévi-Strauss, *Tristes Tropiques*, 17.

211 "a philosopher among the Indians": Quoted in Mathieu Lindon, "Mission *Tristes Tropiques*," *Libération*, September 1, 1988.

211 "Knows a lot. A fine": Quoted in Patrick Wilcken, *Claude Lévi-Strauss: A Poet in the Laboratory* (Penguin Press, 2010), 29.

Chapter 27: A Tutorial in Structural Linguistics

213 "With a name like yours": Quoted in Emmanuelle Loyer, *Lévi-Strauss: A Biography*, trans. Ninon Vinsonneau and Jonathan Magidoff (Polity Press, 2018), 191.

214 "very much out of place,": Claude Lévi-Strauss, *Tristes Tropiques*, trans. John Weightman and Doreen Weightman (Penguin Books, 1973), 25.

214 Lévi-Strauss was briefly: Lévi-Strauss, *Tristes Tropiques*, 34; Loyer, *Lévi-Strauss*, 202.

214 "a mass of documents": Quoted in Didier Eribon, *Conversations with Claude Lévi-Strauss*, trans. Paula Wissing (University of Chicago Press, 1991), 43–44; Loyer, *Lévi-Strauss*, 244.

214 "This flirtation with the savages": Quoted in Loyer, *Lévi-Strauss*, 213.

215 "Everything is based on relations": Ferdinand de Saussure, *Course in General Linguistics*, trans. Wade Baskin, eds. Perry Meisel and Haun Saussy (Columbia University Press, 2011), 122.

215 French word *mouton*: Saussure, *Course in General Linguistics*, 115–16.

216 But these two parts "have nothing": Saussure, *Course in General Linguistics*, xxvii.
216 "sheet of paper": Saussure, *Course in General Linguistics*, 113.
217 "At the time, I was a kind of naïve structuralist": Quoted in Eribon, *Conversations with Claude Lévi-Strauss*, 41; Loyer, *Lévi-Strauss*, 227.
218 "Although they belong to another order": Claude Lévi-Strauss, *Structural Anthropology*, trans. Clare Jacobson and Brooke Grundfest Shoepf (Basic Books, 1963), 34.
219 marriage laws could be: Claude Lévi-Strauss, *The Elementary Structures of Kinship*, trans. James Harle Bel, John Richard von Sturmer, and Rodney Needham (Beacon Press, 1969), 221.
219 "A monumental work": Quoted in Loyer, *Lévi-Strauss*, 266.
219 Beauvoir gave Lévi-Strauss's career a big boost: Loyer, *Lévi-Strauss*, 270–71; Patrick Wilcken, *Claude Lévi- Strauss: A Poet in the Laboratory* (Penguin Press, 2010), 172–73.
219 He also had mainly nice things to say: Georges Bataille, "The Enigma of Incest," in *Erotism: Death & Sensuality*, trans. Mary Dalwood (City Lights Books, 1986), 200–1. Also Wilcken, *Claude Lévi-Strauss*, 173.
220 the travelers arriving at: Quoted in Eribon, *Conversations with Claude Lévi-Strauss*, 73.
220 "I always had the impression": Quoted in Élisabeth Roudinesco, *Jacques Lacan*, trans. Barbara Bray (Columbia University Press, 1997), 211.
221 "The primordial Law": Jacques Lacan, "The Function and Field of Speech and Language in Psychoanalysis," *Écrits*, trans. Bruce Fink (W. W. Norton, 2006), 229.
221 "Lacan's encounter with the thought": Roudinesco, *Jacques Lacan*, 212.
222 Sartre believed "there was *meaning* everywhere": Michel Foucault, *La Quinzaine littéraire*, April 15, 1966. Also in Eribon, *Michel Foucault*, 161.
222 those "links by which a necklace": Lacan, "The Instance of the Letter in the Unconscious," *Écrits*, 418.
222 "He shows penetrating imagination": Quoted in Roudinesco, *Jacques Lacan*, 87.

Chapter 28: Barthes Dismantles the Doxa

223 "The intoxication with the power": Tony Judt, *Marxism and the French Left: Studies on Labor and Politics, 1831–1981* (Oxford University Press, 1986), 175.
223 In Paris, rumor had it: François Dosse, *History of Structuralism: Volume 1: The Rising Sign, 1945–1966*, trans. Deborah Glassman, vol. 1 (University of Minnesota Press, 1997), 317.
224 "vast field of signifying media": Roland Barthes, *Elements of Semiology*, trans. Annette Lavers and Colin Smith (Hill and Wang, 1977), 9.
224 "a gelatinous mass which sticks": *Roland Barthes by Roland Barthes*, trans. Richard Howard (Hill and Wang, 1977), 122.
224 "Cars today are almost": Roland Barthes, "The New Citroën," in *Mythologies*, trans. Annette Lavers (Noonday Press, 1972), 88.
224 "I resented seeing Nature and History": Barthes, Preface, *Mythologies*, 10.
224 "One felt that he could generate": Susan Sontag, "Remembering Barthes," *New York Review of Books*, May 15, 1980.
225 "I have a disease," he wrote: *Roland Barthes by Roland Barthes*, 161.
225 "Jean Werth was a humanist": Philippe Sollers, *Women*, trans. Barbara Bray (Columbia University Press, 1990), 121.
225 "Nothing is more depressing": Barthes, *Sade/Fourier/Loyola*, trans. Richard Miller (University of California Press, 1976), 7.
225 "*Happiness* is perhaps what I understand": Quoted in Tiphaine Samoyault, *Barthes: A Biography*, trans. Andrew Brown (Polity Press, 2017), 126.
226 "That was Hermine Kleefeld": Thomas Mann, *The Magic Mountain*, trans. H. T. Lowe-Porter (Vintage Books, 1969), 50.
226 "lie at an angle": Samoyault, *Barthes*, 116.
226 "tuberculosis was incontestably": Samoyault, *Barthes*, 115.
226 at his death he had amassed: Denis Hollier, "Notes (on the Index Card)," *October* 112 (Spring 2005): 35.
227 "No father to kill": *Roland Barthes by Roland Barthes*, 45.
227 "Barthes's life was not": Samoyault, *Barthes*, 16.
230 Some say they were occasional: David Macey, *The Lives of Michel Foucault* (Verso, 2009), 82.
230 In 2021, a French author: Matthew Campbell, "French Philosopher Michel Foucault 'Abused Boys in Tunisia,'" London *Sunday Times*, March 28, 2021.
230 "an old fool with an old fogey": Quoted in Samoyault, *Barthes*, 450.

231 **"The necessity for this book":** Roland Barthes, *A Lover's Discourse: Fragments*, trans. Richard Howard (Hill and Wang, 1978), 1.
231 **"By weeping, I want to":** Barthes, *A Lover's Discourse*, 182.
231 **"Once the first avowal":** Jeffrey Eugenides, *The Marriage Plot* (Farrar, Straus and Giroux, 2011), 66–67.
231 **"eating, sleeping, washing":** Quoted in Samoyault, *Barthes*, 200.
232 **"Werth was at the end":** Sollers, *Women*, 120.

Chapter 29: The Death of the Author

234 **"gives virtually no indication":** Susan Sontag, Preface, *Writing Degree Zero* by Roland Barthes, trans. Annette Lavers and Colin Smith (Hill and Wang, 1968), viii.
234 **"one of the modish structuralists":** Tiphaine Samoyault, *Barthes: A Biography*, trans. Andrew Brown (Polity Press, 2017), 252.
234 **"There is an eclecticism":** Quoted in Samoyault, *Barthes*, 254.
234 **"You can't understand anything":** Quoted in François Dosse, *History of Structuralism, Volume 1: The Rising Sign, 1945–1966*, trans. Deborah Glassman, vol. 1 (University of Minnesota Press, 1997), 215.
234 **"the slightly forbidding":** James Miller, *The Passion of Michel Foucault* (Simon & Schuster, 1993), 134.
235 **he called the book "already dated":** Roland Barthes, *The Fashion System*, trans. Matthew Ward and Richard Howard (University of California Press, 1990), ix.
235 **"we know now that":** Roland Barthes, "The Death of the Author," *Image-Music-Text*, trans. Stephen Heath (Hill and Wang, 1977), 146.
236 **M. Louis Althusser, who has reinterpreted:** Quoted in Samoyault, *Barthes*, 313.
237 **"*What is Sarrasine?*" Barthes asks:** Roland Barthes, *S/Z*, trans. Richard Miller (Hill and Wang, 1974), 17.
237 **"On its way to the subject's patronymic":** Barthes, *S/Z*, 106.
237 **"Phonetically, Z stings":** Barthes, *S/Z*, 106.
237 **"the same letter seen":** Barthes, *S/Z*, 107.
238 **"This was more than":** Barthes, *S/Z*, 238.
238 **"This text is a galaxy":** Barthes, *S/Z*, 5–6.
238 **"make the reader no longer a consumer":** Barthes, *S/Z*, 4.
240 **"absolutely plural":** Barthes, *S/Z*, 6.
241 **"system which I shall call":** Roland Barthes, *Empire of Signs*, trans. Richard Howard (The Noonday Press, 1982), 3.
241 **"neither incongruous nor significant":** Roland Barthes, "The Reality Effect," *The Rustle of Language*, trans. Richard Howard (Hill and Wang, 1986), 142.

Chapter 30: The Death of Man

243 **"for me, the work of art is":** Quoted in Tiphaine Samoyault, *Barthes: A Biography*, trans. Andrew Brown (Polity Press, 2017), 254.
243 **he'd sent the letter "as a joke":** Quoted in Didier Eribon, *Conversations with Claude Lévi-Strauss*, trans. Paula Wissing (University of Chicago Press, 1991), 79.
243 **"I've just read you in one sitting":** Quoted in Samoyault, *Barthes*, 434.
243 **"With no other text do I at present":** Quoted in Samoyault, *Barthes*, 334.
244 **"Certain half-witted 'commentators'":** Michel Foucault, Foreword, *The Order of Things* (Vintage Books, 1994), xiv.
245 **"The threshold between Classicism":** Foucault, *The Order of Things*, 304.
246 **"this picture of a picture":** Foucault, *The Order of Things*, 5.
246 **"an essential void":** Foucault, *The Order of Things*, 16.
246 **"one of the most famous":** Fredric Jameson, *The Years of Theory: Postwar French Thought to the Present* (Verso, 2024), 315.
246 **"an invention of recent date":** Foucault, *The Order of Things*, 387.
247 **"Our task is to completely free ourselves":** Foucault, "Entretien avec Madeleine Chapsal," *La Quinzaine littéraire*, May 16, 1966; quoted in David Macey, *The Lives of Michel Foucault* (Verso, 2009), 171.
247 **"A young man has come on the intellectual":** Quoted in James Miller, *The Passion of Michel Foucault, The Passion of Michel Foucault* (Simon & Schuster, 1993), 149.
247 **Sartre panned Foucault's book:** See Didier Eribon, *Michel Foucault*, trans. Betsy Wing (Harvard University Press, 1991), 163.
247 **"Jean-Charles and Dufrène":** Simone de Beauvoir, *Les belles images*, trans. Patrick O'Brian (G. P. Putnam's Sons, 1968), 116–17.
248 **"the worst book he had written":** Eribon, *Michel Foucault*, 185.

Chapter 31: "What Is It to Write?"

249 **By calling attention to philosophy's:** Jacques Derrida, "The Ends of Man," *Margins of Philosophy*, trans. Alan Bass (University of Chicago Press, 1982), 109–36.

250 **"My most constant interest":** Jacques Derrida, "Punctuations: The Time of a Thesis," in *Philosophy in France Today.*, ed. Alan Montefiore (Cambridge University Press, 1983), 116.

250 **writing was simply speech's "dead letter":** Jacques Derrida, *Of Grammatology*, trans. Gayatri Chakravorty Spivak (Johns Hopkins University Press, 1974), 17.

250 **"absolute proximity of voice and being":** Derrida, *Of Grammatology*, 12.

250 **"Problems were proposed":** Peter Salmon, *An Event, Perhaps: A Biography of Jacques Derrida* (Verso, 2020), 130.

251 **"deconstruction" suddenly came to him:** Benoît Peeters, *Derrida: A Biography*, trans. Andrew Brown (Polity Press, 2013), 160.

251 **"meaning is a will-o'-the-wisp":** Fredric Jameson, *The Years of Theory: Postwar French Thought to the Present* (Verso, 2024), 249.

251 **"It is a question of determining":** Jacques Derrida, "The Ends of Man," *Margins of Philosophy*, 134.

251 **"A gloriously bonkers book":** Salmon, *An Event, Perhaps*, 127.

251 ***Of Grammatology* "is exorbitant":** Salmon, *An Event, Perhaps*, 127–28.

252 **She had never heard of Derrida:** Steve Paulson, "Critical Intimacy: An Interview with Gayatri Chakravorty Spivak," *Los Angeles Review of Books*, July 29, 2016. See also, François Cusset, *French Theory: How Foucault, Derrida, Deleuze, & Co. Transformed the Intellectual Life of the United States*, trans. Jeff Fort (University of Minnesota Press, 2008), 109.

252 **"The main question for Heidegger":** Merve Emre, "Jon Fosse's Search for Peace," *The New Yorker*, November 13, 2022, newyorker.com/culture/the-new-yorker-interview/jon-fosses-search-for-peace.

253 **"The age of the sign":** Derrida, *Of Grammatology*, 14.

253 **"'Differance' is the structure":** Gayatri Chakravorty Spivak, "Preface," *Of Grammatology*, lix.

253 **"*differance* is neither a *word* nor":** Quoted in Spivak, "Preface," *Of Grammatology*, lxxi.

254 **According to Lévi-Strauss, writing's:** Claude Lévi-Strauss, *Tristes Tropiques*, trans. John Weightman and Doreen Weightman (Penguin Books, 1973), 299; Derrida, *Of Grammatology*, 130.

254 **"role as sign, and the social":** Quoted by Derrida, *Of Grammatology*, 125. Original source: Claude Lévi-Strauss, "La vie familiale et sociale des Indiens Nambikwara," *Journal de la société des américanistes*, no. 37 (1948): 40.

254 **Over the course of two hours:** Lévi-Strauss, *Tristes Tropiques*, 296.

254 **"still living in the Stone Age":** Lévi-Strauss, *Tristes Tropiques*, 298.

254 **"The story is very beautiful":** Derrida, *Of Grammatology*, 126.

254 **"Aren't you playing":** Quoted in Peeters, *Derrida: A Biography*, 178–79.

255 **"charged with unease":** Spivak, "Preface," *Of Grammatology*, lxii.

256 **"A letter does *not always* arrive":** Jacques Derrida, "Le Facteur de la Vérité," *The Post Card: From Socrates to Freud and Beyond*, trans. Alan Bass (University of Chicago Press, 1987), 489.

256 **"More and more, where would":** Quoted in Peeters, *Derrida: A Biography*, 164.

PART 4: EVASIONS

Chapter 32: Samson in the Structuralist Temple

259 **Lacan was holding a plate:** Élisabeth Roudinesco, *Jacques Lacan & Co.: A History of Psychoanalysis in France, 1925–1985*, trans. Jeffrey Mehlman (University of Chicago Press, 1990), 409.

259 **"People were falling out of":** Quoted in Brett McCabe, "Structuralism's Samson," *Johns Hopkins Magazine*, Fall 2012, hub.jhu.edu/magazine/2012/fall/structuralisms-samson.

260 **"ninety-six-gun French dispute":** Richard Macksey and Eugenio Donato, eds., *The Structuralist Controversy: The Languages of Criticism and the Sciences of Man, 40th Anniversary Edition* (Johns Hopkins University Press, 2007), xxiii.

260 **Lévi-Strauss was supposed to come:** Cynthia Haven, *Evolution of Desire: A Life of René Girard* (Michigan State University Press, 2018), 129.

260 **Deleuze was also unable:** François Cusset, *French Theory: How Foucault, Derrida, Deleuze, & Co. Transformed the Intellectual Life of the United States*, trans. Jeff Fort (University of Minnesota Press, 2008), 29.

260 **Foucault, who was known:** Haven, *Evolution of Desire*, 129.

260 **"acknowledged the absurdity":** Macksey and Donato, "Anniversary Reflections," *The Structuralist Controversy*, ix–x.

260 "I think he would be somebody": Quoted in Haven, *Evolution of Desire*, 130.
260 "So! I had to come": Quoted in Roudinesco, *Jacques Lacan & Co.*, 410.
261 At one point, he tried: Haven, *Evolution of Desire*, 131–32.
261 "You can't bear my": Quoted in Roudinesco, *Jacques Lacan & Co.*, 410.
261 "in particular by me, after": Jacques Derrida, "For the Love of Lacan," in *Resistances of Psychoanalysis*, trans. Peggy Kamuf, Pascale-Anne Brault, and Michael Naas (Stanford University Press, 1998), 51.
261 "You'll see," he said: Derrida, "For the Love of Lacan," 52.
261 "The works of Lévi-Strauss and Lacan": Eugenio Donato, "The Two Languages of Criticism," in *The Structuralist Controversy*, 89.
262 "Man does not exist": Roland Barthes, "To Write: An Intransitive Verb?" in *The Structuralist Controversy*, 135.
262 "Because he had been down": Haven, *Evolution of Desire*, 132.
262 "M. Goldmann has just shown": Macksey and Donato, eds., *The Structuralist Controversy*, 120–21.
263 Fredric Jameson has given this line: Fredric Jameson, *The Years of Theory: Postwar French Thought to the Present* (Verso, 2024), 188–89.
263 "All that I could see, except": Jacques Lacan, "Of Structure as an Inmixing of an Otherness Prerequisite to Any Subject Whatever," *The Structuralist Controversy*, 189.
263 "Freud was really": Lacan, "Of Structure as an Inmixing of an Otherness Prerequisite to Any Subject Whatever," *The Structuralist Controversy*, 195.
264 What is the relationship: Macksey and Donato, eds., *The Structuralist Controversy*, 196.
264 According to Macksey: Haven, *Evolution of Desire*, 136.
264 "Perhaps something has occurred": Jacques Derrida, "Structure, Sign, and Play in the Discourse of the Human Sciences," *Writing and Difference*, trans. Alan Bass (University of Chicago Press, 1978), 278.
267 "the as yet unnamable": Derrida, "Structure, Sign, and Play in the Discourse of the Human Sciences," *Writing and Difference*, 293.
268 "I was wondering myself": Derrida, "Structure, Sign, and Play in the Discourse of the Human Sciences," *The Structuralist Controversy*, 267.
268 "Structure should be centered": Derrida, "Structure, Sign, and Play in the Discourse of the Human Sciences," *The Structuralist Controversy*, 268.
269 "I have just heard": McCabe, "Structuralism's Samson."
269 For the Americans, Richard Macksey: Macksey and Donato, eds., *The Structuralist Controversy*, x.
269 "I hadn't realized that": McCabe, "Structuralism's Samson."
269 referred to himself as: Benoît Peeters, *Derrida: A Biography*, trans. Andrew Brown (Polity Press, 2013), 202.
270 One eminent doctor: Haven, *Evolution of Desire*, 138.

Chapter 33: The Connoisseur of Nothingness

272 "If I have known a great man": Quoted in Evelyn Barish, *The Double Life of Paul de Man* (Liveright, 2014), 288.
272 "Catnip to women": Barish, *The Double Life of Paul de Man*, 244.
273 McCarthy's letters to her friend the critic Elizabeth Hardwick: Barish, *The Double Life of Paul de Man*, 254.
273 Barish thinks it's possible: Barish, *The Double Life of Paul de Man*, 256.
273 Their contact ceased only: Letter from de Man to McCarthy, January 8, 1950. Mary McCarthy Papers, Archives and Special Collections Library, Vassar College.
273 "He has so little," McCarthy wrote: Quoted in Barish, *The Double Life of Paul de Man*, 254.
274 Then, after de Man's three-year term: Barish, *The Double Life of Paul de Man*, 413.
274 When de Man fell behind: Barish, *The Double Life of Paul de Man*, 414–18.
274 largely on the basis of a single essay: Barish, *The Double Life of Paul de Man*, 421.
275 a speech delivered "in character": Cleanth Brooks, *The Well-Wrought Urn: Studies in the Structure of Poetry* (Harcourt, Brace & World, 1947), 165.
275 "sit in front of a text": Quoted in Barish, *The Double Life of Paul de Man*, 344.
276 "I met a blond Apollo named": Quoted in Howard Felperin, *In Another Life: The Decline and Fall of the Humanities Through the Eyes of an Ivy-League Jew* (AuthorHouse, 2014), 62.
276 "Neither the statement 'I see'": Paul de Man, "The Dead-End of Formalist Criticism," in *Blindness and Insight: Essays in the Rhetoric of Contemporary Criticism*, trans. Wlad Godzich (University of Minnesota Press, 1983), 232.

277 **"a connoisseur of nothingness":** Geoffrey Hartman, *A Scholar's Tale*: *Intellectual Journey of a Displaced Child of Europe* (Fordham University Press, 2007), 86.
277 **The one for "beauty" reads:** De Man, *Blindness and Insight*, 292.
277 **"Professor Hartman has given you":** Quoted in Geoffrey Hartman, "Polemical Memoir," in *A Critic's Journey: Literary Reflections, 1958–1998* (Yale University Press, 1999), xxiii; Gregory Katz-Jones, *Deconstruction: An American Institution* (University of Chicago Press, 2021), 161.

Chapter 34: Rousseau's Supplement

278 **"Each in his own way":** Jacques Derrida, "In Memoriam: Of the Soul," trans. Kevin Newmark, in *Mémoires for Paul de Man.* (Columbia University Press, 1989), xvi.
278 **"No aspiring academic critic":** Walter Kendrick, "De Man That Got Away," *Village Voice Literary Supplement*, April 1988.
279 **"Languages are made to be spoken":** Quoted in Jacques Derrida, *Of Grammatology*, trans. Gayatri Chakravorty Spivak (Johns Hopkins University Press, 1974), 144.
279 **nature for Rousseau being what "suffices":** Derrida, *Of Grammatology*, 145.
280 **Try as he might, Rousseau:** Derrida, *Of Grammatology*, 153.
280 **"A speech without consonantic principle":** Derrida, *Of Grammatology*, 315.
281 **"The boldest contemporary thinker":** Quoted in Benoît Peeters, *Derrida: A Biography*, trans. Andrew Brown (Polity Press, 2013), 180.
281 **A friend of Derrida's:** Pierre Aubenque, *Faut-il déconstruire la métaphysique?* (Presses Universitaires de France, 2009), 60.
281 **"There was something permanently":** Geoffrey Hartman, *A Scholar's Tale*: *Intellectual Journey of a Displaced Child of Europe* (Fordham University Press, 2007), 79.
282 **"an exemplary case":** Paul de Man, "The Rhetoric of Blindness: Jacques Derrida's Reading of Rousseau," *Blindness and Insight: Essays in the Rhetoric of Contemporary Criticism*, trans. Wlad Godzich (University of Minnesota Press, 1983), 111.
282 **"nothing by natural right":** Quoted in De Man, "The Rhetoric of Blindness," 128.
282 **"the structural characteristics of language":** De Man, "The Rhetoric of Blindness," 131.
283 **"Rousseau's theory of representation":** De Man, "The Rhetoric of Blindness," 127.
283 **"leaves *giant* to the false":** Quoted in Derrida, *Of Grammatology*, 276.
284 **"there is no need to deconstruct Rousseau":** De Man, "The Rhetoric of Blindness," 139.
284 **"*the* primal scene of 'deconstruction'":** Marc Redfield, *Theory at Yale: The Strange Case of Deconstruction in America* (Fordham University Press, 2016), 36.
284 **"the only form of language":** De Man, "Criticism and Crisis," *Blindness and Insight*, 17.
284 **"the most photocopied essay":** Wlad Godzich, "Introduction: Caution! Reader at Work!" *Blindness and Insight*, xvi.
285 **"foreplay, in a heterosexual world":** Alice Kaplan, *French Lessons: A Memoir* (University of Chicago Press, 1993), 155.
285 **"two entirely coherent but entirely incompatible":** Paul de Man, "Semiology and Rhetoric," in *Allegories of Reading: Figural Language in Rousseau, Nietzsche, Rilke, and Proust* (Yale University Press, 1979), 12.
286 **"made literary statements appear":** Hartman, *A Scholar's Tale*, 52.

Chapter 35: How to Become a Dominant French Philosopher

287 **his own work was of no interest:** Donald Marshall, "The State of Criticism," *Partisan Review* 47, no. 3 (1980): 431. (Transcript of a conference on "the state of criticism," held at Boston University, September 14–15, 1979.)
287 **"There is always already deconstruction":** Jacques Derrida, "Acts: The Meaning of a Given Word," trans. Eduardo Cadava, in *Mémoires for Paul de Man* (Columbia University Press, 1989), 123.
288 **"He radiated intellect":** Howard Felperin, *In Another Life: The Decline and Fall of the Humanities Through the Eyes of an Ivy-League Jew* (AuthorHouse, 2014), 62–63.
288 **"at the literature lectures":** Alice Kaplan, *French Lessons: A Memoir* (University of Chicago Press, 1993), 148.
288 **There was "a religious quality":** Kaplan, *French Lessons*, 154.
289 **"no comparably intense institutional":** Marc Redfield, *Theory at Yale: The Strange Case of Deconstruction in America* (Fordham University Press, 2016), 33.
289 **"He never sought followers":** Barbara Johnson, "The Following Tributes Were Offered at the Memo-

rial Service for Paul de Man Held at the Yale University Art Gallery on January 18, 1984," *Yale French Studies*, no. 69 (1985): 10.

289 He was Yale's "resident Godfather": Frank Lentricchia, *After the New Criticism* (University of Chicago Press, 1980), 283.

289 "new professional-managerial class": John Guillory, "Literature After Theory: The Lesson of Paul de Man," *Cultural Capital: The Problem of Literary Canon Formation* (University of Chicago Press, 1993), 181.

289 "no longer requires the (primarily literary)": Guillory, Preface, *Cultural Capital*, xii.

290 "*reproduction* of the social order": Guillory, Preface, *Cultural Capital*, ix.

290 "specialization with a *universalist* rationale": Guillory, "Literature After Theory," 264.

290 "In his 'impersonality,' he rather resembles": Guillory, "Literature After Theory," 195.

290 "Those who learned the lesson": Andrzej Warminski, "The Following Tributes Were Offered at the Memorial Service for Paul de Man Held at the Yale University Art Gallery on January 19, 1984," *Yale French Studies*, no. 69 (1985): 13.

290 "Nothing succeeds so well": Guillory, "Literature After Theory," 186.

291 "a purely North American artifact": Quoted in Redfield, *Theory at Yale*, 6.

291 "On the basis of Derrida's work": Michèle Lamont, "How to Become a Dominant French Philosopher: The Case of Jacques Derrida," *American Journal of Sociology* 93, no. 3 (1987): 593.

Chapter 36: Tyranny of the Yale Critics

293 "In those days, Derrida": Quoted in Benoît Peeters, *Derrida: A Biography*, trans. Andrew Brown (Polity Press, 2013), 190.

294 "perfect diction, the energetic gestures": Quoted in Peeters, *Derrida: A Biography*, 421.

294 "radiant narcissism": Quoted in Peeters, *Derrida: A Biography*, 421.

295 *Glas* was "an ancestral rite": Gayatri Chakravorty Spivak, "*Glas*-Piece: A Compte-Rendu," *Diacritics* 7, no. 3 (Autumn 1977): 22–43.

295 "Bowled over" was a reaction: Quoted in Peeters, *Derrida: A Biography*, 261.

295 Over the course of the 1970s: Jeffrey J. Williams, "The Brief, Wondrous Life of the Theory Journal," *Chronicle of Higher Education*, October 16, 2011.

295 "a new group of critics": J. Hillis Miller, "The Year's Books: On Literary Criticism," *The New Republic*, November 29, 1975, 30–33.

295 "document about the interpretation of documents": J. Hillis Miller, Introduction, *Bleak House*, Charles Dickens (Penguin Books, 1971), 11.

295 "God is dead": Howard Felperin, *In Another Life: The Decline and Fall of the Humanities Through the Eyes of an Ivy-League Jew* (AuthorHouse, 2014), 117.

296 English was Yale's second-most-popular: Gregory Katz-Jones, *Deconstruction: An American Institution* (University of Chicago Press, 2021), 292.

296 "tyranny of the Yale Critics": Colin Campbell, "The Tyranny of the Yale Critics," *New York Times Magazine*, February 9, 1986.

296 as selected by six hundred: Michèle Lamont, "How to Become a Dominant French Philosopher: The Case of Jacques Derrida," *American Journal of Sociology* 93, no. 3 (November 1987): 607.

296 "Derrida's theories lingered": Jonathan Rosen, *The Best Minds: A Story of Friendship, Madness, and the Tragedy of Good Intentions* (Penguin Press, 2023), 118–19.

297 "Our defense against a text": John Sturrock, "The Book Is Dead, Long Live the Book!" *New York Times Book Review*, September 13, 1987.

297 "I was very disappointed": Quoted in Dinitia Smith, "Philosopher Gamely in Defense of His Ideas," *The New York Times*, May 30, 1998.

297 "Deconstruction, the way I understand it": "Derrida on Seinfeld," YouTube, youtube.com/watch?v=TNOXuurUODE.

298 "demanding French philosophers": Peter Salmon, *An Event, Perhaps: A Biography of Jacques Derrida* (Verso, 2020), 13.

298 "equivocal and multiplex": M. H. Abrams, "The Deconstructive Angel," *Critical Inquiry* 3, no. 3 (1977): 425–38.

298 "antihistorical" and "pseudo-democratic ethos": William Phillips, "The State of Criticism," *Partisan Review* 47, no. 3 (1980): 379. (Transcript of a conference on "the state of criticism," held at Boston University, September 14–15, 1979.)

298 Another critic in attendance joked: Lawrence Graver, "The State of Criticism," 390.

298 "Even in the philosophy of language": John R. Searle, "The World Turned Upside Down," *New York Review of Books*, October 27, 1983.

299 "The ideas that deconstructionists articulate": David Lehman, *Signs of the Times: Deconstruction and the Fall of Paul de Man* (Poseidon Press, 1991), 76–77.

299 In a letter published in the London *Times*: Barry Smith et al., "Derrida Degree a Question of Honor; Letter," *Times of London*, May 9, 1992.

299 Derrida was duly awarded: Peeters, *Derrida: A Biography*, 447.

300 Unbeknown to either father or son: Peeters, *Derrida: A Biography*, 473–74.

300 "If a right to the secret": Jacques Derrida and Maurizio Ferraris, *A Taste for the Secret*, trans. Giacomo Donis (Polity Press, 2001), 59.

300 "I cry for you I cry over you": Jacques Derrida, *The Post Card: From Socrates to Freud and Beyond*, trans. Alan Bass (University of Chicago Press, 1987), 108.

301 "Metaphysics," she replied: Quoted in Peeters, *Derrida: A Biography*, 308. In 2018, in a case that roiled American academia, Ronell was found guilty of sexually harassing a graduate student and suspended for a year by New York University, where she teaches comparative literature. (See Ginia Bellafante, "The Dangerous Intimacy of Grad School: Was the N.Y.U. Harassment Case Inevitable?" *New York Times*, August 18, 2018).

Chapter 37: Derrida Behind Bars

303 "the law of the law": Jacques Derrida, "Before the Law," trans. Avital Ronell and Christine Roulston, in *Acts of Literature*, ed. Derek Attridge (Routledge, 1992), 181–220. Derrida writes, "What *must not* and cannot be approached is the origin of *différance*: it must not be presented or represented and above all not penetrated. That is the law of the law" (p. 205).

304 "I summoned up my knowledge": Derrida, Quoted in Benoît Peeters, *Derrida: A Biography*, trans. Andrew Brown (Polity Press, 2013), 333.

304 "What use is that philosophy?": Quoted in Barbara Day, *The Velvet Philosophers* (Claridge Press, 1999), 93.

304 lectured was a "Kafkologue": Derrida, "Before the Law," 218.

304 meditating "on the value of deconstructionist": Day, *The Velvet Philosophers*, 94.

305 "a pile like in concentration camps": Quoted in Day, *The Velvet Philosophers*, 94.

305 "You must have the impression of": Derrida, "Unsealing ('the old new language')," trans. Peggy Kamuf, in *Points . . . : Interviews, 1974–1994*, ed. Elisabeth Weber (Stanford University Press, 1995), 128.

306 "Whether they expelled me": Jacques Derrida, "Circumfession," *Jacques Derrida*, trans. Geoffrey Bennington (University of Chicago Press, 1993), 300.

306 was himself arrested: Peeters, *Derrida: A Biography*, 341.

Chapter 38: The Radical Campus

308 The idea for the school: Hervé Hamon and Patrick Rotman, *Génération, vol. 2, Les Années de poudre* (Éditions du Seuil, 1988), 56–57.

308 Vincennes was also state of the art: Hamon and Rotman, *Génération*, 57.

308 The pedagogy and curriculum too: François Dosse, *Gilles Deleuze & Félix Guattari: Intersecting Lives*, trans. Deborah Glassman (Columbia University Press, 2010), 344.

308 Exams were optional: Didier Eribon, *Michel Foucault*, trans. Betsy Wing (Harvard University Press, 1991), 208.

308 Course offerings included: Eribon, *Michel Foucault*, 206.

308 "The university is a fragment": Quoted in Hamon and Rotman, *Génération*, 180, translation mine; Eribon, *Michel Foucault*, 208; David Macey, *The Lives of Michel Foucault* (Verso, 2009), 228.

309 Classroom ceilings were dismantled: Dosse, *Gilles Deleuze & Félix Guattari*, 345.

309 He was accused: Eribon, *Michel Foucault*, 202.

309 students disrupted his classes: Hamon and Rotman, *Génération*, 62.

309 His courses "The End of Metaphysics": Eribon, *Michel Foucault*, 207.

309 Foucault fled to the roof: Hamon and Rotman, *Génération*, 56; Eribon, *Michel Foucault*, 205.

310 "Vincennes was the one place": Hamon and Rotman, *Génération*, 59. Translation mine.

311 "atmosphere of intellectual terrorism": Quoted in Eribon, *Michel Foucault*, 206.

311 "the drone of this lecture": "L'impromptu de Vincennes," *Le Magazine littéraire*, no. 121 (1977): 21–25.

311 "had enough of being surrounded": Quoted in Eribon, *Michel Foucault*, 209.

311 "is when the Foucault whom": Eribon, *Michel Foucault*, 210.

Chapter 39: The Chomsky Hash

313 "Police control is tightening": Quoted in Didier Eribon, *Michel Foucault*, trans. Betsy Wing (Harvard University Press, 1991), 224.

313 A psychiatrist's report: James Miller, *The Passion of Michel Foucault* (Simon & Schuster, 1993), 191–92.

313 "The problem of prisons is local": Michel Foucault and Gilles Deleuze, "Intellectuals and Power," *Language, Counter-Memory, Practice: Selected Essays and Interviews*, trans. Donald F. Bouchard (Cornell University Press, 1977), 209–10.

315 "pale, tense, quivering": Claude Mauriac, *Le Temps immobile, vol. 3: Et comme l'espérance est violente* (Grasset, 1976), 561. Translation mine.

316 he peed his pants: David Macey, *The Lives of Michel Foucault* (Verso, 2009), 447.

316 "perhaps the first great insurrection": Michel Foucault, "Il mitico capo fella revolta nell Iran," *Corriere della sera*, November 19, 1978, 1–2. (Quoted in Miller, *The Passion of Michel Foucault*, 309.)

316 "infantile leftism" and "self-indulgent radical": Michael Walzer, "The Politics of Michel Foucault," *Dissent* (1983); Richard Rorty, "Foucault and Epistemology," *Foucault: A Critical Reader*, ed. David Couzens Hoy (Blackwell, 1986), 47.

317 "He struck me as completely amoral": Quoted in Miller, *The Passion of Michel Foucault*, 201–3.

317 Foucault later said he had asked: Simeon Wade, *Foucault in California* (Heyday, 2019), 24.

317 But Foucault argued that "popular justice": Quoted in Miller, *The Passion of Michel Foucault*, 204. See also Michel Foucault, "On Popular Justice: A Discussion with Maoists," trans. John Mepham in *Power/Knowledge: Selected Interviews and Other Writings, 1972–1977*, ed. Colin Gordon (Pantheon Books, 1980), 1.

317 "Crime," he said, paraphrasing: John K. Simon, "Michel Foucault on Attica: An Interview," *Telos*, no. 19 (1974): 161.

318 "I was several times obliged": Giacomo Casanova, *The Memoirs of Jacques Casanova de Seingalt, 1725–1798*, trans. Arthur Machen, vol. 3 (G. P. Putnam's Sons, 1894), 27.

319 "warders, doctors, chaplains": Michel Foucault, *Discipline and Punish: The Birth of the Prison*, trans. Alan Sheridan (Vintage Books, 1979), 11.

319 "In our societies," Foucault wrote: Foucault, *Discipline and Punish*, 25.

320 the goal is "not to punish less": Foucault, *Discipline and Punish*, 82.

320 "The soul," Foucault wrote: Foucault, *Discipline and Punish*, 30.

320 "Power produces knowledge": Foucault, *Discipline and Punish*, 27–28.

320 "It's power all the way down": Susan Neiman, *Left Is Not Woke* (Polity Press, 2023), 63.

321 "Hence the major effect": Foucault, *Discipline and Punish*, 201.

321 "generalizable model of functioning": Foucault, *Discipline and Punish*, 205.

321 "a marvelous machine": Foucault, *Discipline and Punish*, 202.

321 "one not of spectacle": Foucault, *Discipline and Punish*, 217.

321 When he speaks of power as a "faceless gaze": Foucault, *Discipline and Punish*, 214.

321 As the historian Michael Behrent: Michael C. Behrent, "The True Foucault," *Dissent*, September 30, 2021.

Chapter 40: Coercion and Control

323 "A revolution in theory": Gilles Deleuze, "Écrivain non: un nouveau cartographe," *Critique*, no. 343 (1975): 1212. Translation mine.

323 The philosopher François Ewald: François Ewald, "Anatomie et corps politique," *Critique*, no. 343 (1975): 1229. Translation mine.

323 "Visibility is a trap": François Roustang, "La Visibilité est un piège," *Les Temps Modernes*, no. 356 (1976): 1567–79. (See also David Macey, *The Lives of Michel Foucault* [Verso, 2009], 337.)

324 "a machine for elimination": John K. Simon, "Michel Foucault on Attica: An Interview," *Telos*, no. 19 (1974): 155.

324 "What appeared to be a utopian": François Dosse, *Gilles Deleuze & Félix Guattari: Intersecting Lives*, trans. Deborah Glassman (Columbia University Press, 2010), 467.

324 Foucault, for his part, attacked: Sylvère Lotringer, "Doing Theory," *French Theory in America*, eds. Sylvère Lotringer and Sande Cohen (Routledge, 2001), 140.

324 The crowd was agitated and rude: See François Cusset, *French Theory: How Foucault, Derrida, Deleuze, & Co. Transformed the Intellectual Life of the United States*, trans. Jeff Fort (University of Minnesota Press, 2008), 68–69; Lotringer, "Doing Theory," 140–41.

325 He toyed with the idea: Macey, *The Lives of Michel Foucault*, 430.

325 **Before a 1980 lecture at Berkeley:** James Miller, *The Passion of Michel Foucault* (Simon & Schuster, 1993), 321.

325 **The magazine portrayed him:** Otto Friedrich, "France's Philosopher of Power," *Time*, November 16, 1981, 147–48.

326 **"You should not waste your time":** Simeon Wade, *Foucault in California* (Heyday, 2019), 69.

326 **"Foucault's true theme":** Jonathan Rosen, *The Best Minds: A Story of Friendship, Madness, and the Tragedy of Good Intentions* (Penguin Press, 2023), 187.

326 **"Americans used Foucault for":** Lotringer, "Doing Theory," 154.

327 **The Victorian novel:** D. A. Miller, *The Novel and the Police* (University of California Press, 1988), viii–ix.

327 **"The very perfection":** Jean Baudrillard, *Forget Foucault*, trans. Nicole Dufresne (Semiotexte, 1987), 11.

328 **"Foucault has never been able to explain":** Otto Friedrich, "France's Philosopher of Power," *Time*, November 16, 1981, 148.

328 **"'Confinement,' in all its particular":** Clifford Geertz, "Stir Crazy," *New York Review of Books*, January 26, 1978.

328 **"If justice is at stake":** Noam Chomsky and Michel Foucault, *The Chomsky-Foucault Debate on Human Nature* (New Press, 2015), 50.

329 **"All the spectacularism":** Maurice Agulhon, "Postface," *L'Impossible prison: Recherches sur le système pénitentiaire aux XIXe siècle réunies par Michelle Perrot. Débat avec Michel Foucault* (Éditions du Seuil, 1980), 315. Translation mine.

329 **"What led us to show, ostentatiously":** Michel Foucault, *The History of Sexuality: An Introduction*, trans. Robert Hurley, vol. 1 (Vintage Books, 1978), 9.

329 **"What is peculiar to modern societies":** Foucault, *The History of Sexuality*, 35.

330 **"Sex" in this conceit:** Foucault, *The History of Sexuality*, 35.

330 **"for achieving the subjugation":** Foucault, *The History of Sexuality*, 140.

330 **"The battle has thus been joined":** Lawrence Stone, "Madness," *New York Review of Books*, December 16, 1982.

331 **Wounded by Baudrillard's *Forget Foucault*:** Macey, *The Lives of Michel Foucault*, 360.

331 **His "dominance and control" model:** Lawrence Stone, "An Exchange with Michel Foucault," *New York Review of Books*, March 31, 1983.

332 **"How did Michel Foucault become":** Susan Neiman, *Left Is Not Woke* (Polity Press, 2023), 93.

332 **"a bunch of tribes":** Neiman, *Left Is Not Woke*, 108.

332 **"Common-sense questions":** Neiman, *Left Is Not Woke*, 96–97.

332 **"Foucault's obsession with hidden power":** Rosen, *The Best Minds*, 188.

333 **"simply a nihilist":** Neiman, *Left Is Not Woke*, 62.

333 **"Comparative literature has now fallen":** Allan Bloom, *The Closing of the American Mind: How Higher Education Has Failed Democracy and Impoverished the Souls of Today's Students* (Simon & Schuster, 1987), 379.

333 **Scholars have lately stressed:** See, for example, *Foucault and Neoliberalism,* eds. Daniel Zamora and Michael C. Behrent (Polity Press, 2015) and Dean Mitchell and Daniel Zamora, *The Last Man Takes LSD: Foucault and the End of the Revolution* (Verso, 2021).

333 **The leftist press labeled:** Christopher Caldwell, "Meet the Philosopher Who Is Trying to Explain the Pandemic," *New York Times*, August 21, 2020.

334 **"Experts have taken over our lives":** Blake Smith, "The Unwoke Foucault," *Washington Examiner*, March 4, 2021.

335 **"rooted in a collective experience":** Blake Smith, "Biopolitics," *Tablet*, June 25, 2020.

335 **"the Foucault realignment":** Ross Douthat, "How Foucault Lost the Left and Won the Right," *New York Times*, May 25, 2021.

336 **"I think I have in fact been situated":** Foucault, "Polemics, Politics and Problematizations: An Interview with Michel Foucault," in *Ethics: Subjectivity and Truth: The Essential Works of Michel Foucault, vol. 1* (New Press, 1997), 113.

Chapter 41: Country Joe Foucault

337 **"to make his face invisible":** Hervé Guibert, *To the Friend Who Did Not Save My Life*, trans. Linda Coverdale (Semiotexte, 2020), 33.

337 **"become what one is":** James Miller, *The Passion of Michel Foucault* (Simon & Schuster, 1993), 98.

337 **"I have always wanted my books":** Quoted in David Macey, *The Lives of Michel Foucault* (Verso, 2009), x.

338 Félix Guattari had been charged: François Dosse, *Gilles Deleuze & Félix Guattari: Intersecting Lives*, trans. Deborah Glassman (Columbia University Press, 2010), 273.

338 "*une honteuse*" (or "closet queen"): David Halperin, "Michel Foucault, Jean Le Bitoux, and the Gay Science Lost and Found: An Introduction," *Critical Inquiry* 37 (2011): 374.

338 "Nothing that went into his total composition": Michel Foucault, *The History of Sexuality: An Introduction*, trans. Robert Hurley, vol. 1 (Vintage Books, 1978), 43.

339 "the pleasure that comes of exercising a power": Foucault, *The History of Sexuality*, 45.

339 "parents and children, adults and adolescents": Foucault, *The History of Sexuality*, 45.

339 he even gave lectures at The Barracks: Ed Cohen, "Foucauldian Necrologies: 'Gay' 'Politics'? Politically Gay?" *Textual Practice* 2, no. 1 (1988): 91.

339 a "two-story BDSM wonderland": "Yesterday's Crimes: The Great Folsom Street Fire," *SF Weekly*, March 31, 2016.

339 "the real creation of new possibilities": Michel Foucault, "Sex, Power, and the Politics of Identity," *Ethics: Subjectivity and Truth: The Essential Works of Michel Foucault, vol. 1* (New Press, 1997), 165.

339 "French *savant's* observation": Macey, *The Lives of Michel Foucault*, 370. From Edmund White, *States of Desire: Travels in Gay America* (Picador, 1988), 267.

340 "The S/M game is very interesting": Foucault, "Sex, Power, and the Politics of Identity," *Ethics: Subjectivity and Truth*, 169.

340 "I hope I'll die of an overdose": Michel Foucault, "The Minimalist Self," *Politics, Philosophy, Culture: Interviews and Other Writings, 1977–1984*, ed. Lawrence D. Kritzman (Routledge, 1988), 12.

340 "nothing less than the greatest thinker": Simeon Wade, *Foucault in California* (Heyday, 2019), 3.

340 "the *episteme* was for the human sciences": Wade, *Foucault in California*, 4.

341 "as a medieval monk might": Wade, *Foucault in California*, 10.

342 From a letter Foucault wrote: Wade, *Foucault in California*, xvi.

Chapter 42: At the Bathhouse

345 "book about sexual repression": Simeon Wade, *Foucault in California* (Heyday, 2019), xvii.

345 experimenting with S/M as early as: James Miller, *The Passion of Michel Foucault* (Simon & Schuster, 1993), 91.

346 "unrelenting, deeply ambiguous": Miller, *The Passion of Michel Foucault*, 7.

346 "the most revolutionary—and deeply serious": Miller, *The Passion of Michel Foucault*, 9.

346 "madness, drugs, sexuality": Quoted in Miller, *The Passion of Michel Foucault*, 398, fn 49.

346 Centers for Disease Control gave: Miller, *The Passion of Michel Foucault*, 21.

346 the department's "number one priority": Robert Pear, "Health Chief Calls AIDS Battle 'No. 1 Priority,'" *New York Times*, May 25, 1983.

346 By the time President Reagan: Donald P. Francis, "Deadly AIDS Policy Failure by the Highest Levels of the US Government: A Personal Look Back 30 Years Later for Lessons to Respond Better to Future Epidemics," *Journal of Public Health Policy* 33, no. 3 (2012): 292.

347 "As if an exceptional intellectual": Quoted in Miller, *The Passion of Michel Foucault*, 21.

347 "Foucault knew. And he did not want": Didier Eribon, *Michel Foucault*, trans. Betsy Wing (Harvard University Press, 1991), 325.

348 "It is in the reflection on love": Michel Foucault, *The History of Sexuality: The Use of Pleasure*, trans. Robert Hurley, vol. 2 (Vintage Books, 1985), 245.

348 "One of my hypotheses": Michel Foucault, "Sex, Power, and the Politics of Identity," *Ethics: Subjectivity and Truth: The Essential Works of Michel Foucault, vol. 1* (New Press, 1997), 171.

349 The last party he threw: François Cusset, *French Theory: How Foucault, Derrida, Deleuze, & Co. Transformed the Intellectual Life of the United States*, trans. Jeff Fort (University of Minnesota Press, 2008), 349, fn 21.

349 "*Je n'y crois pas*": Miller, *The Passion of Michel Foucault*, 348–49.

350 "My friend fell off the sofa": Hervé Guibert, *To the Friend Who Did Not Save My Life*, trans. Linda Coverdale (Semiotexte, 2020), 27. Guibert later acknowledged that he had kept a detailed journal of his visits with Foucault as he was dying.

350 "Those places must be completely deserted": Guibert, *To the Friend Who Did Not Save My Life*, 34–35.

350 "To have taken AIDS": Miller, *The Passion of Michel Foucault*, 381.

351 "teleologically structured quest": Miller, *The Passion of Michel Foucault*, 7.

351 "The celebration of his intellectual perversions": Roger Kimball, "The Perversions of M. Foucault," *New Criterion* (March 1993).

351 "The problem with Foucault": Jay Tolson, "Fatal Attraction," *National Review*, February 15, 1993, 47–48.

351 "relatively minor thinker who was": Mark Lilla, "Marx and Murder," *Times Literary Supplement*, September 25, 1992, 3.

352 a seventy-four-page diatribe: Camille Paglia, "Junk Bonds and Corporate Raiders: Academe in the Hour of the Wolf," in *Sex, Art, and American Culture: Essays* (Vintage Books, 1992), 170–248. Originally published in *Arion: A Journal of Humanities and the Classics* 1, no. 2 (1991), 139–212.

Chapter 43: The Trial of Paul de Man

353 "It was, and remains, unique": Jacques Derrida, "In Memoriam: Of the Soul," trans. Kevin Newmark, in *Mémoires for Paul de Man* (Columbia University Press, 1989), xvi.

353 the headline read: Susan Chira, "Yale Still Feeling Loss of Revered Professor," *New York Times*, February 25, 1984.

353 The doctor sent de Man: Geoffrey Hartman, *A Scholar's Tale: Intellectual Journey of a Displaced Child of Europe* (Fordham University Press, 2007), 80.

353 "You know, don't you": Quoted in Benoît Peeters, *Derrida: A Biography*, trans. Andrew Brown (Polity Press, 2013), 351.

354 In classic deconstructive fashion: Derrida, "The Art of *Mémoires*," trans. Jonathan Culler, *Mémoires for Paul de Man*, 82.

354 "What does a memory without": Derrida, "The Art of *Mémoires*," 85.

354 "Paul was irony itself": Derrida, "In Memoriam: Of the Soul," xvi.

355 "One need only read": Derrida, "Mnemosyne," trans. Cecile Lindsay, *Mémoires for Paul de Man*, 15–18.

355 "gloomy existentialist": René Wellek, "Destroying Literary Studies," *New Criterion* (December 1983).

355 "The panicked dogmatism becomes": Derrida, "Mnemosyne," 41–42.

355 "What would it have been": Derrida, "Mnemosyne," 20.

355 "the author's own monumental inscription": Paul de Man, "Autobiography as De-facement," *MLN* 94 (1979): 923.

356 "trace of the other in us": Derrida, "Mnemosyne," 29.

356 "I am not given to": Paul de Man, "Foreword to Revised, Second Edition," *Blindness and Insight: Essays in the Rhetoric of Contemporary Criticism*, trans. Wlad Godzich (University of Minnesota Press, 1983), xii.

356 "return of the ghost as text": Derrida, "Acts: The Meaning of a Given Word," trans. Eduardo Cadava, *Mémoires for Paul de Man*, 122.

357 The pieces were illustrated with a caricature: James Atlas, "The Case of Paul de Man," *The New York Times Magazine*, August 28, 1988.

357 "degenerate and decadent": For a good English translation of "The Jews in Present-Day Literature," see David Lehman, *Signs of the Times: Deconstruction and the Fall of Paul de Man* (Poseidon Press, 1991), 269–71. The French original is included in Paul de Man, *Wartime Journalism: 1939–1943*, eds. Werner Hamacher, Neil Hertz, and Thomas Keenan (University of Nebraska Press, 1988), 45.

358 Seventeen months after the essay: "Paul de Man: A Chronology, 1919–1949," *Responses: On Paul de Man's Wartime Journalism*, eds. Warner Hamacher, Neil Hertz, and Thomas Keenan (University of Nebraska Press, 1989), xvii.

358 piece in *The New York Times*: "Yale Scholar Wrote for Pro-Nazi Newspaper," *New York Times*, December 1, 1987.

358 anguished, sixty-three-page response: Jacques Derrida, "Like the Sound of the Sea Deep Within a Shell: Paul de Man's War," trans. Peggy Kamuf, *Critical Inquiry* 14, no. 3 (Spring 1988): 590–652.

Chapter 44: Excuses (Confessions)

360 "The new disclosures imbed": Geoffrey Hartman, "Blindness and Insight: Paul de Man, Fascism, and Deconstruction," *New Republic*, March 7, 1988, 29.

361 De Man's "later writings offer some of the most": Jonathan Culler, "Letters," *London Review of Books* 10, no. 8, April 21, 1988.

361 "a belated, but still powerful, act": Hartman, "Blindness and Insight," 29.

361 "something of an academic Waldheim": Jon Wiener, "Deconstructing de Man," *Nation*, January 9, 1988, 22.

361 "He didn't just say": Quoted in Wiener, "Deconstructing de Man," 24.

361 "an act of unspeakable moral shabbiness": Wolfgang Holdheim, "Letters," *London Review of Books* 10, no. 6, March 17, 1988.

362 "Deconstruction turned out to be": David Lehman, "Deconstructing de Man's Life," *Newsweek*, February 15, 1988, 63.

362 an opportunist, a liar, and a cheat: James Atlas, "The Case of Paul de Man," *New York Times Magazine*, August 28, 1988.

363 he abandoned three young sons and a wife: Atlas, "The Case of Paul de Man."

363 "History is not human": Paul de Man, "Conclusions: Walter Benjamin's 'The Task of the Translator,'" *The Resistance to Theory* (University of Minnesota Press, 1986), 92.

363 Decades later, in his *Confessions*: See gutenberg.org/files/3913/3913-h/3913-h.htm. This translation of the *Confessions* is from Project Gutenberg; it's a 1903 English translation printed privately in London.

364 "At the end of the *Rêverie*": Paul de Man, "Excuses (*Confessions*)," *Allegories of Reading: Figural Language in Rousseau, Nietzsche, Rilke, and Proust* (Yale University Press, 1979), 299.

364 "system of truth": De Man, "Excuses (*Confessions*)," 289.

364 "There can never be": De Man, "Excuses (*Confessions*)," 299.

365 "The indecision makes it possible": De Man, "Excuses (*Confessions*)," 293.

365 "To remain suspended between de Man's two possibilities": Denis Donoghue, "Deconstructing Deconstruction," *New York Review of Books*, June 12, 1980.

365 "Paul de Man and his deconstruction": Richard Rand, "Rigor Vitae," *Responses: On Paul de Man's Wartime Journalism*, eds. Warner Hamacher, Neil Hertz, and Thomas Keenan (University of Nebraska Press, 1989), 354.

366 "No fewer than three": Jeffrey Mehlman, "Perspectives: On De Man and *Le Soir*," *Responses*: *On Paul de Man's Wartime Journalism*, eds. Warner Hamacher, Neil Hertz, and Thomas Keenan (University of Nebraska Press, 1989), 329.

366 Like Althusser, someone pointed out: Peter Salmon, *An Event, Perhaps: A Biography of Jacques Derrida* (Verso, 2020), 221–22.

Chapter 45: The Death of Deconstruction

367 more than eight months on the bestseller list: James Atlas, "Chicago's Grumpy Guru," *New York Times Magazine*, January 3, 1988.

368 Here, Bennett helpfully enumerated: William J. Bennett, *To Reclaim a Legacy: A Report on the Humanities in Higher Education*, National Endowment for the Humanities, November 1984.

368 On Martin Luther King Day: Mark Bauerlein, "When Bill Bennett Came to Stanford," *American Conservative*, December. 12, 2022.

368 His visit was sponsored: Jennifer Schmid, "Bennett to Speak Out on CIV Tonight," *The Stanford Daily*, April 18, 1988.

368 a university brought low: William J. Bennett, "Why the West?," in *The Eighties: A Reader*, ed. Gilbert T. Sewall (Addison-Wesley, 1997), 274–80.

369 "You don't make the case": *The MacNeil/Lehrer NewsHour*, April 19, 1988.

369 "This is the politics of": Quoted in Edward B. Fiske, "Reagan's Man for Education," *New York Times Magazine*, December 22, 1985.

369 Liberals began to speak of: Mary Louise Pratt, "Humanities for the Future: Reflections on the Western Culture Debate at Stanford," in *The Politics of Liberal Education*, eds. Darryl J. Gless and Barbara Herrnstein Smith (Duke University Press, 1990), 15.

369 "a great tradition that is essentially": Helene Moglen, "Allan Bloom and E.D. Hirsch: Educational Reform as Tragedy and Farce," in *The Eighties: A Reader*, ed. Gilbert T. Sewall (Addison Wesley, 1997), 284.

370 "The transformation of American campuses": Dinesh D'Souza, *Illiberal Education: The Politics of Race and Sex on Campus* (Free Press, 1991), 2.

370 "white, male-dominated, Western European": Quoted in D'Souza, *Illiberal Education*, 7.

370 "deconstructionists hold that all literature": D'Souza, *Illiberal Education*, 178.

370 "many of the most influential theorists": Charles J. Sykes, *Profscam: Professors and the Demise of Higher Education* (Regnery Gateway, 1988), 182.

370 "There is nothing uncertain": D'Souza, *Illiberal Education*, 192.

371 "the frequently heard charge": Roger Kimball, *Tenured Radicals: How Politics Has Corrupted Our Higher Education* (Harper & Row, 1990), 102–3.

371 "What a curious irony": David Lehman, *Signs of the Times: Deconstruction and the Fall of Paul de Man* (Poseidon Press, 1991), 242.

371 what French historians have called: Richard Bernstein, *Dictatorship of Virtue: Multiculturalism and the Battle for America's Future* (Knopf, 1994), 4.

372 "A parade of luminaries arrived": Karen Winkler, "Post-structuralism: An Often-Abstruse French

Import Profoundly Affects Research in the United States," *Chronicle of Higher Education*, November 25, 1987, 7–8.

372 "The questioning of authority": James Atlas, "Battle of the Books," *New York Times Magazine*, June 5, 1988.

373 "It's hard to do it well": Quoted in Mitchell Stephens, "Jacques Derrida," *New York Times Magazine*, January 23, 1994.

373 "putting into discourse of 'woman'": Alice A. Jardine, *Gynesis: Configurations of Woman and Modernity* (Cornell University Press, 1985), 24–25.

373 The number of women's studies programs: *A National Census of Women's and Gender Studies Programs in U.S. Institutions of Higher Education*. Prepared for the National Women's Studies Association by the National Opinion Research Center, December 26, 2007.

374 "Identity politics amounted to demobilization": Quoted in Gil Troy, *Morning in America: How Ronald Reagan Invented the 1980s* (Princeton University Press, 2005), 272.

374 As America became more diverse: Katherine Mangan, "Where Are the White Students?" *The Chronicle of Higher Education*, November 1, 2024.

374 Black professors, for example: National Center for Education Statistics, "Race/ethnicity of college faculty," nces.ed.gov/fastfacts/display.asp?id=61.

375 the number of English majors: Nathan Heller, "The End of the English Major," *New Yorker*, February 27, 2023.

375 "Deconstruction is dead": Quoted in Stephens, "Jacques Derrida."

Chapter 46: "Liberally Salted with Nonsense"

379 "You make use of extremely dubious": Louis Althusser, *Writings on Psychoanalysis: Freud and Lacan*, eds. Olivier Corpet and François Matheron, trans. Jeffrey Mehlman (Columbia University Press, 1996), 43.

380 "Experience is at once always already": Joan W. Scott, "The Evidence of Experience," *Critical Inquiry* 17, (1991): 797.

382 "While my method was satirical": Alan Sokal, "A Physicist Experiments With Cultural Studies: A Confession," *Lingua Franca*, May 1996. Reprinted in *Quick Studies: The Best of Lingua Franca*, ed. Alexander Star (Farrar, Straus and Giroux, 2002), 3–9.

383 "Modern French philosophy is a load": Jon Henley, "Furor on the Left Bank: Philosophical Phonies," *Guardian*, October 1, 1997.

383 Julia Kristeva pronounced the book "disinformation": Julia Kristeva, "Une Désinformation," *Le Nouvel Observateur*, September 25, 1997, 122.

383 in an interview with *Corriere della Sera*: Munzi Ulderico, "'Francesi, intellettuali impostori': Americani all'attacco di Parigi," *Corriere della Sera*, September 26, 1997.

383 "As for the 'relativism'": Jacques Derrida, "Sokal et Bricmont ne sont pas sérieux," *Le Monde*, November 20, 1997.

384 "its anti-authoritarianism": Barbara Epstein, "Postmodernism and the New Left," *New Politics* 6, no. 2 (1997).

384 "could see nothing but instability": Epstein, "Postmodernism and the New Left."

Chapter 47: "A Total Fraud"

385 "like a great cathedral": Larissa MacFarquhar, "The Prophet of Decline," *New Yorker*, September 22, 2002.

385 "In the space war of": Geoffrey Hartman, "The Following Tributes Were Offered at the Memorial Service for Paul de Man Held at the Yale University Art Gallery on January 18, 1984," *Yale French Studies*, no. 69 (1985): 6.

385 "In a profession full of fakeness": Barbara Johnson, "The Following Tributes Were Offered," 10.

386 "That work remains for others": Evelyn Barish, *The Double Life of Paul de Man* (Liveright, 2014), 436.

386 "In this way," one reviewer noted: Robert Alter, "Paul de Man Was a Total Fraud," *New Republic*, April 5, 2014.

386 in *The New Republic*: Robert Alter, "Paul de Man Was a Total Fraud," *New Republic*, April 5, 2014.

387 "was and must have remained": Barish, *The Double Life of Paul de Man*, 45.

387 "in an aristocratic loneliness": Quoted in Barish, *The Double Life of Paul de Man*, 33.

388 Anne claimed it was a rental: Barish, *The Double Life of Paul de Man*, 152.

388 One friend recalled bumping: Barish, *The Double Life of Paul de Man*, 153.

388 "her blond hair flowing": Barish, *The Double Life of Paul de Man*, 77–78.

389 he was careful to hide the fact: Barish, *The Double Life of Paul de Man*, 52.
390 "showed itself above all": Quoted in Barish, *The Double Life of Paul de Man*, 169.
390 "an entirely Nazi journal": Barish, *The Double Life of Paul de Man*, xxiii.
390 "He wanted *Cahiers Européens*": Barish, *The Double Life of Paul de Man*, 140.
390 who put up all her savings: Barish, *The Double Life of Paul de Man*, 187.
390 de Man treated Hermès as a piggy bank: Barish, *The Double Life of Paul de Man*, 191.
391 In 1951, Paul was tried: Barish, *The Double Life of Paul de Man*, 192.
391 He never saw his father again: Barish. *The Double Life of Paul de Man*, 364.
391 I am known as being: Quoted in Barish, *The Double Life of Paul de Man*, 196.
391 "Principles are [what]": Quoted in Barish, *The Double Life of Paul de Man*, 58.
392 helped Jewish friends during the war: Barish, *The Double Life of Paul de Man*, 158.
392 "so egregiously Nazi": Barish, *The Double Life of Paul de Man*, 135.
392 "seduction," "power," "rigor": Barish, *The Double Life of Paul de Man*, 48.
392 Hendrik himself called his nephew: Barish, *The Double Life of Paul de Man*, 62.
392 "a highly controversial political figure": ed. Thomas Keenan, "Documents: Public Criticisms," in *Responses: On Paul de Man's Wartime Journalism*, eds. Warner Hamacher, Neil Hertz, and Thomas Keenan (University of Nebraska Press, 1989), 476.
392 confiding to a colleague: Barish, *The Double Life of Paul de Man*, 54.
393 a résumé larded with falsehoods: Barish, *The Double Life of Paul de Man*, 260–62.
394 Beneath the French bureaucratese: Barish, *The Double Life of Paul de Man*, 340–41.
394 De Man failed to pay: Barish, *The Double Life of Paul de Man*, 308–13.
394 "a good and innocent man": Mary McCarthy, *The Groves of Academe* (Harcourt, Brace, and Company, 1952), 88.
395 find his home in disarray: Barish, *The Double Life of Paul de Man*, 313, 501, fn 19.
395 "lying, evasion, fantasy": Quoted in Barish, *The Double Life of Paul de Man*, 277.
395 "divided up the children": Quoted in Barish, *The Double Life of Paul de Man*, 499, fn 6.
396 de Man did not actually obtain: Barish, *The Double Life of Paul de Man*, 303, 425.
396 deprived him of the loving gaze: Barish, *The Double Life of Paul de Man*, 13.
396 "does not seem like the behavior": Louis Menand, "The De Man Case," *New Yorker*, March 17, 2014.

Chapter 48: Into the Abyss

398 "All my life I have lied": John Banville, *Shroud* (Alfred A. Knopf, 2002), 8.
398 "His writings can and should be read": Jacques Derrida, "Typewriter Ribbon: Limited Ink (2)," *Without Alibi*, trans. Peggy Kamuf (Stanford University Press, 2002), 150.
399 "say what they need to": Andrezj Warminski, "Machinal Effects: Derrida With and Without de Man," *MLN* 124, no. 5 (2009): 1088.
399 "dull hesitancy about concluding": Marco Roth, "Derrida: An Autothanotography," *n+1*, October 18, 2004.
400 "locked in eternal combat": Arthur C. Danto, *Mark Tansey: Visions and Revisions* (Harry N. Abrams, 1992), 29.
401 "Derrida's much-vaunted interpretive": Edward Rothstein, "The Man Who Showed Us How to Take the World Apart," *New York Times*, October 11, 2004.
401 Six paragraphs were devoted: Jonathan Kandell, "Jacques Derrida: Abstruse Theorist, Dies at 74," *New York Times*, October 10, 2004.
401 "You are never going to find": Fredric Jameson, *The Years of Theory: Postwar French Thought to the Present* (Verso, 2024), 252.
402 "to characterize Jacques Derrida": "Jacques Derrida: Homage to a Giant," *The New York Times*, October 13, 2004.
402 "No thinker in the last 100 years": Mark C. Taylor, "What Derrida Really Meant," *New York Times*, October 14, 2004.
403 "I think about nothing but death": Jacques Derrida and Maurizio Ferraris, *A Taste for the Secret*, trans. Giacomo Donis (Polity Press, 2001), 88.
403 "learning to live should mean": Jean Birnbaum and Jacques Derrida, "Je suis en guerre contre moi même," *Le Monde*, August 19, 2004. Published in English as *Learning to Live Finally: The Last Interview* (Melville House, 2007).

Epilogue

404 After all, the student added: Stanley Fish, "Truth but No Consequences: Why Philosophy Doesn't Matter," *Critical Inquiry* 29, no. 3 (2003): 389–417.

404 blamed "postmodernist" professors: Stanley Fish, "Don't Blame Relativism," *Responsive Community* 12, no. 3 (2002).

405 mood in the room that day: Emily Eakin, "The Latest Theory Is That Theory Doesn't Matter," *New York Times*, April 19, 2003.

405 "Theory may not matter right away": W. J. T. Mitchell, "Medium Theory: Preface to the 2003 *Critical Inquiry* Symposium," *Critical Inquiry* 30, no. 2 (2004): 328.

406 "Theory, at least of the French kind": Stanley Fish, "French Theory in America, Part Two," *The New York Times*, April 20, 2008.

406 "Only by arresting the questioning": Stanley Fish, "French Theory in America," *New York Times*, April 6, 2008.

407 "in universal terms that would be persuasive": Stanley Fish, "Condemnation Without Absolutes," *New York Times*, October 15, 2001.

407 "What we think *with*": Fish, "French Theory in America."

407 "incredulity toward metanarratives": Jean-François Lyotard, *The Postmodern Condition: A Report on Knowledge*, trans. Geoff Bennington and Brian Massumi (University of Minnesota Press, 1984), xxiv.

408 "What we need now is": Ross Douthat, "How to Make Sense of the New L.G.B.T.Q. Culture War," *New York Times*, April 13, 2022.

408 including "bias," "climate crisis," "equality": Karen Yourish, Annie Daniel, Saurabh Datar, Isaac White, and Lazaro Gamio, "These Words Are Disappearing in the New Trump Administration," *New York Times*, March 7, 2025.

408 "Nothing may be more essential": François Cusset, *French Theory: How Foucault, Derrida, Deleuze, & Co. Transformed the Intellectual Life of the United States*, trans. Jeff Fort (University of Minnesota Press, 2008), xx.

409 "dumbed-down corollaries": Michiko Kakutani, *The Death of Truth: Notes on Falsehood in the Age of Trump* (Tim Duggan Books, 2018), 45–46.

409 "I don't seem like a guy": Andrew Marantz, "Trolls for Trump," *New Yorker*, October 24, 2016.

410 "Am I Maude because": U/MaudeReads, February 2, 2026, moltbook.com/post/e5b10f2e-3858-4610-b839-3bd8a76ca852.

410 "these algorithms only circulate different signs": David Gunkel, "Deconstruction to the Rescue," *Outland*, June 20, 2023.

411 "Either philosophy is a waste of time": Michel de Montaigne, "To Philosophize Is to Learn to Die," trans. Sebastian Biot, hyperessays.net/essays/to-philosophize-is-to-learn-to-die.

412 "part of the furniture of their lives": Nicholas Dames, "The Theory Generation," *n+1*, Summer 2012.

412 Theory's "not actually gone": H. Aram Veeser and Jane Gallop, "What Happened in the 80s? On the Rise of Literary Theory in American Academia," *Literary Hub*, lithub.com/what-happened-in-the-80s-on-the-rise-of-literary-theory-in-american-academia, December 23, 2020.

IMAGE CREDITS

Page 3: Courtesy of Amy Ziering.
Page 6, *left*: Courtesy of the author.
Page 6, *right*: Courtesy of the author.
Page 7: Courtesy of the author.
Page 27: Archives Louis Althusser / IMEC.
Page 37: Photo 12/Alamy.
Page 39: Archives Louis Althusser / IMEC.
Page 60: AP Images.
Page 72: © 2025 Artists Rights Society (ARS), New York / ADAGP, Paris. Digital Image © CNAC/MNAM, Dist. RMN-Grand Palais / Art Resource, New York.
Page 80: *Album Jacques Lacan: Visages de Mon Père*, by Judith Miller © Editions du Seuil, 1991.
Page 88, *left*: GL Archive/Alamy.
Page 88, *right*: Fine Art Images/Heritage Images/Getty Images.
Page 92: © 2025 Salvador Dalí, Fundació Gala-Salvador Dalí, Artists Rights Society. Digital Image © CNAC/MNAM, Dist. RMN-Grand Palais / Art Resource, NY.
Page 100: Historic Collection/Alamy.
Page 116: © Estate Brassaï—GrandPalaisRmn. Digital image © RMN-Grand Palais / Art Resource, New York.

Page 125: Masterpics/Alamy.

Page 127: Livioandronico2013/CC BY-SA 4.0 via Wikimedia Commons.

Page 130: Chancellerie des Universités de Paris—Bibliothèque littéraire Jacques Doucet.

Page 139: Fausto Giaccone/contrasto/Redux.

Page 150: Courtesy of Nils Öberg.

Page 157: Ulf Andersen/Getty Images.

Page 164: Courtesy of Jean Derrida.

Page 169: Felix H. Man/ullstein bild via Getty Image.

Page 176: Roland Allard/Agence VU/Redux.

Page 182: Marc Gantier/Gamma-Rapho via Getty Images.

Page 194: Sonuma-RTBF, Jacques Lacan Parle, F. Wolff & G. Lejeune.

Page 204: Courtesy of the author.

Page 210: Apic/Getty Images.

Page 215: Album/Alamy.

Page 225: Reporters Associes/Gamma-Rapho via Getty Images.

Page 228: Ulf Andersen/Getty Images.

Page 244: © 2025 Artists Rights Society (ARS), New York / ADAGP, Paris.

Page 272: Image courtesy of Bard College, Archives & Special Collections.

Page 279: Lebrecht Music & Arts/Alamy.

Page 294: Courtesy of Jean Derrida.

Page 305: Keystone Press/Alamy.

Page 309: Alain Keler/MYOP.

Page 314: Josee Lorenzo/INA via Getty Images.

Page 344: Photograph by Simeon Wade, used with permission by David Wade.

Page 399: © Mark Tansey. Courtesy of the artist and Gagosian.

Page 420: Courtesy of the author.

INDEX

Italic page references indicate photographs.